Drop Dead

performance works

SERIES EDITORS
Patrick Anderson and Nicholas Ridout

This series publishes books in theater and performance studies, focused in particular on the material conditions in which performance acts are staged, and to which performance itself might contribute. We define "performance" in the broadest sense, including traditional theatrical productions and performance art, but also cultural ritual, political demonstration, social practice, and other forms of interpersonal, social, and political interaction which may fruitfully be understood in terms of performance.

Drop Dead

Performance in Crisis,
1970s New York

✦

Hillary Miller

NORTHWESTERN UNIVERSITY PRESS
EVANSTON, ILLINOIS

Northwestern University Press
www.nupress.northwestern.edu

Printed in the United States of America

10 9 8 7 6 5 4 3 2 1

Library of Congress Cataloging-in-Publication Data

Names: Miller, Hillary, author.
Title: Drop dead : performance in crisis, 1970s New York / Hillary Miller.
Description: Evanston, Illinois : Northwestern University Press, 2016. | Series: Performance works | Based on the author's thesis (doctoral)—City University of New York, 2013.
Identifiers: LCCN 2016031995 | ISBN 9780810133884 (pbk. : alk. paper) | ISBN 9780810133891 (cloth : alk. paper) | ISBN 9780810133907 (e-book)
Subjects: LCSH: Theater—New York (State)—New York—History—20th century. | Performing arts—New York (State)—New York—History—20th century. | Theater—Economic aspects—New York (State)—New York. | Performing arts—Economic aspects—New York (State)—New York. | Recessions—New York (State)—New York. | Nineteen seventies.
Classification: LCC PN2277.N5 M43 2016 | DDC 792.09747109047—dc23
LC record available at https://lccn.loc.gov/2016031995

CONTENTS

ACKNOWLEDGMENTS

This book owes much to the doctoral program in theater at the Graduate Center, City University of New York (CUNY), where I had the great fortune to work with remarkable scholars and dedicated educators. David Savran consistently encouraged my research pursuits, and his advice never failed to deliver insights and, when needed, skepticism. While I had long looked to his scholarship for inspiration, his commitment to this book and support of my research have been valuable beyond measure. Marvin Carlson's astute observations in response to my writing always advanced my questioning in new ways. Jean Graham-Jones was a thoughtful sounding board from my earliest theoretical engagements with theater and the city. I benefitted from her leadership as executive officer of the program, and remain indebted to her perceptive critiques of my work. I thank also the many other faculty members at the Graduate Center with whom I studied theater, politics, and culture, including Alison Griffiths, David Harvey, Judy Milhous, John Mollenkopf, Mike Wallace, Maurya Wickstrom, and Jim Wilson. I am grateful to Mimi D'Aponte, professor emerita, for her generous sharing of materials related to the Everyman Street Theatre. To the Theatre Program's assistant program officer and academic program coordinator, Lynette Gibson, and to so many of my colleagues at CUNY who aided my progress throughout this research, thank you.

Mikhail Gershovich and the phenomenal team at the Bernard L. Schwartz Communication Institute at Baruch College, as well as Jana O'Keefe-Bazzoni in the Communication Studies Department at Baruch, allowed me to complete the research for this book while enjoying stimulating teaching and work. I was proud to be a member of the inaugural cohort of the Provost's Digital Fellows at the Graduate Center, directed by Matthew Gold, which provided essential support in my final year. A grant from Andrea Ades Vasquez at the CUNY New Media Lab supported my preliminary investigations into the changing geographies of theater in downtown Manhattan.

Jonathan Berger, Scott Bukatman, and Janice Ross, my colleagues in Stanford University's Immersion in the Arts: Living in Culture (ITALIC) program, provided encouragement and an unparalleled academic adventure as I finished work on this project. Kim Beil, Mary Doyno, Jared Hoffman, Katherine McDonough, Aaron Shkuda, and many others made my two years in the Bay Area a true gift. I thank former Program in Writing and Rhetoric (PWR) Faculty Director Nicholas Jenkins, Director Marvin Diogenes, and all of the dedicated PWR instructors and staff members for creating such a stimulating environment within which to develop teaching and research. I thank as well the inspiring undergraduate students with whom I shared the frustrations and satisfactions of writing about the arts, and especially Tina Vachovsky, who provided careful assistance with bibliographic entries. This project benefited greatly from a PWR Research Award, funded by the office of Harry J. Elam, Jr., Freeman-Thornton Vice Provost for Undergraduate Education at Stanford.

As I was completing the final revisions of this manuscript I met new colleagues in the Theatre Department at California State University, Northridge. I am especially grateful for the support of colleagues Ah-Jeong Kim, Garry Lennon, and Interim Dean Dan Hosken of the Mike Curb College of the Arts, Media, and Communication. Thanks to them, probationary faculty research funds supported the end stages of my work on this book. Administrative Analyst Alicia Lawrence's patient assistance made that support a reality.

Numerous research institutions provided time and materials, and I am indebted to the librarians at the archives I accessed: the Municipal Archives of New York City, the New York Public Library for the Performing Arts and their Document Delivery Services, the Schomburg Center for Research in Black Culture, the Brooklyn Historical Society, the Brooklyn Academy of Music Archives, the La Mama Archives, the Social Welfare History Archives at the University of Minnesota, the Judson Memorial Church Archive at New York University's Fales Library, and the Municipal Assistance Corporation for the City of New York Archive at Baruch College's Newman Library. I also made use of the extensive visual resources available through the Coney Island History Project, the Museum of the City of New York, and the Municipal Arts Society, and I am grateful to the Lower East Side History Project for materials about East Fourth Street.

The artists, activists, and administrators with whom I spoke during the course of my research left a strong imprint on the final manuscript. I thank everyone who generously shared memories of past productions and cherished collaborators: Jan Barry, the late Bernard X. Bovasso, Woodie King Jr., Janet Langsam, Val Orselli, Albert Poland, Charles Reichenthal, and Mical Whitaker. I thank also my (Save) Coney Island interlocutors with whom I shared lively discussions related to the city and the finer points of C7 zoning.

I acknowledge also the editors and publishers of academic journals where I continued to revise and refine some of these ideas. Specifically, chapter 2 was derived in part from an article published in *Performance Research* 20, no. 4 in August 2015, "Institutional 'Landing Sites' and Uneven Cultural Development: Planned Shrinkage and La Mama E.T.C.," available online: http:/www.tandfonline.com/, DOI: 10.1080/13528165.2015.1071038.

My deep gratitude goes to friends and colleagues who stepped forward as willing readers and discussants, including Linell Ajello, Grant Barnes, Lindsey Mantoan, Shayoni Mitra, and Catherine Young. Michael Shane Boyle, a generous scholar and great resource during my first year out west, provided thoughtful feedback on two chapters. Annabelle Winograd's rigorous reading of a chapter draft came at an important phase of revision. Her larger contribution throughout the life of this project was as a loyal and tireless force for good: reframing and reminding me of the priorities in theater research, writing, and historical inquiry.

Mike Levine at Northwestern University Press has been so patient at every step of this process that I hardly believed he was real until we met face-to-face. His early excitement about the topic, and his careful shepherding of this manuscript, were indispensable to this book's completion. I benefitted greatly from the support and advice of series co-editors Patrick Anderson and Nicholas Ridout. I thank them for their belief in this work, and also for incisive (and often quite funny) comments on the manuscript. Their detailed feedback helped me to better understand my own ideas and my approaches to communicating them. I thank the two anonymous readers who provided succinct and clear feedback on the manuscript. While the deficiencies in the final text are all mine, I am grateful to Maggie Grossman, Marianne Jankowski, Nathan MacBrien, and everyone at Northwestern University Press who contributed to its steady improvement throughout many months. I was fortunate to have Daniel Gundlach's encouragement and careful preparation of the index. I thank photographer Shalmon Bernstein for his permission to use one of his beautiful images as the cover for this book.

I am sure I will not be able to properly thank the friends and family who endured my complaints and my confusions, not to mention missed vacations. Great affection and love go to the Miller, Bloom, and Hazas families: Samantha, Warren, Amelia, and Jake, Sean Devlin, Charlotte, Jerry, and Mike Hazas. Special words are reserved for my remarkable parents, Robert and Estelle Miller, who schlepped me to cultural and political events around New York throughout my childhood and continue to support my every personal and professional step. My friends have all conspired to keep me healthy and happy. But especially: Nell Boeschenstein, Chris van Ginhoven, Lily Gurton-Wachter, Jordan Kirk, Oliver Kramer, Kate Lieberman, Zoe Lister-Jones, Alexis McGuinness, Rebecca Poretsky, Nik Steinberg, and Kristjan Thor.

The achievement of this book is shared with Tracy Hazas, with whom I've enjoyed countless adventures. Together we've shifted coasts and created new homes, pursued new challenges and built a life. Her tireless faith and phenomenal humor provide daily inspiration.

Several people who influenced this project are not here to celebrate its completion. This includes Michelle Meyers, a committed educator with a passion for social equity through institutional reform. Dan Gerould had a distinctly empathetic curiosity and wisdom that guided me through my earliest inquiries into urban development and theater. My grandmother, Yolanda Miller, was a funny and tough Brooklyn woman who taught me much about neighborhoods. My aunt, Fern Devlin, had a great passion for New York, from its garment district to its galleries and Broadway houses. She regarded the city as a muse, and exerted considerable influence on my work. I dedicate this to them.

Introduction

✦

City in Crisis / Performance in Crisis

> It cannot be gainsaid that the fight for meaningful employment, decent housing and freedom from hunger must preempt the fight for "Arts" in our list of priorities.
>
> —Vinnette Carroll

> When I asked my boss for a raise in pay,
> He shook his head and replied, "No way!
> I must refuse for the good of the nation,
> We're in a recession and a raise is inflation."
>
> —*Don't Bother Me, I Can't Cope*

The bluesy "Harlem Streets" from Vinnette Carroll's 1972 musical, *Don't Bother Me, I Can't Cope*, tells the story of a young man who lives in an apartment with rats, falling plaster, and wintry drafts through broken windowpanes. The jazz and funk-inflected libretto rebukes racial stereotypes and calls for self-determination, while it communicates contradictory and nuanced feelings about the city. This New York is a malevolent one, hardened by deindustrialization and national recession. In 1964, Title VII of the Civil Rights Act created the United States Equal Employment Opportunity Commission, and the Equal Employment Opportunity Act of 1972 attempted to codify and strengthen its effectiveness.[1] Yet the gains of the legislation did not improve conditions for the inhabitants of *Don't Bother Me, I Can't Cope.* The protagonists faced daily injustices: city officials condemn tenements in favor of landlords, civil servants condescend to the unemployed on the line for relief, and bosses use excuses of an economic recession to withhold equitable pay. Characters demand wage increases only to be told that gains will have to wait until the "big freeze thaws." By the time the play closed in 1974 after 1,065 performances on Broadway, New York City's unemployment rate surpassed 10 percent, and residents faced widespread layoffs across the public sector. The "big freeze" would not thaw for another decade.

During this period in New York's urban history, policy makers transformed the politics of growth into regimes of scarcity. The ensuing political battles pitted defenders of New York's identity as a progressive social welfare state against those who depicted the city as a "fiscal junkie" that needed to be tamed by austerity and shrinkage. The infamous *Daily News* headline from October 29, 1975—FORD TO CITY: DROP DEAD—captured the response of an infuriated polis after President Gerald Ford initially denied federal assistance to the bankrupt municipality. (Ford later changed his mind and signed legislation to provide federal loans to the city.) New York was an island within a country that took an anti-urban and anti-cosmopolitan stance toward the city, whipped to a fever pitch during its most desperate hour. This was not an attitude confined to President Ford, for whom it helped appeal to his conservative constituency. Democrats in Congress joined the chorus and responded with enmity: "There is a general negative feeling toward New York City," North Carolina representative Richardson Preyer said. "New York City had a certain overtone of sinfulness about it."[2]

City and state officials turned to the business establishment for counsel, and hastily created a state-backed corporation, the Municipal Assistance Corporation (MAC), to restore the city's finances. Headed by investment banker Felix Rohatyn, MAC took direct control over the city sales and stock transfers. With "Big MAC" in charge of the city's economic policy, New York entered into a receivership model that would control budgetary surpluses for years.[3] A three-year plan implemented in 1976 included wage freezes to uniform forces and educational personnel, tens of thousands of layoffs, salary cuts, and furloughing, all sold to the public as steps to avoid bankruptcy.

In the predominant narrative of the time—and one that still persists today—the largest city in the United States could not meet its financial obligations: billions of dollars of short-term debt reflected long-standing deficits and poor accounting practices. Missing from the headlines was the ideology that tied the fiscal crisis to certain populations, the same ones who would also soon pay a steep price under resulting austerity frameworks. Politicians and analysts blamed the "influx of impoverished blacks, Puerto Ricans, and other immigrants" after World War II who "demanded a greater range of services than any other city provides."[4] Robert Fitch opens his book, *The Assassination of New York*, with an anecdote that further captures this thinking: when on assignment for *Mother Jones* in the mid-1970s, he called a public relations official from the MAC to ask about the underlying reasons for the fiscal problems: "It's the fucking blacks and Puerto Ricans. They use too many city services and don't pay any taxes."[5] In more polite parlance, this was identified as a "job-skills mismatch," produced when the city shifted from manufacturing to white-collar industries just as new arrivals to the city needed work. The cultural ideologies of the crisis transcended accounting ledgers and financial statements. They inculpated a supposedly unruly populace that wasted municipal resources and brought disrepute to the formerly glittering metropolis. Many New Yorkers who blamed fellow residents for draining city services and not contributing enough tax revenue also saw the protection of elite arts culture as an essential step in the recovery.

Drop Dead investigates theater in New York during this mid-1970s fiscal crisis[6] period and analyzes the frameworks of austerity constructed during and after the city's near-bankruptcy, when theater mediated conflicts over public resources, spatial inequities, and community identity. Across the five boroughs of New York, theater artists, community leaders, and agency officials battled, fueled by the confounding logic of austerity. Many of the cultural initiatives intended to be temporary—such as the TKTS discount ticketing program on Broadway—were in fact institutionalized, while others created new tensions and new points of encounter between neighborhoods and theaters. This book explores the associated debates around performance, location, and access: arguments over money for grassroots theaters versus a flagging commercial theater; accusations of parochialism, radicalism, and traditionalism; advocacy on the part of playwrights and theater owners to create spaces for the theater in a city locked in crisis conditions; and, finally, hostilities over the very identities of neighborhoods, as defined by growing cultural institutions.

While this book pays careful attention to the material conditions of specific plays and performances, it emphasizes the cultural consequences and social implications of the fiscal crisis. *Drop Dead* argues that the policies implemented in the wake of the crisis calcified ideologies of austerity across the theatrical landscape, and constrained the distribution of theater across the city and its movement toward decentralization that began in the 1960s. Rather than track these dynamics through a single lens on the budget sheets of city-funded organizations, or top-down analyses of political regimes, I follow the careers of theater artists working in specific communities to show the arc of changes, some positive and some distinctly negative, encompassing patterns of production and reception.

While *Drop Dead* maintains a focus on one city, the crisis was part of a worldwide recession; banks in New York had tremendous exposure to New York City paper, third world debt, and bankrupt corporations. Historian Mike Wallace argues that they leaned on the city itself through a "proto-IMF strategy," and treated the city as a developing nation that needed to be reprimanded for wasting funds on social services, an area in which New York City had been historically liberal.[7] Theater's relationship to austerity figures differently throughout the various instances offered in this book, but the use of austerity as a punitive tool with which to reform the city's activities remains a constant. In this, the historical moment about which I write holds similarities with more recent international financial crises. Lenders in contemporary Greece, including the IMF and European central bankers, employ tactics reminiscent of New York's crisis period: hard-line backers of austerity chastise Greece for "living beyond its means," while the international elite of large banks and European Union governments protect their assets.

As critics of the creditors' proposed demands have noted, this narrative of overspending provides justification for socially destructive bailout measures. While steps were taken to safeguard investors, the great majority of Greek citizens (and the Greek economy) experienced devastating effects, including social crises throughout the city of Athens.[8] As in 1970s New York, a particular political project was advanced under the guise of economic necessity. Yet theater's relationship to austerity is not confined to examples of theaters resisting cutbacks—although that certainly existed. Theater offered opportunities for public debate about the principles of economic value and the arts; it became a rallying point for a changing notion of public services. In some cases, theater became compensation for austerity, as when politicians would shore up cultural resources to improve the city's cosmopolitan image. This, in turn, made theater a *part* of austerity, and a shaper of the city neighborhoods it most directly affected.

These notions extend, then, to the practices of communities and artists. While New York's crisis has been most frequently analyzed for its repercussions in the municipal sectors of hospitals, schools, and union workers, many other workers—including artists—absorbed the shocks of austerity. The cover art of Robert W. Bailey's book, *The MAC, The EFCB, and the Political Impact of the Crisis Regime,* depicted two balding, spectacled officials of the MAC and the Emergency Fiscal Control Board (EFCB). They handed soup to a breadline of stunned laborers: a police officer, sanitation and transit workers, a New York University professor, an orchestra member, and an actor holding a copy of *Backstage*. The image suggests that everyone was in it together, but the downturn touched certain populations and sectors more than others. Policy makers and government officials deployed particular rhetoric to hide the artificial aspects—and uneven distributive effects—of the crisis, controlled by and targeted against certain groups. The politics of "austerity discourse"[9] therefore remain central to any analysis of this chapter in New York's history and the response to a downturn that reflected the contradictions within capitalism, not simply sloppy ledgers. "Particularly in times of crisis, those who impose programs of austerity tend to present them as technocratic solutions to merely financial problems, rather than as social processes shaped by struggle and contestation," social theorists Craig Browne and Simon Susen write in their study of contemporary austerity-related contestation.[10] While mindful not to conflate 1975 with 2008, their insights are applicable across the last forty years of urban dynamics, when developments in the public and private sector inverted postwar social-democratic policies. This particular historical phase in struggles between capital and labor has been understood as part of a shift toward "neoliberal politics," and the early development of this model (in the United States) can be apprehended through the technocratic crisis management strategies of the 1970s.[11] Alongside urban sociologists and cultural geographers, theater scholars are increasingly seeking to elaborate the impacts of neoliberalism within cities and city-regions.

I began researching this project armed with questions about performance, urban neighborhoods, and the fiscal crisis, which intersected within a tangle of interdisciplinary research. Why did the city's 1975 economic crisis—which did so much to remake and reshape New York City for decades to come—factor so thinly in studies of New York theater, yet so prominently in other disciplines? Historian Joshua Freeman describes its broad significance, writing that the fiscal crisis "proved more damaging to New York social democracy than the Cold War. Beneath the cover of assumed economic necessity, a wholesale shift in power and normative values took place."[12] What were the shifts in power and values in the theatrical workplace during this period? How did these shifts alter the relationship between theaters and their audiences? Economic and cultural changes operated as a determining force for theatrical production both then and now; how might one analyze theater as a social practice during that time of municipal crisis?

Another goal of this book is to redress the perfunctory treatment previously afforded to the dynamics of 1970s theater in New York. Tom Wolfe's essay, "The Me Decade and the Third Great Awakening," published in 1976, has widely influenced perceptions of the 1970s and convinced many chroniclers that narcissistic consumerism had irreversibly corroded American culture. Will Kaufman suggests that rethinking this position can lead to a "re-evaluation of the markers that these critics use to identify narcissism, such as nostalgia, irony, and individualism."[13] When scholarly accounts conjoin the economic crisis and theater, they frequently portray artists as fleeing the city or weaseling their way into its cheap housing stock. Studio 54, Andy Warhol, and Pop Art loom large in cultural histories of the period: the 1970s as a "me" decade is remembered as relentlessly superficial and self-obsessed. Yet the excesses of urban neglect presented a far more urgent set of contingencies for most residents. Untested definitions of the decade as hedonistic and self-indulgent can obscure a particular scale of inquiry into the scope of cultural production of the period. While not disregarding the significance of national political movements or aesthetic trends, I argue that in New York City, the performance and politics of neighborhood beg equal consideration. Theater companies that gave voice to local concerns and the dynamics of urban dispossession often operated on the boundaries between community-based, amateur, and Off-Off Broadway performance. How did the relationship between neighborhoods, audiences, and theaters change as a result of austerity ideologies? And, as city officials sought to promote a vision of New York's cosmopolitan culture to improve its image as it ascended out of the crisis, what were the implications for theaters?

Interest in these questions, of course, proceeds with the assumption that performance practices are entangled with municipal infrastructures. Geographer Matthew Gandy's eloquent writing about water in the metropolis is worth quoting here at length for its articulation of the ways in which urban infrastructure presents a "stage" for analyses of class relations, power, movements, economic justice, and security:

> Water is not simply a material element in the production of cities but is also a critical dimension to the social production of space. Water implies a series of connectivities between the body and the city, between social and bio-physical systems, between the evolution of water networks and capital flows, and between the visible and invisible dimensions to urban space. But water is at the same time a brutal delineator of social power which has at various times worked to either foster greater urban cohesion or generate new forms of political conflict.[14]

It is possible to substitute "performance" (or, for that matter, "theater") for every instance of the word "water" in Gandy's passage; indeed, performance scholars have interrogated the relationship between performance, the complexity of urban infrastructures, and the social production of space.[15] Judith Hamera writes of the "relational infrastructure" of dance technique, and begins her study of dance and urban life with the observation that "dancers make cities as friends, as partners, as *corps* and, in so doing, remake themselves, their audiences, and each other every day, day after day."[16] I share this contention, and superimpose on Hamera's list the labors of remaking neighborhoods.

As a corollary to this work, numerous scholars have excavated linkages between the growth of neoliberal political ideology in the 1970s and changes to the quality of local spaces—streets, theaters, and architecture. These investigations discern the contours of neoliberal dispossession through urban performance practices, and reflect growing concern with "the bitter quandaries of neoliberalism that affect the pasts and the futures of theatre and performance research in particular, and with social welfare as a whole."[17] In post-Fordist New York, the emergence of neoliberal governance was experienced, across space, differently (often unevenly) from place to place.[18] The intimate interrelation between the rise of neoliberalism and the implementation of austerity "packages" has been strategically articulated in the arena of the city through urban initiatives. Where does this large-scale restructuring connect with the theatrical production of specific localities?

Uneven Cultural Development

At the time, New York City's $13.5 billion budget was the largest municipal budget in the United States and the third largest overall governmental budget in the country; with 7.5 million residents, New York was the most populous city in the nation, with more than 6,000 miles of streets across five boroughs.[19] Its budget is an accounting tool—a public statement that should reflect the priorities and political philosophies of the mayor and the City Council. Keeping in mind the decisive role of the material realities of many theatrical productions, my primary space of investigation is not the budget sheet, but the spatially and sectorally uneven sites of crisis. Surpluses or fiscal crises: both create questions of value. Examples of how that value was discussed, discerned, fought for, and represented, constitute this book. "Crisis is not objectively bad or good; rather, it signals systemic change whose outcome is determined through struggle," writes Ruth Gilmore.[20] She also encourages thinking about political economy "in an everyday way" to understand local manifestations of economic and political restructuring.[21] Theater and performance texts (which include plays alongside annual financial reports) comprise essential reading in this research.

Most introductory textbooks for economics and the public sector, for example, clarify the different branches of the government and the federal and local structures. But these local structures—education, police and fire, libraries, sewage, garbage—will often not include the arts or analyses of culture, representation, and the city's public realms. These same textbooks will discuss the necessary trade-off between efficiency and equity; the difficulty of measuring costs of benefits from their savings. Economy, scarcity, and culture: *Drop Dead* demonstrates that all three intersected with rhetorical, performative, and historical dimensions and repercussions.

New York was "the prototypical New Deal city in the prototypical New Deal state,"[22] and its orientation toward the arts earned it a similarly progressive reputation. Throughout the 1960s, New York State pioneered a model for arts funding, which, on the state level, originated with Governor Nelson Rockefeller's 1960 creation of the New York Arts Council, now known as the New York State Council on the Arts (NYSCA). The federal government adopted a similar approach in 1965 with the creation of the National Endowment for the Arts (NEA). On a city level, in the late 1960s, the funding stream inched beyond mainstream arts organizations such as the Metropolitan Museum of Art, with monies directed toward new programs that reflected some of the city's ethnic and racial diversity.[23]

This constituted a "powerful shift in the geography of culture" during the 1960s and early 1970s, a span of time coextensive with the two mayoral terms of John Lindsay (1966–73).[24] Mariana Mogilevich argues that the Lindsay administration transformed the arts from a "vehicle of exclusion" to a cultural dimension accessible to a wider public, a political program explicitly spatial, as well as cultural.[25] Admirers of Lindsay's policies point to his ability to soothe volatile conditions amid a national context of wars, rights movements, urban unrest, and financial troubles inherited from his predecessors. His critics maintain that "limousine liberal" Lindsay's two terms had catastrophic results for the city, and lay the blame at his feet for not doing more to recognize and stem the city's economic deterioration. This view similarly attributes "white flight" out of the city to Lindsay's acquiescence to wage and pension agreements, his concessions to militant political organizations, and a perceived fiscal promiscuity.[26] That narrative, however, reproduces misunderstandings of the city's municipal crisis, as well as twin national recessions (1969–70 and 1973–75). More to the point, discontentment with his socially and culturally progressive programs fostered divisions that obscured the accomplishments of his tenure.

Lindsay in fact implemented changes of great significance to the primary concerns of this book—not just through an altered map of available art and culture, but through the production of new representations of the city. Coupled with a decisive push toward consolidating the city's cosmopolitan credentials, the eight-year period of Lindsay governance established a trend toward decentralized yet robust support for the arts, a balance swiftly destabilized during the fiscal crisis. Lindsay's expansion of the arts via a redistribution of programs across urban space comprises a crucial historical context for this book, with many developments of the 1970s forming a reaction to the decade before: the fiscal crisis conditions arrested the decentralization process and (albeit controversial) neighborhood empowerment programs.

This "democratization of the arts" led some to fear that established cultural assets would suffer a reduction in support and a concomitant decline in artistic quality. Protestations against decentralization feared a dislodging of theater from "a concentrated and competitive environment," and the irrelevance of the traditional sites of high art.[27] Advocates of decentralization framed their argument as expansion and equity: an in-progress movement with distinct political underpinnings, begun in the 1960s, when neighborhoods and ethnic groups campaigned for greater shares of city resources. Artists demanded local facilities for their own brand of training, experimentation, presentation, and audience building. These actions inherently critiqued antiquated notions of delivering "beauty to the ghetto" through touring productions of the classical canon. The movement for community control of arts resources reached a pinnacle in the late 1960s and early 1970s, after which the philosophy became more vulnerable to accusations of provincialism and divisive radicalism, running counter to the city's new image agendas.

In addition to this overriding theme of decentralization during the 1970s, another recurring factor to consider is the process understood as suburbanization. Though frequently conceptualized as the exodus out of the city that began in the postwar period, this operated in multiple ways, across multiple sites, and had ramifications for many spheres of the city's cultural life. As a consequence of both the real and perceived results of this phenomenon, many city officials and mainstream producers sought to attract the spectral "lost audiences" that had abandoned the city for the suburbs. Due to the city's near-bankruptcy, public services were vilified in political and popular discourse, while demographic shifts led to angst-ridden discussions of "white flight." Films like *The Out of Towners*, *The Warriors*, and *Taxi Driver* showcased a violent and even apocalyptic side of the city: the villains of film and television narratives were the people themselves, with shadowy and unsafe neighborhoods typifying modern urban ruin. Max Page identified the trend of imagining New York City's demise through narratives of disaster as helping to resolve society's anxieties during the fiscal crisis period.[28] But these films excluded austerity measures themselves; the sensational snapshots of crime and fear overwhelmed the dull reality of bank notes and interest rates, as well as the struggles for power that motivated the decisions to restructure the city's debt.

The case studies chosen for this book present different narratives of the city's neighborhoods at this time. All germinate in the realm of embodied, live performance across the geography of the five boroughs. They offer the opportunity to analyze the interplay between institutional forms and emergent neoliberal philosophies as New York City and state progressed through the stages of the "Long Default." The heaviest burdens of the profound retrenchment program implemented in New York following 1975 were imposed upon the consumers of municipal services,[29] and many city expenditures were suspect (it was during this period that officials abolished the 150-year tradition of tuition-free City University). One primary preoccupation of *Drop Dead* is, therefore, theater as a city service. Producer Joseph Papp's famous evocation that theater should be as essential as garbage removal framed theater as a public "service" at the very moment when political pressure first sought to eliminate even the services already *accepted* as essential. "A city living on the precipice of national disgrace," Bernard Gifford opined, "is hardly in the position or the mood to equate expenditures of funds it does not have with the public good."[30] Across all neighborhoods, theater artists, communities, and city officials waged battles over retrenchment. This transformed and expanded the long-standing "turf wars" over control of resources into a larger conflict over the identity of the city and its discrete neighborhoods. The politics of representation were central to this confrontation over the economics of representation.

Because of this, these chapters explore a cross-sectoral vista of theatrical activity, looking to Broadway, Off, Off-Off, as well as neighborhood theaters. In *Social Work: Performing Art, Supporting Publics* (2011), Shannon Jackson opens her study of contemporary art practices by questioning models of political engagement that "measure artistic radicality by its degree of anti-institutionality," encouraging scholars and artists to instead imagine sustainable social institutions.[31] Support systems frayed during this era in New York, when the interdependent social networks of which Jackson speaks—labor, sanitation, welfare, and urban planning—disintegrated within the urban ecosystem. Street corners piled with garbage, union leaders battled against cuts, and the civic discourse questioned the very stability of the city's welfare protections. It is within this context that major institutions strained to achieve relevance and stability, while fledgling 1960s arts organizations embarked on institutionalization.

Since World War II, city boosters staked much of New York's urban identity (and economic vitality) on its status as an international arts hub.[32] But when former city Comptroller Abe Beame was elected mayor in 1974, the future of New York as both a cultural capital and a solvent city were understood as linked to the ability of the city to revive "the nation's cultural heart."[33] Throughout the late 1960s, many of the cultural jewels of the city, Broadway and Times Square, civic centers like Lincoln Center and the Brooklyn Academy of Music, confronted issues of declining reputation and reception. Once the city's public relations efforts sought to consolidate investor confidence and the credit market's perception of the city, arguments to bolster the big-ticket cultural life of the city gained traction. Fred Ferretti referred to the people behind this campaign as inner city technicians—"they spoke of the beauties of Central Park, the cultural context of Lincoln Center, the glories of the city's museums, the fact that the Broadway and off-Broadway theatres were the gardens in which the seeds of acting greatness were planted."[34] In addition to the institutionalization of theater, this decade also laid the groundwork for contemporary assumptions about the instrumentality of performance.

Nowhere is this more clear than in the discourses of the "creative city," and, more broadly, contemporary urban cultural policy. City governments seek to generate specific attributes of this creative city as business development tools, concomitant with the expectation that theater activities must be legitimated in economic terms.[35] Arlene Dávila argues in *Culture Works* (2012) that these culture-based strategies do not necessarily mitigate inequalities: "far from an added-on ornament that 'softens' or ameliorates the social inequalities of neoliberal polices, culture becomes imperative to their production," especially when culture is the primary tool "to convey a sense of inclusion and the illusion of representation."[36] Often, "creative city" strategies focus more on producing a display of creativity as a cultural *asset* rather than supporting existing coalitions of theaters and developing the myriad ways in which artistic activity intersects with urban space and city residents. Further, as Laura Levin and Kim Solga argue, two of the questions that emerge from inquiry into the "creative city" are also central to the larger project of urban renewal: how and who determines what it means to be "from" a city, and to feel "at home" in the city?[37] The complex reality of the role of artists in urban redevelopment has been acknowledged by academics since the mid-1980s, yet all too often detailed analyses into theater's role within these transformations have been neglected in favor of highly polarizing characterizations.

The trumpeting of New York's culture as the city's finest export during the 1970s had a dark side; few people mentioned the services that the city offered its own people in the same glowing terms. Programs (from the city's welfare load to its free university and municipal hospital system) were blamed, and yet its cultural riches were defended. This period also tested the depth of commitment to the professed values of urban renewal projects like Lincoln Center: art for the public good became interpolated as art from the public coffers. A range of interconnected trends gathered strength in the city's financial collapse, as issues of growing national and international concern were evaluated: escalating costs of federally sponsored and locally delivered social and cultural programs were high among them.

During the 1973 mayoral election, the *New York Times* presented the candidates with a series of questions about the role of the city as an arts center, and all projected predictably arts-friendly stances, with revealing shadings of distinction. The candidate running on the Conservative party line, Mario Biaggi, expressed distress about the deterioration of "the whole quality of theatregoing in New York," and pledged to restore it to "what it once was," a reference to the perceived need for change on Broadway.[38] Other candidates spoke of decentralizing cultural opportunities: "I want Tebaldi to sing in the Bronx," said the Liberal-backed candidate, State Assemblyman Albert H. Blumenthal, in an effort to emphasize opportunities away from Manhattan.[39] That the arts would have a role to play in New York's rejuvenation was assumed; what models this imperative to intervene required, what the role of artists themselves might be, and how government agencies should react, were all less clear. These conflicts amounted to a struggle for the very identity of the streets. The social, political, and economic implications of performance in urban space ultimately influenced the perception of culture in New York at a time when the fiscal crisis threatened the stability of any and all cultural enterprises.

This defense of New York's cultural sphere did not lead to a single outcome, or a single set of policy provisions. The crisis did not decimate all performing arts funding, and it also did not bolster the strength of every elite institution. Rather, it enacted conditions of uneven cultural development across fields of performance practices. I adapt this concept from geographer David Harvey's term, "uneven development," and his contention that the one persistent fact within the complex history of uneven neoliberalization "has been the universal tendency to increase social inequality and to expose the least fortunate elements in any society—be it in Indonesia, Mexico, or Britain—to the chilly winds of austerity and the full fate of increasing marginalization."[40] With that in mind, and given that no theater company depended wholly on city funding for its livelihood, my emphasis here is not exclusively on the budget sheets of city-funded arts organizations. It is on the ways in which innovations in performance infrastructures connected to municipal infrastructures, as well as on shifts in audience composition between and throughout certain neighborhoods of the city. My immediate interest is with the interlocking of municipal priorities and performance: how it decentralized across the city (or did not) through material and immaterial connections with other companies, institutions, and agencies, for survival and for growth.

Urban Process / Urban Performance

To their critics, the urban policies of the period (including the controversial "planned shrinkage" approach to urban redevelopment) were little more than thinly veiled attempts at a spatial reordering of the city. In the most nefarious interpretation, these aimed at the displacement of less desirable residents—newly arrived African American laborers from the South, recent Caribbean immigrants—who could not find employment. Since the late 1960s, population shifts had changed audience composition but went unacknowledged by many, especially those on the Great White Way. In 1973 Joseph Papp, the head of the New York Shakespeare Festival (NYSF) and the Public Theater, argued that theater in New York operated in denial of "the exodus of great numbers of white middle class to the suburbs," and the wall of poverty that separated "vast numbers of people from the arts."[41]

As a consequence, new collaborations emerge as a defining aspect of this period; desperate conditions and declining audiences led, for example, to Papp's artistic decisions at the helm of Lincoln Center's Repertory Theater, as well as to the creation of the TKTS booth in Times Square. It also prompted the Brooklyn Academy of Music (BAM) to open its doors to a range of theater groups for dynamic collaborations in which residents of the outer boroughs, fueled by the decentralization of arts training, appeared on stages alongside the avant-garde programs that would later comprise the bulk of BAM's offerings.

Performance *in* crisis refers to these machinations, and yet the questions raised are as old as the ones Plato considered during the twilight of Athenian democracy regarding the city. What is the role of interest groups in the city? How do the city's institutions function? How does the city government respond to dissension? What is democracy and what is merely democratic propaganda? Jean-François Pradeau, reflecting on Plato's political philosophy, argues that the underlying subject of any inquiry into city life must be "the nature of life lived in common, the way to live a communal life."[42] Otherwise, city life is understood simply as one of conflict and power struggles, with politics little more than a technique of domination. Many instances in these chapters—such as Ellen Stewart's work at La Mama, or Vinnette Carroll's Urban Arts Corps—provide insights into the functioning of institutions and the ways in which performance operates in relation to this communal imperative. During the 1970s, many theaters and theater companies vied for the civic stage: this book is titled performance *in* crisis because competition for resources (money, theater space, spectators, new plays, new talent, political favor) aided, abetted, and exaggerated the multidimensional "fiscal crisis." In the case of Stewart, Carroll, Papp, and others, its force was resisted and occasionally blunted through performance practices.

This contention finds support in a long line of theorizations about the city. In the mid-1980s, urban sociologist Manuel Castells observed with approval the increased acceptance of the idea that cities are shaped by class interests and the change in perspective across his field: "The matter is not who has power *in* the city, but who controls (and whose interests are fulfilled by) what happens *on* the city."[43] Cities are far more complex than their accounting systems, and scholars have endeavored to analyze this crisis as a social process of structurally conditioned conflicts. Since Castells noted this change, understandings of the city have continued to shift; political systems analysis moves alongside neo-Marxist perspectives inspired by Michel de Certeau; Peter Marcuse's writings on the "right to the city" integrated the arguments of Henri Lefebvre to introduce new theories of urban space and justice; radical geographer Edward Soja utilized the lens of spatial justice in order to recompose "our lived spaces of representation as potentially nurturing places of resistance."[44] In theater's relatively recent spatial turn, "the city" as a site of performance has been theorized in multiple ways. Jen Harvie emphasizes cities as urban process, something ever changing; as a social activity, theater does more than just demonstrate the structures and social power dynamics of politics and economics, but is also part of the urban process, as a set of cultural and labor practices.[45] These imaginings allow the tensions in the city—private space and political freedom, urban space and neighborhood change, and contested definitions of "public"—to emerge.

If this framing appears overly invested in the decisions of government actors and too far removed from performance practices, that reflects my desire to, as Shannon Jackson has written, analyze social practice that inevitably engages "a range of political orientations and social goals," situated within debates about "social systems of governance and human care."[46] Here the term "agency" takes on new meanings, as the interrelations between city agencies and theaters during this period performed such crucial labors of city building. Jackson's interest in the "non-autonomy of human beings" and "projects that imagine agency not only as systemic disruption but also systemic relations"[47] leads, in this study, to the close analysis of theater companies in tandem with systems of performing arts labor and social welfare during the 1970s. My argument positions this decade as one rich in a range of models that made clear the imbrication of theater and the city. The anti-authoritarian philosophies of the 1960s did not merely expire as separatist movements dissolved, but often flourished into remarkable arts institutions with deep civic ties—from the Chelsea Theater Center to La Mama E.T.C. to the Urban Arts Corps to the Public Theater to the Everyman Street Theatre Company. How did new political matrices revise the performance practices of the 1960s?

Initiatives aimed at the support and delivery of cultural goods sought to redress structural inequities, and these, in some senses, dominate *Drop Dead*. By the close of the decade, however, largely due to incoherent and disorganized cultural policies coupled with the ideological fallout from the fiscal crisis, the outcome remained decidedly contradictory. Neil Brenner and Nik

Theodore build upon David Harvey's work to identify particular concepts as concomitant with the early 1970s, and remind us of the unpredictable nature of the transformations of industrial cities in the United States:

> The creative destruction of institutional space at the urban scale does not entail a linear transition from a generic model of the "welfare city" towards a new model of the "neoliberal city." Rather, these multifaceted processes of local institutional change involve a contested, trial-and-error searching process in which neoliberal strategies are being mobilized in place-specific forms and combinations. . . . Neoliberal strategies of localization severely exacerbate many of the regulatory problems they ostensibly aspire to resolve—such as economic stagnation, unemployment, sociospatial polarization, and uneven development—leading in turn to unpredictable mutations of those very strategies and the institutional spaces in which they are deployed.[48]

Performance sowed urban cohesion as frequently as it generated political conflict—sometimes both in the same instance. With astonishing rapidity, the years of the fiscal crisis adjusted and revised the trend of experimental and investigational support for new institutions, and, on a broader scale, new systems of cultural dispersal across the city that attended to the goals of urban improvement. As federal monies and political enthusiasm for such programs lagged, municipal support reverted to a safer model, one focused on the activities and edifices of established institutions. Like its well-publicized move to save Radio City Music Hall during a moment of extreme fiscal stress, the administration looked to red-letter institutions that could garner sympathy around the country and behind the doors of boardrooms. Due to the dynamics of funding, support, and urban unrest, for theater artists, the perils and pleasures of institutionalization reoccur throughout each case study in this book. How did competing concerns play out on the level of city and civic support?

Part 1: Ideologies of Austerity

One danger of writing about a distinct temporal period of crisis is that crisis tends to be a descriptive rule, rather than exception, in historical studies of post–World War II theater and performance. Mike Sell writes of 1960s countercultural performance trends such as the Living Theatre, early U.S. Performance Art, and the Black Arts Movement as a "performance crisis" that permanently altered aspects of American culture.[49] This book does not disagree; in fact, *Drop Dead* is as much about the 1960s as it is the 1970s, and its case studies straddle city administrations that crossed the threshold of the decades. Much of the "meat" of fiscal crisis alterations functioned as reactions and responses to the upheavals of the Swinging Sixties. Additionally, given the developments of "abundance" within the larger landscape of the 1960s cultural field—the spread of university training programs, the growth of large repertory theaters in major cities, the formation of the NEA and the expansion of the Ford Foundation[50]—the crisis of 1970s performance in New York is far more intricate than a yawning trench of austerity.

This book attempts to massage tricky matters of periodization, particularly the tendency to oversimplify the tumble after 1960s-era radicalisms into identity politics. As James Harding and Cindy Rosenthal note, any study of the political theater of the 1960s reinserts the "deceptively simple question of legacy."[51] In addition to Sell, one the strongest appraisals of these complicated legacies is found in their anthology, *Restaging the Sixties: Radical Theaters and Their Legacies*. The authors describe the group theaters that emerged in the 1960s as responding to issues of authority and community, both "vis-à-vis society at large and vis-à-vis theatrical practice in particular."[52] The preoccupation of many theaters of the 1960s with issues of authority and community makes the artists examined in *Drop Dead* excellent examples through whom to revise, resist, and subvert the troubling retrenchment ideologies that crept into the discourses and materiality of arts provision in the 1970s.

The first part of this book tracks the contours of these "ideologies of austerity" through case studies in two locations: downtown Manhattan, where the Off-Off Broadway (OOB) movement had created new modes and spaces of performance; and Times Square, where theater owners panicked over the effects of suburbanization on Broadway houses. A tension stretches between these two chapters, and it is found in much theater scholarship about 1970s New York: on the one hand, some chroniclers pass over the decade as a veritable artistic wasteland, while on the other, scholars employ narratives of economic instability as breeding enhanced creativity—as if artists received immunity from material concerns. These structures of loss often turn on the diminished strength of the OOB movement (and Broadway theater production) as paralleling the decline of the Lower East Side and the deterioration of Times Square. Both narratives, however, obscure the fecundity of the 1970s; in part 1, I look into the expansion of La Mama E.T.C. on OOB and the debate over audience development in the Broadway theater district.

Will Kaufman argues that 1970s theater encompassed both private and public conflict, and dwelt "as much upon social exclusion, isolation and exhaustion as upon solidarity and faith."[53] In the realm of experimental or alternative theater, for Theodore Shank (as well as theater historians Arnold Aronson and Christopher Bigsby), the period is typified by the professionalization of theater, during which the aforementioned "abundance" (union contracts, GI Bill university programs, increased institutional structures) contributed to the limiting of barrier-breaking, experimental avant-garde theater.[54] As I explore, these factors were indeed decisive, but not always as limiting as some contend.

It is of course true that OOB, which once symbolized a new role for alternative theater, experimental writing, and production styles, had, by some measures, disintegrated by the early 1970s.[55] Yet in Arnold Aronson's look at the avant-garde of the 1950s through the 1980s, his section on the 1970s in New York focuses on solo performance art that emphasized the individual over the commodified object. Aronson describes an increased self-reliance (equated with self-reference) in avant-garde works, and an overall shift in political sensibilities: "By the 1970s . . . the impetus seemed more attuned to the self-absorption of the 'me generation' than to larger sociopolitical concerns."[56] Herbert Blau described the decade's theater as "a participatory period of improvisational method and instant gratification," and for Shank, "self-as-content" was a prominent mode of theatrical exploration at the time, found in companies such as the Hungarian Squat Theater or Richard Foreman's Ontological-Hysteric Theater.[57] Because the rise of identity politics occurred in the 1970s, the output of companies like the San Francisco Mime Troupe, El Teatro Campesino, and the Negro Ensemble Company are frequently (and valuably) analyzed as collectives within the prism of identity politics, responding to the Vietnam War, the civil rights movement, and, eventually, feminist and queer struggles. The very necessary labors of institutionalization, however, are submerged in histories of downtown theater that focus on 1970s political separatism on the one hand, and myopic investigations of the self and identity on the other.

As Stephen Bottoms and Wendell Stone both acknowledge, many artists of the OOB era matured into new formations after 1968, and, as I demonstrate, worked across the five boroughs of New York to formulate new performance practices, while many others kept an eye trained on the stages of Broadway. As the production expenses of Off-Broadway continued to rise,[58] the wave of experimental theater that had taken root on the East Side of downtown entered its second—and for playwright Julie Bovasso, third—decade with new demands for space, money, and visibility. This coincided with increasingly decentralized funding streams that supported theater initiatives in the very neighborhoods where basic city services had historically been neglected. Meanwhile, specific locations in the city—like Times Square—became targets for pro-growth officials desperate to enact visible change and encourage tourism.

For some in the OOB movement, institution-building came at a price; the whiff of something *dirty* hovered over the consolidation of real estate and depositing of Rockefeller money in company coffers. The remembrances of Caffe Cino inscribe the 1960s playwrights explosion as insulated from critical or popular approval, but by the early 1970s this was patently not the case among many writers and theater owners. Playwrights sought producers, producers sought theater spaces, and theater spaces sought audiences. And everyone, it seemed, sought a greater level of financial support. The valorization of seemingly oppositional and autonomous 1960s performance practices can cloud analyses of 1970s theater as a "selling out" into a triumphal embrace of pacifying governmental monies.

Yet the funding decisions of the NEA, NYSCA, and the city's Department of Cultural Affairs (DCA) in the early 1970s reflected—and refracted—the political and social gains made during the preceding decade: social turmoil forced change in the areas of funding, geography, and critical attention. Previously marginalized theater artists and organizations transferred spheres of legitimacy and enjoyed credibility through publicity and endowments. By the late 1970s, however, as the city strategized ways to repair its image deficit, the model of centralized culture gained ground: the administration restructured its cultural affairs apparatus around economic development and rerouted its support to a centralized model. For some, the newly politicized funding process presented opportunities to seize the attention of government officials and clarify their demands. In these instances, their relationships within a crumbling urban ecosystem posed a great threat to the theater's financial survival yet also constituted its most crucial institutional connections. Other organizations focused locally, unwilling to reframe their performance practices within a city-sponsored vision of a new New York.

Part 2: Affective Inequalities

On the other side of generalizations of the "Me Decade" lies a recurring nostalgia for the sequined glory days of 1970s bohemia. Allan Tannenbaum, chief photographer during the run of the *Soho News* (1973–82), assembled a remarkable compendium of photographs that richly catalogs memorials to John Lennon and Studio 54, anti-nuclear, anti-draft, and anti-heroin demonstrators, gay pride marches, urban decay in the South Bronx, the Ching-A-Lings motorcycle gang in an empty storefront, and drivers lined up for gas during the oil embargo of 1973. "The cultural and political revolution of the 1960s gave way to the hedonism and decadence of the 1970s," writes Tannenbaum.[59] Andy Warhol's glib proclamation that the 1970s "are very empty" animates this common narrative.[60] In it, the depths of New York's economic crisis led to a "different kind of prosperity" for visual arts, music, theater, dance, and cinema that hinged upon cheap spaces, artistic freedom, and a spirit of community and ingenuity that flourished "amidst the dilapidated buildings and mean streets of downtown Manhattan."[61]

This book takes a different approach to thinking through the mean streets and the efforts toward renewed definitions of prosperity. Throughout *Drop Dead*, I do not draw generalizations about the vast population of artists in the city, but rather attempt to dismantle the myth that the economic downturn necessarily delivered conditions for creativity. Indeed, portrayals in popular culture tend to depict only the Warholian sensibility and omit the 1975 bankruptcy altogether or cast it in a nostalgic register. One of my original impetuses in undertaking this research was a desire to complicate two misperceptions that persist even today: that artists flourish during times of urban crisis, and that the goal of government involvement in the arts is to foster eventual economic self-sufficiency on the part of cultural organizations. Elizabeth Currid-Halkett argues that economic factors during the 1970s "created an environment that allowed artists to cluster in the same neighborhoods, paying rents so cheap that instead of working a second job, they were able to focus completely on performing and exhibiting nonstop in rock venues, clubs, galleries, and cafes. The downturn in the economy that negatively affected much of society was significantly positive for creativity in the long term."[62] This may have been true for Hilly Kristal, the founder of the legendary club CBGB, who recalled low rents and fertile congregations of artists like Patti Smith, Allen Ginsberg, Jeff Koons, and Warhol. But this formulation positions artists outside of the reach of social, cultural, and economic conditions when in fact, in the case of many Off, Off-Off, and Broadway theaters, a plurality of crisis narratives emerged, with other urgent variables.

The theaters analyzed in this book directly confronted the intense racial turmoil of urban centers during this period. Kimberley Johnson analyzes the political and cultural milieu of the city "when demands for African American autonomy and community control were increasing," motivated by genuine desire for positive change as well as "rank opportunism."[63] As politicians, foundations, and activists all responded to the urban crisis, they engaged in a vibrant, and often contentious, discussion in media venues about the form and function of cultural production. This included newly launched theaters inspired by the artistic impulses of the mid-1960s Black Power movement. Mike Sell argues that when the Nixon administration slashed government funding for experimental arts and the national economic crisis of 1973 struck hundreds of community theaters across the United States, "many of the practical links forged between art and politics were sundered—but the theory survived in those educated by the Black Arts Movement."[64] To a degree, the same can be said for the ethos of many street theater groups, experimental interracial theaters, and neighborhood arts groups, all of which feature prominently in *Drop Dead*. Yet as Kimberly Phillips-Fein has documented, austerity measures involved not only actual cutbacks, but also inflicted damage on the mood and imagination of artists and other citizens, threatening their very capacity to make demands on the state.[65]

With systemic disruptions, so too were there meaningful, constitutive relations. I employ John Brown Childs's term, "transcommunality," as well as Kathleen Lynch's concept, "affective inequality," to discuss some of the significant coalitions that formed during this period. Much of the extant language to describe small, independent, or neighborhood theaters tends to reinforce the very divisions they hope to clarify; Jan Cohen-Cruz describes well the word soup of performance that "engages" community: for example, the subtle differences between community-based and grassroots theater. One of her questions points to my reason for continually seeking new terms throughout many of these chapters, and occasionally borrowing from urban sociologists, such as Childs and Lynch, to do so: "What is the line between institutionally-based and community-based art?"[66] Neither of the terms that I put forward here are intended to erase the reality that these are *arts* organizations, but rather to set my analysis apart from the descriptors that relegate this work to a kind of transaction—art for (or from) the community. This transactional view of neighborhood arts not only obscures the role that institutions can (and often do) play in such performances, but also the nature of this art as "local." This "local" branding can lead to erroneous assumptions about its aesthetic value, as well as its role and function within urban processes.

Part 3: The Performance of Neighborhood

I continue to connect theaters, neighborhood, material conditions, and the reigning economic order through two case studies in part 3 in which the tensions between a centralized model for urban rejuvenation through the arts—in civic centers on city-owned land—created bold experiments in audience, performance, and the public. A careful excavation of performance practices in neighborhoods across the city shows contradictory ramifications of austerity ideologies—spatially, racially, and culturally coded. The "performance of neighborhood" emerges through more dimensions than just narratives of decline, rebirth, or revitalization. For many artists, particularly those in under-resourced communities, the cumulative effects of initiatives only exacerbated the spatial inequities across city blocks. In a rousing speech at the 1974 First American Congress of Theatre (FACT), Hazel Bryant, the founder of the Afro-American Total Theatre Arts Foundation (1963) and the Richard Allen Center of Culture and Art (1968), as well as the president of the African-American Federation of Arts and the Black Theater Alliance (1971), described how fiscal instability was experienced differently across the field:

> What we are really talking about is the haves and the have-nots. What we have brought to this conference is people who have money and people who do not and people who do not have the slightest idea how to get the kind of money you are talking about, and people who glory in finding ways to do what they want to do without money. . . . In a society where money is so desperately important, it becomes very difficult for people who do not have money to have a strong voice. That is one of the ways that you who have money can help us. . . . So now it is about how do we make all of us important and by so doing, we make people important.[67]

Bryant presented a cogent plea on behalf of artists committed to and representative of small-scale institutions and their audiences—the grassroots, radical, or neighborhood theaters. While large-scale institutions like BAM weathered their own fiscal crisis tumult, the city's disinvestment hit small-scale institutions triply: in their theater companies' operations, on their stages, and in their communities. I have therefore focused on the material development of the idea (or ideology) of culture, to understand "how the idea of culture functions within systems of production and reproduction in the contemporary city."[68] How has "the idea of culture" been developed and deployed as a means of attempting to order, control, and define "others"? And how did cultural producers in turn create their own structures, definitions, and representations?

Chapter Organization

Robert W. Bailey acknowledged—with some exasperation—that measuring the impact of New York's near-bankruptcy is "easier said than done."[69] To do so within a large city's formidable cultural sphere is no less challenging. The reader knowledgeable in the performance landscape of the period may find unfathomable omissions. How could the Performing Garage not take center stage in any discussion of neighborhood, cultural equity, and performance in the 1970s? I omitted a great many companies that seemed "perfect" for inclusion in this study: from The Wooster Group to the Jean Cocteau Repertory to Barbara Ann Teer's National Black Theatre to Theater for the New City, all vital contributors to the theater during the time of my focus. I have attempted to avoid reproducing a tendency to write about theater in New York in the post–World War II era with a Manhattan-centric mindset. The host of assumptions within theater history that privilege the borough of Manhattan and the development of Off and Off-Off Broadway downtown also produces a polarizing notion of the "edges" and "centers" of cultural production. While I begin my study in downtown Manhattan, the nexus of so much theatrical innovation, from there I travel to multiple neighborhoods across the map of the city. Throughout, I attempt to iterate the "centralized" city institutions (BAM, Lincoln Center) as landmarks to orient the reader, but also to call attention to the profusion of theater occurring far from those sites. Thanks in part to the rise of Brooklyn's global brand, the outer-boroughs have only recently enjoyed a cultural renaissance in the popular media. This study, however, gives prominence to the long history of outer-borough performance, and, in doing so, questions the often totalizing narrative of "urban decline."

While being mindful of each city's historical development, there are similarities between post-industrial cities during this period, and this book is illuminated by corollary research into performance and economic restructuring in other city centers, such as that of Michael McKinnie, Loren Kruger, and Jen Harvie. Still, "New York exceptionalism" has dogged New York studies, and the city has been argued to be a poor model for extrapolation. My personal biography plays a role in compounding this, as is so often the case in scholarship; thanks to a childhood in Brooklyn, I for a long time viewed Manhattan as the unimpeachable "center"—it was the destination for after-school playwriting workshops and discount musicals through Theatre Development Fund (TDF) subscriptions. But through the years I began to question that bias as much as someone living in Chicago, Summers County, or San Francisco might. What about the outer boroughs? How and why did major theater locations remain so centralized when artists necessarily lived across the five boroughs? Why did a city with such a rich history of activist and grassroots performance boast so few remaining grassroots, neighborhood theaters? These early questions inspired me to structure *Drop Dead* in such a way that pushes beyond some of the companies and artists that have been incredibly important and productive—from The Wooster Group to Stephen Sondheim—but remain overexposed in the writing about late twentieth-century performance in New York. In fact, it was during this period that the diversity of institutional structures for the production and consumption of theater became salient.

In chapter 1, I pursue La Mama E.T.C. during the 1970s from three angles: the venue itself, playwright Julie Bovasso (one of Ellen Stewart's "kiddies"), and the sociopolitical context of the neighborhood. For Roger Starr, the emblematic policy maker in this equation, the LES bristled with a "wave of newcomers, displaced from peasantry" chopping up "New York's cosmopolitan heart."[70] Stewart pursued a philosophy of expansion at a time when the dominant urban buzzword was "shrinkage." While the economics of everyday life were indisputably changing, many artists renewed their commitment to work on the LES. A central aim of this chapter is to explicitly define those developments in theatrical communities of the 1970s that were wrought by the preceding decade of Off-Off Broadway transformations and evolved in a dialectical relationship with municipal forces. Many of its playwright advocates—including Julie Bovasso—revealed the obstacles at the intersection of funding battles, local politics, space, and critical reception.

As conditions changed downtown, OOB playwrights looked to other neighborhoods to stage their work, and envisioned a resurrection of the moribund theatrical giant, Broadway. Times Square as a collection of blocks and Broadway as a stretch of theatrical dynamism needed renewed attention if it was to survive, and yet for many, downtown theatrical production and Lincoln Center's growth threatened to upend the visual map of commercial theater production. In chapter 2, "TKTS and 'Lost Audience' Anxiety: Fiscal Crisis Times Square," I home in on the anxiety that convinced theater producers of the need to lure "old audiences" back to a neighborhood that many viewed as a rotting appendage on the body of the city's cultural production.

Specifically, I analyze a public/private initiative, the TKTS discount ticketing program, which, while intended as temporary, in fact became permanent, and staged an encounter between neighborhoods, theater, and the public during a period of great demographic change.

City power players—from prominent producers, to the *New York Times*, to mainstream critics, to downtown theater impresarios, to politicians—fought over the future vision of Times Square. Advocates who argued for fundamental adjustments to the structure of Broadway (locational, operational, and aesthetic) were ultimately overpowered by city officials and developers focused on a Times Square renewal rooted in the mystique of its historic theaters. While perhaps an unlikely player in the development of Times Square, one influential figure introduced in chapter 2 is the economist William Baumol. His impassioned explanations of the "cost disease" theory and its implications for Broadway regularly went unheeded, but his influence was felt through the FACT conference and the TKTS discount ticketing initiative.

In chapter 3, "Vinnette Carroll's Urban Arts Corps and the Inevitability of Interdependency," I analyze the "uneven development" of theatrical practices and resources in the city, through the trajectory of the Urban Arts Corps. The struggle between seeing the arts as a "coolant" for inner city passions rather than as a provocative and even combustible force lasted through the decade. I employ the terminology of "affective inequality" to look at artists working against the dismantling of the few equality infrastructures that had been put in place for the city's cultural sphere. This chapter also offers a counter history in its tracing of national and statewide War on Poverty programs as germinal to revisions of flawed and problematic "inner-city" arts initiatives.

Unsurprisingly, the climate of austerity exacerbated the competition between theater companies, and inflamed fissures between theaters with different ideological, aesthetic, and political positioning. As with Vinnette Carroll and Micki Grant's *Don't Bother Me, I Can't Cope* characters, smaller arts organizations felt the harsh winds of fiscal insolvency before they suffered alongside the rest of the city as it confronted the depth of the problem. Carroll was, of course, not alone: there was a network of artists who worked across neighborhoods and cultural barriers to curate and cultivate multi-ethnic, community-based theater in the face of cuts and an environment of political separatism.

In chapter 4, I visit Coney Island and Lincoln Center to chart the growth of street theater occurring in the early 1970s. Coney Island was a honky-tonk amusement destination for the laboring classes, but by the fiscal crisis period it was known largely for its ailing reputation and crime and unemployment statistics that outpaced the rest of the city. This chapter examines the work of the Everyman Street Theatre company as the nexus of a performance trend in this working-class neighborhood/amusement district that once inspired the early inventors of cinema and nineteenth-century immigrant entrepreneurs, but by the second half of the twentieth century typified the uneven cultural development of New York City.

This is also the first of two chapters that incorporates the cultural landmark, Lincoln Center. By the 1970s, the scale of the Lincoln Center development held ramifications for uptown, downtown, and outer-borough theater. Marvin Carlson writes of the ascendancy of the arts complex phenomenon, where performance structures were clustered together to form "a kind of supermonument, an entire artistic enclave within the city."[71] During this period of profound neglect and divestment in Coney Island, Lincoln Center regularly invited street theater companies to perform as part of its free outdoors program, bolstering the exposure of the troupes as well as the institution's own profile as responsive to community needs. Demographic change contributed to new pressures on organizations to engage the increasingly multiethnic communities surrounding their physical plants.

Chapter 5, "How the Public Became a Public: Joseph Papp's Civic Building," examines Joseph Papp, a masterful engineer of city support during the 1970s. As a producer, Papp embraced failure as a necessary ingredient for success in his operations, a strategy poorly suited for a publicly funded theater during a fiscal crisis. Yet some city heavyweights saw in Papp a city redeemer. His free productions of classical plays reinforced a sense of continuity for parks and open-air Shakespeare, and his bold statements about art and urban life attracted attention across the country, and even the world.

Papp's influence extended from downtown theater to uptown and outer-borough theater, and his work during this time presents a compelling case study of how and to whom city monies were allocated, and which theaters were singled out for support, and to what end. His projects galvanized a wide-ranging audience of city politicians, philanthropists, and parkgoers, all engaged in a discussion about the definition of accessible theater, theater for the people, and theater for the city. The promise of Papp's marriage of his New York Shakespeare Festival with Lincoln Center had been to reverse the decline in its audiences; to do so, he attempted to confront anxieties circulating about changes in the city, as well as the elite sheen of Lincoln Center's past theatrical programming.

Chapter 6, "The Brooklyn Syndrome: BAM and Outer-Borough Arts," examines BAM's programming experiments before the Next Wave Festival to demonstrate that the institution was not the stable center of rebirth, but rather part of many intricate and overlapping zones of performance activity that reshaped contested urban spaces.

Policies favored a centralized vision of Brooklyn "culture" to counteract its image as an outer-borough backwater. In downtown Brooklyn, developments during this period assisted in the rebuilding of a broken neighborhood, but also evacuated community theater groups from the very stages that anchored the resurgence. The fiscal crisis strained all arts organizations across the city, but it crippled a neighborhood arts movement that had connections to the Black Arts Movement, avant-garde theatrical practice, street theater, and community-based arts. This chapter considers the expansion of "downtown" theater into the outer boroughs through new networks of theaters in downtown Brooklyn. I conceptualize the growth of downtown Brooklyn as a theater hub through the formation of coalitions, alongside an impassioned neighborhood arts movement that sought to exert community control over cultural production. These companies created new models of collaboration, which sometimes complemented—and at other times contradicted—a national and citywide trend toward a civic center model of cultural development.

Part One

✦

Ideologies of Austerity

Chapter 1

✦

Planned Shrinkage and the New Theater

Ellen Stewart, La Mama E.T.C., and Julie Bovasso

> Whatever contribution has been made, it is not because I take La Mama anywhere, it is because La Mama takes me.
>
> —Ellen Stewart

Julie Bovasso's *The Moon Dreamers*, a play that inaugurated a new decade and a new theater space at La Mama E.T.C. in 1969, scrambled the conventions of Off-Off Broadway performance. The new Lower East Side (LES) multi-theater space, named after La Mama's founder and figurehead, Ellen Stewart, presented *The Moon Dreamers* in its giant, garage-like interior with brick surfaces and rough lumber scaffolding. Bovasso's script calls for "an architectural hallucination" and smoke rising from the floor as a succession of bewildered chorus members gather on stage, beginning with a crippled, bloody soldier. Three black stockbrokers follow, and, after them, an Indian Chief (who is really, the stage directions indicate, a Zen Buddhist priest), a Beggar Groom and his Beggar Bride, a Gold Star Mother, a lawyer in a raccoon coat and a straw hat, and six cherubic angels. Each waves a tiny American flag. The music: military marches, 1930s foxtrot, patriotic World War I anthems, 1920s ragtime. Ziegfeld Nurses arrive to dance a Hospital Ballet with the soldiers; next, the stockbrokers engage in a soft shoe dance competition with the bandaged men, who can muster only an imitation of the brokers' prowess. *New York Times* critic Dan Sullivan compared this horror-filled musical prelude to "a floorshow in hell."[1] At its close, six angels dance on the stage furniture and ineptly set the props: the protagonists, Rene, Sandra, and Mimi, enter, "playing at being themselves as the actors, not the characters," and tussle violently with a demented angel. Finally, the play begins: "Well, I guess this is it."[2]

The plot—for lack of a better term—revolves around a simple conflict: Rene has cheated on Sandra with Mimi, but cannot determine who should be forced to leave the apartment. A mad parade of supporting characters hunt for an elusive resolution: lawyers, police, stockbrokers, cousins, doctors, Buddhists, and poets. At the end of the labyrinthine three-hour play, the deus ex machina arrives in the form of Ira, a capitalist astronaut. He implores the remaining ragtag characters—an unhappy couple, a midget Police Chief (played by later *Fantasy Island* star Hervé Villechaize), a Jewish mother, their lawyers, their accountants, and a Swedish-speaking Geisha—to join him on the Moon, where various Ministries awaited their new ministers.

Analyzed on the scale of the nation, the play commented on a deluded and exhausted country anesthetized by Doublemint gum commercials while aspiring to intergalactic colonization. The dramaturgy of *The Moon Dreamers* also presented a cautionary tale: the New Yorkers in the play forge ahead with clueless ambition, suggestive of a city full of demented bureaucrats and megalomaniac poets no better than their Napoleonic police. Bovasso, who also directed the production, crammed forty-three principals onto the stage, nearly as many players as there were seats in La Mama's previous theater space. But it was not just Actors' Equity rules and cramped basement theaters that the Bovasso aesthetic mocked; on the downtown performance scene, a restless and expansionist avant-garde outgrew its playgrounds to find a Tower of Babel awaiting them. The characters speak English, Swedish, Chinese, Italian, and gibberish; their desires are hysterical, their conflicts self-reinforcing. "What do you mean, dream's over?" a desperate lawyer asks a psychiatrist, holding tightly to the fantasy of Jungian interpretation. Bovasso's writing and direction stressed the uncanny contours of loss, experienced through the performers' resistance to their roles, and the playwright's insistence on a fraudulent dramatis personae. The play laughed in the face of those who saw this theater—and La Mama itself—as amateurish, inessential, minimal, predictable, traceable to any single tradition or mode.

Some critics, however, discerned the corruption of OOB's cooperative approach in La Mama's new foundation-funded premises, "businesslike" ticketing policy, and uptown press coverage.[3] La Mama had stepped boldly into a new decade on the LES, committed to the production of new space as much as new theater. Stewart's choice of Bovasso as one of the inaugural playwright/directors in the Ellen Stewart Theatre announced as much. While reviewers attached blanket labels of "experimental" or "avant-garde" to Stewart's venue with frequency, Bovasso's theatrical language aligned with La Mama's curatorial hand. Stewart herself referred to the work at La Mama as "New Theatre," which she described in early interviews as "subliminal theatre" interested in "unconscious receptivity."[4] For some, this New Theatre formed out of the residue of an Old Theatre—Bovasso, for example, directed the first stateside productions of Genet and Ionesco at her Tempo Playhouse on East 8th Street in 1953, after briefly working with the Living Theatre in 1952. The works of Beckett, Pinter, Ionesco, Brecht, and Tennessee Williams appealed to Stewart's interests, but as the 1960s drew to a close, Stewart used her theatrical platform to feature bold auteurs with sweeping visual spectacle and pronounced musicality. The new building at 74A East 4th Street facilitated and advanced this "big-set" aesthetic.

This marked a major turning point in the history of Off-Off Broadway theater; of the four main venues of OOB (Caffe Cino, Theatre Genesis, Judson Poets' Theater, and La Mama), only La Mama survives today.[5] La Mama had opened its doors as a basement theater/café with Tennessee Williams's *One Arm* in 1962. Money from the Ford, Rockefeller, and Doris Duke Foundations funded the purchase and renovation of the dilapidated building on East 4th Street in 1969. While some OOB theaters confronted the demands of institutional durability with ambivalence, La Mama entered the 1970s with transformative conceptions of space and urban cultural cohesion, raising the question: what is at stake when theaters just can't wing it anymore? What if, in addition to the OOB artist as trailblazer, as nuisance, and as disrupter of set patterns, the narrative is also of a particular institution, one built, aggregated, and consolidated by theatrical labors? Stephen Bottoms declares that by 1969, La Mama decisively "won the race for institutionalization," yet the real process of "sustainable assimilation into existing economic structures" required more than foundation funding and ticketing policies: it necessitated an even deeper connection to the community, something that onlookers argue La Mama severed by 1969.[6] Rather than inaugurating the betrayal of her underground roots and off-off ethos, this contradictory turning point prepared La Mama to withstand the pressures of the arduous 1970s on the LES. La Mama did not institutionalize through structural trappings alone but produced new relationships within the brittle urban ecosystem. The theater defied socially destructive municipal policies through interdependence and collaboration—between artists, their funding sources, and municipal systems.

While the security of a foundation-funded space assisted in Stewart's ability to protect her theater, these relationships proved decisive. La Mama company members began touring internationally in 1965 and Stewart initiated early play exchanges with artists from Denmark, India, and Poland. But La Mama New York remained loyal to one site: the Lower East Side. It was there that La Mama became what Brian Massumi, drawing from Madeline Gins and Arakawa, calls "a landing site," an urban form that offers useful connections and platforms for possible action.[7] The uncertain encounters of the Situationists—in which group members arrived at street corners at predesignated times, destined only for the possibility of an appointment—inspired Massumi's theorization. His essay applies these "virtual appointments" of the Situationists—pregnant with the potential for recognition—to contemporary art interventions. Here, the descriptor illuminates La Mama as a performance site that altered the perceptual conditions of local space and crystallized "unaccustomed possibilities" for the neighborhood.[8] Elsewhere, with Erin Manning, Massumi emphasizes the *process* of landing, an interfusing of "agency and patience,"[9] two elements characteristic of Stewart's strategies toward institutionalization.

The significance of this landing is found in La Mama's ability to both connect itself to the machinations of the city and also create the frameworks to withstand them. On La Mama's stages throughout the 1970s, the abundant spectacles of its artist innovators (such as Bovasso, Andrei Serban, the Tokyo Kid Brothers, Wilford Leach, and Playhouse of the Ridiculous director John Vaccaro) presented "a 'more' postulating the existence of an elsewhere, beyond the conventional logic of that place."[10] Why did La Mama perform this postulation? What necessitated this push beyond the conventional logic of place? Why engineer the "existence of an elsewhere" if *there* was where La Mama wanted to be? And if, in this definition, a landing site is somehow "sculpted" to the needs of the human body, what function did La Mama fulfill within the needs of the city or neighborhood?

Any answer must take into account the relationship between La Mama's institutionalization and the fraying of support systems during this era in the city, when interdependent civic and social networks disintegrated within the urban ecosystem. Dolores Hayden's definition of "cultural landscape" situates the theater on the LES:

> The history of the cultural landscape is about larger environments, collectively formed, changing over time. It is the story of how places are planned, designed, built, inhabited, appropriated, celebrated, despoiled, and discarded. Indigenous residents as well as colonizers, ditch diggers as well as architects, migrant workers as well as mayors, housewives as well as housing inspectors, are all active shaping the urban cultural landscape.[11]

The notion of "landing sites," linked to Hayden's definition of cultural landscape, renders Stewart's work more visible as a shaper of the LES, and the LES as a shaper of her theater. The LES at this time confounded a usual assumption of urban space: the sites of the city could no longer be trusted. Urban policies divested swaths of blocks and dictated cutbacks to neighborhood-based programs. Inequitable development practices spread, and the public resources available to certain neighborhoods (the South Bronx, the Lower East Side, Bushwick) thinned.[12] "Planned shrinkage" was the darker edge of a deluded urban policy that ultimately overwhelmed entire segments of the city with neglect. This touched many spheres of existence: from health care to morale to crime to infrastructure to housing stock to the life of the street to local cultural practices.

La Mama's institutionalization connects directly to this particular moment in New York's urban history. As a growing institution, La Mama resisted policies dictating shrinkage and closure. Because the geographic location of a performance venue "anchors theatre practice in social, cultural, and historical contexts,"[13] the processes of neighborhood divestment and theatrical institutionalization developed concurrently, and the complexity of their interactions obscured La Mama's contributions to the neighborhood itself. Media coverage imbued Stewart's theater with certain narratives, many of them fabricated, others merely superficial. They accused Stewart of staging chaotic works that mirrored and even exacerbated the perceived decline of the downtown area.

Following Hayden, however, La Mama's (theater) workers were central to "building" the city, a claim that should redress La Mama's absence from academic discourse and mainstream arts reporting. Cindy Rosenthal proposes that Stewart's resistance to categorization played a role in this omission, as did her reputation as a "catalyst" rather than an artist.[14] Yet while the latter might explain elements of her artistic legacy, it does not account for La Mama's conflicted legacy as an institution, embodied not only by its thin representation in the relevant scholarship, but also in the funding agencies that gave repeatedly to New York's "Big Daddies" of the theater—"Mayor" Joe Papp and Harvey Lichtenstein—on a scale not afforded to La Mama.[15] We have looked to the "Big Daddies" for our civic institutions, and, as David Savran has argued, our avant-garde.[16]

It is not just the questionable consecration of the avant-garde that muddies the role of La Mama and its geographic specificity. In some narratives of OOB, creative freedom leads to vulnerability, and monetary success victimizes. This dominates analyses of the Caffe Cino, established in 1958 by Joe Cino, a former dancer, in a shoebox of a storefront on Cornelia Street in Greenwich Village, celebrated for its "Dionysian magic madness" and shows put on without "paperwork, subsidies, or corporate grants."[17] The "free theater ethos" of the 1960s included freedom from more than just expensive ticket prices: "free of creative interference from backers; freewheeling, reciprocal collaboration between artists."[18] The horizon of performance on the other side of this decade hardly sounds appealing. This also reflects a criticism leveled at Stewart by some of her contemporaries: after she received the foundation checks that allowed her to purchase her new multi-theater space in 1969, some in the OOB scene expressed ambivalence about La Mama turning "professional."[19]

New theater premises and ticketing procedures signaled Stewart's long-held desire to push beyond the skeletal financial model of La Mama's early years. She never romanticized a vision of her theater wholly supported by her earnings as a fashion designer. By 1968, Stewart already expressed deep grief over having her actors work "all day on a cup of instant coffee,"[20] a telling confession at a time when many theater artists viewed autonomy from commercial concerns as an essential ingredient of OOB. Politically hard-to-categorize theaters like La Mama (whose work did not receive sustained analysis until Cindy Rosenthal's 2006 article in *TDR: The Drama Review*) and artists like Julie Bovasso operated on the margins of the dramatic canon and yet functioned centrally in the development of performance practices on the LES during this period.

The fiscal crisis enacted an aggressive incursion into a tumultuous period in downtown theatrical production, and the fracturing of the LES coincided with the death knell of its prodigious playwrights wing. As members of a vibrant yet nascent phenomenon, the leaders of OOB fought to expand beyond the small theaters of downtown and to gain some measure of financial security after years of shoestring operations. City agencies and neighborhood politics pushed the West Village incarnation of OOB to the East Side of downtown, and then, once there, artists ran headlong into the city's "triage" urban policy of the 1970s. For the coterie of playwright-directors working out of La Mama, the spirit of the prior decades necessitated new models of autonomy and survival. Playwrights joined together in coalitions as opportunities for staging their work rapidly disappeared while community activists agitated against the displacement of low-income, working-class tenants. The spatial restructuring of the LES across the 1970s had decisive repercussions for theaters, which could not exempt themselves from the complex economic transitions (and fractional politics) of the fiscal crisis period. In this chapter, La Mama as landing site provides a conceptual frame for analyses of the performance work on its stages, as well as Stewart's resistance of dominant austerity ideologies.

Triage

> Suppose a consortium of foundations erected a replica of the East Village somewhere in the badlands of the Dakotas, a place where all the heroin anyone could want would be placed neatly in his veins. Would that draw dangerous street criminals away from the cities, as the Western frontier drew off some of the city's less docile residents in the nineteenth century?
>
> —Roger Starr[21]

As urban creatures go, Ellen Stewart and Roger Starr represent utterly divergent worlds and worldviews. Starr was a Manhattan-born conservative-leaning commentator on urban affairs who served three mayors, was New York City's Housing and Development administrator from 1974 to 1976, and later enjoyed a lengthy career on the editorial board of the *New York Times*. Stewart was born in Louisiana in 1919 with a childhood spent in Detroit and Chicago, culminating in a 1950 migration to New York with dreams of attending fashion design school.[22] She opened her café theater in the basement of a tenement on East Ninth Street in 1961, became a fixture on the alternative theater scene, and in 1985 received a MacArthur Fellowship "Genius" Grant for her efforts.

During a time of municipal retrenchment, Starr crafted an ideology of austerity, espoused through a series of essays and policy prescriptions. Four years after he described his fantasy of wiping East Village residents off of the city grid, Starr argued "that the golden door to full participation in American life and the American economy is no longer to be found in New York."[23] He embodied a municipal philosophy in the early 1970s that preached divestment as the responsible solution to the problems miring the city's declining industrial neighborhoods.[24] Starr reasoned that city funds should focus on repairing areas that were not experiencing population decline; planning was consigned to new development, while older neighborhoods were left to the forces of urban decay until private investment deemed them valuable again. While some city officials publicly rejected the letter of Starr's policy suggestions, in practice, a version of his philosophy became a rational approach in a time of dwindling city funds—a phenomenon that was later reproduced around the nation. According to Joshua Freeman, this "planned shrinkage lite" meant that priority in public investment, tax relief, and economic development were given to the central business district, "while leaving outlying areas, including those undergoing devastation, to fend for themselves."[25] Residents, in turn, experienced diminished public transit, cutbacks in police and fire protection, and curtailed sanitation services. Rather than renewal through incremental public investments (such as restoring older housing stock), "internal resettlement" of deteriorating neighborhoods plagued by job flight became a goal. Within this setting, the traditional interpretative context applied to the OOB theaters of the 1960s and 1970s—experimentation, hedonism, and counterculture radicalism—does not apply. La Mama's path toward institutionalization instead requires the conceptual lenses of shrinkage, economic polarization, and urban institution-building.

Since the mid-1980s, scholars have identified the particular ravages of these policies on the LES, and Peter Marcuse's 1982 description of "triage urban policy" remains an apt descriptor for the city's approach. Once an area was considered undesirable for either capitalist investment or housing-related profit, there existed a ready-made justification to withhold additional public expenditures. The result of this triage policy accelerated the destructive process of population and housing loss. Some critics predicted this destructive spiral and denounced planned shrinkage as aimed at displacing residents. Stewart arrived in New York City in 1950, when many artists traveled between West Village and East Side performance spaces, and theaters moved just as frequently due to municipal licensing regulations. The now-legendary bars and clubs in Greenwich Village were magnets for poets, jazz and folk musicians, students, beatniks, boho tourists, and anyone looking to escape the normative encasings of the 1950s. By the 1960–61 season, the Village café scene regularly presented plays in addition to the jazz and poetry that already inhabited the intimate spaces of Take 3, the Café Roue, the Café Manzino, and Phase 2. The popularity of the neighborhood as a tourist destination fermented conflicts with the local residents, who demanded increased regulations for the new establishments.

OOB grew as a polyglot network of independent café theaters with a clear commonality: triangulation with city officials. Its establishments confronted fires, licensing violations, and homophobic police raids.[26] Accounts by writers and artists (particularly those of color) cite an eastward movement partly motivated by conflicts borne of racial and cultural differences with older (white) immigrant residents and old guard bohemians that functioned alongside political differences.[27] The tinderbox dynamic between the café (and bar) culture, youth culture, and the authorities reached a zenith with Stonewall in 1969, but the regulation of theaters by authorities was more than a cat-and-mouse game; it extended larger cultural policies. Between the 1960s and the 1970s, a complex mix of neighborhood politics and real estate troubles pushed New York's alternative theatrical production away from the coffeehouses of the West Village to the East Side of downtown. This geographic shift rendered it particularly vulnerable to the distributional consequences of services and benefit cutbacks.

Stewart coped as a "moving target," and labored toward greater staying power on the map of downtown. She opened La Mama Café, a thirty-seat basement theater, on East 9th Street in 1961. Since 1963, when she calmed a rowdy audience with the ringing of a cowbell swiped from the prop stand of Paul Foster's *Hurrah for the Bridge*, Stewart greeted most La Mama audiences with a cowbell and an entreaty: "Welcome to La Mama E.T.C., Experimental Theatre Club, dedicated to the playwright and all aspects of the theater." With this guiding philosophy, La Mama grew rapidly throughout its first decade, providing an early home to young experimental American theater artists such as Lee Breuer, Tom Eyen, Tom O'Horgan, Sam Shepard, Megan Terry, and Lanford Wilson. Stewart was evicted from multiple early theater spaces, but with each move rebuilt her hospitable café environment marked by intimacy and artistic freedom. "Each space," Stewart reflected, "triggered the imagination a little more and a little more."[28] In 1966, in an effort to evade authorities demanding she obtain a theatrical license, Stewart shifted to a "private club" admission policy for her 74-seat theater (with a one-dollar membership fee).

She also created a performance ritual that incorporated old-fashioned stoop-sitting with the defensive posture required of an underground venue; in Stewart's "nightly vigil" on the front stairs of La Mama (then located at 82 Second Avenue), she sat on the lookout for authorities or inspectors who sought to interrupt the show.[29] For La Mama's playwrights, this tradition communicated Stewart's total trust in her "kids." For New Yorkers, "stoop sitting" could be an act of boredom, of intimidation, of community, of being present at the dance of the street. As a social act, it signified Stewart's persistence in a contested neighborhood: stories abound of neighbors reporting Stewart's business to authorities as a suspected brothel, of her myriad entanglements with city inspectors, her nights at the New York Women's House of Detention when convicted of offering entertainments without a license, harassment from Con Edison, the Fire Department, and the police, and of her negotiations with area kids who watched her building in exchange for rooftop pigeon-breeding space. Her stoop-sitting marked the street with her body at a time when she fell victim to racism at work and at home,[30] and when city authorities relentlessly pursued downtown performance cafés as illegal.[31] Her conflicts with municipal authorities motivated her tactics into the 1970s; Stewart faced the paradoxical reality of "downtown" theater as radical, permissive, and yet surveilled.

Stewart fixed her sights on a legal venue for her growing circle of playwrights, directors, designers, and actors. In 1969 she showed W. McNeil Lowry of the Ford Foundation the building at 74 East Fourth Street, and foundation money from the Ford, Rockefeller, and Doris Duke Foundations enabled her to purchase the building. This marked a major step in her theater's history, and symbolized her new strategy in her adopted neighborhood after 1969. One of the first productions in the new Ellen Stewart Theater, New York native Julie Bovasso's *The Moon Dreamers*, was also the first La Mama show to have the financial underwriting of the Theatre Development Fund (TDF), a nonprofit organization whose primary mission was to help build new audiences for theater. TDF purchased $10,000 worth of tickets to Bovasso's "demonic saga of American life, with funky music and a truly rotten chorus," and distributed them at a discounted rate to schools, colleges, youth groups, settlement houses, and churches.[32] Stewart chose Bovasso's play to launch her TDF collaboration, but also to announce the continued spatial and theatrical disordering at the heart of La Mama's enterprise.

Playwrights Advocacy

> The history of Julie Bovasso is the first and most fundamental fact I know about off-Broadway theatre.
>
> —Jerry Tallmer[33]

Julie Bovasso lived on the east side of Tompkins Square Park between First and Second Avenue. Her preferred watering holes with cast members included Pete's Tavern near Gramercy Park, Phebe's on the Bowery, and late nights at Max's Kansas City. In 1961, she and a friend snuck into McSorley's Old Ale House on East Seventh Street to protest its "men's only" policy; Bovasso dressed in drag and supposedly the prank worked—until her mustache fell off, one beer in.[34] Bovasso's LES years overlapped with major transitions in the neighborhood, stemming from forces outside the women's liberation movement; real estate agencies coined "the East Village" to create prestige spillover from neighboring Greenwich Village during a 1960s period of middle-class spread into the formerly working-class area.[35]

For many, the use of the "Lower East Side" is synonymous with a commitment to the neighborhood's working-class character. The name connects it to its past as a nineteenth-century residential and industrial area that boasted the origins of the labor movement and all shades of left-wing organizing through the decades. This past was also distinguished by some of the earliest examples of community input in urban planning,[36] as well as markedly heterogeneous fields of cultural production, with nineteenth-century halls and theaters that presented farce, musical comedy, melodrama, dime museums, and vaudeville.

By the 1930s, many factors had slowed the influx of immigrants into the neighborhood; the population dropped as older immigrants left the crowded conditions of the Lower East Side for other landscapes (and new social status). Janet Abu-Lughod stresses the legislated decline in immigration to the United States in the 1920s that had a dramatic impact on the population until Puerto Ricans moved to the area in increased numbers in the 1950s.[37] After 1960, the "East Village" became accepted parlance to describe the area that once was just a corner of the larger LES. "Loisaida" refers to the Puerto Rican enclave east of Avenue A formed in the 1950s and early 1960s, a name attributed to a 1974 poem by Nuyorican actor, playwright, director, and activist Bimbo Rivas.[38] The 1965 U.S. Immigration Act brought the waning of Little Italy and the growth of Chinatown. The symbolic weight attached to the naming of this neighborhood indicates the very real struggles for control that transpired: of space, of political power, of resources, and of rights.

Rosalyn Deutsche and Cara Gendel Ryan warn against the distortion produced when equating the experiences of past waves of European immigrants and the attrition experienced by internal migrants, African Americans, Puerto Ricans, and others on the LES, due to demographic and economic transformations.[39] Without the city's burgeoning manufacturing industry and the kind of upward mobility that characterized past immigrant experiences, there are fundamental differences between the distinct phases of "slum" histories on the LES. Unquestionably, however, these waves of newcomers shaped its theatrical histories and determined its climate of pluralistic performance. Radical, avant-garde, and political performance concerned with national, international, and local conflicts converged in the concentrated area of the LES, and for all classes and communities, "theatre literally *saturated* the neighborhood."[40]

Born in Brooklyn, Bovasso's background aligned with the working-class roots of the LES; her personal geographies spanned from Rome, her mother's birthplace, to the LES, her father's. After attending the High School of Music and Art, she enrolled at the City College of New York. She acted in theaters downtown, and in 1953, at age twenty-three, Bovasso opened the pioneering Tempo Playhouse on East Eighth Street between Second and Third Avenues. There she managed, produced, and acted in Jean Cocteau's *The Typewriter*, Eugène Ionesco's *Amédée*, and Genet's *The Maids*, as well as in plays by Gertrude Stein, Arthur Schnitzler, and Henrik Ibsen. The Tempo Playhouse received a special citation from the Obies in 1956, after Bovasso mounted the first New York production of *The Maids*. *Village Voice* theater critic Jerry

Tallmer described it as the energetic spark for the first season of the Obie awards, 1955–56, at which Bovasso received the first Obie for best actress.[41] For Tallmer, the work on stage was as noteworthy as the location of the Tempo, a tiny hole-in-the-wall "up a rickety set of iron stairs at 4 St. Mark's Place in what was not yet called the East Village, though it soon would be."[42] Bovasso too faced frequent closures of her theater due to licensing issues.

After introducing many plays of the Theater of the Absurd to avant-garde audiences at the Tempo, Bovasso gained respect as a playfully loudmouth and formally innovative playwright in Ellen Stewart's cadre. In La Mama she found a landing site, and in Ellen Stewart she found an artistic kinship; Bovasso mashed high and low with stage pictures dredged from dreams and the subconscious, and chaotic pastiches that employed elements of 1940s film culture, war imagery, and satire. Like Stewart, Bovasso could not find full faith in the misleading contours of language, and she wrote plays thick with the agonies wrought from the inability to communicate. Any theatergoer traveling to the LES for *The Moon Dreamers* found an entirely new world—one that parodied the philosophizing of Happenings, the sexism of the old neighborhood, the ambitions of immigrants, the camp cult of musicals, the vapidity of 1930s film culture, the soap opera genre, the creep of corporate advertising. Digging even deeper at a sense of her audience's security, the play lampoons Freudian psychology and the comforting notion that one can interpret dreams—and theater—into a recognizable space of knowing. Throughout *The Moon Dreamers*, every character doubts every other character's identity—"maybe he's wearing his social mask?"—and with good reason, as the confusion of "character" permeates the play's knotted hijinks. The audience, Bovasso seems to maintain, should give up its frenzied hunt for meaning on *any* stage. "Let's drop the social mask and get down to facts," a lawyer begs in an effort to find clarity.[43]

Bovasso's fortunes became increasingly tied to La Mama's. She directed the 1968–69 Obie ceremony, which even its sponsor, the alternative newsweekly *The Village Voice*, described as "bizarre."[44] The evening featured glimpses of Bovasso's past productions at La Mama, which included ballet dancers posed beneath colored lights as the audience gathered to the strains of "Les Sylphides," likely a nod to the absurdity of a proper awards ceremony for the vanguard of theatrical experimentation. In an irreverent swipe at the bushwhacking artist persona, Bovasso herself took the stage in a cowboy hat and bush jacket to introduce the judges.

It was at this time that Bovasso took on a new role, as a decrier of the diminishing field of opportunities for playwrights who had once been heralded as the dramatists of the future. This is decisive in understanding *Gloria and Esperanza* (1969), the second full-length play of Bovasso's mounted at La Mama. Critic Jerry Tallmer wrote: "[*Gloria and Esperanza*] justifies everything La Mama and Ellen Stewart—and Julie Bovasso—have been struggling for all these years."[45] The play showcased Bovasso's affinity for chaotic revues within complex narrative structures. In it, Bovasso borrowed elements from the Follies and presented them alongside men in chicken costumes, hysterical secretaries, mad psychiatrists, uniformed officials, and IRS representatives. The play puzzled audiences and critics, yet Ellen Stewart picked the sprawling three-hour epic to open the first season of another foundation-funded space, and to transfer to Broadway at the ANTA Playhouse (245 West 52nd Street) in February 1970.

Gloria and Esperanza is a playwright's primal scream. It spared no one in its indictment of the quagmires entrapping the artist. In the play, a fragile poet and novelist, Julius, is taken for all that he is and owns until he descends into madness. Gloria Gilbert, his petulant girlfriend and the ostensible heroine (played by Bovasso), steals his poetry, and schemes with Fred the Mailman and their landlord Terry Wong Fu to publish the work surreptitiously, making a fine profit along the way. When the nosy Internal Revenue man, Eric Von Schtutt, comes calling, Gloria attempts to bribe him with Julius's new novel, but Julius has already escaped to an alternate world, where his exploits later constitute his secret novel. In between, chickens prance on stage, an ice cream seller doles out popsicles to mad men, and scenes are buttoned with grandiose chorus numbers. Julius is a writer victimized by his vulgar mistress and a slew of random, undeserving, and obnoxious characters who "live high off the hog of the writer's back," representing only a means of money for parasites who steal from him.[46] Julius's genius is both co-opted and mocked, relegated to the halls of the insane asylum and the (mad) psychiatrist's office, the dignity and stability of the writer utterly compromised.

In his excellent discussion of La Mama's programming at this time, Stephen Bottoms presents an engaging summary of *Gloria and Esperanza* as "a kind of demented, showbiz version of the apocalyptic fears apparent in the writings of many American playwrights."[47] Those anxieties likely included rejection by a chorus of random know-nothings freely weighing in on the creative process: the play can be viewed as a protest against the changing production process for new writers. (Gloria's tax inspector advises her to overhaul the secret book with more conventional literary devices if she ever hopes to sell it.) Actor Kevin O'Connor remembered Stewart seated outside on most opening nights, regardless of the stage: when *Gloria and Esperanza* moved from La Mama to the ANTA Theatre on Broadway, Stewart sat on the backstage stairs through the early performances. "This act I know she repeated for most of her biddies' moves to more commercial ventures."[48] Yet Bovasso and her La Mama contemporaries—Paul Foster, Tom Eyen, Megan Terry, Maria Irene Fornes, Adrienne Kennedy, Leonard Melfi, and others—resented paltry production opportunities and frequent critical dismissal of their work. When theaters received money for new spaces, playwrights' dramaturgical and directorial services went unmentioned and often uncompensated; their labors of institution-building disappeared in the drive for theaters like La Mama to find a supply of new artists.

As much as the further success of her playwrights remained essential for Stewart, these tensions grew. The LES theaters were being squeezed; La Mama's nurturing could not possibly be expected to provide the kind of mid-career support playwrights required. Moreover, grants frequently supported buildings, not individual shows, creating friction between a theater expanding and offering new stages and spaces but few new resources. La Mama's work toward its own livelihood often traveled along parallel tracks with its playwrights throughout the 1970s; a building of theatrical infrastructure did, however, create a form of network that playwrights soon attempted to turn into an organizational machinery. Bovasso's involvement in these playwright advocacy efforts of the time—such as the New York Theatre Strategy (NYTS) and the Women's Theatre Council (WTC)—presents another dimension to this period of downtown theater's precarious standing in the city. On the LES, parallel with grassroots political activism, playwrights banded together as advocates for the needs of Off-Off dramatists. After the flush of 1960s federal and foundation funding, the avenues for support for the explosion of new playwrights became harder to locate.

Julie Bovasso's home became mission control for this wave of 1970s artist organizing. In 1972, over a dozen playwrights from Off and OOB (Ken Bernard, Rosalyn Drexler, Maria Irene Fornes, Paul Foster, Robert Heide, William Hoffman, Terrence McNally, Murray Mednick, Leonard Melfi, Rochelle Owens, Robert Patrick, Sam Shepard, David Starkweather, Jeff Weiss, and Lanford Wilson) met at her apartment to create the NYTS, which they described as "a playwrights' production company."[49] More than a few of those playwrights were already affiliated with theaters; most had been produced at La Mama. But the writers identified an infantilizing production landscape, recognizing the inequitable arrangement that had them contributing to performance spaces but sharing in few of the rewards.

In discussing the rationale for the 1972 formation of the NYTS, Fornes described frustrations not dissimilar from those of Julius in *Gloria and Esperanza*, which began when OOB transitioned into doing plays in the commercial theater. As funding and numbers of theaters increased, these small theaters began accepting submissions, creating a new flank of gatekeepers to production. "I thought that I would never submit a play to this person, who would be somebody I felt had no great sense of what theatre was, no great intelligence, no great knowledge, no great taste—nothing."[50] Fornes recognized the absurdity in this exchange: these theaters had no capital to invest in the play, or to pay Fornes (or the actors, for that matter). Horrified by a situation that would impel playwrights to gift their plays to someone who offered little more than flyers and a barebones set, the NYTS vowed to control the context and conditions of their play productions.

But how was it that productions continued to multiply, theaters received funding, and yet the precarious conditions for its most prominent playwrights increased in severity? Richard Schechner identified one facet of the core problem as early as 1965, and it reverberated throughout the 1970s. National foundations insisted on providing money for certain categories of need and not others, which meant that La Mama acquired new theater spaces courtesy of the Ford Foundation, but then assumed the full burden of attracting a sustaining subscriber base during a time of neighborhood divestment. In this complex arrangement, the neighborhood accrued certain benefits—if the city itself would not provide the resources to overhaul empty buildings, foundation money could, and artists trained in the 1960s principles of "sweat equity" then stepped in to complete the work. This, however, compounded a dangerous equation that left artists to labor within processes of institutionalization that contained little possibility for a feedback loop.

The stakes of OOB therefore changed with the influx of foundation money and the decimation of local place-based monies. "We seem to be inaugurating theatres left and right on East 4th Street," Bovasso wrote in a letter to a member of the Rockefeller Foundation on July 3, 1969.[51] Yet foundations, Schechner argued, created an "impossible relationship" between artist and institution by only supporting institutions that they deemed able to support themselves as permanent cultural resources.[52] The ideas and values that emerged from the political movements of the 1950s and 1960s could not have a voice in the theater without permanent support, and permanent support was against foundation policy. "Whatever hopes one might have had for a multi-class audience have been denied by foundation stipulations for matching funds and black budgets."[53] This model of a top-down management impressing a particular benchmark of "fiscal responsibility" on the arts institutions of the city soon became a dominant element of the cultural discourse. Its reach was not confined to downtown performance; the uptown theaters of Broadway and Lincoln Center could not achieve black budgets, either.

In response, playwrights formed hopeful coalitions, lionhearted attempts to confront the debilitating twin issues of finances and theater spaces. In 1972, with a group of female playwrights (Rosalyn Drexler, Adrienne Kennedy, Rochelle Owens, and Megan Terry), Fornes and Bovasso established the WTC.[54] They announced that they were in the process of securing $400,000 for their first season, with the goal of finding a 300-seat theater that would allow them to produce six plays in rotation, each running for six weeks, regardless of reviews or reception.[55] If the season of inclusion of formerly marginalized artists was to have a lasting effect on the theater, the theaters presenting those works needed stability. In a remarkable essay in the *New York Times* in September 1973, playwright Tom Eyen celebrated the NYTS, a collective of twenty-three OOB playwrights seeking to produce their own work.[56] The writers' co-op aimed to "dilute the divinity of agents and producers," and their first outing was a month-long festival of plays at the Manhattan Theatre Club in the spring of 1973.[57] The ultimate objective of the group was self-determination, to be achieved in the form of a writers' theater—a goal that remained elusive during the cooperative's five-year run.

Eyen's essay describes a fictive downtown dinner party, with all twenty-three playwrights gathered around a waterbed to eat a dinner served by actress Madeleine Le Roux. This festive gathering is quickly dampened: having arrived at La Mama for their meal, the lights suddenly go out. "We sit in silence. No one moves. We cannot find the food. Years pass. An era is over. An entire generation of Off Off Broadway playwrights emerged silently in the '60s and there were so few to realize the importance of the movement."[58] The imaginary power failure signaled the material insufficiency of La Mama; the champions of unsanctioned theater spaces risked appearing disloyal to Stewart, but still demanded more. Eyen identified an unsustainable aesthetic and economic equation at the center of OOB's relationship to professional theaters: the playwrights of NYTS did not write the inexpensive five-character, one-set comedies deemed financially feasible on Off-Broadway, or Broadway. The latter routinely celebrated a recycling of the past suited to older critics seeking plays in the mold of 1950s realism, a style to which Eyen and his compatriots could never warm.

Nevertheless, the beginning of the 1970s seemed to hold the promise of a second act for these writers; Eyen imagines the walls of his dining room opening not into a do-it-yourself café stage, but the 1,675-seat Palace Theater, one of the Nederlander Organization's nine Broadway theaters in the heart of the Theater District, on Broadway and Forty-Seventh Street. They are all on stage, but haunted by an empty auditorium. Had the playwrights forgotten to invite the audience? The writers of the NYTS took nothing for granted—spectators, productions, or a future for McNally, Wilson, Owens, Kennedy, and Ed Bullins. This coalition cut across racial and gender divisions, and revealed a surprising current of optimism regarding the expanding categories of representation in the theater after the social movements of the 1960s. Eyen's fierce article takes a celebratory tone in writing about new spaces, new representations, and new arrangements between producers, audiences, and playwrights.

But what might that look like? While the WTC did not succeed in raising the money to support their productions, in a lengthy article published in *New York* magazine in early 1974, Bovasso struck an upbeat note and described a process—ten years in the making—that allowed a "new breed" of New York actor to emerge, one more individual, independent, and representative of the city itself.[59] Stage actors were finally placing themselves at the center of the business process. While meaningful roles for women beyond "hookers, wives, or mothers" remained rare, opportunities for actors who had before been ignored "in the background slicing pizza" emerged: "Apart from the problems of staying alive and the discouraging employment statistics from Actors' Equity, this period impresses me as one of the most important and exciting times for actors in New York. I can't help feeling that something new and quite extraordinary has finally taken shape and is finding its way onto the scene."[60] After two decades of performing in New York City, what prompted this ebullience? For one, the emergence of homegrown actors, from many ethnic backgrounds and every borough, signified a reprieve for actors traditionally ignored in the casting process: "Irish from Queens and Brooklyn, Jews from Brooklyn and the Bronx, Puerto Ricans from the Bronx and Manhattan, blacks from all the boroughs."[61] The theaters along East Fourth Street were prolific showcases for this trend.

Across the street from La Mama and next to the Playwrights Unit, Bruce Mailman's new theater, Truck and Warehouse Theatre, opened in 1970 with *Billy Noname*, a well-reviewed musical about the maturation of a young black man in 1936. Johnny Brandon wrote the music and lyrics; William Wellington Mackey wrote the book, Talley Beatty choreographed, and Lucia Victor directed the all-black company. *Times* critic Clive Barnes praised the large performance site as "a genuine acquisition for New York . . . looking rather like the Mermaid Theater in London, which is a fine example for this kind of theater. (But couldn't it call itself the Rialto, or at least something a little more ritzy than Truck and Warehouse Theatre?)"[62] The Old Grey Lady already compared an OOB theater on East Fourth Street to the Mermaid in London, expecting it to strive for "something a little more ritzy" than its drab, industrial moniker.

Truck and Warehouse developed a record of production that supports Bovasso's positive estimation of the opportunities available to a wider pool of actors. While the cast of *Billy Noname* was unknown to Barnes, one of its stars, Urylee Leonardos, had previously appeared on Broadway, and William Wellington Mackey quickly garnered a reputation as an emerging African American playwright. Truck and Warehouse distinguished its programming through a diversity of perspectives, communities, styles, and genres. A dark comedy by Bruce Jay Friedman, *Steambath*, earned Héctor Elizondo an Obie award for portraying a Puerto Rican attendant at a steambath on the LES (who is later revealed to be God). In his review of *Steambath*, Barnes describes the play as a reflection of its location, with characters that mimic "typical New York neurotics . . . scared representatives of urban blight."[63] The third production, in December 1970, would be John Guare's first full-length play, *The House of Blue Leaves*, and later shows included Tennessee Williams's *Small Craft Warnings*, Al Carmines's revue *Faggots* (1973), and Tom Eyen's *2008 ½ (A Spaced Oddity)* (1974) and *Women Behind Bars* (1976). For seven years, the Truck and Warehouse producing team mounted politically conscious theater with consistently mixed-race casts, and even occasional activist imports. "Quick, send your money while it's still worth something," began a small blurb in the *Village Voice* on July 3, 1973, that encouraged readers to donate to a San Francisco Mime Troupe tour to the theater.[64] The last company to perform at the theater in its "Truck and Warehouse" incarnation was Charles Ludlam's Ridiculous Theatrical Group before Mailman succumbed to the financial burden of the theater's operations and closed the theater in 1977.

Summer 1974, 66–68 East Fourth Street

> It's still nailing and hammering and carrying water and everybody pitching in.
>
> —Ellen Stewart[65]

After thirteen years and five other locations, La Mama, E.T.C. acquired its Annex building in the summer of 1974. Ellen Stewart had relentlessly pursued the city in a bid for the empty Manhattan Plaza building that sat down the block from the La Mama flagship at 74A East Fourth Street. The city granted her (and two other tenants) a dollar-a-month renewable lease. The space that would soon hold the new 200-seat theater annex, at 66–68 East Fourth Street, formerly housed a boxing club, catering hall, and a television studio before the city took it over for urban redevelopment. Whereas the Ford Foundation and other private grants supported La Mama's 1969 move from St. Marks Place to 74A East Fourth Street, La Mama's 1974 expansion into the city-owned building would not have been achieved without collaboration with the city government. With lease in hand, Stewart faced renovation costs of $50,000, but her OOB venue would finally claim space for rehearsals, workshops, dressings rooms, offices, and storage. "It isn't Lincoln Center or the Public," Stewart commented, "but it's all right for us."[66] Her choice of comparison is apt: both Lincoln Center and the Public sat on city land, enjoyed the benefits afforded to official civic cultural institutions, and laid claim on their cultural landscape.

Though it was only the fall of 1974, and the scope and depth of the city's money problems remained under debate, that summer independent audits of the city's comptroller's office had disclosed numerous accounting concerns. The mayor, a former city comptroller himself, took to the airwaves to convince the citizens of New York City that the reports amounted to distortion and manipulation.[67] Anxiety increased in financial circles, interest rates for bonds began to rise, and the collision course toward the brink of financial collapse had been set. What journalists described as "dimming the beacons" of New York City had begun: the few cultural institutions in neighborhoods like the South Bronx and the LES, already devastated physically and socially, understaffed and underfinanced, would sustain cuts.[68]

A legacy of triangulation existed between city agencies and experimental theater venues; while La Mama relied on relationships with local community members and organizations, city officials had never provided it with support. La Mama's one-dollar annex lease signified a major change from the prior decade, when officials regularly acquainted Stewart with the Women's House of Detention in Greenwich Village for offering entertainments without a license. This provided recognition of small theaters as more than entertainment or experiment, and requiring more than grant packages. An outpost, the physical presence of La Mama represented an incursion into new urban territory, not as a brittle independent formation, but as a structure connected to the moving parts of urban policy.

In theater studies, dominant paradigms used to historicize theaters of OOB measure their radicality—in terms of politics, or the commercial theater, or prior stage conventions—through a model of autonomy and resistance to institutions. There is something to this nostalgia, particularly given its economic arrangement; the 1960s liberation politics that rode sidecar to new performance practices thrived in a particularly alluring form of creative exchange. A celebration of amateurism, in both management style and aesthetic, is enshrined as resistance, with or without an explicit political agenda: from the comic camp stage aesthetics of Joe Cino's café to the corporeal anarchy of the Living Theatre to the refusal and rebuttal of Amiri Baraka's revolutionary theater. While the principles of opposition and dissent factor centrally in any narrative of post–World War II theater and performance in New York, this reading threatens to devalue issues of place, space, and, moreover, institutionalization.

While Bovasso observed with relish both the activity on East Fourth Street and the opening of opportunities for once-marginalized New York performers, the realities of life on the LES clashed with the optimism of actors ascending. With the onset of the fiscal crisis between the summer of 1974 and April 1975, a different kind of social, political, and fiscal tumult awaited. Roger Starr's 1972 recommendation that a new East Village in the Dakota Badlands might relieve the city of some of its unsavory characters represented a rhetorical prototype to the fiscal crisis discourse. A now infamous statement made by President Ford's press secretary in response to New York's appeals to the federal government for federal aid in 1975, compared the city to a "wayward daughter hooked on heroin. You don't give her $100 a day to support her habit. You make her go cold turkey to break the habit."[69] The federal government was not alone in its putative stance toward the liberal capital of the United States; the city's own government targeted certain neighborhoods with "benign neglect," particularly those with residents that contributed to the perceived problem of the low-skill, low-wage segment of its industrial mix. The crisis ideology operated on the belief that an ailing and irresponsible public sector could not undertake resource provision. Every debate boiled down to one seemingly incontrovertible fact: the government "does not receive enough wealth to sustain the city at the level to which its citizens have been accustomed."[70] In response to the litany of crisis symptoms, Starr proposed a third, less familiar solution than taxation or cuts: New York City could continue to be a "world city" if it shrinks its population. "We could simply accept the fact that the city's population is going to shrink, and we could cut back on city services accordingly, realizing considerable savings in the process."[71] Starr suggested that the federal government might assist in relocating residents to areas of the country where jobs exist, rather than expending services on deteriorating neighborhoods that are not at full capacity. He blamed local community groups that too often pressured the city to make futile investments and improvements; internal resettlement could be "a natural flow" out of these areas.

One of the most prominent groups fighting Starr's contentious proposal was the Cooper Square Committee (CSC), an organization that worked with residents in a small square of the East Side that included La Mama's locations. CSC viewed benign neglect as one more plot twist in a long drama of urban planning on the LES after World War II. CSC had formed in 1959 to oppose the city's urban renewal designation; while the aims of urban renewal were progressive (deeming existing public housing in the area at that time to be inadequate), the city's approach to Cooper Square would have resulted in the displacement of tenants and businesses. CSC strove to maintain the diverse social and physical aspects of the neighborhood, encouraging tenant rehabilitation with protections and the safeguarding of residential communities most vulnerable under the city's changing plans for the area. The CSC's vision of the LES as it is expressed in their proposed alternative to urban renewal in 1970 is a methodical approach to maintaining the heterogeneity of the area through planning. It gave special consideration to artists—a reflection of the artist-citizens who were active in the CSC, as well as a less volatile relationship between artists and other residents.[72]

Five neighborhood activist organizations formed the LES Joint Planning Council (JPC) to continue their fight for control of neighborhood land against the tides of federal, state, and municipal fiscal problems. The city adopted the CSC's alternate plan for the LES in 1971, over a decade after the area first received its blanket urban renewal designation. But the drying up of federal spending for subsidized housing—thanks to a 1973 moratorium by President Richard Nixon—put a halt to the implementation of the community-led plan in Cooper Square. City and state agencies soon deemed CSC's proposal unacceptable, arguing a theory of the "tipping point." Val Orselli, a longtime housing activist in the area, explains:

> Tipping point means if you have a white neighborhood, and you start moving more and more black or Hispanic families in, you reach a certain point that the whites start leaving, and therefore you create a ghetto—that's the theory behind tipping point. But how was that

> applicable to the Lower East Side?—we have Black, White, Asian, Ukrainian, you name it we have it—so it could not be a racial tipping point, because the people that we wanted to house were already here.[73]

It was, rather, an economic tipping point—the belief that if a certain number of low-income people or moderate-income people were to be housed, the larger neighborhood would decline economically. Based upon this premise, the city forced the CSC to modify many of their proposed percentages for low-income versus middle-income apartments—a compromise Orselli now regrets. When the city and state went into fiscal crisis, there was no money to build; the housing organizations attempted to keep the housing occupied, even if it meant breaking in to city-owned properties.[74] Incidents of arson multiplied, creating abandoned buildings where drug dealers proliferated; a reduction of police presence exacerbated the perfect storm of conditions.

The downturn in the fortunes of the CSC would coincide with an upturn in the consolidation of Ellen Stewart's work at La Mama on the LES. William Sites explains that while urban leaders refocused New York's development vision on central business districts, local government was forced to assume ownership of abandoned properties; more than 500 were located on the LES.[75] This introduced enormous complications and sparked bitter clashes. When the CSC's plans could not go forward because of the lack of funds for affordable housing, the city made buildings slated for demolition available to cultural groups. During this process, La Mama acquired its annex. Thanks to its month-to-month lease below market rates, La Mama moved forward, while housing activists met renewed municipal obstacles. At a time when residential displacement loomed as a very real threat, this inequity did not go unnoticed by community groups. Ellen Stewart, meanwhile, took on the renovation of the city-owned 1871 building that had "a leaking roof, a buckled floor, vandalized plumbing," and a rent of a dollar a month.[76]

La Mama's roots strengthened on the LES as the dynamics of the neighborhood were changing and local political activism surged, but critics missed the resonance of her focus on cultural exchange. While internationalism had long been an element of La Mama's repertoire, Stewart's global focus intensified throughout the decade as she built transnational institutional connections. In addition to artists such as Andrei Serban, Tadeusz Kantor, and Kazuo Ohno, her full-time resident companies included the Third World Theatre Institute, the American Indian Theatre Ensemble, and La Mama Chinatown (directed by Wu Jing-jyi and Ching Yeh). Isolationism on the part of the National Endowment for the Arts (NEA) and other national funding sources meant that foreign governments were more likely to support La Mama than the United States; the NEA criticized Stewart's "insistently international programs" when it cut its funding to her theater in 1979.[77] "I feel there ought to be some kind of reciprocity," Stewart said in 1977. "There are festivals in South America, in India, Europe; even Africa just had a festival. But America doesn't do this."[78] Stewart's move into a city-owned space as she redoubled her commitment to international tours and guests did not present a contradiction.

On the contrary, an embrace of the intercultural mix of New York City into her theater seats and stages required flexibility and expansiveness; the local ethnic Ukrainians who wanted to rent her theater, the Hell's Angels down the block, the Korean troupe presenting *Hamlet*, Peter Brook's International Centre for Theatre Research, companies from Poland, Japan, Italy, and Portugal. All of the variegated performance practices interrupted the bland descriptions of her theater's neighborhood as "one of the most depressed areas of Manhattan,"[79] and replaced them with the unlikely performance of a redefined cosmopolitanism. When Broadway actress Zoe Caldwell had an improbable hit at La Mama with *Colette*, Mel Gussow mused cheekily, "*Colette* and Miss Caldwell are not only theatrical successes—they may also be leaders in urban redevelopment."[80]

In January 1975 a Kathakali dance troupe inaugurated a new season at La Mama, and, on January 15 the theater produced a series of one-act plays by Julie Bovasso: *The Super Lovers, Schubert's Last Serenade, The Final Analysis*. (Mid-month, Ellen Stewart's re-creation of the Cotton Club, *Cotton Club Gala*, became a tradition.) In *Standard Safety*, Bovasso departed from the aggressive structures and chaotic stage pictures of her full-length plays. She observed the unities of time and place in a disarmingly average office setting: she replaced bohemians and lunatics with tidy insurance types. The action takes place at the World Trade Center (which had opened in 1973), in the company cafeteria of the Standard Safety Insurance Corporation, Inc. Soft muzak hums in the background while two members of the auditing department discuss their bouts of unexplained fatigue, depression, and memory loss. At regular intervals, their lunch is interrupted by a public address sound system that berates the employees with a range of infractions, birthday announcements, and inane bureaucratic requests. The office workers yearn to defy the choking hierarchy and pervasive weight of authority, but they are covered in a paralyzing pall; they can merely daydream about taking up painting and running out to have illicit lunches outside of the cafeteria (against company policy).

The time indicates "the present," but the world of the play maintains an allegiance to a conservative mentality that bears more resemblance to the 1950s than to 1975. Behind the carefully orchestrated procedures of their office lives, a blunt racism and chauvinism simmers, as when an attractive executive seeks a more attractive secretary and quizzes the prospective candidates on their ethnic and racial identity, or when Mr. Weinrib, the company president, reveals his own repressed homoerotic desires for the godlike young executive. The company, however, does boast a ballet team, led by its recreation director, a Monsieur Jacques Le Fracques, who has trained the gentlemen from Fidelity Bonds and Surety to fandango. Mr. Weinrib's son delivers a speech in his mother's memory before the performance. After describing her dashed dreams of becoming a ballerina—she was not tall and thin with high cheekbones—he makes an impassioned plea for the arts:

> And so she became a victim of injustice, a victim of a stupid prejudice; but she vowed in spite of that to carry out her inner vision which told her that everybody can dance. Everybody, ladies and gentleman, has ballet in their bones—regardless of height, weight, size or shape . . . regardless of sex, religion, nationality, race, or economic background . . . I share my mother's vision, and I feel that it is up to the leaders of industry, like my father, to develop and nurture a golden age in which art, music, drama, poetry and the Dance will flourish, in the place of football, baseball, ice hockey, and the Military.[81]

His speech reads as a naive espousal of the arts as pseudo-spiritual uplift rather than craft, seeded in the independent artist. The play takes aim at the titans of business who dully sponsor maddeningly out-of-touch philosophies for the arts. Phillip's is a milquetoast and acceptably pluralist one, contingent, of course, on the clueless leaders of industry who wrap even the announcement of office birthdays in red tape.

Bovasso may have felt optimistic about the new breed of actor, but *Standard Safety* protests emergent visions of the arts in New York City at a time when its full fiduciary responsibility would soon be transferred to unelected businessmen (and a few women). By mid-1975 the major banks refused to market the city's debt, and in the logic of austerity, the frenzied embrace of the private sector in politics and culture became the solution to a public sector unable to provide. This framework established private industry as the ultimate giver of resources, and, in Bovasso's world, the arbiter of everything from birthdays to dance lessons to sexual indiscretions. Gone are the lively and unpredictable artist characters of *Gloria and Esperanza*, replaced by the concern not for the artist's livelihood, but the unholy fandango between business and the arts. The space of the office replaces the multitudinous wash of old stage pictures. Her image of a culture that exiles art as lunchtime "recreation" to be enjoyed in the company cafeteria might have seemed distant from the new annex theater at La Mama, yet it was right around the corner. As the bigotry of the past marched up the ladder in the offices of Standard Safety, the company men looked to art to smooth over their rough edges. In a city left to appeal to the private sector for funding with city and state coffers off limits, the short play offered a sterile vision of an encroaching reality. *Standard Safety* scoffed at the antiquated notions of creativity in the corporatized city, and it was a poignant final play for Bovasso to stage at La Mama.

Ellen Stewart Will Come Through

> The agony of it is people always believe that Ellen Stewart will come through. Most of the time I do, but it gets harder to do instead of easier. I sometimes wonder how we'll go on.
>
> —Ellen Stewart, 1980[82]

By 1979, theaters in Lower Manhattan deflated from the difficulty of fund-raising during a fiscal crisis, and the perception of the LES neighborhood projected by the media verged on comically dismal. A custody dispute between a part-time actor and his state employee and artist ex-wife cited the factors of crime, pollution, and burnt-out buildings as an unfit geography for child rearing.[83] (The mother insisted that the cultural and ethnic diversity of the neighborhood made the LES an ideal locale to raise a child.) The decades following the fiscal crisis fulfilled Roger Starr's hope that the powers of the market would deem certain neighborhoods of "value," but as scholars have noted, this was often to the detriment of populations who endured years of diminished city services.[84] The city continually postponed elements of CSC's alternative plan until the organization's vision of heterogeneity became compromised by more than just lack of federal funds. The reality of retrenchment meant that the city's cost-saving measures—even in small decrements—added up to large-scale deterioration in the quality of life for local inhabitants,[85] and this became true across swaths of downtown neighborhoods. The day-to-day existence of the LES choked under tax delinquencies, arson, and the abandonment of housing in neighborhoods with an already high poverty rate.

Ellen Stewart won an influential position with the Comprehensive Employment Training Act (CETA) Artists Program, and La Mama in turn received funds from this groundbreaking federal program designed to support unemployed artists across many fields during the recession. The Nixon and Ford administration created CETA in 1975, and at its height in 1979, the Department of Labor estimated $200 million dollars invested in CETA arts jobs alone. (Reagan ended the employment program when it was pilloried as one that enabled "taxpayer-subsidized employees goofing off in painting and theatre workshops.")[86]

CETA transferred funds and decision-making to grassroots officials, ostensibly tailoring the use of its resources to local needs, a boon for proponents of a decentralized labor policy. Yet while La Mama enjoyed this newfound role in job creation activities, other agencies in the national government pulled their support for her theater; the NEA abruptly decreased its funding, arguing that the panel could no longer "afford the luxury of providing one third of the La Mama budget."[87] That same year, the *Village Voice* mounted a scathing critique of Stewart and the work of the theater, after Stewart used grant money to purchase a building on Great Jones Street, to be utilized for rehearsals:

> It seems that La Mama has become less experimental an institution, more interested in the acquisition of assets. Very little radical theatre happens at La Mama these days. Whenever some agency wants to invest in some remembered notion of the avant-garde, however, Stewart is there with a proposal to absorb some of the funding. Having the right connections, she got her piece of the CETA art lines. When the City divested itself of abandoned property, she was there to propose a neighborhood renaissance.[88]

At this time, however, cultivating neighborhood performance activity and generating projects for theater workers was in fact a radical practice. In 1978 Stewart utilized CETA funds to mount Goethe's *Faust I* directed by a leading director at the Weimar Nationaltheater, Fritz Bennewitz. She forged ahead with the mission of the funds to support unemployed artists and positioned the cultural strength of the community as a cornerstone of the production through the hiring of 22 actors, an 8-person chorus, 6 musicians, dancers, and an 18-member crew. After sifting through over 4,000 applications for the available positions, the "very ethnography of Manhattan's talent pool" coalesced on La Mama's stage: Jamil Zakkai, of Syrian descent, played Faust; James Leon, a white actor, Mephisto; Christine Campbell, a Caribbean immigrant who grew up in Harlem, and Marilyn Amaral, both black, Gretchen and Martha.[89] Bennewitz enveloped the casting choices into his production concept and process, as the actors became intimately involved in shaping a final performance text from Walter Kaufman's translation. David C. John argues that the creative team behind *Faust I* incorporated the actors' cultural history and the performance's immediate inner city context, and quotes Bennewitz's personal notes about the production:

> What are the basic reasons for doing the La Mama-Ceta FAUST?
>
> To see if the values of the play as a stage event can be a theatrical reality.
>
> To take the challenge of getting the play alienated from its historical, cultural, and local vicinities since history is everywhere.
>
> . . . To remove the play from a prejudiced context to represent the typical.[90]

In order to do so, Bennewitz addressed three audiences: "the neighborhood folk of New York's Lower East Side, to whom the CETA program was primarily directed, the people for whom for Campbell the Gretchen figure stood," as well as the OOB and political theater audiences and university-affiliated spectators.[91]

Perhaps because of this tripartite understanding of audience, mainstream critics yearned for the familiar La Mama playwrights throughout the mid-1970s; even Julius Novick, in his review of Andrei Serban's "amazing," "beautiful," and "magnificently presented" *Greek Trilogy*, questioned Stewart's waning commitment to the "playwrights of the post-Beckett generation."[92] The artists and collaborators at La Mama had endured long years of financial instability, which continued regardless of the infusion of CETA funds or the acquisition of a new building. Rather than receive praise for her tactics, Stewart met criticism for being too well funded, for attending too much to the hallmarks of longevity, for slipping in the assumed standards of aesthetic experimentation.

As the 1970s progressed, theater reviewers were not alone in criticizing Stewart's approach to spatial consolidation. La Mama and many of the theaters along East Fourth Street became embroiled in conflicts with one another and their neighbors, creating an uneasy coexistence of politics, neighborhood identity, and, most crucially, resources.[93] The surrounding community on the LES dug their heels in for battles on the local and city level for self-determination in matters of housing and community control. "It's not that we are against artists; it's that we have no places to put them," said one Loisaida resident at a Board of Estimate hearing about proposed artist housing on the LES.[94] The fiscal crisis set the conditions for an invidious alignment between once-persecuted artists and a desperate city. For one, the progressive politics of the 1960s represented a direct contradiction to the austerity approach, and a grand conflict quickly emerged: agencies regularly produced reports urging the expansion of city funding for theater downtown and a wider decentralization of cultural programming across the city, but officials responded haphazardly at best.[95] The proliferation of plays and playwrights, rather than understood as a positive opening out onto a field of new representations, became theatrical "inflation" that ignited tensions between fractured communities and resident artists.

Regardless of La Mama's profound work at the fulcrum of municipal politics and performance, these tensions have often led to associations between La Mama and negative urban processes occurring on the LES in a way that few other performance venues have. Many urban histories of the 1970s in New York City do not contend with the OOB movement, and when they do, it is cast as a contributing problem. The loss leaders of the experimental theater have been portrayed in various ways: hippies, bohemians, anarchists, beatnik intellectuals, but often in opposition to the goals of working-class tenants and activists. Of La Mama, for example, Christopher Mele writes that the lack "of pressures of commercialism" allowed performers to embrace "taboo issues . . . such as homosexuality, and presented the stories of marginal, underworld characters—pimps, prostitutes and drug dealers."[96] This is an updating of a reactionary criticism that began in the late 1960s and only increased in virility through the cultural turn into the 1970s: "La Mama's playwrights have turned contemporary culture into a condemned playground, a place of desperate masquerade and hysterical revel, an arena of total metaphysical neurasthenia where nothing is sacred except some unachieved or betrayed human possibility," wrote Jack Kroll.[97] Yet La Mama more frequently offered the opposite; a place of possibility separated from the burden of reflecting the streets. The theater reconfigured the assumptions made within the logic of austerity that created a deceptive causality between artists and city spaces. Certainly, economic and social conditions on the LES offered benefits to "bohemians" seeking adventure, artists evicted from the old venues of the West Village, or just those seeking a more manageable cost of living. But generalizations about the composition of a monolithic artist class relegated some of the work created on the LES into the category of a nomadic hippie counterculture invested only in translating downtown experience with little regard for community betterment or social movements unfolding right down the street.

Stewart, the figurehead of La Mama for nearly fifty years, earned (and claimed) a maternal honorific: Mama. Virtually any profile of Stewart and her theater emphasized nurturing, caring, and caretaking as central to its operations.[98] The first line of Richard Schechner's obituary for Stewart articulated this enduring element of her style: "Ellen Stewart had more children than anyone I ever heard of."[99] As artistic director, Stewart lived in an apartment above her theater, and provided many collaborators with food, enthusiasm, and space to develop their work and the labors of creating La Mama. Shannon Jackson notes that "domesticity has not fared well as analytic paradigm," and perhaps as a consequence, theatrical genealogies after World War II obscure Stewart's labors.[100] Rather than connecting her institutionalization as part of this caring approach, many critics equated her effective deployment of foundation money with commercialization and lukewarm politics.

Yet these material achievements led to stages of new possibility for the LES. La Mama forged interdependence: an awareness of collaboration not just between artists, but between artists and their funding sources, and theaters within municipal systems. This facilitated its eventual installation as a city venue, initially made official by the building purchased from the city in 1974. To borrow Massumi's terms, La Mama's version of environmental theater remained not "site-specific but *relationship-specific*."[101] These relationships extended beyond La Mama and her playwright "biddies," and tied the theater to the social and cultural fluctuations occurring on the LES. All of these relations operated on an inherently political level, with contradictory connections to local neighborhood dynamics.

The logic of austerity rendered government spending on arts—especially experimental theater—preposterous. Yet Ellen Stewart's eclectic programming and her early embrace of intercultural exchange and local theater spaces anchored her commitment to expanding definitions of both New York performance and local space. This is particularly true given her fidelity to heterogeneous performance and a neighborhood with an established legacy of sheltering people and places, even against the wishes of the municipality. Roger Starr defended his argument for planned shrinkage by obtusely suggesting that neighborhood attachment was a superficial preoccupation easily sloughed off.[102] Yet, just as community groups vociferously protested this concept, so too did La Mama embody the countering philosophy of spatial centrality and neighborhood abandonment. Across the 1970s, population decline rocked all of New York City's neighborhoods, as labor and migration patterns led to demographic composition changes.[103] In order to fully interrogate the institution-building activities of theaters like La Mama, attention must be paid not just to population upheaval, but to the systematic divestment of the LES and the energies of those who remained. Overemphasis on a version of artistic "white flight" from downtown areas calcifies the 1960s in a nostalgic register, and conceals the equally important role of artists and activists resisting the dismantling of a neighborhood.[104]

To understand downtown theater movements as interconnected with the changes in the urban ecology is, then, to understand La Mama as adopting a stance at odds with the official urban strategy of fracture and division, valued and undervalued territories. An analysis of the uneven cultural development rampant in neighborhoods like the Lower East Side eschews the neat outlines of census districts in favor of the urban network and reality of spatial flows and political coalitions. At the intersection of cultural institutions, audiences, and the government, Stewart's most masterful "producing" was, then, of the neglected relations of care in the neighborhood.

Chapter 2

✦

TKTS and "Lost Audience" Anxiety

Fiscal Crisis Times Square

> The real question is should Broadway continue to exist? Should it continue to exist as a neighborhood? Should it continue to exist as an economic operation, a particular kind of exploitative producer-director dominated economic arrangement? One must ask whether the whole structure must be ripped down or allowed to die.
>
> —Richard Schechner, *First American Congress of Theatre*, 1974

During the summer of 1973, Broadway producer Alexander H. Cohen went abroad with a pile of theater-related reading. Protracted conversations with the League of New York Theatres and Producers weighed on his mind; that spring, Cohen and others in the league had engaged in a contentious search for solutions to Broadway's great quantity of problems. Hit shows did not sell out, fewer plays opened, new projects lacked financing, and dark theaters proliferated as fast as the theories of the causes behind the troubles.[1] Some producers blamed the industry's defects on the legitimate theater's home, Times Square. They changed curtain times to appease skittish audience members and lobbied the city for more law enforcement, but the oncoming financial crisis created deaf ears at City Hall. Cohen and fellow producer Gerald Schoenfeld dismissed piecemeal solutions, and rallied around the idea of a citywide theater conference that might address the vast industry and build political momentum on its shared problems. Old-guard producers recognized the need for substantial change to Broadway's status quo; when Bernard B. Jacobs, president of the Shubert Organization, became responsible for the seventeen Shubert houses in 1972, only eleven were lit.[2] The commercial theater's argument for government funding—the ailing tourist district needed stimulation in the midst of the corrosive fiscal period—caused consternation among nonprofit administrators. Broadway already received foundation subsidies through TDF for its risky ventures.[3] Small, underfunded theater organizations viewed the argument that it deserved more as disingenuous. All theaters experienced the effects of urban deterioration on theater attendance.

Cohen's fervor for such an event only increased after his summer travels, when he read journalist Margaret Croyden's volume on experimental theater, *Lunatics, Lovers & Poets*.[4] The book defined the surrealist and symbolist antecedents of contemporary experimental performance, and presented dispatches from Happenings, Jerzy Grotowski's work, the Open Theatre, environmental theater, and Peter Brook. Stuart Little described Cohen's revelatory reading of Croyden's study: "Here was a world of theatre unknown to him although in his own backyard, whose influence had spread, and whose ideas indirectly affected him and his colleagues."[5] The conference that Cohen convened, the First American Congress of Theatre (FACT), ultimately revealed great depths of divisiveness between artistic communities. FACT delegates and panelists argued over recognition, subsidy, and support, in a city poised to enter one of the largest municipal bankruptcies in the nation's history.

In the ongoing battle for resources during a time of reappropriation, nonprofit and experimental theaters perceived Cohen and his co-conveners as late to the table and motivated by self-interest, not the good of the city's rapidly diversifying citizenry. Joseph Papp argued that Broadway was not yet awake to "the exodus of great numbers of white middle-class to the suburbs," or the wall of poverty, ignorance, and historical conditions that "separates vast numbers of people from the arts."[6] Since the late 1960s, population shifts had changed audience composition but went unacknowledged by many producers on the Great White Way.

Mayor John Lindsay had his own vision of the future for Times Square. To some, he exuded a blend of star power and patrician charisma more suited to Broadway than City Hall. Lindsay harbored fantasies of a stage career, as well as a belief in theatrical activity developing west of the heart of Times Square. With an eye toward westward development, the Lindsay administration ushered in the decades-long refiguring of Times Square, a protracted process that activated long-standing competition between the industries of performing arts, real estate, and sex.[7] Studies of the area have traced its history as a center for commodity speculation as well as flourishing subcultures and social diversity, performative desire and regulated behavior, risqué entertainment and mainstream diversions.

By the early 1970s, terms such as "legitimate theater" and even "Broadway" lost their utility as geographic locators; in small theaters downtown, scouts searched for ways to duplicate the boundary-crossing successes of *Hair, Godspell*, and *A Chorus Line*. Downtown playwright Tom Eyen, for example, was heartened by the handful of writers who had already made inroads in legitimate theater houses, an indication that new plays and perspectives would increasingly be seen on Broadway. Eyen's 1973 op-ed piece, "The Discreet Alarm of the Off Off Broadway Playwright," revealed his own wish to play Broadway's 1,675-seat Palace Theatre and leave behind the tiny stages of La Mama and Caffe Cino.[8] The cadre of writers who had plied their trade in Village cafes and cabarets with few thoughts of remuneration were due for an upgrade; the alternative, Eyen feared, would be to turn the gilded theaters of Broadway into museums: "The past had a beauty we'll never find again, no matter how many old musicals they revive."[9] The municipal crisis introduced city intervention in a moment of theatrical upheaval that can only be seen as a contest for territory and audiences, manifested in disagreements over producing choices, audience outreach, and the major initiative of the period, the TKTS Discount Ticket Booth.

The widespread media coverage of the crisis created an imperative for municipal involvement in the theater district beyond the clean-up campaigns and city planning initiatives of the 1960s.[10] By the time Mayor Abe Beame took office in 1974, a chorus of voices argued that more was needed to convince residents and out-of-towners that the Big Apple's entertainment center was one worth visiting. This coincided with a difficult time for financing Broadway shows, and in her history of adult musicals—a genre that thrived just before and during the fiscal crisis—Elizabeth Wollman describes the heavy toll of economic pressure on creative output when it came to the commercial theater in 1970s New York. Weakening attendance and stagflation caused producers to "slash the costs of production and increase ticket prices."[11] Yet Irving W. Cheskin's analysis of the forty-three "tax-paying" theaters demonstrated that in nominal dollars, Broadway increased its grosses by about 300 percent between 1971 and 1981 after a period of intense decline after 1968.[12] How did legitimate houses achieve this gain during declines in financing, swaths of retail taken over by topless bars and massage parlors, and the near-extinction of a standard producing model?

In the late 1960s, producers panicked as they watched traditional audience profiles decline; controversial initiatives like the TKTS discount ticketing program, created in 1973, signaled a competition over the future orientation of the neighborhood and audience composition. This case study presents a compelling series of contradictions unique to the period: grosses increased during a national recession and citywide fiscal crisis, and the municipal government marshaled resources to support commercial theater while smaller theaters criticized these for-profit strategies as unjust and outdated. Many of these contradictions grew out of contrasting responses to white flight and broader demographic change, a twin phenomenon legible in the street scene of Times Square and the self-preservation efforts of major producers. The onset of fiscal contraction coupled with perceptions of Times Square's fading glory led the power brokers of the area to furiously consolidate the centrality of the legitimate theater within a cozy continuum of historical Broadway. Through these campaigns and clashes over audience and location, the fiscal crisis years in Times Square reshaped the relationship between spectatorship and neighborhood.

The Garden of Earthly Delights

Cohen was correct that worlds of theater previously unknown to him now played in his backyard. Back in 1968, Charles Ludlam, the ambitious and off-kilter actor, playwright, and director, still had a number of itinerant years to go before his Ridiculous Theatrical Group would settle into a long-term space at One Sheridan Square. *Turds in Hell*, a bawdy midnight camp extravaganza written by Ludlam and Bill Vehr (featuring Ludlam in the role of Saint Obnoxious), performed for three weeks at the Gate Theatre downtown. The play received rave reviews from the alternative press, although the *New York Times* would not consent to a print advertisement until they changed the title of the show to *Garden of Earthly Delights*. When the Gate owners raised their rental fees, Ridiculous admirers and art critics Stefan Brecht and Frederick Ted Castle found a new venue for *Turds in Hell*: "one of the porno theaters on West 42nd, where they watch 'beaver' films."[13] The Ridiculous team jumped at the chance.

Turds in Hell opened at the Masque Theatre, 440 West Forty-Second Street, between Ninth and Tenth Avenues, in December 1968, running through the spring of 1969. Just a few avenues west of the nerve center of Broadway, the small theater offered the essentials: dressing rooms, a sloped auditorium, built-in seating, and a free stage every Friday and Saturday night at midnight. A porn theater on the far west side of Times Square provided an ideal environment for the play, a carnivalesque fable adapted from the *Satyricon*, rife with scatological references and Ridiculous imagery: sexually confused lesbian nuns sing and dance while saints engage in orgies with the Devil, rich men defecate money on a yacht bound for the underworld, and a sex maniac in search of his true parentage ultimately turns to cannibalism. But in the summer of 1969—against the backdrop of Woodstock and the Stonewall Riots—Ludlam lost the Masque Theatre when his ticket sales dwindled and the tightrope balance of using box office revenue to pay for rent and ads finally snapped.

On the edge of the 1970s, Ludlam's stint at the Masque provides an apt prelude to the fiscal crisis in Times Square, a period of turmoil for a theater district convulsing with desires for the new within the domain of the old. Ludlam's perch in midtown put a fine point on his incessant mocking of the once-tidy categories of Broadway, Off-Broadway, and Off-Off-Broadway. He harbored little interest in performing his burlesque and vaudeville-inflected shows in the alternative spaces of the Off-Off Broadway movement. He wanted a "real theater" in which to pay homage to the traditions of theatrical history.[14] The Ridiculous dangled the tantalizing proposition that fresh uses might transform hackneyed theaters with downtown energies and producing arrangements. Ludlam's foray to midtown revealed a side of Broadway that was both assiduously ignored and generally feared: the tearing down of the gatekeepers of taste and the prior assumptions about audience. He melded the upper and lower registers of the tourist neighborhood and the city, poking fun at the opportunistic morality crusades of public officials who alighted on Times Square just long enough to condemn its poor taste. For some, Broadway in the late 1960s showed signs of anemia, but to Ludlam, its empty stages intimated potential beyond antiseptic notions of preservation or urbane nostalgia.

For the city, Times Square equaled a black hole of missed opportunities on the development map; the theaters that survived into the second half of the twentieth century were "totally depreciated and paid relatively low taxes."[15] When compared to the revenue that medium-sized office buildings provided to the government in property taxes, Times Square was untapped potential. Its high-crime reputation meant that it could not attract the kind of private investment that the city envisioned for the area, only isolated speculation and minimal small-scale investment activity. Yet standing in the way of Times Square as an anchor to revive the city was Times Square itself: the "crossroads of the world" defied coherence. As a landmark, it encompassed more diversities than certainties, more fringes than centers. In order to consolidate the area's fictive centrality in the nation and the city, the formerly liminal space—with its capacity to both represent and challenge the mainstream—had to be rendered intelligible.

Part of this process required enforcement; historian Themis Chronopoulos demonstrates that the intensity of police interventions through the late 1960s and into the 1970s did not occur because Times Square was central to the city's actual spatial and economic organization, "but because of its centrality to the image of New York City."[16] The struggle to reconfigure notions of "centrality" had clear battle lines in theater practices. Would Broadway continue to emblemize homogenized taste? Could the appeal and reach of the legitimate theater extend into the ailing neighborhoods of the city, or would the fruits of its success always remain regenerative for Broadway itself? Was the very concept of a legitimate theater in the "center" of the city relevant to audiences or merely another spectacle orchestrated by old-guard commercial producers?

The 1971–72 season reflected a changing Broadway. Its subjects included Vietnam, war resistance, colonial violence, and poverty, presented in plays including *Sticks and Bones*, David Rabe's tragedy about a Vietnam veteran; the Off-Broadway transfer *The Trial of the Catonsville Nine*, a play by draft resister Father Daniel Berrigan; and two musicals from Melvin Van Peebles that depicted the tribulations of an African American neighborhood, *Ain't Supposed to Die a Natural Death* and *Don't Play Us Cheap!*[17] The influx of popular movie houses as well as downtown theatrical transfers brought new patrons to Times Square. Some individual producing teams grew adventurous in their appeals to target audience members—especially the under-fifty crowd. The desperate fiscal environment encouraged certain kinds of artistic risks, and new hit plays that had succeeded Off-Broadway, such as Joseph A. Walker's *The River Niger* at the St. Mark's Playhouse, surprised critics and producers with a strong showing on Broadway, winning the Tony for Best Play in the 1973–74 season. Popular shows like *Purlie* (1970) and *The River Niger* led to a swelling of new work written and directed by African Americans on which producers were willing to take a chance, including the musicals *Raisin* (1973) and *The Wiz* (1975). This held particularly true for revues with minimal production requirements like *Don't Bother Me, I Can't Cope* (1972), *Bubbling Brown Sugar* (1976), *Your Arms Too Short to Box with God* (1977), and *Ain't Misbehavin'* (1978).

In the categories of representation and sheer artistic heterogeneity, Off and Off-Off activity in the previous decades had altered the relationship between uptown and downtown theater, and led to a reckoning: how to discern the imprint of these changes on audience composition? It is here that austerity ideology, fiscal crisis anxiety, and white flight paranoia overlapped with producing choices and government support. The need to attract new theater patrons to the area was of paramount concern; in addition to the perception of the district as unsafe, demographic studies showed that the age and profiles of Broadway audiences were stagnant. Producers, critics, and some government officials maintained that the audiences lost to suburbanization needed to be lured back to a tourist-friendly Times Square; others argued that to appeal to the diversity of residents living in New York City neighborhoods would be a stronger, more durable path to urban regeneration.

The producers of Forty-Second Street feared irrelevance within the cultural life of the city, and further than ever from an American middle. If Times Square once held the capacity to cater to this middle, the 1970s comprised an exhaustive drive to push it into the upper registers of culture—as producer Gerald Schoenfeld explained, to give it a more "statesmanlike" character[18]—that would rescue it from the fringes of the cultural, aesthetic, and geographic imagination of the city and the nation. The legitimate theater fit perfectly with this philosophy of cultural upgrade as a path to economic revitalization; to achieve this, the restoration of "the legendary Great White Way" drew upon romantic imagery of a theater district that Alexander Reichl argues had only a "slight basis" in reality.[19] Whether the theaters should be relocated, preserved, or demolished was a matter of extensive debate, shadowed always by their potential to provide the city with more money in tax revenue and tourist dollars. While government officials seized on the nostalgic heyday-rhetoric of landmark theaters to argue for their overhaul of a contested neighborhood, many artists and independent producers argued for a decentralization of city support away from the staid legitimate theater. Richard Schechner typified the attitude of emergent theater artists in response to the calls to preserve a commercial theater industry built upon a troubled Forty-Second Street: "Why should we be working to decentralize the theatre and then centralize it again?"[20]

After the 1971–72 season, critic Otis Guernsey imagined the coming decade on Broadway as one marked by newly divided audiences. The "massive majority" now confronted the prior decade of experimentation, and old audiences would either be ready for "the adventure of change," or repelled by the new forms and theatrical language of the 1960s.[21] Statistics indicate that they were at first repelled: at the beginning of the 1970s, the Broadway theater suffered a decline, and from 1971 to 1973, season attendance dropped from 6 million to a little over 5 million, with ticket sales falling by $10 million.[22] Irving Cheskin, executive director of the Broadway League, attributed the figures to the deteriorating atmosphere of Times Square, lack of action on the part of public officials and the general public, and the "archaic" operations of the industry itself, including cash-only, in-person ticketing, outdated marketing techniques, and out-of-touch advertising.[23] Broadway producers and many of the city's institutions, including relatively new arrivals like the Theatre Development Fund (created in 1968), depended upon the longevity of a legitimate theater on Forty-Second Street. It was their collective influence that led to a prioritization of business incentives for theater owners in lieu of confronting the issues that economist William Baumol identified as the real problems of Broadway: not the much talked-about issue of pornography, but economics.

While frequently characterized as an iconic low in the history of legitimate production, the turning point of the 1970s transcended questions of pornography and respectability and hinged upon changing demographics, commercial engineering of theater audiences, and governmental influence on the cultural position of entertainment and aesthetics. Forty-Second Street earned its nickname of "the Deuce" (as in "forty-deuce") during the 1970s: this late-twentieth-century moniker referred to its seedy underbelly and thriving subcultures. But the fiscal crisis period in Times Square is distinguished not by its relationship to an underground, or by its usefulness to anti-pornography activists, but by a struggle for the center—on the part of producers and city leaders seeking a stable hub in a bruised city. This quest faced myriad pressures: New artists and new producers demanded consideration downtown, while Lincoln Center's growth uptown threatened to unsettle the visual map of commercial theater production. Crime and the purported ills of the street further challenged the vision that sought to be the Big Apple, rather than its rotting core.

Paranoid Urbanism: "Lost Audience" Anxiety

When he won the 1973 mayoral election, Abe Beame was loath to be associated with an area "overrun by pornography, drugs, and street crime" until one of his aides suggested that they target Forty-Second Street as a signature issue.[24] Intense lobbying from old-guard Broadway producers contributed to Beame's change of heart:

> I had a conversation with Gerald Schoenfeld, who told me the reason the industry of Broadway was still in such financial straits and now was in danger of being totally dismantled, theatre by theatre, was that 42nd Street had become the porn capital of America. This disturbed me quite a bit and that same year I asked Schoenfeld to chair a new organization, the Mayor's Midtown Citizens' Committee to help me revive the area.[25]

This pat explanation for Broadway's precarious financial position remained a matter of debate. According to economist William Baumol, the view that pitted the porn capital against Shubert's Alley was a misconception, or, at the very least, an exaggeration. Baumol argued that something endemic to theatrical production also required attention. With economist William Bowen, Baumol coined the phenomenon of "cost disease" to argue that live performance faces unique financing problems as unit costs rise and a "productivity lag" persists. A play will always take the same amount of physical output per work hour; the very conditions of live performance create this static productivity because "the work of the performer is an end in itself, not a means for the production of some good."[26] "The Baumol Effect" threatened to both liberate and flatten the constraints of theaters, for it held the economics of theatrical reality as the ultimate leveler.

Baumol insisted on a reckoning with the financial impoverishment of New York theaters. In a 1974 opinion piece, Baumol and his coauthor, Hilda Baumol, dismissed the problems of featherbedding by stagehand unions, the profiteering of greedy producers, and unsavory urban conditions—none of which, they argued, could be described as "critical."[27] Transportation was not impossible, the crime rate was declining, and neither lascivious entertainment "nor Runyonesque characters" were newcomers. (Ticket prices were also not the culprit, although the perception of prices had some bearing: when theatergoers believe ticket prices to be high, producers avoid raising ticket prices to reflect production costs.) Baumol and Baumol argued that the two fundamental problems were competition from the mass media and cost disease. Due to the progressive nature of the latter, the commercial theater "will need more and more subsidization if it is to survive and provide a product of substantial quality."[28] Mayor Lindsay had previously attempted to zone Broadway into a renewal and Mayor Beame attacked its public relations problems; neither considered "cost disease" or meaningful levels of subsidy.

Beame's efforts to instill law and order in the peep show district led to a flurry of citizen committees (the Mayor's Midtown Citizens' Committee, the Midtown Enforcement Project, and the Mayor's Office of Midtown Planning and Development), police raids, and tourist-ready spaces, all achieved under severely curtailed budgets for enforcement. The idea of cost disease was relegated to the sidelines as major initiatives waded into the battleground of porn, usually through raids of establishments. "Going in would turn my stomach," Beame said as he taped a vacate order on the doors of yet another topless bar. "We can make Times Square the Great White Way that it used to be."[29] The crowds heckled ("Forget porno. We need jobs!"), the press covered them as overblown stunts, and Beame looked foolish when many of the closings were overturned.

Still, many ignored systemic analyses of theater within a market economy in favor of interpreting the social factors of crime and indecency. The rot of Times Square was considered so detrimental to the patterns of theatergoing that critic Walter Kerr published his vision of a twentieth-century change of location for the legitimate theater. In an emotional nine-page article in the *New York Times* magazine, Kerr advocated plucking up Broadway "by the roots" and planting its theaters along the East River, "nearer audiences, nearer where films are now, nearer busy department stores and flourishing restaurants, nearer highways, possible parking and all of that."[30] Kerr's plan was not just impractical from an economic perspective (he conceded that the price tag would near $400 million), but also from a policy stance, given the commitment to a westward pattern of development across the city. His wish for a theater district nearer to highways and parking also ran contrary to the long-held belief that Times Square's proximity to a major transit hub was one of the defining features of the "crossroads of the world." This, Kerr argued, had changed. "People simply don't want to come into midtown Manhattan at night any more."[31] Kerr's bid for a new address for Broadway was a wish for Robert Moses–era master planning, as well as a masked scare tactic. Since his position at the *Times* made it unlikely that he would propose a serious challenge to Broadway's zip code, his scenario sought to compel readers to equate the entire theater district with the respectable families fleeing the city for the suburbs. Would the Great White Way give way to the Great White Flight, or could the tide be stemmed? His argument pushed for a reinstatement of values, not an inversion or upturning of geographic positioning or aesthetic norms.

Kerr's relocated Broadway revealed one articulation of the "lost audiences" theory. This was a largely spectral force that also motivated the choices of producers and officials. The persistent attachment to an "old" Broadway audience—or, more to the point, the resistance to embrace a new audience—animated the notion that the financial realities of theater producing would be irrelevant if the audience were right. Kerr sought "Broadway's audience—the old Broadway audience, the big Broadway audience," and he was not alluding to the quantity of spectators alone:

> We need a vast number of people to keep an expensive production alive, we need them concentrated in one place and not dispersed in small pockets across the land, we need them where influential critics can depend upon a theatergoing habit to get them to attend the

> "best" . . . we need a focal point, an apex, a professional top. We need busyness and business, contrast and competition, one thronged center where the ultimate struggle toward quality can be fairly thrashed out.[32]

Kerr disregarded the prior two decades of Off and Off-Off experimentation and clung to a central marketplace and standard (one established and judged, presumably, by the paper of record). This position was bound up in the very ethos of Kerr's employer, the *New York Times*, which had its own stake in the future (and past) identity of Times Square.[33]

Kerr's argument against the decentralization of theaters and audiences assumed that Broadway ticket-buyers needed to be "concentrated in one place," as a bulwark against the kind of heterogeneity downtown and outer-borough artists argued for so passionately. If Tom Eyen was interested in Broadway's dark theaters as playgrounds for unpredictable downtown upstarts, Kerr argued that Broadway existed in order to exclude them. The outlands needed something to aspire to, and without Broadway in Times Square, work might go on being done, "but standards will be vaguer, parochialism come to prevail."[34] This attachment to Broadway as a professional apex represented a mainstream anxiety that the terra firma of clear critical judgments and a legible, recognizable audience rose and fell together. Kerr, Richard Barr, and others voted to abandon the lowbrow elements of Times Square in an effort to reclaim audiences that had abandoned the city. Perhaps this suburban audience could be wooed back if Times Square was aesthetically closer to the aggressively elite Museum Mile?

These configurations have the earmarks of "paranoid urbanism," a phenomenon identified by Matthew Gandy, in which confidence in the city's infrastructure, such as its transit system, fell to such a low point that it overshadowed the reality of government neglect of that system itself. In his writing about the water system in New York City, Gandy observed that the "maintenance of physical infrastructure represents only one side" of the water crisis; "the other dimension is provided by declining public confidence in the safety of the drinking water."[35] Broadly, "paranoid urbanism" is one response to the urban crisis of the late 1960s and 1970s, when fears of social disorder began to resurface.[36] Gandy's theory is particularly instructive when applied to the approach of many city planners, residents, and critics toward Broadway and the city services that facilitated it, from the transit system to policing to the upkeep of city property. These fears about Times Square, with its abandoned theaters and vanished audiences, provided the other side of the city's disinvestment in theater architecture and pressing infrastructure needs.

The language employed throughout the 1970s encapsulates the depth of these anxieties, as old metaphors of disease and illness returned to public discourse: the body of a sick municipality choked theaters with its symptoms. Times Square had been overrun by an illegal and dangerous street culture:

the neighborhood as a "cancer" defined its contaminants and necessitated surgery.[37] This legitimated a view of Broadway as one coherent—albeit ailing—district, disconnected from a network of artists, theaters, and audiences that might themselves be the picture of health. Richard Schechner, frustrated by these assumptions at the 1974 First American Congress of Theatre, admonished, "If this is the First American Theatre Congress [*sic*], it should not start out with the assumption that we have this invalid that has to be resurrected. Maybe the terminal disease is very good, and maybe the institution has served its purpose and now we can say rest in peace and let's get on with the work of the theatre."[38] To be fair, debates over the health of the theater had traded in these metaphors since Moss Hart and George S. Kaufman wrote *The Fabulous Invalid* in 1938, but commentators revived these terms in the 1970s to declare Broadway beyond recovery. The fiscal crisis amplified this trend, as many referred to the city itself—and even the country—as afflicted with a "malaise."[39] If the problems stretched nationwide, New York City formed the apex.

Crime-in-the-streets publicity had the little-known ability to hurt Off and Off-Off Broadway even more adversely than Times Square "because its little theaters are scattered in many dark corners" of Manhattan.[40] High-tourist and high-traffic areas were often more safe, operating in a zone of surveillance that could have comforted, rather than concerned, the average tourist. Yet critics like Kerr jumped on the white flight panic bandwagon, and his rhetoric signified a dangerous nadir during the time of fiscal crisis: as costs rose, the *New York Times* already held sway in the fate of productions—and now critics used their pulpits to proclaim the death knell of an entire neighborhood. Otis Guernsey and other Broadway boosters published vehement accounts arguing that instances of crime inflamed perceptions as much as the bigotry of commentators too jaded by their own racism and norms of cultural segregation to look more deeply into the mix of social forces and entertainments occurring in Times Square.

The emphasis on "lost audiences" was itself a strategy, one that sidestepped discussion about how the patrons of Times Square and Forty-Second Street had changed, perhaps even for the positive. Hundreds of thousands still passed through the area every day for work, pleasure, entertainment, and leisure, and one of the most oft-cited sociological studies conducted at the time considered Forty-Second Street's appeal across racial and ethnic lines to be an asset of the area.[41] There was a market for "all forms of popular culture" including jazz, dancing, sports, ethnic entertainment, and programming for children, with crossover between the profiles of clients patronizing all of its offerings. They also noted three reasons for optimism, and none were related to office development. In 1978 the Off-Off Broadway Theater Row was inaugurated; Manhattan Plaza, the rental building for artists, had a waiting list of 3,000; and there was a third consecutive year of record theater sales for Broadway theaters.

The decline of legitimate entertainment along the Forty-Second Street corridor predated both the rise of television and the metropolitan demographic shift that accounted for the racial and ethnic change in the street; a report on pedestrian traffic along West Forty-Second Street indicated that "during the peak entertainment hours black, latin, and white working-class populations are the dominant groups who seek entertainment there."[42] This was, however, the minority opinion; the majority saw little need to distinguish between the "large groups of young black and Latin men" who were there for movies and those who were part of the drug traffic, prostitution, or con games. Lower- and middle-class moviegoers and homosexuals, pimps, prostitutes, and petty criminals were considered part of a large and unchecked population of urban detritus.

The marking of certain bodies in the Times Square area as "deviant" through official mechanisms such as sweeps and police dragnets has been well documented. Historian Themis Chronopoulos established that the mass arrests that occurred in Times Square at this time may have been aimed at decreasing crime numbers but in practice blurred the definition of undesirables—vagrants, homosexuals, and loiterers were lumped together under broad charges that were often later declared by the courts to be invalid; still, police used them to arrest people who "simply happened to be in public space."[43] Alexander Reichl argues that the racial integration of the Square was viewed as a "minority takeover," and that the definition of a loiterer had grown so vast, so politicized, and so fear-based that even shoeshine men were included.[44]

Theater producers, however, did not uniformly share these assumptions regarding the patrons of Times Square and the need to recapture lost audiences. In order to broaden the audience for legitimate theater, some targeted the new population of moviegoers in the hopes that they could be lured from the movie seat to the theater seat. In discussing his plans for the Vivian Beaumont Theater at Lincoln Center, Joseph Papp explained: "Special attention will be given to the casting of black plays with the purpose of bringing into the theater not only those blacks who are already theatergoers, but those who attend movies only."[45] Papp both heeded and contributed to the upsurge of black artistic participation in the commercial theater that was credited in 1975 with bringing "a new spirit and a new audience to Broadway."[46] The prior decades of civil rights activism and work by leading black artists had loosened the media stranglehold and produced a surge of new representation on television and in theater. While *The Jeffersons* and *Good Times* succeeded in prime time, theater patrons finally had "a choice among Broadway shows that offer [black audiences] something to identify with."[47] Articles that heralded (and alternately denounced) this trend proliferated, and observed that the "predominantly black crowds, and particularly families with young children" now greeted passersby near West Forty-Fourth Street, thanks to shows like *The Wiz*.[48]

Related attempts to mollify reluctance to venture into Times Square also signified a proactive step toward culling audiences from neighborhoods that might not have a tradition of Broadway attendance, but might begin at an all-black revue like *Don't Bother Me, I Can't Cope.* The long-running Vinnette Carroll and Micki Grant musical offered ticket purchasers from all New York City boroughs (except Staten Island) a free taxi ride one way, either to the theater or home after the show.[49] Those who sought to emphasize the dangers of Times Square as a pretense for aid to the commercial theater ignored the frequently novel marketing and promotion strategies of these new plays.

There was a tension between the drive to make Broadway more appealing to wider audiences, and the rampant conflation of young people of color with the unsavory aspects of the area. Alexander Reichl argues that the politics surrounding the redevelopment of Times Square was led by a fear of diversity: while the dominant narrative of public and political discourse clung to the definition of Times Square as a symbol of urban decline, lurking beneath the surface of redevelopment was a potency borne from racial anxieties.[50] Many producers, however, were desperate to stimulate theatergoing and widen the geographic audience profile beyond limited segments of brave Manhattanites and intrepid tourists.

The knotty questions of audience composition and ticket access led to audience development initiatives. These corresponded to efforts to tackle the sociological problems of the area. In 1972, three city agencies announced that they would implement the recommendations of a citizens committee convened under the auspices of the New York State Council on the Arts (NYSCA) and the New York City Cultural Council.[51] Jaquelin Robertson, director of the Office of Midtown Planning and Development, remarked that among the physical improvements to the streets and the lighting, the removal of "undesirable characters from the area and a special zoning designation" would provide a physical "face lift" to the theater district.[52] The committee lobbied for federal and city subsidies to "the serious and classical theater, such as Lincoln Center," the establishment of better ticketing methods, and a repeal of regulations. Within a year, a new system of ticket distribution, the Times Square Theatre Center (TKTS), would be created.

TKTS and the Myth of Broadway's Decline

The marketing initiative TKTS opened on June 25, 1973, under the sponsorship of state and city agencies and the Theatre Development Fund (TDF).[53] The program distributes unsold seats for same-day Broadway and off-Broadway shows at a discount, and was rightly lauded for improving box office sales at a crucial moment of flagging confidence in both Broadway offerings and Times Square viability. As a study by William Baumol attested, the program was a dramatic success from its very first year—for relatively little cost. Theater artists and producers, however, did not uniformly support the new program; some felt that it ran counter to their initiatives to expand the audience for legitimate theater. At a time when Off and Off-Off theater companies, plays, and playwrights were beginning to make inroads in Broadway houses, TKTS—primarily marketed to tourists and out-of-towners—threatened to undermine full-price ticket sales. At its best, it provided a renewing jolt of energy to the midtown theater district, and claimed Times Square for Broadway into the future. At its worst, it represented a missed opportunity to effectively expand audience demographics and constrained the possibilities of production and aesthetic choices on Broadway for decades to come.

Today, TKTS is virtually inseparable from the experience of Broadway, but at the time of its inception, it was an experiment directed toward easing the fiscal strain at the heart of Baumol's cost disease in the performing arts. In its earliest years, the TDF staff studied the operation of the booth, and, with Ford Foundation money, William and Hilda Baumol worked on a comprehensive report.[54] Initially, TDF and Mayor Lindsay's Office of Midtown Planning and Development created a barebones capital budget for TKTS that left two enterprising designers with only $5,000 and a can of paint to create the original structure.[55] The architects, John Schiff and Robert Mayers, used rented pipes from a scaffolding company in the Bronx, stretched panels, and a donated trailer. In a large Helvetica font, they painted "TKTS" in letters six feet high. To protect against the wind, they used steel cables with concrete anchors at each corner. This simple construction would become a central box office that sold tickets to Broadway, Off-Broadway, Lincoln Center, the Brooklyn Academy of Music, City Center, and others.

The Negro Ensemble Company (NEC) provides a case study in the intersection of audience analysis, cost disease, and TKTS adoption. At about the same time that the plan for the TKTS booth was hatched, economic troubles mired the NEC. With production costs rising and an original grant from the Ford Foundation gone, even standing-room-only audiences at their St. Mark's Playhouse could not generate enough revenue to meet the budget. They took drastic steps to ensure that some elements of their activities could move forward: the resident company was disbanded, salaries were deferred, training programs were canceled, and the staff was cut during the 1972–73 season.[56] The creative team decided to produce one new play a year, and the first play, *The River Niger*, by Joseph A. Walker, proved to be their largest success yet—one that ultimately helped support the company into the next ten years.

The play opened on December 5, 1972, at the St. Mark's Playhouse, and after 120 performances and three Obie award wins (two for distinguished performance, one for best play), on March 27, 1973, it became the first NEC production to move to Broadway. A review in the *New Yorker* described the unlikely ascent of this intimate rendering of a Harlem family whose alcoholic patriarch confronts his golden child, an air force veteran who has returned from his training a changed man:

> A considerable risk was involved in moving from the pleasantly ramshackle little St. Marks Playhouse . . . to the commodious Brooks Atkinson, with its touch-me-not, unbridgeable gulf between the audience on one side of the proscenium arch and the actors on the other. The risk has proved eminently worth taking, and the play speaks to us with undiminished zest and power, just as *That Championship Season* proved able to do after making a similar journey uptown.[57]

The play won Walker the 1974 Tony Award for Best Play and critical accolades. Notwithstanding the challenges, *The River Niger* enjoyed an eight-month Broadway run, sustaining 280 performances before closing on November 25, 1973—five months after the TKTS booth opened.

Why did the head of the NEC and the director of Walker's play, Douglas Turner Ward, refuse to participate in the ticketing initiative with *The River Niger*? One reason might have been an aversion to the focus on tourists in TKTS marketing, which was inconsistent with the aims of independent companies like the NEC. The ticket incentive deal could have had a deleterious effect on their precarious financial standing, especially if the booth did not substantially attract new audiences, but rather provided deals to old ones. (Some sellout shows at the time—like *Uncle Vanya*, *Pippen*, and *A Moon for the Misbegotten*—initially chose not to participate because they found it superfluous.)[58] For small theaters with high running costs, money lost on discounted tickets would not be easily absorbed when audiences dwindled.

The issue, however, was cultural as well as financial. Woodie King Jr., producer and founder of the New Federal Theatre, expressed his own reservations at FACT about programs that built audiences through discounted seats: "We can say there are cheap seats, but that is exactly what the audience doesn't want. His whole life has been a series of cheap seats."[59] Producers resisted making meaningful changes to their operations in accordance with demographic factors, and instead supported ticketing initiatives geared toward calcified target audiences. "I see middle class whites vacating the city for the suburbs and leaving it to the blacks and Puerto Ricans, but the theater owners don't want to leave the theaters to blacks and Puerto Ricans," lamented King.[60] This extended to the marketing and publicity choices of producers who relied exclusively on mainstream press outlets. Not only was an ad in the *Times* too expensive for King or Ward's theaters to afford, but it also did not target their core audiences. TKTS advertising practices located billboards at airports and railroad stations where full-price-paying tourists could be found, a strategy that ignored and discounted the ways in which other communities were learning about plays.[61] Successes of the time indicated that many black audiences attending commercial shows like *The Wiz* most frequently learned about productions through word of mouth.[62] The Harlem-based Audelco (Audience Development Committee) began devising theater parties for both commercial and noncommercial productions in 1973, impatient with the myopic view of out-of-town audiences as the sole Broadway customer. In 1975 Eleanor Lester in the *New York Times* credited Melvin Van Peebles's two shows in the 1971 season with bringing black audiences in larger numbers to Broadway.[63] Van Peebles's efforts to publicize his shows to niche audiences—through commercial spots on radio stations that mainstream producers usually ignored, for example—were then copied by individual Broadway shows. There is no evidence that this model influenced TKTS.

Ward observed upticks in their white audience numbers after praise for *The River Niger* arrived in the mainstream press, but he too chose to develop advertising innovations to attract new black audiences to the theater. "The white component might contract according to what the critics say but our core audience come because what we're doing on stage is in one way or another relevant to them. With *The River Niger* on Broadway it was the black audiences that kept us running for as long as we did."[64] Years later, Ward expressed continued frustration at the difficulty of undertaking serious audience development given the reality of Broadway ticket prices, which even in 1973 were quite high.[65] That difficulty, he argued, transcended geography; Ward equated the audiences at the Brooklyn Academy of Music (BAM) with those on Broadway, and suggested that the repercussions from these politics of reception were found in the plays themselves:

> Whether it's BAM or the New Wave or whoever, who are they playing to? Shit, as an artist, a black artist on Broadway, who the fuck am I playing to? What audience am I playing to? Nothing much, I'll tell you. Not a goddamn thing. So except for making me personally rich to have a Broadway quote hit there's just no reason for me to have a play done there with the ticket prices being what they are. That's why when we did *The River Niger* there we insisted that we keep a certain amount of ticket prices down so that they were affordable to our core constituency. We made them the price of what people were paying for movie tickets because we wanted to go directly to the black public and get them to witness what was being presented. In that way our artists write and play to a real public. Because you have to ask yourself: who are those others playing to? They don't think that because they want to idealize their audience. They want to think that everybody wants to come out and see a play by Shaw. That everybody wants to be cultured in some way. That's bullshit of course. Fuck being cultured. Who are they playing to?[66]

Ward aimed to divert audiences who flocked to Times Square for entertainments other than theater, and celebrated the altered nature of Times Square in 1973: "Drive through Broadway on a Saturday night . . . and it's like 125th Street."[67] The TKTS booth presented the perfect opportunity to experiment with this goal. But Ward opted out of the program, likely because his question—who are they playing to?—could not be answered through its channels.

The evaluation of the TKTS program illustrates its tendency toward partial discernment. From the first page of their TKTS study, Baumol and Baumol discuss the reservations of some members of the theatrical community, which existed alongside a reliably favorable reception from patrons: "While it has been welcomed as a means to attract new and more varied audiences, and its financial support has been partly underwritten by theatrical groups, some persons have felt that it undercuts the normal, full-price sales of the theatre."[68] This notion of "more varied audiences" was relative; TKTS clearly brought in new patrons, but it also enticed those who would have paid full price. (Baumol and Baumol provide primarily anecdotal evidence that this was inevitably the case—they describe meeting the president of a top corporation who gleefully recounted his experience buying half-price tickets at the TKTS booth.) Other theater members feared that the booth would habituate patrons to buying at a discount, leading to fewer profits for theaters. If patrons begin to see the half-price sale as the normal transaction—and as a guarantee for most shows as they near closing—only a smash hit could protect itself. (Theater producers were "particularly appalled" at radio spots that invited ticket buyers to "beat the system" with TKTS.)[69] Additionally, more last-minute purchases meant that the risk borne by theaters would increase, as a snowstorm could have acute consequences for unplanned theatergoing. Still others did not see the logic of advertising the fact that a show was not a sellout.

Amid these factors, location—of advertisements and TKTS box offices—emerged as a point of contention in debates about the viability of the program. Baumol and Baumol reported and then dismissed the suggestion that the booth should be relocated "out of the theatrical district where the purchasers can conveniently stroll from TKTS" as "obviously intended primarily to undermine the operations of TKTS altogether."[70] But producers like Papp, King, and Ward evolved in distinctly different theater traditions than the major Broadway producers, and in addition to the political movements of the prior decade, King and Papp shared a love for radical left-wing art movements of the 1930s and 1940s. They operated with strong philosophies of the "popular," and TKTS booths positioned across the entire city would have seemed necessary components of an outreach program seeking to reach the people. Although not within strolling distance of Broadway, booths outside of the theater district might have been nearer to where some of the fifty-two member theaters of the Black Theater Alliance were located, for example, or in one of the parks where Papp's Mobile Unit toured free summer Shakespeare.

Satellite booths and accompanying public relations campaigns elsewhere might have cultivated a wider geographic spread of audience members for Broadway. Yet patrons from Manhattan were understood to be the desired norm, regardless of population numbers or contiguous arts outreach programs at the time. Branches of TKTS in Brooklyn, or the Bronx, or on a university campus would not be desirable without "the volume to justify the undertaking," Baumol and Baumol concluded.[71] Like many initiatives begun during the austerity period, TKTS was meant to be temporary, and its underestimation of cartographic expansion reflected its short-term goals, as well as its vague definition of target "new audiences." Baumol and Baumol gathered evidence that TKTS patrons came from a "wide variety of areas" around the city and tri-state area. In the year studied, ticket purchasers hailed from Manhattan (between 20 and 31 percent), other boroughs (between 15 and 20 percent), Long Island (between 9 and 11 percent), other states (17–29 percent), as well as New York State and abroad, in lesser numbers. Their surveys did not pursue the question of residence further; the Manhattan-centric orientation of the study precluded this, and assumptions about Broadway's audience composition were therefore built into TKTS as well as its officially sanctioned study. In 1974 another Manhattan TKTS box office opened in the financial district; clearly their vision of expansion toward potential ticket-buyers looked like *something*.[72] Brooklyn did not receive a ticket booth until 2008, in the Metrotech Center.

By many standards, the TKTS booth was a massive success—in one year, it sold 450,000 tickets and paid $2 million to participating theaters (compared with a total Broadway gross of $46 million).[73] In the summer of 1974 it was selling 14,000 tickets per week, and the profile of newcomers to theater and to TKTS was a heartening 9 percent of the sample. The booth did attract people who had not previously attended the theater, including impulse buyers who considered attending only days before. "It seems to take a convulsion of nature to keep the impulse buyers away," marveled Baumol and Baumol.[74] To determine the characteristics of the TKTS audience, 375 patrons of the booth were interviewed, in August 1973, February 1974, and May 1974. Across all three interviews, median age (thirty), income (roughly $15,500), and education (four years of college) were "remarkably consistent."[75] In comparison with the general Broadway audience, TKTS users included a higher share of professionals (60 vs. 56 percent) and a higher proportion of blue-collar workers (5 vs. 3 percent). TKTS users were also younger (median age thirty) than the Broadway audience, and better educated (70 percent having completed college, as opposed to 45 percent). TKTS users seemed to be less affluent (median income $15,800) than the Broadway audience as a whole (median income $17,100), although this appears likely to be correlated with age, rather than class identity. While the study attended to age, economic, and educational characteristics, race was not mentioned once in the report. This is a significant omission, especially given the plays on Broadway at the time of their study. Baumol and Baumol also did not analyze which plays were selling TKTS tickets in what proportion.

While TKTS clearly contributed to audience size, it did not reach that sought-after goal of modifying audience demographics. And, as Baumol and Baumol repeatedly note in their report, while the discount box office attracted some numbers of lower income groups and occupations ordinarily less inclined to attend the theater, it also sold to many patrons who could afford to pay full price. This aspect fulfilled the worst fears of theater producers in that it did compete with the theater box offices for customers—two-thirds of those who attended the theater before the booth opened switched their purchases to TKTS from theater box offices. This finding renewed anxieties circulating around the value of theater: if a corporate executive chooses to purchase discount theater tickets, what are the implications for the perceived worth of a Broadway show, when production costs were rapidly rising? Additionally, the small volume of Off-Broadway and Lincoln Center tickets sold had held "fairly steady apart from the first month of operation,"[76] so the booth was doing very little to encourage or streamline ticket purchasing for performance outside of the Times Square area.

Baumol and Baumol's study attempted to determine how the effects of the booth would continue into the future, but it is noteworthy that it continued at all. Despite the "unfortunate state of the nation's economy," the summer of 1974 on Broadway was relatively prosperous.[77] As with so many adjustments made during periods of fiscal crisis, the TKTS booth founders intended it to contribute to the short-term relief of financial problems. The donated city trailer with holes cut into it and electricity taken clandestinely from a nearby street light did not smack of permanence, yet it achieved Cohen's wish for a centralized ticket area and marked Times Square as a theater "center." Long lines of tourists and vacationers waiting to purchase tickets staked a claim on the streets of a contested area and performed a defiant show of confidence: the theaters were open for business and the space declared public. Although TDF originally launched TKTS "to increase accessibility of their performances for less affluent individuals," the development of Times Square ultimately meant that TKTS soon became viewed as another service for a targeted tourist sector.[78] Commercial theater operators warmed to TKTS as a tool to buttress Times Square as the geographic center of the legitimate theater. It was through initiatives like TKTS that city agencies, developers, and theater owners clung to a vision of "uptown theater" that had a stable center in Times Square. Throughout, the cash-strapped city supported changes to the district aimed at improving theatergoing and altered patterns of audience composition. Artists, particularly those in downtown theater communities, continued to question whether this vision of Broadway offered any real structures of inclusion and possibility for theatrical innovations nurtured elsewhere. Situating the performing arts as one of the main pillars of the city's larger economic development—even as the theater itself also cried out for economic salvation—was one path to maintain the legitimate theater's geographic positioning at Forty-Second Street and leave its conventions, artistic or otherwise, unchallenged.

Safe Excess

Susan Bennett describes the significant changes between the tourist environment of Broadway in 1975 and that of 1995 as a testament to the flourishing of corporate spectacle over aesthetic and literary values, and important within that conclusion is the work of the city brand.[79] Up until the late 1970s, however, it was not clear that legitimate theater would even remain in Times Square, let alone that its future would be written in the gleaming smile of Mickey Mouse. The district had been slated for economic redevelopment for many years before the fiscal crisis neutered the possibility of large-scale overhaul, especially one government-led. Once New York crawled out from the shadow of its near-bankruptcy, it became "ripe politically and economically for new investment," and, aided by a new political order, engineered the explosive real-estate boom that came to define the 1980s.[80]

While the full arc of the legitimate theater's development in Times Square was a complex and protracted process, the growth of New York City during this period was surprisingly quick, especially as the strong public/private coalitions formed in the crisis developed rapidly.[81] It took two decades to transform Forty-Second Street from a symbol of urban decline to a "Disneyspace," and scholars have chronicled the impact on the Broadway musical, alongside its potent blend of nostalgia, consumerism, tourism, and commodification.[82] Once the thirst for more and more tax revenue in the form of lucrative, large office spaces and other corporate uses took over, the limited protections instituted in the late 1960s and 1970s for the theater district in the form of zoning and historic preservation of houses proved as ineffectual as many had feared.

In 1971 the architect of planned shrinkage, Roger Starr, viewed the future course of Times Square through the lens of cosmopolitanism versus what he dubbed the "contemporary spirit." The latter term signified backwardness and the denial of cultural values. In the struggle between these two poles of his devising, decentralization threatened to mar the entire city through the elevation of neighborhoods over the elite:

> While the cosmopolitan spirit exalts the importance of the city as a whole, the contemporary spirit exalts the importance of the specific neighborhood, the particular block, the individual house. While the cosmopolitan spirit accepts the importance of taste, and fosters style established by an elite, whether selected by birth, by wealth, or by cultural attainment, the contemporary spirit decries taste, calls

> imposed patterns of behavior hypocrisy, and puts what used to be secret in the windows of 42nd Street.[83]

Starr's formula is rigorously top-down, one that upholds stable standards for aesthetic life as set by an established elite. Times Square represented a front in a larger ground war that could unseat or reinstall this upper-class style for the metropolis—the return of *good taste* to a muddied cultural field, and "known" audiences to plush seats. Decentralization was equated with a rebellion against standards and a general disorderliness in the urban environment.

Paranoid urbanism motivates Starr's conceptual link between hedonism and the choice to exalt a specific neighborhood (and its residents) seemingly over the good of the entire city. But many city officials shared the belief that New York could be buttressed through the magnification of a city center. The trade-offs have been debated ever since. Times Square was undeniably safer: its streets, many believe, improved for the better. Within the realm of performance, however, the identity of Broadway as a theatrical nucleus, and its value to residents of the five boroughs, remained contested. Further, Starr's definition of cosmopolitanism did not anticipate—or align with—the consumerist spectacle delivered by the entertainment monoliths that later gravitated to Times Square. The center held, even if its price was a transformation into a "benign amusement center where locals and tourists attended Disney shows and bought food and souvenirs at restaurants and stores owned by Disney, Warner Brothers, ESPN, and other national corporations."[84] By 2000, the Great White Way remained a champion of urban rebirth, roundly criticized for its bloated ticket prices and a specialized, upper-middlebrow consumer base, necessarily focused on tourists and featuring relatively few Off or Off-Off Broadway transfers. This contradictory outcome—the vibrancy of historical Broadway whose constituent parts are corporate products—resonates in the public imagination, and is exemplified by the institutionalization of TKTS.

In March 2000, two Australian architects won an international competition to create a new TKTS booth in Duffy Square. The designers admitted that they had only visited the city once—their design was based on impressions from film and television culture.[85] That they were inspired by the "visual buzz" rather than embodied experiences in the space only intensified the opposition to the project. Father Duffy Square, neighborhood activists argued, should retain characteristics of a public space memorializing something other than snaking lines for half-price tickets to musicals. Preservation advocates questioned the wisdom of removing the original TKTS booth, lauded for its innovative and thrifty design, and its status as a relic from the penny-pinching 1970s. The booth, "that wonderful, ramshackle, pipe-and-canvas construction which has come to represent Broadway theater to an entire generation since its inception 26 years ago," deserved landmark status, they argued, even if it had not yet reached its thirtieth year.[86] The TKTS booth represented the protracted and contentious development process that evolved across those many years: Mayor Rudolph Giuliani referred to it as one of the "symbols of the renaissance" of New York City, while actor Ron Silver, then chairman of the New York City Millennium Committee, called it "Times Square's centerpiece."[87] It also, however, signified a simplicity of scale that harkened back to the diversity of the neighborhood, before Mark Sussman's term, "static festival," aptly described the "safe excess" of its massive towers and corporate insignias.[88] The *New York Times* took an ambivalent stance, both contrary and mournful, as it contemplated the loss of yet another structure from Broadway's architectural past, a continued erosion of "what was once a splendidly pungent esthetic amalgam, made of dozens of incongruous icons layered one on top of the other."[89] The controversy focused more on buildings than on audience analysis, more attached to the structures than attentive to individuals.

If the battles to save dozens of Broadway's iconic theater houses had been lost decades before, so had the battle to diversify the Broadway audience and offerings. Decades earlier, during Mayor John Lindsay's rezoning of Times Square, theater artists feared office encroachment into Broadway, and these fears were now realized. The decision of preservationists to defend a tin can for ticket sales constituted a last stand in those conflicts. The area that in 1932 had boasted ninety theaters in the blocks between Times Square and Columbus Circle had only forty-eight by 1987.[90] Save The Theatres Inc., formed in 1982 to prevent the razing of the Helen Hayes, Morosco, and Bijou theaters, had failed in its mission. The cries of outrage over the small TKTS booth a decade later articulated and instigated new and not-so-new disagreements about the small district.

By the time TDF popped the champagne on the $19 million redesign of the TKTS booth and Duffy Square, it was October 2008. After eight years of cost overruns, political squabbling, and construction problems, public officials celebrated "a new standard for the public realm in Times Square."[91] The centerpiece of the redesigned TKTS booth is a red cascading glass staircase of 27 steps that rises 16 feet above 12 ticket windows and functions as a public amphitheater for visitors to admire a refurbished Duffy Square. In addition to the enlarged costs of the project (of which the city paid $11.5 million), more urgent concerns detracted from the opening day festivities. Lehman Brothers, whose (former) headquarters was visible two blocks north, had collapsed just weeks before. A *New York Times* reporter commented optimistically on the importance of the polished staircase with the "kinetic panorama" of Times Square on view for all, and a quote from Tim Tompkins, president of the Times Square Alliance, revealed the cruel symmetry between the contexts of the new TKTS booth and its rickety predecessor: "And could there be a better moment for a truly public amenity, where the price of admission is zero, than now, when the clouds of a long recession are gathering? 'It's a bright light in a dark economic time.'"[92]

Part Two

✦

Affective Inequalities

Chapter 3

✦

Vinnette Carroll's Urban Arts Corps and the Inevitability of Interdependency

> Mayor Beame could not be there yesterday morning because of such pressing matters as the city's new budget, but, if he had he would have observed his Commissioner of Cultural Affairs in a hand-clapping foot-stomping dance with cast members of *Don't Bother Me, I Can't Cope.*
>
> —*New York Times*, May 16, 1974

This unexpected musical routine took place on a platform in front of the Edison Theatre on West Forty-Seventh Street, where Vinnette Carroll and Micki Grant's hit show, *Don't Bother Me, I Can't Cope*, was enjoying what would become a two-year run on Broadway. The occasion was the announcement of a new program, "Broadway in the Parks," which brought free performances of *Cope* to twelve parks and community centers across the five boroughs, including Central Park, Tompkins Park in Bedford-Stuyvesant, the Store Front Museum in South Jamaica, Queens, and the Henry Street Settlement on the Lower East Side. The Pepsi-Cola Company, in cooperation with the Parks, Recreation and Cultural Affairs Administration (PRCAA), sponsored the program. The musical, with lyrics and music by Grant and choreography by George Faison, marked a turning point for Carroll's troupe, the Urban Arts Corps (UAC). Previous UAC shows toured parks and housing projects, but *Cope* traveled from a new base: Broadway.

Carroll's Urban Arts Corps developed *Don't Bother Me, I Can't Cope* at the troupe's artistic home, a second-floor "miniature theater" in a former factory at 26 West Twentieth Street, in Chelsea. But the company branched out across the neighborhoods of the city every July and August, with Carroll's Urban Arts School summer program. UAC evolved with the "educational laboratory theater" as one of its inspirations,[1] but Carroll did not design the company as a grassroots theater for beginners, or as a youth or community theater. It aimed to aid performers stymied by lack of training or available roles. This interlocked with Carroll's desire to transform the staid relationship between city-sanctioned performance and inner-city neighborhoods.

City tours became a constitutive element of UAC's development process—not just of plays, but of actors and neighborhood spaces.

Vinnette Carroll described the activity of "coping" as "a basic commitment of a mature, purposeful, involved human being . . . that happiness is a by-product, not an end product."[2] By 1975, the troupe had toured *Don't Bother Me, I Can't Cope* through outdoor locations across the five boroughs, the Off-Broadway Playhouse Theatre, and the Edison Theatre on Broadway.[3] While the predominantly corporate sponsorship of the "Broadway in the Parks" program was unique to the 1970s, tours of earlier UAC shows traveled through the city's five boroughs in the 1960s, as well. *Cope* proved that theater in the streets did not exist at the behest of city officials desperate to prevent riots; by 1974, UAC had created a dialectical relationship between the city's streets and the Broadway hit. In his 1974 memoir, City Parks Commissioner August Heckscher described most city-sponsored theater in the streets as "cut-down versions of Broadway musicals" with "little relevance to the lives of the people they were supposed to entertain."[4] *Cope* made a mockery of these attempts. The music-filled play drew its energy from ritual traditions, Brechtian presentation styles, and the bitter pill of urban life. In "All I Need," the character Sheila sings alone:

> I don't need your platitudes
> I don't need your pity
> I don't need your Gallup polls or your ad hoc committee
> I don't want your sympathy without respect
> I don't need your study groups or your benign neglect.[5]

Mainstream critics were complimentary but not quite sure what to make of *Cope*'s mixture of humor and "militancy." The play eventually found its audience through a lengthy path of revision and remounting, from the streets to Off-Off to Off.[6] By the time it reached Broadway in 1972, Grant's lyrics succinctly rehearsed local frustrations. Within a revue structure, each song sliced a sharp melody through obstacles to secure housing, employment, and human dignity. From the Kafkaesque bureaucracies of city government to the dull ache of discrimination, the cast of six singers and six dancers "coped":

> The landlord sold my building without asking my consent
> And my brand-new landlord told me to vacate or pay more rent.
> I said, "Man, do you think I'm some kind of dope?
> This place ain't fit for occupancy
> The way I see it, you owe me!
> Now get out of my doorway 'cause I can't cope!"[7]

Carroll had spent two years conceiving and directing *Cope* with "the Core"—her name for her semi-regular collaborators at UAC.[8]

UAC's vibrant production history during this period attests to a changing approach from the state-sponsored "Ghetto Arts" programs to the city-supported "cool streets" initiatives of Mayor John Lindsay, culminating in an abandonment of comparable support for the company's activities by the late 1970s. Carroll demonstrated the ways in which city, state, and federal programs could collaborate with director-educators to benefit aspiring and underserved performers while collapsing the fictional boundaries separating performance and place. Carroll shaped the company as a professional training ground devised to protect artists of color who might win gigs with raw talent but not secure a career without intentional support.

Her core of mostly black and Latino actors frequently hailed from the five boroughs. Many young artists arrived at UAC after graduating from New York's public high schools; others emerged from conservatories, or met Carroll through friends. She auditioned new actors with a simple command: sing something a cappella. (Jennifer Holliday chose "God Will Take Care of You." Others nervously clung to "Happy Birthday.") Carroll encouraged her performers to "find some solutions . . . and a sense of values that enables [them] to cope in the jungle."[9] Actor James Earl Jones, one of Carroll's students, recalled the pragmatism of her pedagogy: "Even though us young ones were in there to learn the craft better to make a better living, we were never deluded to think that we were going to be fed by anybody else but ourselves. That was the reality, especially in those days."[10] Kathleen Lynch's writing on "affective inequality" provides a framework to theorize Carroll's labors within a landscape of uneven cultural development. This transcends superficial treatments of "inner city" arts of the period, or cynical readings of Carroll's work as somehow complicit with state-sponsored mechanisms. In fact, since the category of "community theater" fails to capture the multileveled nature of Carroll's theater, or to properly convey the manifold energies that she contributed to the period as an actor, director, teacher, and producer, the labors of "caring" fill an ontological gap.

Lynch's definition of "affective inequality" illuminates Carroll's methods of creating and devising. On an instrumental level, it provides a reminder that UAC's work addressed deprivations. "Being deprived of the capacity to develop supportive affective relations, or of the experience of engaging in them when one has the capacity, is therefore a serious human deprivation and injustice; it is a form of affective inequality."[11] Institutions either enable or undermine these affective relations; Carroll's theater did not treat love and care as private or outside of the realm of a theater company, but rather placed them at the core of her performance practices. "Affective inequality" scholarship eradicates the erroneous assumption that care is a private matter (and not a form of work), thereby extending the theory to dominant conceptions of citizenship. Carroll modeled a performative urban citizenship for young artists who felt at best ignored and at worst abandoned by the mechanisms of city government.

UAC utilized a phenomenon Lynch and Walsh describe as "the inevitability of interdependency."[12] UAC built upon interdependence as a strategy to redress systemic affective inequality at a time when inequitable resource provision across the neighborhoods of New York City was widely discussed, from councils to city agencies. Carroll's troupe achieved success through performance initiatives committed to expanding arts "access" and representation beyond the status quo. Analyzing UAC as labor in the affective domain is meant to underscore its process, outcomes, and influence, as social and relational.

The use of these theories to reinforce the labors of caring and solidarity within UAC's operations does not intend a specific relation to Carroll's bedside manner; she was notoriously demanding in rehearsals, and could be merciless in her expectations of her "instruments"—young actors. Another UAC alumni, actor Nora Cole, wrote of the director's difficulties and defenses: the thunder of her tirades, the fear felt by actors who daily attended rehearsals uncertain if they had been cut. "Hers was a system that devastated many a young actor. . . . Vinnette's way of working was tedious and draining."[13] Still, as Cole attests, UAC offered an uncommon place for artists to expand their range, and to fail under the tutelage of a professional with insight. Carroll substituted *support* in the place of passive empathy, and molded structures to address affective inequalities she identified in both neighborhoods and the theater industry. In her long career, she created elaborate plays with extended production lives, in a world of elite, white, Broadway producers. To do so, Carroll revised the outdated structures of "Ghetto Arts" programs and worked within the shells of governmental initiatives to create theater about the fundamental interdependence of artists, and the residents in the city.

UAC's consolidation occurred against a backdrop of change in the city government's orientation toward the arts. Mariana Mogilevich describes the alterations across John Lindsay's two terms as mayor (1966–73), during which the arts were used as "a central vehicle and a metaphor in Lindsay's spatial politics of democratization and decentralization."[14] This was simultaneous with efforts to reinforce the arts at key sites, such as Times Square and the Brooklyn Academy of Music. Carroll demonstrated that initiatives to shore up centralized performance venues could, in fact, bolster the process of decentralization. Efforts that took seriously culturally vibrant spaces outside of Manhattan could lead to innovations miles away on Broadway.

Numerous theater companies in the 1970s shared Carroll's motives, but few enjoyed her outcomes.[15] These companies often had characteristics in common: their leaders began careers at social service organizations, day care centers, and high schools. They did not focus exclusively on distinct, privileged performance sites, but rather assumed as desirable the participation of audiences across the entire map of the city. They developed networks from city agencies, YMCAs, settlement houses, acting training programs, and schools. Their priorities blended theories of 1960s racial pride and political subjectivity with a drive to educate young artists to withstand the trials of the arts professions. Most crucially, a focus on communicating the nuances of the deteriorating "urban condition" emerged as central to the process of creation: the streets were not merely their stages, but also their incitement. Carroll's performative mechanics of survival brought her company to Broadway, Lincoln Center, and the steps of City Hall.

Cooling It in the Streets

> The deprivation imposed by the white community on the Black Artist is not only crippling to the Deprived, but also to the Depriver.
>
> —Vinnette Carroll[16]

The same element that proved decisive for Café La Mama on the Lower East Side also shaped the origins of UAC: government, corporate, and private foundation grants opened their funding streams to a more diverse population of theater artists during the 1960s, and the map of cultural support widened. These were, Alvin Reiss observed, "the enlightened years" between 1965 and 1968.[17] In reports and grant applications, the revolutionary phrasings of 1960s autonomy manifestos created a new institution-speak, as in the 1968 Rockefeller report articulating the diffuse energies and tensions produced by the overthrow of previous assumptions: "The new viewpoint looks at 'culture' not as a commodity but as a condition. . . . The growth in number of elaborate cultural centers has been matched by the growth of neighborhood arts centers—many in ghetto areas—which have sprung up in churches, housing developments, schools, garages, and store fronts."[18] These late 1960s funding surges were created in response to—and in collaboration with—the demands of cultural leaders influenced by radical politics, settlement legacies, and experiences in antipoverty programs.

Alongside her card-carrying credentials as an acolyte of Erwin Piscator, Carroll's performances can also be positioned within the lineage of these federal antipoverty programs. The architects of President Lyndon Johnson's War on Poverty searched for solutions that would be local, diffuse, and not dependent on state government or Congress. Antipoverty packages commonly consisted of a preschool program (Head Start), an economic development program, and a "recreational" arts and culture piece. The performing arts became a popular component of the latter, as it generated "a better head count of both participants and audience."[19] This transformed the cultural politics of space and place, as federally funded organizations with more mainstream goals, such as the Puerto Rican Forum, clashed with activist groups like the Young Lords, committed to mobilizing citizens around principles of self-reliance and place-based urban identity.[20] In New York, programs incorporating arts practices received an infusion of federal monies, and constitute a valuable context for theater programs with troubling pretenses of "riot prevention" as a top layer and professional training and artistic development as a guerrilla layer of cultural activism.[21]

The highly bureaucratic intrusion of the community action programs during the Great Society garnered many detractors.[22] Yet they also led to unexpected successes, and as theater producer and director Woodie King's Mobilization for Youth (MFY) on the Lower East Side demonstrated, these cultural programs provided important institutional frameworks to be deployed in successive performance projects. King remarked, "[MFY] was supposed to be a program designed for failure, but we made it something viable and meaningful."[23] From the summer of 1965 until 1969, MFY paid youth to train with jazz artists (Kenny Dorham), dancers (Rod Rogers), poets (Diane Wakoski), and playwrights (Lonne Elder, III). The Office of Juvenile Delinquency funded his Cultural Arts Program, and King considered other antipoverty programs, Harlem Youth Opportunity Unlimited (HARYOU) and the Bedford-Stuyvesant Redevelopment Corporation, his sister organizations.[24] Under a bureaucratically thick program, theaters managed to form intermediaries between the state's definition of citizen participation and more radical dimensions of political mobilization.

In 1970, Bertram Beck, the director of the Henry Street Settlement (HSS), hired King to run the "Arts for Living Program" at HSS. A dance company had access to the Playhouse at the time, so King took the workshops into the community, and often rented La Mama's Ellen Stewart Theatre on East 3rd Street. He ran workshops in black theater, dance, Hispanic theater, Asian theater, and Jewish theater, surrounded by the tenements and slum buildings of the Lower East Side, until one of those tenements was torn down and a new Arts for Living Center erected. With support from the New York State Council on the Arts, King launched his "multiracial New Federal Theater" (NFT) to develop new works and new talent. "To understand our program," King wrote, "you must understand the community it represents. Its residents are the classic urban American mixture—Jews, Puerto Ricans, Blacks, Chinese, Italians, and many others, brought together by choice, by the immigrant tradition, poverty."[25] NFT instituted an open-door policy, and admission remained free for its first six years; later, they often set aside free tickets for community members, with paid tickets for other spectators. In 1974, King explained his ticketing policies as a response to resistance against his chosen art form:

> Low income people in New York cannot deal with the term theater. The word must be destroyed (as far as they are concerned). Having grown up in the city, theater means to them Broadway where the Kennedys and the Javitses go before or after dinner. And the cost

> of that theater they relate to the word theater no matter where it's located.[26]

Advancement toward greater cultural equity in the realm of professional neighborhood theater was essential at a time when many low-income neighborhoods considered the police force, one of the most visible government mechanisms, a tool of suppression. King's company members and audiences witnessed the injustices meted out by the Police Department's Tactical Patrol Force, "which represents the thoughts and feelings of the establishment exclusively. When the Tactical Patrol Force visits our neighborhood, the only piece of equipment they don't bring is a tank."[27] The NFT's performance practices stood in opposition to harsh and discriminatory operations of the NYPD, but King did not distance himself from cultural coalitions, foundations, or even federal or state-sponsored models of delivery. The city, however, remained an exception: NFT did not receive city funding.

One of King's early productions was *Charades on East Fourth Street* by Lonne Elder, III. The play depicted an urban phenomenon that received little attention: the sexual abuse of teenagers by neighborhood police. *Charades* takes place in midsummer, in the basement of an old movie house on the Lower East Side. The bare stage has a few chairs and benches; five teenagers wear white eye-masks to protect their identity. A police officer in uniform is slumped, unconscious, chained and handcuffed to an old swivel chair on rollers. In the movie theater above, a community meeting has been convened with residents and the city police force to confront the "age-old problem of police-community relations" on the Lower East Side. The boys in the basement have taken matters in their own hands, ambushing the police officer and planning to torture him until he admits his misdeeds to the assembly upstairs. One boy, Manuel, believes the officer raped and impregnated his sister. Another teen, Cliff, accuses the officer of beating his brother and wanting to "goose up one of them young girls" on the street:

> You came up to my sister one night while she's with her boyfriend the Horse—You beat Horse and you run him away—Then you tell her you're goin' to run her in because you say she's a whore—You put your hands all over her body and told her if she didn't let you screw her, you was going to take her over to the precinct and book her as a streetwalker.[28]

In each scene, the gang advances a new method of mental and physical torture on the cop. During tense exchanges with the terrified officer, uncertainty builds: do they have the right man? Elder masterfully dramatizes their rage, both dulled and sharpened by their youth and frustration. In moments of fear, the boys are undone by their anger, their mistrust of their ringleader, even their suspicion that they have miscalculated the extent of the individual cop's power. As they decide how to best humiliate the officer into confessing, they hear snippets of the community meeting above them through the speaker system—neighbors relay tragic stories of police brutality, and plead for sanity and sensibility in the face of the "blue devils."[29] The solidarity between the teenagers erodes through the chaos of their doomed kidnapping scheme. They follow through on their plan to humiliate the officer—posing him in compromising positions with their female friend, scaring him with an antique guillotine—but ultimately remain divided over the proper punishment to inflict as their revenge.

Elder based the play on his documentary interviews with teens, and King produced it alongside Maryat Lee's *Dope!* during the MFY phase of King's operations. For King, neighborhood welfare was secured in part through the fulfillment of local cultural production, professionally and independently functioning. "Our arts program isn't interested in the arts and culture projected by Doris Day, Rudolph Nureyev, or Andy Warhol."[30] King's progression—from the training programs of MFY, to the workshops within HSS, to the performances at Abrons Arts Center—advanced a model of theater production that tied the promulgation of black theater to the sustainability of local performance spaces. "If black theatre is to continue to mature or be infused with new ideas, new forms, and new points of view, it must find a way to sustain neighborhood theatres," wrote Lindsay Patterson in the same year.[31]

While grassroots theater movements developed new organizational and communication methods that sought to "address the failure of national and international organizations and to map the contours of local concern,"[32] much theater activity at this period also scrutinized and modified the standard bourgeois-liberal state arts structure. When civil rights protests gripped the South, and New York and other northern cities, city governance was still largely in the hands of old, white ethnic "machine" politicians. Clarence Taylor emphasizes the importance of Mayor Lindsay's appointment of young black leaders to positions in local agencies, alongside the creation of his Urban Action Task Force, intended to redress the fact that there existed "no channels of communication between City Hall and remote city neighborhoods."[33] One of those agencies was the Department of Cultural Affairs (DCA); Courtney Callender had served as deputy commissioner of the DCA and was appointed in 1966 to run the Parks Department's first office of Community Relations (he was also the agency's first high-ranking African American official). Callender laid the groundwork and set the pace in the decentralization trend that fueled the neighborhood arts movement.[34] He defined decentralization as inextricable from the demand for local facilities, motivated by desires for a richer quality of life in all neighborhoods. He defended this strategy against an old guard that demonized decentralization as symptomatic of a crisis in its focus on quantity, not quality, "opportunities" over merit.[35] Calls for decentralization constituted an arts rebellion, waged in tandem with efforts toward greater representational power.

Under Callender's leadership, the Parks, Recreation and Cultural Affairs administration sponsored a growing number of street theater groups who required little more than a platform stage and a generator truck to perform on pavements from Evergreen Avenue in Bushwick to Mount Morris in Harlem. In 1966 the city financed four groups, and by 1971 that number was twenty.[36] The summer of 1970 boasted 1,250 performances and a budget of $800,000 from Parks.[37] The Parks Commissioner, August Heckscher, "thought the proliferation of street theater groups, reaching into poor neighborhoods, had helped the city 'cool' during potentially explosive hot summers."[38] Callender challenged that idea: "I don't have much faith in keeping people cool by entertaining them, but maybe that's because I'm black. But people do give money for that reason and we're happy to take it."[39] He expressed this view more forcefully in the years to come: the arts in New York City had undergone a great change since 1966, and severe fiscal problems—including the fallout from the recession in 1969—meant that the cultural resources of the city were highly dependent on the quality of leadership at City Hall. Further, Callender realized that the city's small grants were not an insignificant source of support for the city's minority artists; two-thirds of the twenty troupes financed in 1971 identified as black or Puerto Rican companies.[40] Some, like UAC, presented theater during the summers as corollaries of their broader performance activities, with one funding stream feeding the other. While contested, these changes on a municipal level held great repercussions for many companies in the years to come, particularly those that became part of the fabric of the city's cultural affairs through institutionalization.

For Carroll, "art for the people" was hardly a new concept. By the time she launched UAC she was a seasoned performer, educator, and administrator. Having grown up in Sugar Hill, she had studied and worked as a psychologist and a teacher, knew the halls of state government, the school system, and the theater industry. For some artists, Mayor Lindsay's attempts to improve communication between the city government and its "troubled" areas raised a question: Could performance act as a conduit? Could the communication flow both ways?

Without networks of politicized, trained theater makers, state and city funding councils, and neighborhood service organizations, the prior models—which had fed widespread inner city distrust of authority and frustration with nonresponsive decision-making bodies—could not have been disrupted. Yet a detrimental aura of condescension emanated from functionaries who valued performance on unruly street corners—particularly during hot summers—as pacifying balms for young people of color, not tools for political mobilization. As some artists and activists negotiated the implications of creating neighborhood-based theater sanctioned and funded by federal, state, and city mechanisms, official support of decentralized opportunities unsettled many members of the city's establishment elite. In 1972 the Lindsay administration formed experimental "neighborhood governments," which had precedent in the earlier Neighborhood Task Forces, created in the late 1960s to pacify animosities in inner city neighborhoods.[41] Politicians, law enforcement, and budget makers (all largely white) expressed reservations about this continued consolidation of local organizations. Paul Screvane, the City Council president who organized the city's role in President Johnson's War on Poverty, argued against funding too many groups that could influence—and even control—governmental policy:

> We have been in the process over the last few years of doling out pieces of the City of New York to various groups that would come to it, such as MFY, Haryou Act, Youth in Action in Bedford-Stuyvesant, and a number of others that have been formed since. . . . What would happen ultimately . . . we would have a number of little private governments in the City of New York . . . I am not confident at all that we would be able to solve all of the problems we have with this kind of approach.[42]

In the performing arts, however, this fear—of lost control—constituted a decisive ingredient in the progression beyond tired models of fostering culture in underserved communities. The implication that new mechanisms of expression might chip away at an existing order relied most of all on the maintenance of fictive stability in the cultural sphere. Carroll reworked the stale expectations of what "culture" might bring to "ghetto areas," and recalibrated the standard institutional structures and procedures for state-supported performance, beginning with the Ghetto Arts Program (GAP).

New York Governor Nelson A. Rockefeller founded GAP in 1966, and in 1967 John B. Hightower, the executive director of the New York State Council on the Arts, appointed Vinnette Carroll as director.[43] Carroll's UAC emerged in 1967 as a pilot project of GAP, and its initial members were black and Puerto Rican students aged seventeen through twenty-two, from public schools and youth agencies.[44] Carroll directed a $350,000 budget, and immediately undertook two projects: UAC and Summer on Wheels, the latter of which brought free traveling performances to city residents. This critical development occurred after NYSCA supported Carroll's study of cultural needs in Harlem and Bedford-Stuyvesant. In response to the cultural privations identified in her study, Carroll established UAC with two missions: to provide direct collaborative performing arts experiences to culturally underserved urban communities, and to develop a major repertory company that produced new plays. The former was not to be misconstrued as therapy, or social work, but an arts program capable of developing technical and artistic relevance. All of this depended upon Carroll and her collaborators to establish professional standards, effective teaching methods, and a focus on process and product.

Carroll viewed GAP as an overdue and yet potentially misguided undertaking. She recognized its problematic and imperialist overtones, and did not want the project "to be an ineffectual community unit because of Eurocentric male autonomy in the governance of the program."[45] However, she also saw GAP in light of the needs identified in her study; she approached the state apparatus with a muted hopefulness in the face of its potential dangers. Hightower heeded Carroll's warnings, and they founded GAP on a radical premise: "to find out what the ghetto community wanted rather than what we, as an outside agency, decided it should have."[46] Carroll was the right person to negotiate these challenges; a trained clinical psychologist, she studied acting with Piscator at the New School and with Lee Strasberg and Stella Adler at the Actor's Studio. While working as an actor in New York, she taught drama at the High School of Performing Arts (1955–66), and briefly worked with the federally subsidized Inner City Repertory Company in Watts, Los Angeles.

Under Rockefeller's leadership, New York State was at the forefront of experiments in neighborhood-based arts, largely motivated by dismal youth employment numbers.[47] Junius Eddy of the Ford Foundation argued that emphasizing youth employment was a necessary tactic to dislodge the category of "arts and culture" from calcified notions of cultural "enrichment," which followed a troubling philosophy:

> [A] kind of loosely organized exposure of poor youngsters (mainly nonwhite) to enriching experiences from the Western middle-class cultural tradition, intended to compensate for presumed deprivation in their own lives and backgrounds. One does not have to deny the true richness of the Western cultural tradition to point out the presumptuousness, arrogance, and racism inherent in this simplistic approach to the culturally different person in our pluralistic society.[48]

Eddy's contemptuous critique is well placed; this approach exemplified many of the educational programs supported by Title I of the Elementary and Secondary Education Act of 1965, as well as the youth agencies spread across urban America. Cultural enrichment indicated certain passive practices: agencies underwrote entertainment and admission costs, or sponsored popular entertainers in stadiums or parks. Performing arts organizations were occasionally utilized to present productions of classical drama, music and ballet, and opera, and a third variation employed touring mobile versions of such productions.

New York and a handful of other cities moved beyond these models. "Instead of bringing 'culture' to the people of the ghettos, or ghetto youth to cultural events," municipal arts agencies began to invest more of their hard-pressed budgets to support arts activities "established and run by ghetto artist-leaders themselves."[49] Carroll's approach conjoined this philosophy with her desire for a repertory company and a view of the streets as yet another audience, undifferentiated from commercial venues. "We never thought of it as being Broadway or not, or Off, or anything," Carroll explained.[50] With GAP, Carroll animated a counterthrust to passive forms of support. Yet she also discerned the extent to which GAP's funding hinged on the belief that creative outlets in communities could "cool" slum areas, a benefit she publicized in interviews. She echoed the hopes of nervous city officials and parlayed them into further support: "[Art] helps to divert hostility. . . . I think the whole thing with art is that anger is healthy because it's a positive state. If you can find a way to harness it, I believe you'll have fewer riots."[51] She hopped on the bandwagon of riot prevention, yet in practice she elevated training, professionalism, and craft as foremost principles of the statewide project.

These departures necessitated a liberation from the domination of classical canon delivery. Hightower and Carroll underscored participation as the antidote: "There is no interest in rehashed versions of *Our Town* or *The Matchmaker*," declared Hightower. "The themes are drugs, Black-White intransigence, family strain. Theater can articulate these concerns in a way that other things don't. The aim is for participation, not just spectator audiences."[52] This valorization of community theater defined by the challenges of its environment facilitated the funding for UAC, yet also delimited Carroll's performance practices in ways that would have little bearing on the work she later conceived and directed at the Urban Arts Theatre. These expectations, however, shadowed the long (and difficult) career of UAC in which Carroll continually fought to reframe the conversation around the exigencies of urban neighborhoods, to push past Hightower's laundry list of urban foes to expand the repertoire of possibility, in form, function, and location.

Carroll eventually sustained a core of twenty-five performers, and the project expanded from summer to year-round, working at the forefront of a movement to extend and institutionalize practices initially fashioned as "pilots." Would they survive into the next decade? There was evidence that a robust demand for such activities existed, and a growing awareness that low-income areas did not suffer only from low employment and housing shortages: the imprecise question of "access" captured the multidimensionality of needs, and the injustices of "service provision." Top-down reports attempting to quantify the scale of the problem proliferated. *Arts and the People*, a 1973 report sponsored by NYSCA and the National Research Center of the Arts, indicated that within the state's urban areas, a "culturally inclined coalition" was not actively engaged.[53] Among urban residents with a high school education level, blue-collar workers, and those in the low-income brackets, proportionally "non-white," there was a clear pattern of "cultural frustration."[54] Regardless of New York's international reputation as a post–World War II culture capital, those who lived in the city felt even more strongly than upstate dwellers that they did not have access to the arts. The study also revealed that preferences for *types* of performance differed: 75 percent of the "nonwhites" polled favored seeing amateur actors from the neighborhood or community, and one-third of New York City residents said it was important to have activities that they "could take part in."[55] All New Yorkers surveyed expressed a desire for culture, yet some felt that it was not within their reach.

More striking was the study's finding related to the definitions of community and proximity. While respondents consistently placed personal importance on cultural facilities in their community, the data suggested that feelings of ownership over public culture varied.

> Significant percentages of people living in the five NYC boroughs . . . feel a real lack of access to cultural facilities. . . . . Conversely, the data suggests that a person's "horizon" of what constitutes a neighborhood or community expands as income and education increase, and for this reason the higher socio-economic groups tend to see the availability of cultural facilities in broader terms.[56]

Class identity and geographic location therefore became accepted as indicators of arts access and need. This pointed squarely toward the development of neighborhood arts resources and away from centralized, big-ticket arts complexes, regardless of their engagement initiatives. Carroll understood that "access" remained a subjective concept; street theater was not enough of a solution. Park theater, playground theater, parking lot theater, prison theater, church theater, library theater, art gallery theater, and theater theater: Carroll tried them all in her effort to expand the "horizon" of neighborhood and address the stark disconnect between who was on stage, who was in the audience, and who was in the city.

A contemporaneous study of "artistic impulses" in poorer neighborhoods deemed the wave of "arts democratization and decentralization" necessary because only "a very special speck" of the general population attended mainstream arts offerings in Manhattan.[57] The survey proceeded with the assumption that the arts, wherever presented, would achieve unity across the city, linking sites through performance. Carroll's theater, however, did not envision harmony as an outcome—she saw the exercise of rights in inner city neighborhoods as social democratic practice, not a passive enjoyment of citizenship conferred by federal programs. In redressing affective inequality while maintaining an awareness of the agonistic struggle as a component of both urban arts and cultural affairs, Carroll developed a company that responded to the complexity confirmed in the surveys, and known intuitively all along.

Carroll, in her work with GAP, intervened in a period that Harry Elam Jr. and other scholars identify as one of intense social protest performance activity. Yet Carroll distanced herself from the incendiary theatrics of some 1960s protest theaters, even while representations of "power, community, cultural identity, and collective consciousness"[58] remained organizing principles of her work. This was a delicate balance for a director free of the delusion that an arc toward democratic consensus was possible or desirable in her theater. When "nerve ends are raw . . . feelings are close to the surface . . . [and] racial pride as well as hostility are at their height," new ideas and forms need to push beyond the myth of an "ethnic monopoly" on art: "an artist cannot fully develop in an apartheid society," she wrote in 1969, and a sentiment she carried forward with her decision to develop UAC as an interracial company.[59]

Her administrative labors sought to reform social institutions, though the plays she conceived rarely addressed the oppressor as primary. Mike Sell's concept of "counterspectacle" describes representational strategies that "challenge the conceptual, aesthetic, and ethical boundaries of Euro-American political drama" through an emphasis on emotional excess, virtuosic music, and intricately intertwined vocal performances.[60] While *Cope*'s buoyant revivalism is undeniably worlds away from Amiri Baraka's *Slave Ship*—the play Sell discusses in his explication of counterspectacle—the absence of "shock value" in *Cope* does not preclude its vibrant repudiation of mainstream theatrical conventions, be they toothless productions of Shakespeare or saccharine Broadway smashes. Carroll's plays confronted these contested terrains, particularly through her use of counterspectacle to have fun in the face of the dominant culture. The emotional excess of her plays conveyed a theatricality reliant on the boisterous and the interactive, and not always participatory.

What Carroll gleaned from Piscator fed her passions for producing, and compelled her to explore Brecht's inquiry: "what ought our representations of men's life together look like?"[61] Through the 1970s she revised her strategies in order to achieve levels of institutionalization while also keeping the artistic mission of the company fixed between her sights: constant development and creation of new work, often based in cultural signposts, from the poetry of Langston Hughes to the Gospel of Matthew to the reality of housing discrimination.

Defiant Parochialism

> Thinking of catching a performance? You might try your own neighborhood.
>
> —*Cue* Magazine, 1971[62]

One of UAC's first touring shows of the 1970s was *But Never Jam Today*, Carroll's adaptation of *Alice in Wonderland* with a cast of fourteen actors, and original music by Howard Roberts infused with gospel, calypso, and American folk music. Lindsay's Urban Action Task Force funded the tour with additional monies donated by the composer Richard Rodgers's wife, Dorothy, an early supporter of both NYSCA and UAC. Carroll had already resigned from GAP to develop the Corps, and changes in city government facilitated the group's continued foothold in the city, including new dramatis personae (such as Callender) in some municipal corners.

In 1971 *Croesus and the Witch*, conceived and directed by Carroll and dramatized by Grant, traveled the city's neighborhoods, touring parks and streets before returning to its West Side location.[63] Carroll adapted the play from a folk tale, creating a taut and energetic one-act musical that manipulates the sparse production requirements of traveling performance to teach its audiences about the pleasures of watching theater. At the opening, the narrator, backed by a drummer, pianist, chorus, and dancers, addresses the audience and prepares them for storytelling time. The lyrics announce mysteries to come: they will be taken "someplace that you've never been . . . another time and . . . back again." The play is adeptly pitched to the predominant summer youth audience demographic, and slants the participatory toward the pedagogical with a Brechtian structure and staging. Characters prep the audience in the conventions of theater, and walk them through the imaginative process. In conversational dialogue, the narrator introduces each dancer, and each dancer introduces the role that she will play—deer, acorns, forests, corn, the stuff of storybooks, not the concrete jungle. The actors set out the provisions necessary for the audience to open to the theatrical experience, before developing the plot, organized around a man named Croesus, "as poor as Job's turkey." Croesus's philosophy changes the course of his life and inspires the most rousing (and reprised) number of the musical, "You Can Do What You Wanna Do."

> No use sitting, waiting for something to happen
> Sitting, twiddling your fingers and your toes,
> You can be out making your own thing happen
> Instead of sitting at home scratching your nose.
> You can get what you wanna get
> You can go where you wanna go
> You can do what you wanna do
> By doing it
> Today will be yesterday tomorrow
> If you want to sit around and wait
> You will just be hungrier tomorrow
> And you won't have any grits to put on your plate.[64]

Croesus's buoyant mantra motivates his journey through the woods. While this play has a fairy tale arc and fantastical imagery, Carroll routinely displayed dexterity in her ability to shift between vastly different projects and audiences. The 1973 musical *Step Lively, Boy!* satisfied her long-standing desire to mount an antiwar statement with the source material of expressionist writer Irwin Shaw's 1936 *Bury the Dead*.[65] In the play, deceased soldiers refuse to be buried, and haunt their fellow comrades, up the chain of command. Her adaptation is dark and disturbing, but has a musicality and wryness that nears Shakespearean: humor among the gravediggers. It typifies the shadows—never fully eclipsed by pessimism—that inhabited her work, pieces so often misunderstood as simplistic with their uplifting, catchy "hand-clapping," "finger-jabbing" tunes.

Carroll's desire to cultivate professional theater in accordance with a dispersal model of arts provision did not emanate from the thin stuff of grant requirements. Carroll was adamant that without state subsidy for UAC, her only stage life would be "that 'Dinner is served' stuff."[66] She had already won an Emmy and multiple awards for her work as a director and actor, on and Off Broadway, between 1955 and 1966; she no doubt knew that the implementation of her particular vision for UAC would make it challenging for the company's repertory work to garner mainstream attention. The tensions created by Carroll's twin desires for her company—training and repertory, professional and decentralized—were not limited to UAC: prejudices and critical biases weighed heavily on artists fighting for recognition throughout the 1970s. Many mainstream critics dismissed inner city arts initiatives and redistributive models of arts development. In a public debate between Robert Macbeth of the New Lafayette Theatre and critic Mel Gussow of the *New York Times*, Macbeth chided Gussow for referring to a production at Macbeth's Harlem theater as "defiantly parochial." Although Gussow wrote a glowing review, Macbeth took exception to the suggestion that the theater

> would have been more universal "on or off Broadway". . . . Gussow, it seems, is saying that Black artists can and will and should only achieve full presence in his view when they are performing in *his* theatre, for *him* and *his audience*, like it was during slavery time . . . and still is for some. Then he would be spared the long journey to the "narrow province" of Harlem. Harlem would come to him. And the artists of the province would insure that a transistorized translator would interpret their petty offerings for his "more universal" intelligence.[67]

Reviewers still labeled performance venues in certain locations "parochial," and they maintained a cheery elitism even after they consented to widening the scope of their reviewing. These critics traversed formerly rigid geographic boundaries but held tightly to the fiction that theater in certain contexts remained anti-cosmopolitan and, by extension, unprofessional. Through these rules of engagement, critics reordered the priorities of the work, and artists like Macbeth refuted the assumptions therein. The political associations attached to many theater operations—militant theater, community theater, nationalist theater—occluded the movement of some productions to wider audiences. This would be one obstacle Carroll learned to circumvent through the evolution of UAC.

Every morning at 6:00 a.m., Vinnette Carroll rode her bicycle from her studio loft on West Seventeenth Street to Central Park, forty-two blocks uptown. "Her two-wheeler presence," described a 1972 UAC profile, "is a wedge in the fossilized snobbery of the bridle path—a joyfully vital sign that the times . . . they are indeed a-changing."[68] The same journalist described *Cope*'s progression from a modest project in a 66-seat house to a Broadway hit as a reflection of Carroll's career: "from unlikely to inevitable." Clive Barnes, reviewing *Don't Bother Me, I Can't Cope*, opened his review with the line, "It is the unexpected that is the most delightful." While critics responded to Carroll's presence on the theater scene in the 1970s with surprise, she maintained that the struggle was not new—its reception was.

Carroll's most significant collaboration of the 1970s was with lyricist, composer, writer, and performer Micki Grant. Writer and dancer Glory Van Scott introduced Grant to Carroll, and at the end of a hectic day spent planning the musical version of Irwin Shaw's *Bury the Dead*, Grant played Carroll some original songs. Carroll knew her search was over, and she made Grant artist-in-residence at UAC, beginning a new direction and focus for the company. The work that resulted tongue-tied reviewers in their attempts to categorize it: ritual theater? Gospel revue? Song play? Musical?[69] *Don't Bother Me, I Can't Cope* transferred to Broadway in 1973, where its jazz and funk-inflected songs vented the rage of citizens trapped between contradictions and expectations: "Love, hate Uptown, downtown Separate state. If I sit in I get arrested. If I break in I get arrested. If I shout nobody answers. If I knock I'm Uncle Tom. Questions!" Confused characters—"so many voices preaching"—navigate conflicting desires for peace marches and militancy, violence and passivity, standing tall and bending. "Fighting for Peace" demanded a break from the fighting, on the street, in the supermarket, across the country, and across the globe; "Good Vibration" bounded back with a jubilant, evangelical joy.

The musical critiqued governmental programs that encircled neighborhoods with the stance of distanced anthropologists while usually missing the point. The characters push back against bureaucratic dimness and institutional condescension:

> I can't use a course in etiquette
> When my rent is due
> I don't need your Dr. Jensen
> To study my I.Q.
> I don't need your theories
> From some book you've read
> I don't need your social worker
> Peeping under my bed.[70]

The Grant/Carroll collaboration valorized resilience in its lyrics, its staging, and its performance schedule, as it snaked from the streets to the UAC theater, Off Broadway, other cities, Broadway, and right back out into the boroughs. Carroll's subliminal argument leveled the hierarchy of neighborhood versus professional stages in a desire to deliver its message across the parallel hierarchies of taste. Injustice, power, mystery, ethics; an exuberant score gave voice to a disheartened city, while poking fun at its irrational fears:

> Now all the good white folks have gone and left town
> For it wasn't fun any more,
> When those fun colored folk left the cocktail party
> And bought the house next door.[71]

Grant and Carroll's plays experimented with ways to incorporate audiences into their structure. *Cope* hides its own performative pedagogy, such as "History of Dance," which begins as a slow blues and then unfolds from the Charleston to the Hustle, from the jitterbug to acid rock, only to melt into the mournful "Billie Holiday Blues": "Anything worth knowin' you knew it all by then / Where some folks are still goin' is already where you been."[72] Carroll's notions of address, interconnection, and interdependence manifested in the divergent and atypical audience demographics she cultivated through the years of UAC's touring. McCandlish Phillips of the *Times* described the audience for one of UAC's shows in its Chelsea loft theater space: "The audience, half-black, half-white, included boys off the playground in tee shirts and sneakers in the first row, college-age youths in open-neck shirts in the second row, middle-aged couples, an editor, and at least two artist's agents scouting talent. The range of sophistication was as broad as that of the Manhattan telephone book."[73]

Martin Segal and the Dollar Approach to Culture

> We hang on by our nails down here.
>
> —Vinnette Carroll, 1976[74]

By the time *Cope* closed in October 1974, New York City's unemployment rate surpassed 10 percent, and residents faced widespread layoffs across the public sector. In March 1975 Carroll's group again performed on a public stage, this time at the New York Hilton, to an audience of 1,000 government officials and business leaders, in a spoof of the city's fiscal problems. Since 1923 the Inner Circle, an association of city beat reporters, annually performed a song-and-dance show lampooning city politicians. If the mayor accepts the invitation to attend this black tie event, the rules allow for his administration to prepare a rebuttal in the form of a skit.[75] After a city official saw UAC's adaptation of a Jamaican folk tale, Carroll's company secured an invitation to perform Mayor Beame's rebuttal to "Abie's Irish Woes." In the night's three-act play, the main character, a laid-off zookeeper, lambasted the mayor's job cutbacks to the tune of Jim Croce's 1973 pop hit, "Bad, Bad Leroy Brown":

> It transpired, I was fired,
> Me and several thousand more
> Me and cops and sanitmen [*sic*]
> And firemen were going out that door,
> But it's funny that the money
> That they took from our backs
> Went right down to the party's clubhouse
> As a raise for all the hacks.[76]

The *New York Times* declared the performance a successful "marriage of politics and theater with a more polished veneer than the theatrical politics common to City Hall."[77] But the cutbacks were real, the unemployed city worker a new trope. The politics of retrenchment affected zookeepers and arts groups alike; UAC and so many others relied on relatively limited amounts of municipal funding for their operations. The City Hall performance did not alter Carroll's fortunes; just one year after the Inner Circle appearance, Carroll commented on the frustrations of being a Tony-nominated director who was unable to pay the rent on her theater space. When asked her greatest artistic need, she replied: "For more money."[78] UAC enjoyed the recognition from *Cope* and its prolific output of plays, but this did not translate into meaningful support for a company that needed funds for space, operations, and for its training component and repertory.

As a candidate for mayor, Beame had called for a "major Renaissance" of the arts.[79] Once elected in 1973, he quickly implemented two of his campaign proposals: eager to dismantle the "superagencies" that Lindsay had created, Beame separated the city's Department of Cultural Affairs from Parks and Recreation, and created an advisory committee on Culture and the Performing Arts. The former effectively abolished the "Parks, Recreation and Cultural Affairs" monolith that Beame deemed incompatible with city needs due to its submerging of cultural affairs within the administrative overlay of the massive agency.[80] The turf battle over dominant visions for the city's cultural affairs advanced one more notch with his new advisory committee on cultural policy, helmed by Martin E. Segal, then president of the Film Society of Lincoln Center.[81] A gregarious Russian immigrant, Segal made a fortune in business and was a regular fixture at cultural events and galas, with a signature red rose in his lapel. Once installed in an advisory position with the city, Segal used his bully pulpit to argue that much was amiss in municipal support for its arts. In 1974 Segal's commission reported that the performing arts had been inconsistently funded in New York to a disturbing degree, and singled out the producing realities of theater as necessitating its frequent deficits.[82] He communicated a delicate position: to argue that all was not well, yet what *was* going right constituted an essential plus during the economic crises.

Segal's committed advocacy motivated Beame's pro-arts zeal, and together they reformed the business of the arts in the city, with the greatest emphasis placed on the performing arts. The goal was to confer value beyond "expression," to convince both city officials and the nation at large that New York City deserved to be bailed out of its fiscal crisis because of its contributions as an "entertainment center." In 1975, at the height of crisis negotiations, Mayor Beame spoke passionately about the economic importance of the arts on the national stage: "There's nothing like New York, a factor that assumes even greater urgency when money is short."[83] His confidence was undergirded by Segal's initiatives to install the performing arts as a central weapon in the city's arsenal against its multidimensional perception problems. This twinning of "culture" as both unique attribute and saving grace signified the new approach to the arts as an economic development tool across the city, not just for traditional tourist destinations like Times Square. This could not have been achieved without Segal's efforts to attract the attention of lawmakers as Mayor Abe Beame struggled to balance austerity zeal with steps that would redeem the faltering image of what was once "Fun City." These policies, however, took shape as community cultural centers and neighborhood arts programs were still relatively young. The financial crisis provided city leaders with the excuse to back off from expansionary policies of program development, in order to focus more narrowly on the economic role of culture for the city at large, not its individual communities.

Coalitions of public and private interests began to work together to manage the image crisis that was threatening New York's identity as a global media capital.[84] In 1971, the Association for a Better New York (ABNY) and the Convention and Visitors Bureau (CVB) initiated the "Big Apple" publicity campaign to retain skittish corporations and attract tourists. (It was retired in 1974 with the onset of fiscal crisis, but was embraced again between the summers of 1976 and 1977.) This public relations campaign drew on "mythic, transhistorical representations of the city as a national and global capital."[85] The municipal restructuring that Beame and the Department of City Planning devised in 1976 was spelled out in an economic recovery report, which created the new Office of Economic Development (OED), the "first city-wide administrative division devoted entirely to generating new income for the city through its dealings with the private sector."[86] This new office merged previously separate departments like Cultural Affairs, Public Events, and Budget and Finance, all under the jurisdiction of a new "Deputy Mayor for Economic Development." This position of authority, Miriam Greenberg notes, was second only to that of the mayor himself.[87]

A battle for representation developed; the city dispatched the new OED to broadcast assurances of a safe and productive financial district, one without blackouts, strikes, deepening inequality, arson, or closed hospitals. For theater uptown, downtown, midtown, and outer borough, the perspective of the OED was now automatically folded into decisions of cultural policy. A similar trend played out in Washington, as once-symbolic aspects of urban culture became conceived as "material" shapers of cities and an emerging area of "instrumental politics."[88] The Carter administration (1977–81) decided to locate their special assistant to the secretary for cultural affairs, Louise Wiener, within the Commerce Department, a placement that underscored the strategy of looking foremost at the arts in economic life—as a philosophy but also as a legitimization of the arts as a contributor to the nation.

The relative health and productivity of arts institutions—however the city chose to define them—became both a harbinger and an engine of the fiscal crisis rebound. For artists, the processes of dispensing city support were labyrinthine: red tape mired applicants as they scrounged for funding, a reality that did not diminish the sense that the city's machine politicians represented an old guard incapable of understanding the plurality of artistic practices in New York. Architecture critic Ada Louise Huxtable accused city servants of being too entrenched in outdated models to adapt to a new arts landscape: "While the avant-garde struggles somewhere out there, the rear guard holes up in City Hall."[89] Janet Langsam, who served in three mayoral administrations and was the first deputy commissioner of cultural affairs under Beame, remembers Segal's influence during a time of upheaval:

> By the time I got to Cultural Affairs . . . there was a whole group of organizations that were important to the city that were new and fledgling but were not part of the system. They were getting some funds from Cultural Affairs through some other competitive process, through member items from the Board of Estimate or that kind of thing. So at that point, [Martin] Segal was able to move the idea that culture in New York City was important to the economy—or should be seen as economic development and certainly should stand on its own as an agency.[90]

As problematic as the prior motivating philosophies of "cooling the streets" remained, it had succeeded in setting up a loose framework for experimentation around performance practices that found new analytical and organizational strategies. The new dollar approach to culture would not be as flexible, or as open to coalition building. This argument from *New York* encapsulates this diluted message—and mission—of Cultural Affairs:

> New York's cultural life at all levels is what makes the city visible to the rest of the country and modifies the hinterland's resentful

> willingness to let the city slide into fiscal ruin. For New Yorkers, culture is the spiritual topping on the gritty, grinding reality of daily survival. It not only helps stabilize neighborhoods but also generates the largest part of the city's tourist industry. Churning up an estimated $3 billion of economic activity every year, tourism is second only to the $13 billion garment trade.[91]

The idea that the arts spared New York from the harsh judgment of the rest of the country eventually became a truism, but in practice, the emphasis almost always weighted toward tourism and away from local arts resources.

Beame instituted drastic steps to reduce city spending, leaving cultural advocates in an awkward position. Amid various waves of threats and cuts and austerity plans, in October 1974 Beame ordered a freeze on most city hiring and pay increases; shortly thereafter, he ordered large-scale layoffs. The new Department of Cultural Affairs's budget had been decreased by 45 percent in the city's "crisis" slash, and received no restorations. Undeterred, in 1975 Segal presented a larger cultural budget to the City Council, but dubbed it "an austerity budget," justified by "a $3-billion cultural industry in the city that created $100 million in taxes, with some $40 million in direct support funding by the city of cultural institutions."[92] Members of the council responded with indignation that Segal could propose a larger budget for a new agency in such "parlous times."[93] Segal continued to articulate the assumed paradox that the arts uniquely deserved assistance during times of crisis and as a close advisor and friend to the mayor, he undoubtedly influenced policy: "the dollar approach to culture inspired Beame."[94] Yet Segal's protestations arguably had more significance in the long-term approach of the city than in short-term successes. Just a month after Beame publicly advertised his "optimism" about the cultural life of the city, it was reported that the crisis was "deeply affecting its cultural institutions and their services to the public." Cuts of 10 percent were followed by more cuts of 8.5 percent, and news articles predicted that cultural institutions would have to leave the city.[95] Just one year later, the new chief of Cultural Affairs, Claude Shostal, anticipated bruising battles for money between Cultural Affairs, fire, sanitation, and police—the department's budget was down again due to the cuts.[96] The conversation had changed; the arts were now pitted squarely against the essential services of the city.

For UAC, the 1970s delivered unending fiscal stress, but through every material setback, Carroll, a chronic workaholic, created at a dizzying pace. If *Cope* delivered the sounds of the city through gospel influences, *Your Arms Too Short to Box with God* deposited its audiences directly to the "church of good faith." The Italian government commissioned *Your Arms Too Short to Box with God* for the Spoleto Festival, where Carroll presented an early version of the play. The musical, based on the biblical book of Matthew, comprised a compelling follow-up to *Cope*, this time with music and lyrics by gospel singer "Professor" Alex Bradford and Micki Grant. As with her other works, *Box* showcased the agility, discipline, and coherence of her ensemble. The music of *Box* is more furious, more complex, but the libretto tells the 2,000-year-old story in highly theatricalized and presentational language. The play carries messages of peace throughout, with the same thematic resonance Carroll brought to Broadway with *Cope*. Strength through storytelling, and a metaphor for performance: you got yours, I got mine, I shout joy, you shout. *Box* became an extended metaphor for what is possible when seated in the house of good faith, and the play ran on Broadway for 429 performances between 1976 and 1978, with multiple Tony Award nominations in 1977.

From New York to Chicago to Los Angeles, reviews across the country praised the show as "infectious" and "joyous" and "passionate."[97] While most reviewers captured the historical themes—the citation of medieval morality plays and pageantry in particular—all missed the fluidity with which Carroll always staged her environmental theater, designed for both the street and stage, regardless of its ultimate production context. The critical establishment never quite acknowledged the gravitas in Carroll's work, and preferred instead to revel in its celebratory, "toe-tapping" qualities, filing it away as "a gospel revue." This diminished a most important frame for UAC's prior work: the street. True to her earliest convictions, Carroll again created a counterspectacle that spoke about the streets just as much as it commented on the stage.

After Broadway shows, Obies, Tony nominations, national tours, and a popular summer street performance repertoire, new owners evicted UAC from its building at 26 West Twentieth Street, the company's rented sixty-six-seat theater. Carroll, Grant, and their collaborators boasted long resumes—awards and distinctions, more than one hundred plays presented in its eleven years, and prominent alumni Sherman Hemsley and Jonelle Allen. But "Black groups don't get the kind of funding the larger groups do," Carroll observed.[98] Her managing director, Anita MacShane, fretted over the future of the corps' twenty-five actors and technical staff. "We're only a reflection of our times," said MacShane. "We're not funded like [Joseph] Papp [of the New York Shakespeare Festival] and not everybody wants to rent to a minority group. We're a minority group on two counts; we're a theater and we're a black theater."[99] Once seen as an arm of the city's policies to invest in urban neighborhoods, UAC was now just another company begging for help in the *New York Times*. The inevitability of interdependence cut both ways for Carroll's troupe, making way for the reality of vulnerability. "We can't afford the failures that other groups can," she explained. "We don't get the kind of money that Circle in the Square or the Shakespeare Festival get."[100] Carroll recognized that the funding landscape was far from equitable, but that more money also did not signify improved costumes or sets or even advertising—true support meant stability of place, along with room to develop and fail. True support meant a position in the priorities of the metropolis, for her theater, her work, and her audience. Their nonprofit budget of $120,000 per year was nurtured by funding from NYSCA, box office receipts, Carroll's and Grant's royalties from *Cope*, and contracts from the city to perform during the summer in city parks—although that money dried up as funding for street performance waned during the fiscal crisis.[101] This animated the trap of instability that fluctuating city arts policies (and philosophies) abetted. Carroll never achieved what Joseph Papp so craved—a line on the city's budget.

Carroll had developed municipal alliances, but urban regime shifts led to artistic instability. Michael McKinnie, writing about the "edifice complex" prevalent in Toronto after World War II, notes that while some companies "privileged theatre space as an administrative issue (as a 'container' for its theatrical activity), theatre space did not disappear as an artistic issue."[102] UAC confronted this conflict throughout its life span. Temporary funding from Pepsi-Cola undergirded occasional tours, as corporate interests had a clear stake in cultivating seemingly business-friendly streets. This filled funding gaps when NYSCA and Cultural Affairs budgets got slashed, but could not re-create an entire municipal ethos in which Carroll's troupe would be valued on the level of city policy. The group remained at the mercy of the state legislature, a government body that once employed her to command their fledging GAP program. "The NY State Council on the Arts gets cut every year," she explained in 1977, "so naturally the groups they service get cut."[103]

Many factors made UAC's accomplished trajectory possible: a strengthening of the interdependence between government agencies and theater groups that began during Lindsay's tenure; the maturation and dedication of artists like Carroll, who had performed on stage and screen from the mid-1950s onward; and new strains of thought pertaining to the generative role of the arts for the youth of the city. A local confrontation with inequitable sociocultural opportunities led to a radical reimaging of summer theater and youth education, suffused with the sensibilities of industry-tested actors. "Don't be seduced," Carroll repeated as a mantra: "don't be seduced," she warned her casts, regardless of how many standing ovations they received.[104] Historian Clarence Taylor argues that the most racially charged episodes during Mayor Lindsay's mayoralty—the fight over a civilian complaint review board for the police, or the attempt to create community control of schools—"laid the ground work for important structures by giving people an opportunity to make government agencies work for them."[105] This had a striking parallel in performance practices; Lindsay's Urban Action Task Force expressly linked neighborhoods, communication, and performance. Carroll's institution fostered affective equality, and created a poetics of solidarity in her plays; she built frameworks strong enough to extend far past Mayor Lindsay's time in office, overlapping with a new regime in City Hall. The circular tributary—between the small "Core" theater to neighborhoods to Broadway—weakened as the fear of race riots faded, Lindsay left office, and Task Force and state funding drained. Sponsorships from corporations like Pepsi-Cola went from outlier to necessity, and emerged more prominently than ever before; by 1978, the city merely acted as a middleman to raise private funds, dissociating itself from past levels of support.

Chapter 4

✦

The Theater of Poverty

Everyman in Coney Island

> For years, I have been struck by the artificiality of the barriers created by the divisions between experimental, political, intellectual, and popular theatre, each with its own code, audience, and way of life.
>
> —Peter Brook, 1974

By the early 1970s, decades of failed policies had transformed much of Coney Island into a graveyard of large-scale urban projects and weathered icons. The seaside district's Victorian-era amusement parks, Dreamland, Luna Park, and Steeplechase, were defunct, and the shells of storied performance spaces remained. The World of Wax Museum and the disreputable Surf Hotel occupied the famed vaudeville venue, Henderson's Music Hall. The Shore Theater, a seven-floor, 2,400-seat picture palace, operated as an adult movie house (and closed permanently in 1973). The Parachute Jump, Ferris Wheel, and Cyclone roller coaster still dotted the horizon, sentimental landmarks to World Fairs and the golden era of leisure time. Memoirists and urban sociologists alike have investigated the decline of Coney Island, while performance scholars uninterested in popular amusements neglected the area until the neo-burlesque revival arrived on its shores in 1983. Over a decade prior, however, Coney Island was the site of a series of inspired performance experiments. Three radical street theater companies chose Coney as a locus for their operations in the early 1970s: Peter Schumann's Bread and Puppet Theater, Marketa Kimbrell's New York Street Theater Caravan, and the Everyman Street Theatre.[1] The latter created performances led by neighborhood residents, and attracted hundreds of participants and thousands of spectators to street corners, while also infiltrating elite arts venues across the city. Everyman intervened in a fragmented terrain of street theater activity and created a new space for shared performance practices: the Everyman-Community Theater Festival at Lincoln Center, which grew from a ten-day program with 650 performers in 1971 to a two-week festival with 1,500 performers and 30,000 spectators in 1973.[2]

As with many arts projects initially supported by Mayor John Lindsay's Urban Action Task Force, the Everyman Street Theatre inhabited a fraught position as quasi-state-sanctioned performance, vulnerable to misguided mandates from a bureaucracy eager to alleviate urban racial dissension. In 1968 Lindsay invited a large group of prominent New Yorkers active in the arts to Gracie Mansion and put forth an appeal: "Can all of you think of anything to do this summer? Because it's going to be a very bad one."[3] Actress Geraldine Fitzgerald sat on the city's Cultural Council, and the Urban Action Task Force elicited ideas for arts programs to "help the people in ghetto areas."[4] A Franciscan Brother and theater teacher, Jonathan Ringkamp, had since 1967 been working with the Brooklyn Arts and Cultural Association (BACA) to create plays for Twilight Theatre in Prospect Park. Fitzgerald and Ringkamp both felt frustrated by the inability of the Cultural Council to "directly affect" the quality of life on New York City streets.[5]

Lindsay's meeting with arts dignitaries only aggravated their dissatisfactions with the pace of change on the city level. "There was a lot of talk and we noticed that no one listened to what we said, so we decided to go off on our own."[6] They purchased the script of the medieval morality play *Everyman* and went out to Coney Island. In concert with members of BACA, they led neighborhood youth in theater exercises in a room above Nathan's Famous Hot Dogs in the evenings, and held rehearsals outdoors on the Boardwalk and in the parks and upstairs in the Tilyou Theater.[7] Between 1969 and 1975, more than 500,000 spectators in New York City saw the Everyman Street Theatre's first production, *Everyman and roach*.[8] An energetic theatrical repertoire carried the company through a decade of productions, from 1968 to 1979.

The work of Everyman shares characteristics with a particular category of grassroots performance that valorizes "local life aware of itself," Dudley Cocke's term for the deployment of adaptive imagination within local culture.[9] Clifford Geertz's notion of "local knowledges" can be similarly applied to describe Everyman's work: a renunciation of the authority that comes from "views from nowhere," replaced with a "particular variety of view from somewhere."[10] While mindful to avoid romanticizing forms of local cultural production, Everyman's "particular view" performed decisive maneuvers to widen the frame of representation of urban neighborhoods. The "Everyman Street Theatre concept," when duplicated across the city, supported the very interactions and embodied practices that changed and produced urban space. Fitzgerald and her Everyman coproducers acknowledged—and were involved in—a great variety of community theaters but considered Everyman a vehicle for the furtherance of a specific concept of street theater, one distinguished by total openness, with no auditioning. By 1971 Everyman had five borough branches, a reflection of its fundamental performance philosophy that validated a local, particular view and turned away no one. This undertaking developed into a theater festival that conjoined the street life of disparate neighborhoods. In 1972 the *New York Times* reported that street theater was "springing up like neighborhood baseball teams."[11] Although the athletic league comparison captured the quantity and geographic spread of street theater troupes, the uniqueness of the Everyman concept enabled individual groups to distinguish themselves, and proved effective as an organizing principle capable of bringing them together.

Ringkamp and Fitzgerald consciously distanced Everyman from recent iterations of street theater—particularly the guerrilla theater of the 1960s that directly agitated for social change—in order to emphasize the epic themes of theater history, conformed to its participants:

> Rather than talking to people about the things that were making them unhappy in their environment, we spoke, rather, to the bigger issues—life, death, money, love, power. . . . Once you go deeper, if you go beneath the problem of bad housing you come smack into the problem of living.[12]

In addition to the traditions of Greek drama and medieval pageant wagons, Everyman derived from the more recent history of artists negotiating with bureaucracies to support and implement community arts projects. Its members were all variously invested in the potential of antipoverty arts programs sanctioned through official mechanisms, whether it was the New York State Council on the Arts, the Parks Department, or Mobilization for Youth.

Mical Whitaker, the director of the Harlem-based East River Players, instigated the Everyman-Community Street Theater Festival at Lincoln Center with Fitzgerald, Ringkamp, and Hazel Bryant.[13] He considered the War on Poverty's Mobilization for Youth projects not only an essential training and pipeline to his own career in theater, but as decisive in the artistic progression of companies that grew out of its early funding.

> It gave summer work, and therefore summer dollars, to youth who would otherwise be engaged in something else, and probably something not quite as culturally profound as theater. But it served both purposes, for the audience that it reached and for the people participating. Not to mention those who really found a career, like myself, in the theater.[14]

Together, the four collaborators pursued an open, unrestricted approach to street theater. In his first Everyman job, Whitaker served as a production coordinator for the Harlem Everyman Company, and translated his prior knowledge of theater into street theater of neglected neighborhoods. He secured yards to use for costume changes, convinced church facilities or friendly residents to provide bathrooms, chose the orientation of the stage, and even cajoled car owners to point their headlights toward the action when their barebones lighting equipment failed to arrive.

In its early years, the Everyman-Community Street Theater Festival at Lincoln Center facilitated the maturation of a generation of street performance: the companies involved maintained their particularistic and rooted affiliations while returning to the civic platform of Lincoln Center's outdoor spaces. Mainstream media outlets emphasized the chasm between the elite venue and the street theater groups, and dubbed theirs "the theater of poverty"[15] due to the economic profiles of the troupes' home neighborhoods. Yet the festival advanced not just the individual companies and participants, but also the image and operations of the arts complex.

In the penurious topography of 1970s Coney Island, Everyman introduced a transcommunal performance ethos. Sociologist John Brown Childs originated the phrase "transcommunality" to describe a mode of progressive organizing that emphasizes not identities but "affiliations."[16] Inspired by influences including indigenous models of alliances in the Americas, Martin Luther King Jr., bell hooks, John Dewey, Simone Weil, Paolo Freire, and Martin Buber, Childs's theory seeks to create constellations of inclusive cooperation, without duplicating hierarchies of domination. He is especially concerned with cities in the United States too often devoid of constructive projects, left self-defensive and territorialized.[17] As a conceptual framework, transcommunality contrasts impoverishment with interaction.

At a time when its neighborhood theaters sat underutilized, street performance offered Coney Island (and Lincoln Center) a form rooted in both representation and mobility. The traversing of distances—geographic, cultural—reoccur as a theme throughout their activities. Through street performance, Coney Island toured the city during a moment of extreme isolation from the larger city. For this reason, the fight over improved transit, the budgeting of public funds, and the crimes of urban renewal all figure centrally in this period of street performance in Coney Island. The deployment of minimal cultural resources to "calm" urban youth followed the erosion of municipal services in the area. In defiance of politicized boundaries between cultural spaces, Everyman and its festival delivered a brief reprieve from a dispiriting narrative about the culture of the city and its residents. This chapter analyses the processes and production methods of Everyman to consider the labors of post-segregation-era street performance, and to investigate the formation of the Everyman-Community Street Theater Festival as an instance of transcommunal urban performance.

Sinking Surf Avenue

Coney Island of the 1970s was in many ways unrecognizable from the late nineteenth-century seaside resort location, when visitors swarmed its dance halls, piers, barrooms, and bathhouses. Rem Koolhaas famously rendered this fiery scintillation as "fabulous beyond conceiving, ineffably beautiful," and argued that the strategies and mechanisms that later shaped Manhattan were tested in the laboratory of Coney Island.[18] The second half of the twentieth century in Coney played out like a cruel inversion; its amusement area gutted, transformed into imposing ruins, a trajectory halted and reversed. Once a monument to leisure, innovation, and Koolhaas's "attractive artificiality," the more apt term became "monumental dereliction."[19] For this reason, some read Coney Island as a counter-site, or even a "non-site" with characteristics akin to Foucault's "heterotopia."[20] While these analyses provide insights, the category threatens to reproduce disconnections between Coney Island and the rest of the city, and to mute the very subjective toll of urban neglect, in favor of the amusement park's carnivalesque characteristics.

As a "stage" for the city, the vast amusement area historically attracted people of all classes and backgrounds. By the early 1900s, fashionable hotels and homes sidled up against middle-class Brighton Beach, and working-class West Brighton Beach. It was a site to which laborers would journey from Hester Street sweatshops, "a place where the poorest man can take his family and get a little draught of ozone and real life with it," while also enjoying its "hopelessly urban" attributes.[21] The long subway ride from Manhattan to the island offered the chance to see Broadway and Third Avenue for five cents, and, once there, amusements based on new technologies of transportation, from time travel to simulations of lands far away. On the map of the city, Coney Island perched on the Atlantic Ocean and symbolized both escape and arrival.

Scholars have expanded at length on this period in Coney Island, and every account of its Golden Age rightly emphasizes the vast local variations that comprised its heterogeneous cultural production.[22] Coney Island's historical amusement areas were geographically bound; class divisions were encoded in the highly differentiated visual and physical styles of diversions offered. Steeplechase's "ten hours of fun for ten cents" ethos catered to a more working-class clientele, while Luna Park catered to the middle class.[23] Steeplechase featured rides that transformed patrons into performers: the Wedding Ring, the Flopper, Human Roulette Wheel, the Blow-Hole Theater, and the Barrel of Love utilized spinning platforms, high speeds, and craftily placed air vents, resulting in entanglement among the disoriented participants. The other two parks, Luna Park and Dreamland, highlighted foreign travel, spectacular exhibits, realistic drama, and aesthetic sights, and coexisted with shooting galleries, freak shows, and picture arcades. Dreamland, with its religious panoramas and disaster spectacles, closed in 1911 after a fire. Luna Park closed in 1944, after a blaze at the Dragon's Gorge, a roller coaster that traversed Africa, the North Pole, the Grand Canyon, and even Hades.

After World War II, Parks Commissioner Robert Moses's furious highway building commenced in earnest, and many middle-class residents bypassed the peninsula to seek recreation outside of the city limits. The Coney Island of the second half of the twentieth century is dominated by Moses's legacies in more ways than one. Appointed commissioner of the New York City Department of Parks under Mayor Fiorello LaGuardia in 1934, Moses made radical changes to Coney Island in accordance with his urban renewal philosophy. His negative feelings about the area were clear: "I wouldn't want to sink Surf Avenue, but just get rid of about a third of it," said Moses.[24] In the early 1950s Moses began construction on one of his biggest superblock high-rise housing projects, the Coney Island Houses. Moses, at the head of the city's Slum Clearance Committee, had swaths of land rezoned for these projects, and replaced many older and middle-class houses. Conditions in Coney Island deteriorated after the implementation of the city's plan to devote large sections of the neighborhood to high-density residential uses. Marshall Berman describes this period of modern urbanism as one in which the government viewed "the diversity of people, places and activities in the city" as an incitement to control urban life.[25]

In 1964 Steeplechase suffered a tortured demise when Moses sold the land to Fred Trump, who envisioned beachfront condos. But after the Lindsay administration denied Trump's rezoning requests, the developer bulldozed Steeplechase in 1966 to keep the city from anointing it with landmark status. (He later sold the land back to the city in 1969, for a profit.) The destruction of Steeplechase hastened an advanced phase of the displacement of both working-class people and popular amusements from the area. The West End of Coney Island was declared a "poverty zone" in 1967, and ten days after James Earl Ray assassinated Martin Luther King in 1968, riots broke out in Coney Island. Writer Charles Denson argues that this marked the beginning of a negative publicity onslaught, from which Coney Island could not recover.[26] The dismal state of the under-maintained subway system discouraged park-goers and tourists from traveling the long ride on the MTA to the area; politicians blamed the transit authority while threats from "unruly bands of teenagers" dominated the headlines.[27] The decline of mass transit meant that fewer New Yorkers viewed traveling to Coney Island as pleasurable or safe.

Residents often experienced the worst effects of excessive police responses to the unrest through patrols that blanket-targeted young people who lived in the neighborhood and frequented public areas. In her study of race and the decline of amusements after the 1964 Civil Rights Act, Victoria Wolcott writes of a crucial shift in the battlefield over access to recreation. "Increasingly, whites viewed integrated urban recreational facilities as dangerous and crime-ridden spaces. Large-scale recreation riots seemingly legitimated these fears, and in response many whites retreated into private or suburban spaces of leisure."[28] To many residents of the city (and tourists), Coney Island became synonymous with disorder. This characterization intensified as population changes and relocations brought increased numbers of African

American and Latino/a residents to the housing in Coney Island as well as its beaches. These factors reemerged as decisive during the fiscal crisis period, when populations of residents were demonized as a cause of the depletion of city resources without the qualification of the contemporaneous industrial job drain.

These developments in Coney Island coincided with a high point in the promotion and support of street theater troupes across the five boroughs of New York City. As the evolution of Vinnette Carroll's Urban Arts Corps demonstrates, this was not a coincidence; regardless of its varieties, street theater descended directly from the concerns of artists and activists who argued that "public space belongs to the people, whether for performance or protest."[29] In the early 1960s, Joseph Papp's Mobile Theater Unit was one node of this movement; the Street Theatre of the Black Arts Movement represented another. Yet the motivating ideologies behind them cannot be elided. Strains of street theater groups differed in politics as well as methodologies and performance philosophies; theater performed in the streets with little input from residents emerged as easily distinguished from performances that arose directly from the communities in which they played.

Tensions between ethnicities, neighborhoods, and even individual streets rendered the gulf between approaches of individual theater companies of great consequence. The work of playwright Maryat Lee, a pioneer of urban street performance, constitutes a strong precedent for the Everyman Street Theatre.[30] In April 1951 *Dope!*, her play about the drug trafficking that proliferated in Harlem after World War II, performed over five nights to thousands of people outside of a decaying tenement on 100th Street and Lexington Avenue. Later, when Lee taught a course in street theater at the New School, a VISTA volunteer familiar with *Dope!* connected Lee with a high school in East Harlem that had one of the highest addiction levels in the state. Lee's collaborations with the students became East Harlem's Soul and Latin Theater (SALT).[31] They created scenarios that Lee developed and rehearsed with the neighborhood's teenagers, always motivated by social problems: *After the Fashion Show* (sexuality); *Day by Day* (drugs); and *The Classroom* (impoverished schools). Yet Lee's work with SALT remains an anomaly, and not representative of the wider perspective toward "inner city" arts, traditionally reliant on canon delivery.

Joseph Papp, for example, brought free Shakespeare to neighborhoods across the city with his Mobile Unit. A 1965 report commissioned by the liberal think tank, the Twentieth Century Fund, provides a valuable account of one of its summer tours, *A Midsummer Night's Dream*. The study authors critiqued the "complete failure of the institutions of the performing arts to reach individuals in the lower-income—or what used to be called the 'blue-collar'—groups," yet their research questions indicated a troubling (and dominant) perspective toward theater in the streets:

> First, will the masses come to hear and see high culture if it is made available to them?
>
> Second, if they do come, will they know how to behave properly in the face of high art?
>
> Third, will they understand and appreciate what they have seen and heard?
>
> Finally, if the answer to the first two questions is yes, but that to the third is qualified, will not the presentation of high culture to the masses lead to its ultimate debasement as it strives to please them?[32]

Two factors preoccupied the researchers: audience "comprehension" and "behavior." They express anxiety about the influence of television, and the ethical imperative to counteract its reach with the "great masterpieces of civilization." The study's findings suggest that these distractions were misplaced, shaped as they were by cultural condescension, rather than knowledge of the specific environments into which the Mobile Unit entered.

As a consequence, the researchers did not anticipate the unrest the shows fomented. Local gangs felt unjustly usurped by the Mobile Unit, and claimed the playground performance spaces as their exclusive territory. Youths often registered their complaints with rocks thrown at the stage. Confrontations between social spheres in the neighborhood dominated their analysis of the event. The authors argue that peer pressure influenced patterns of attendance: "whether or not [neighbors] turn out for the play may depend . . . on what the 'gang' has to say."[33] The conflict between taste and performance aesthetic went unremarked.

Similarly, Theater in the Street, a multiracial (and often bilingual) company led by Joseph Papp's mentor, Phoebe Brand, faced unruly crowds and, the newspapers suggested, ungrateful reception of their open-air theater.[34] Neighborhood teenagers threw empty liquor bottles (and even old mattresses) from the roofs of nearby buildings during performances of Leopoldo Santiago Lavandero's Spanish-language adaptation of Chekhov's *The Marriage Proposal*, narrowly missing actor Raúl Juliá.[35] One of the architects behind the push for more theater in the streets, Cultural Affairs official Courtney Callender, emphasized the need for sensitivity around neighborhood placement and cultural boundaries. "If a musical group playing nothing but hepped-up muzak comes into a black neighborhood it may be met with fruit, eggs, rocks."[36] This remained a difficult concept for some theater advocates to accept. To them, the notion that theater did not always unify spectators, but rather exposed fractious neighborhoods and frustrated youth, intimated a failure of artistry. It also threatened to undo certainties related to universal masterpieces of established cultural worth. This, of course, threatened in turn the very organizations supporting these initiatives, and compelled some to defend the arts even more vociferously as a neutral mechanism for uplift, not a platform for indigenous neighborhood culture.

Professionals should not be involved in street theater as performers, Everyman's cofounder, Geraldine Fitzgerald believed, but "first-rate directors, choreographers, choral directors" enabled audiences to see "a company yearning to be released."[37] In this respect, another theater relevant to the work of Everyman—particularly in its keen awareness of neighborhood boundaries—was Enrique Vargas's Gut Theatre (Teatro de Tripas) formed in the late 1960s and comprised of members from two street gangs, the East Harlem Thunderbirds and the 110th Street Bachelors. Vargas operated out of the James Weldon Johnson Community Center on East 110th Street, then the epicenter of the heroin scene in Spanish Harlem. The Colombian playwright, trained in anthropology and dramaturgy, moved uptown after a stint at Café La Mama: "Everyone said I was 'great.' Someone should have said, 'Vargas, you're lousy.' I had a feeling of unreality. So I came up to East Harlem."[38] On Park Avenue he watched the Gents, a street gang, perform among the tomatoes of La Marqueta, a marketplace under the elevated railway tracks between 111th Street and 116th Street on Park Avenue. He absorbed the protocols of the neighborhood: when to ask permission, to respect discrete territories, to bring candles and prayers from La Botanica when teenagers felt restless.

Vargas knew well that many local gangs despised the housing projects for their dangerous elevators, and would not go near the community center, "primarily because it's superimposed on the community from above."[39] He tried to decipher the dramatic games of the neighborhood youth, the street festivals of the community, and the spatial politics of the gangs that led police to misunderstand their intent as criminal, rather than social or cultural. When he brought his performers to see Papp's Mobile Theater, although it was only a few blocks away, Vargas's group lacked permission from the block leaders to cross their turf. This constituted trespassing and required circumnavigating territories. Theater interrupted the cartography of neighborhood antagonisms, and the solution, Vargas argued, was to

> incubate indigenous theatre. Everyone wants to bring culture to East Harlem. There's plenty of culture right here, but there's very little communication. I want to have traveling troupes of East Harlemites. Their improvisations grew out of life in East Harlem. That's culture.[40]

In the gap between Vargas's vision and the NYSF's professional Mobile Theater, the work of Everyman inhabited a middle ground. They remained dedicated to classical material—particularly tragedies—as the germinating source for their adaptations but highly attuned to the loyalties and antagonisms of the neighborhoods in which they worked.

These methods avoided assumptions about inner city performance and audience decorum, and instead acknowledged creativity on the part of the youth using urban space to construct meaning. Geraldine Fitzgerald considered some attempts at theater in the streets to be less successful than others, and she harbored a desire to do things differently:

> [Other street theaters] were usually on little trucks that would go to Harlem and do bits of this and that. And people would throw everything at them that wasn't edible. We didn't want to do that, because it was quite clear that that didn't bring happiness to people. So we went out to Coney Island to the high school graduations and announced that we were starting a theatre, that we would like them to come, and that they should take note of two things: one, we were going to do musicals and they could help create them, and two, no one would be tried out and no one would be turned away.[41]

Yet Coney Island offered both a hostile and a fertile terrain for street performance. After the federal government cut off funding for the urban renewal area that stretched across almost all of Coney Island, a "wasteland of unfinished projects" remained.[42] The city owned 410 vacant lots, but had no money to construct the thousands of units of low-rise housing that were planned when the city began acquiring the land. Nearing bankruptcy, the municipal government refused to help with tax relief; businesses closed or were burned. Where beach bungalows once stood, drug treatment centers and nursing homes moved in, and Surf Avenue West became a haven for prostitutes and gang activity, with a 112 percent increase in crime between 1968 and 1973.[43]

Amid these troubled conditions, the Parks and Recreation Department did not commit funds toward the promotion of the few amusement attractions that still existed. Charles Denson describes this as a decade of transition and revolution in the neighborhood, when it seemed "as if the city government had abandoned the island, just cut it loose, hoping that it would float away."[44] In a 1974 survey of New Yorkers about their affective relations with different parts of the city, 48 percent agreed that "no one should go" to Coney Island.[45] News outlets disregarded the continued popularity of the beachside area among some communities and glorified its worst attributes. A desegregation crisis at a nearby junior high school prompted an official 1974 report to describe Coney as a neighborhood scarred by "neglect, nonplanning, and bubble-headed decision[s]."[46]

The engineers of the Everyman Theatre recognized and contravened these three characteristics. The Irish-born Fitzgerald was a major force behind the troupe's longevity and success. In 1971, at age fifty-seven, after a long career largely absent of critical accolades, she received adulation for her portrayal of Mary Tyrone in a Broadway revival of Eugene O'Neill's *Long Day's Journey into Night*. In a *New York Times* profile that celebrated this professional apex, a journalist also detailed her passion for street performance: "Theater should belong to everyone . . . it can *not* be elitist, arcane . . . *anyone* who needs to share it must simply go and do so."[47] Fitzgerald's celebrity impelled media outlets to heed Everyman; the stature of her husband, Stuart Scheftel, in business and civic circles obliged city officials to respond to her entreaties.

Fitzgerald's inspiration for the Everyman Street Theatre concept stemmed from her admiration of Sean O'Casey and similar playwrights who moved Irish theater away from "a kind of poetic notion of an Irishman" toward new plays that presented "the twentieth-century Irishman" of the Dublin streets.[48] Convinced that theater might capture past and future together, Ringkamp and Fitzgerald's modernized version of the medieval play *Everyman* became their first and oft-produced folk-rock play. The development of the play typified their working methods, which borrowed heavily from a pastiche of influences—street protest, agitprop theater, Irish drama, the Black Arts Movement, and, as evidenced by the company's work with Peter Brook, avant-garde and ritual performance. Within this mix, however, Ringkamp insisted that the street theater movement could support a multiplicity of ideological facets—"we're built around the idea that we're not political," he said of the Everyman community theater companies.[49] This, he believed, allowed them to maintain their requirement that no one be turned away if they wanted to join the company.

Fitzgerald and Ringkamp's initial introduction to Coney Island began as many community-based performance attempts do: feebly. After requesting that community leaders hang promotional fliers around the neighborhood, Fitzgerald and Ringkamp arrived at the first meeting of their new street theater—at a neighborhood Y, in a rainstorm—to find only four sullen teenagers. They utilized the four as ambassadors to other teens and guides to better venues, and joined them on recruitment trips to high schools and graduations. With the help of BACA publicizing their workshops, 50 to 100 people attended the next sessions, held in a room over Nathan's restaurant in the evenings. To devise their first play, Ringkamp began with exercises like "CHANGE & SUPPORT," designed to teach the group "trust essential for both physical and vocal improvisation."[50] He led auditions for vocal principals, open rehearsals, and company discussions. BACA administrator Charles Reichenthal remembers the location as "perfect for putting together a mixed group of young people. Nobody was turned away. It was a multiethnic, multiracial, multieconomic production, which was the purpose."[51]

Fitzgerald and Ringkamp inscribed adaptability into their play texts, and part of *Everyman and roach*'s efficacy hinged on its changeability. This allowed for the insertion of references to city politicians like Mayor Lindsay, or more local political figures. Mutable sections of dialogue changed according to the place of performance. When the Preacher introduces Everyman to the audience, the stage directions indicate: "Preacher opens a very large book inscribed with large letters, 'Who's Who In Brooklyn.' The entries in the 'who's who' can be adapted to suit the various communities in which each production takes place."[52] (Everyman's occupation also changed depending upon the locality.) The style of the music in certain versions echoed the jazzy, bluesy rock of *Hair*, with deep bass lines and lively keyboard, but the musical medium of the play was flexible as well, to be performed in the most common musical idiom of the audience. This strategy suited the company's philosophy as well as its nomadic performance schedule, which included indoor venues (La Mama E.T.C., the Society for Ethical Culture, Brooklyn Academy of Music), and the frequent practice of Everyman splinter organizations adapting the same play in another borough. In the summer of 1971, 300 New York City teenagers performed in five Everyman companies, with some companies numbering 80 to 100 people. All inhabited donated spaces, including an unused police precinct.

As the Everyman Street Theatre concept disseminated across the city, directors devised different methods with which to solve the dilemmas of the work. Hazel Bryant identified characteristics of 1960s protests—resistance and instruction—as embedded in the Everyman model. Her time spent training with the Student Non-Violent Coordinating Committee (SNCC) and the Congress of Racial Equality (CORE) incorporated theater techniques and used plays, skits, songs, and improvisations to disseminate information. Yet Bryant, a trained opera singer with a formal theater background, admitted to being unprepared for the task of directing an Everyman company, and experienced a kind of "culture shock" during her transition to collaborating with the group.[53] The first company Fitzgerald and Ringkamp requested Bryant to direct had ninety children; faced with the difficulties of communicating with that many young people, Bryant recalled her preacher father and adopted an evangelist's delivery. She stretched the limits of her voice and her conceptual tools in order to make every direction a lesson, using music, movement, and speech. She worked on numerous plays with Everyman, including two original plays, *Sheba* and *Making It*. Bryant's experience speaks to the development of street theater techniques through the years of the Everyman Theatre Company's evolution. Ringkamp blended commedia dell'arte–influenced acting techniques with ensemble work, aimed at building performers' dexterity to face the logistical demands of the street. With sound equipment a rare amenity, actors desperately needed vocal training. In locations equipped with amplification, Ringkamp and Whitaker devised methods for participants to play serious scenes even while accommodating a clunky microphone. Their choreographer, Elizabeth Keen, evaluated each young person and incorporated their strengths and limitations into the dance: if all you could do was run, she featured your running ability. In this way, the companies embellished the proficiencies of the participants and established a system to work within, not in spite of, the streets. "We had to learn about the streets in order to do a play there," explained Ringkamp.[54]

A filmed 1972 performance of *Everyman and roach* at the Lincoln Center Community-Street Theater Festival demonstrates this approach. At the top of the show, a band of musicians and a chorus of young people gather around the Preacher/narrator figure: they form the choreographed death machine that goes from town to town, "and up and up and up, it don't care who you are, when your number's up." The Preacher steps forward and cautions the audience about mortality, the great equalizer: "It's a funny thing about death, your name might be John V. Lindsay, trying to get all the rats and all the roaches to pay taxes, so he can get policy parity. You're gonna die."[55] The Preacher introduces Everyman, the owner of "A Small Place" dance hall, and his crew, the ensemble: Amico, his best friend and eventual betrayer; No-Count, his business manager; Broad, his girl; three bodyguards, Bull, Whip, and Knife; and roach, a young boy undeserving of even a capital letter in his name, "the poorest, lowest creature they know."[56] The crew shuns roach, who nevertheless idolizes Everyman. Everyman treats roach with disgust; he is condescending and pompous, as when he lectures roach on his theory of social hierarchies:

> You a friend of His. I bet. Well now, every so often, about twice a month. He starts makin' himself a big man. Now He takes this one big man and He places him over there. Then He makes another and places him over here. Now that first one he might call. . . . (*Insert appropriate name of important person known to community*) an' that one over there He might just call him . . . . (*Insert name of President of U.S.*). . . . . But now, after He makes a few big men like that God goes out an makes hisself a real big man. He makes one of them about every ten or twenty years. An' you know who one of those big men is?[57]

Everyman's business is lucrative, but he schemes for a larger discotheque that will yield more patrons and higher profits. In order to finance the new space, Everyman calls in all of his small loans, which, Amico reminds him, are with his oldest friends. Everyman tortures his debtors to extract the cash—hookers, fat men, and the junkie Harry the Head. Each time he demands his money, Everyman yells his magic word, "SOCKIT." Dolores the Gypsy (occasionally played by Geraldine Fitzgerald in performance) summons the police, but they never arrive. The play's turning point is an act of violence: Everyman's hired thugs stab Harry the Head when he is unable to pay his debt.

The play infuses the "call and response" of dialogic art[58] with the politics of territorialism and community loyalties. The energy and brutality of the play derives from the same source: crowds. Crowds of bodyguards, children, debtors, dancers, and onlookers shadow Everyman, taunt one another, alternately pleading for help and direction. The device of the "Death Machine"—created through improvisation in rehearsals—"became the brilliant means of maintaining the company's policy of including, on any evening, any newcomer who might wish to be a performer."[59] If twenty people arrived in the middle of rehearsals, the play could absorb them with specific parts—Suicide, or Old Age—in the Death Machine. This was the case in many of their shows, and contributed to the growth of the company. Everyman's rock music satire of *Macbeth* featured an army of spirits invoked by witches. This play, entitled *Mr. Esteban* when Ringkamp and Fitzgerald created it, became *Mr. Duvalier* when Mical Whitaker adapted and produced it in Harlem; he transported Ringkamp's *Mr. Esteban* to the West Indies. Later, Brooklyn's Everyman Company presented *Mr. Esteban* outdoors at Lincoln Center the same year the Harlem Everyman Company presented *Mr. Duvalier*.[60]

In this way, the adaptability of the material translated the life of the street into a theatrical language. In one scene of *Everyman and roach*, the crowd mollifies Everyman with facile praises, and the stage directions indicate "general jubilation and fast dancing" as the "noisy unruly crowd yells, 'sockit sockit sockit.'" The repetition fades into a slow movement of pot-smoking, with lethargic action and intonation of "Everyman" as the crowd screams, insane with panic. When the police finally arrive, no one reveals the crimes they witnessed, and the police exit, satisfied. Everyman is suddenly overcome with nightmares of catastrophe. He hears voices and receives visions, for which the crowd provides a contorted and eerie soundscape. The Ghost of Harry the Head mocks Sockit and his life, "a bag of worms."[61] Each individual member of the Death Machine that stalks Everyman throughout the play represents a dimension of mortal demise: disease, time, suicide, accident, violence, fear, superstition, old age, and pallor. The "crowd" of the Death Machine doubles as spectators for the main action. When Everyman intones the name of his new disco, "The End Is Near," their chanting gains strength, and the Angel of Death arrives with dire proclamations.

The church bell tolls and the Death Machine finally summons Everyman. In a concluding attempt to avoid this fate, he throws money at the debtors and hanger-ons in his crew. Devoid of pity for him, they shout insults that rise to a frenzied incoherence.[62] Roach loyally accompanies Everyman to the Death Machine, but Everyman, in his lone act of generosity, prevents roach from sacrificing his life. The Preacher returns, and announces that it is up to God to decide Everyman's fate; he then queries the audience for their judgment. The text provides for two possible endings—Everyman is killed, or spared—depending upon the answer of the audience assembled. "After the response is given and repeated so that all may hear, the Preacher says, 'so be it.' According to what God determines one of the following two endings is played."[63] In this coda, the spectators—and the people of the street—engage directly in the decisions made in the public sphere. The structure of the play concurs, and implies a deeper implication to this participation: whereas Everyman lived with a belief that God (and a few big men created in his image) exists to surpass (and suppress) others, the Preacher locates God with the audience.

This embodiment of spiritual agency in the audience—which mirrored the performers—celebrated the capability and cogency of youth culture alongside neighborhood aesthetics. Theater scholar Mimi D'Aponte notes the significance of an Everyman younger than traditional depictions of Everyman. "His youth is epitomized, of course, by the young players who, by virtue of their willingness to improvise in a street theatre experiment, became co-authors of an allegorical drama in which their own potential destinies were under discussion and, theatrically speaking, at stake."[64] When Fitzgerald and Ringkamp first produced *Everyman and roach* on a corner of Surf Avenue in Coney Island, the cast was huge and the sidewalks barely contained the audience. The Parks Department commissioner at the time, August Heckscher, includes in his memoir a recollection of viewing *Everyman and roach*:

> I journeyed, this time to Coney Island, to see the results. At the end of the afternoon, in a street whose every outward experience was of sordidness and neglect, the play was scheduled to take place. The actors and the audience were from the block and the near neighborhood. . . . And what talent there was! It belonged to that block, and as the block progressed it seemed to wash away the block's ugliness, as it must have washed from the individuals taking part the sense of the city's loneliness and despair.[65]

Heckscher interprets the event (and its location) as a kind of melodrama; talented kids crying out amid loneliness and despair. Producer and director Woodie King Jr.'s skepticism of much street theater critiqued such an audience response—liberals "not interested at all in the real play, the real theatre. They want the Moynihan Report confirmed, all those reports from the Welfare Department verified. If all this happens, then intellectual discussion can be set."[66] King referred to the racist and damaging 1965 report by sociologist Daniel Patrick Moynihan, then assistant secretary at the U.S. Department of Labor, which argued that the family structure of black America constituted the most dangerous social problem facing the county. "The Negro family in the urban ghetto is crumbling. . . . for vast numbers of the unskilled, poorly educated city working class the fabric of conventional social relationships has all but disintegrated."[67] The report denounced, warning of national liability, the "tangle of pathology" that caused delinquency and alienation.

Coney Island was the object of fetishization on the part of both city planning and private developers, and to defend against this peril of "the Moynihan Report confirmed," *Everyman and roach* offered residents a range of representational devices in a very public realm. Ringkamp and Fitzgerald's second play, a satirical rock-opera version of Macbeth, *Mr. Esteban*, played to standing-room-only crowds on corners in Red Hook. A *Village Voice* reporter who finally caught up with *Mr. Esteban* on a street corner commented on the production's ability to bring "together black, white, and brown ghetto residents—young people who might not otherwise be inclined to speak—into a working relationship."[68] His search for the performance location is not unlike Heckscher's long journey out to Coney Island; the men were guests as much as they were spectators. What they found when they arrived was a performance of coauthorship, and an experiment in creation as well as reception. A visitor's ability (or inability) to discern King's "real theatre" became secondary to the labors of the performers and their interactions within their own neighborhoods. The editors of a collection of feminist scholarship on social change and the metropolis articulate the stakes of visibility in such a context:

> Physical zones are read through psychological landscapes of comfort and danger so that neighborhoods experienced as the simple—if sometimes frustrating—everyday by their inhabitants are fetishized as unlivable by other populations. Such fantasies of danger normalize neglect and decay, justify the implementation of development plans without the input of neighborhood residents and regulate bodies marked by race, gender, sexuality and disability, among other things.[69]

In a neighborhood threatened by the normalization of neglect, the activist cultural production of Everyman troupes disputed economic devastation and top-down decision-making. As Sonja Arsham Kuftinec describes, even small-scale productions can challenge narratives, animate difference, perform and reform culture, and attest to a community's "inherent instability."[70] In many respects, the Everyman Theatre—with its local variations and broad coalitions—achieved a model for communicating these functions.

In addition to the risks of perpetuating structures of urban malaise through their performances, the company also guarded against the stigma of "social work" that followed troupes working with adaptive texts and discursive formations. Clive Barnes of the *New York Times*, for example, diminished the achievements of Everyman as "more in the realm of sociology than art."[71] While the cofounders of Everyman debated these criticisms alongside other street theater practitioners, the company evolved somewhat apart from the expectations of city officials and critics. The decentralized structure of the Everyman concept allowed individual troupes to confound facile assumptions, and its organizers upended the one-way flow of culture *into* troubled neighborhoods through collaboration with larger institutions. Two of these interventions took place at organizations redefining their own relationships to decentralization and audience participation: Lincoln Center and the Brooklyn Academy of Music.

Peter Brook in Brooklyn

Everyman worked with British director Peter Brook and thirty members of his International Centre for Theatre Research during Brook's residency at the Brooklyn Academy of Music (BAM) in 1973. Ringkamp studied and admired experimental directors of Brook's generation, and he had already designed the Everyman project in Coney Island using a related set of inquiries and assumptions.

Brook's arrival in Brooklyn concluded a three-year phase of research for his company that began in 1971, when his Paris-based international theater group put their experiments "to the acid test of whatever specific conditions the particular questions required."[72] Their travels encompassed a shantytown outside of Paris, tombs in Persia, villages in Nigeria, Cesar Chavez's strike meetings in California, asylums, cliffs, camel markets, street corners, community centers, museums, and zoos. "Everywhere, we were asking one question, 'What is theatre?' "[73] Brook and his company settled for five weeks in the newly renovated ballroom of BAM—a versatile black box theater, the Lepercq Space—and used it as a home base for their work. There they collaborated with La Mama's Native American Theatre Ensemble and the National Theatre of the Deaf. In their work outside of BAM, Brook's company traveled by station wagon to a park in Bedford-Stuyvesant, a drug prevention center in Sheepshead Bay, a street corner in Canarsie, a courtyard in the Brooklyn Museum. In these public places, the company showed up unannounced and improvised plays with spectators, unrolling a large carpet as a point of focus to define and begin the work. A journalist described the process, initiated by actors playing instruments, once neighborhood children gathered:

> The cast lined up on the carpet and the audience was asked to choose one of the actors to play God, another the Devil, and the third an ordinary mortal. A contest began—two gigantic monsters fighting for the soul of Mr. Man. Slowly the audience became more involved, cheering each side, making jokes, and, encouraged by the actors, occasionally joining in the action.[74]

Brook's improvisations traded in mythic constructs easily communicated through imagery. Relying on morality tales as a foundation to improvisation, these efforts were not dissimilar from Ringkamp and Fitzgerald's preferred theatrical shorthand. For all, spontaneity and spectacle piqued the interests of neighborhood youth and opened into a process-oriented session of interaction. "Where milk trucks used to load up," wrote a critic, "Mr. Brook's people found their way, effortlessly, unstagily, into the lives of some teenagers. A stereo set was throbbing with The Who one afternoon. Helen Mirren, an English blonde with an important film or two to her credit, began trying her own thing to the music near where a boy was doing the same, and the two of them compared steps."[75]

Both Everyman and Brook dissociated the core of their work from "reflecting ghetto conditions," or delivering a message of uplift to inner city neighborhoods. Ringkamp would never be held in the same regard as Brook, a revered master at flummoxing "traditional" theater audiences through his search for mythopoeic languages to connect across cultures. Yet Brook's visit inspired Ringkamp's notions about performance, barriers, and methodologies when working across the city.

Indoors, at the Lepercq Space, Everyman and other community groups had the opportunity to work with the company. During their residency, Brook and the Centre commenced at 10:30 a.m. with private demonstrations and exercises. In the afternoon, they invited an audience to participate in improvisation and debate; in the evening, the day culminated with a performance of *The Conference of the Birds*. This, according to Brook, was not so much a play as "a possibility." The idea was "to make, in a very special form, something that really comes from the people and the place—and everything that's in the air at the time of the performance."[76] Most of Brook's experiments during that period originated in *The Conference of the Birds*, a piece that drew from avian movement and form, based on a twelfth-century Persian poem.

Brook admitted that the grueling nature of their travels, coupled with meetings and events, left the company depleted for these evening performances. Perhaps as a consequence, while Brook's company garnered plenty of press during their New York residency, the critics responded harshly to the in media res version of what they expected to be polished evening showings at BAM. Brook defended his troupe's uneven output and enjoyed a measure of insulation from the criticism—their free performances were consistently oversold. "The strain was frightening, the quality erratic, but at the same time we were trying to make a statement, affirming that a day in the life of a theatre group can and must be more generous and many sided than if it lets itself get locked into any one theatre slot."[77] While not explicit, this called attention to the labors of Brook's troupe as well as those of Everyman; outreach takes time, as does the practice of remaining open to failure. Brook made visible the material demands of this work, visiting stretches of the city that did not have any performance infrastructure available. Moreover, his sense of theater as spiritual activity—disciplined and deep—resonated with the Everyman organizers, who operated according to similar principles. In Brook's residency they recognized the minimal production requirements, the theater spaces created via delineated consecration, the parks bathrooms turned into dressing rooms. Dan Sullivan described *The Conference of the Birds* improvisations as attempts to achieve "life" in the theater through hard work and the combination of "the immediacy of street theatre with the depth of modern and naturalistic acting."[78] The work was abstract and uncomfortable, fused with questions and conflict, not answers and artifice.

Fresh from their workshops with Brook (who had directed the Royal Shakespeare Company's *A Midsummer Night's Dream* in London in 1970 and on Broadway in 1971), Ringkamp resuscitated the Everyman Street Theatre version of *A Midsummer Night's Dream* with renewed inspiration, using exercises developed through the teachings of the International Centre for Theatre Research. In his program notes for the Everyman's January 1974 production of *A Midsummer Night's Dream* at BAM, Ringkamp traced the production's conception from a Grotowski workshop with students at Bishop Ford Catholic High School in Park Slope, Brooklyn, four years prior. Using *Towards a Poor Theatre*, Ringkamp followed Grotowski's exercises, with *A Midsummer Night's Dream* as their guiding text. "Peter Brook was an inspiration. His gentle persuasiveness and genuine concern for art, plus his real desire for research and discovery, affected us all."[79] They dedicated their production to him.

The unique interaction between Brook and a street theater company from the edges of Brooklyn revealed one of the pressing questions posed by the Everyman's later activities: how can performance practices that germinate in neighborhoods "meet" new audiences and new stages? The social relations of theater both demonstrate and produce the city; BAM's role as a presenting organization with the resources to bring Brook's company together with Everyman, at a venue where Everyman performed months later, suggests a model for symbiosis between the two. At the height of the fiscal crisis, Fitzgerald and Ringkamp transcended limiting bureaucratic assumptions and instead enlivened the stages of BAM, an institution with strong municipal support, as a future cultural anchor and neighborhood revitalizer. Everyman enjoyed the opportunities this relationship conferred, and in turn complemented and refined BAM's developing mission. For many residents and theatergoers, desperate for signs of optimism, Everyman's profile—at once do-it-yourself and collaborative—projected a path to urban redemption through the arts. The Everyman-Community Street Theater Festival became another site, as well as a structure, that could connect the home neighborhoods of street theater troupes with the performance practices developing on stages throughout the boroughs.

Lincoln Center's Grand Gesture

While Coney Island's economic bases deteriorated, the Upper West Side neighborhood around Lincoln Center saw rising property values and retail expansion. This was in part due to Robert Moses's Lincoln Square Urban Renewal Project, the largest in the country, completed in 1969.[80] Although Lincoln Center symbolized for many a failed model for the building of new theaters, it still retained the cultural capital of an elite performance destination. The complex housed the Metropolitan Opera, the New York City Ballet, the Juilliard School, and seven other cultural organizations. Situated in walking distance to Central Park, its venues were frequented by the bow-ties-and-pearls set. This, as Marvin Carlson reminds us, is not a new formulation. The monumental theater (and especially the opera house) still function as "highly visible signs of civic dedication to the arts"—as defined by high bourgeois culture—which led many nineteenth-century theorists (Richard Wagner and Romain Rolland among them) to imagine instead populist theaters.[81]

The Lincoln Center Community-Street Theater festival mashed a populist undertaking with a "high art" civic center, and consequently altered perceptions through its presentation of both street theater and Lincoln Center. As an institution, Lincoln Center strained to build a reputation as a community resource, not destroyer. Given this, the street theater festival was a remarkable development in its history. Since the Mayor's Slum Clearance Committee (of which Robert Moses was chairman) designated Lincoln Square for urban renewal in 1955, the ambitious and idealistic arts project exhibited both the promise and the perils of the government program.[82] Moses admitted that the public purpose of Lincoln Center "was not to build theatres or to build anything else. The public purpose was to clear slums."[83] It was the 1970s by the time the majority of Lincoln Center's physical plants and programming initiatives launched, and it faced considerable financial hurdles and tumultuous leadership changes. The indoor theaters of Lincoln Center battled against budget deficits and cost overruns. Infrastructure problems required expensive solutions, paid for by the city, and challenged the bedrock commitment of the government (and its residents) toward the complex.

In August 1971 Fitzgerald, Ringkamp, Whitaker, and Bryant, co-coordinated the first Everyman-Community Street Theater Festival. Twice per day during the length of the festival, street theater troupes performed on an open platform in the Lincoln Center plaza, with the Metropolitan Opera building providing a majestic backdrop. Businessmen, mail carriers, day care groups, tourists, arts supporters, and teenagers all circulated through the square, stopping to take in the Harlem Children's Theater's *The Liberation of Mother Goose*, the People's Performing Company's *Power*, and the Cuban Cultural Center's *Fuera del Juego*.

In its first year, 3,000 audience members gathered in the plaza for the presentations by participating companies, which included Everyman companies, the Festival Repertory Company, and the Alonzo Players (*400 Years Overdue*). Yvonne Madison (also known as Lubaba Lateef), a student of Amiri Baraka, participated with her Brownsville Laboratory Theatre (*Variations of Freedom*). By the 1973 summer festival, troupes from Washington, D.C., Vermont, Maine, and Michigan joined a dizzying lineup of community and street theaters from around the city: Total Theater Company (*Street Show*), Brothers and Sisters United Repertory Theatre (*Insight*), Voices, Inc. (*Journey into Blackness*), Bed-Stuy Theater (*The Happy Ending*), Harlem Everyman Company (*Mr. Duvalier*), Puerto Rican Traveling Theatre (*Noo Jall*), and Afro-American Total Theatre (*Jimmy's Paradise*).[84] This mix produced interactions between neighborhoods and street theater groups, inverting the social structure of gangs spreading through the boroughs. John Brown Childs's language of "rooted affiliations" offers a set of strategies to move beyond "constraints imposed by interethnic fear, racism, misunderstanding," and captures the heterogeneity and cooperation so central to the success of the Everyman Street Theater Festival. Participants maintained their "emplacements of affiliation" while developing ties through the "shared practical action" of street performance festivals and touring plays.[85]

Historian Julia Foulkes describes the annual summer street festival as one of Lincoln Center's attempts to align its original, populist definition—to expand the definition of the arts and democratic ideals—with dramatic changes in the city's demographics.[86] In 1971 Lincoln Center hired a full-time liaison for community relations, Leonard de Paur, who pledged to "try to dissipate the resentment some people still have against Lincoln Center as a place only for the well-to-do."[87] The executive director of NYSCA, Eric Larrabee, feared since its inception that the arts complex "would become an isolated fortress, sealed off in monolithic separation from the city," and admitted that he "must have said all the mean things one can think of about Lincoln Center."[88] Through its outdoor hosting of performance groups representing some of the diversity of the city, Lincoln Center facilitated a transcommunal event that eventually forced Larrabee to admit to "eating crow" as an "enthusiastic convert" for the complex.[89]

Mel Gussow of the *New York Times* and mainstream theater critics wrote approvingly of the featured companies as "vital grass-roots community centers," but never quite acknowledged the full extent of their geographic and ideological diversity. The work at the Street Festival could not be easily categorized on the Off or Off-Off Broadway spectrum. Gussow expressed ambivalence about evaluating the street theater performances, which had a potential "traumatic effect on the audience" if it was the viewer's first encounter.[90] Many reviews ascribed antagonistic politics or militancy to the plays, and did not recognize or cite the clear stamp of Grotowski, Brook, or Baraka in many of the experiments. They rarely provided contextualization for the challenging works, such as Peter Copani's dark antidrug rock musical, *The Blind Junkie*, presented two years in a row at the street theater festival.[91] August Heckscher questioned this phenomenon of critics visiting Lincoln Center daily to write about the open-air performances, yet would not "bestir themselves to come into the streets" to watch the companies perform in their own neighborhoods.[92]

Just as most critics would not see a Brownsville company in Brownsville, or the Everyman Company on Surf Avenue, the companies hosted in Lincoln Square would never be transferred to one of the official Lincoln Center theaters. The separateness produced by this static inside/outside boundary remained a characteristic of the Street Theater Festival: small theaters fought for community control of spaces in their own neighborhoods, argued for critical recognition of their work, and then found a platform performing in the front yard of a centralized arts space. This fraught relationship between space and social relations birthed a performance of simultaneous inclusion and exclusion; the incongruity of an alternative theater group traveling from Coney Island to perform in the plaza of the master builder, a liminal space between the street and highbrow performance culture.[93]

The co-conveners of the Street Theater Festival discussed the drawbacks and dangers involved in collaborating with an "establishment" arts venue, but deemed the trade-offs worth the risks. Through the festival, companies met and influenced each other, performers learned that a structure existed for their work, and young people discovered *their* Lincoln Center. Ringkamp safeguarded its integrity by resisting monetary return. "As long as we don't charge people and as long as it doesn't get cornered into an arena in the streets, where there's a ticket taker—once you have a ticket taker, then I think the establishment will take it over."[94] This belief led to basic difficulties in the festival's continuing operations when outside support proved inconsistent. Though the festival doubled in size in its second year to include 1,500 performers, and its 1973 summer festival achieved record audience attendance and number of performances, it struggled with a drastically reduced budget. That year, festival organizers scrounged for donations of free sandwiches for their young performers while tens of thousands of spectators attended the outdoor events. De Paur had provided "seed money" in the festival's early years, but budget restrictions placed the burden on individual companies; they needed to cover their own transportation and lodging, and troupe organizers complained that their honorarium barely covered subway tokens for local companies. The United Brands Company supplied part of the $53,000 budget in 1972 (and also distributed free root beer and bananas), but after supporting two festivals, declined to sponsor the 1973 summer.[95]

Reviews remarked on the vulgarity of the language, the boldness of the material, and the antics of the boisterous crowds, who often shouted back to the actors on stage and at times even joined them on the platform. Amyas Ames, then chairman of the Lincoln Center Philharmonic-Symphony Society, described the Street Theater festival as equal in importance to their Mostly Mozart festival. Yet he contended with (and publicized) a "mounting crisis for the performing arts," which he distilled as one in which private sector gifts could no longer bear "the public burden of inflation."[96] These were, Hazel Bryant argued, merely excuses for the complete lack of financial support for the festival, a product of very specific decision-making. "The fact that the establishment has kept street theatre so poor has made it possible for us to still be very imaginative and very independent and still pretty much do what we want to do. Because we must, in order to make it happen at all. So, I don't see any great impressions on the horizon which point to big money and big buildings and Lincoln Centers of street theatre."[97]

Soon, however, street theater would not even enjoy a big outdoor stage. In August 1974, a new two-week festival replaced the Everyman Street Theater Festival: "Lincoln Center Out-of-Doors." On the surface, the 1974 and 1975 festivals echoed prior summers. At the 1974 opening event, 3,000 people gathered on the plaza. There were ice cream cones and colored balloons; senior citizens basked in the sunshine and mothers pushed their infants in strollers through the square. Geraldine Fitzgerald still held court, wielding a navy blue umbrella against the sun. The Exxon Corporation, NYSCA, and the Parks, Recreation and Cultural Affairs Administration sponsored an expanded lineup that now included jazz, chamber music, dance, and cabaret. Members of the Alliance of Latin Arts presented highlights from their musical, *Kismet*. Newly elected mayor Abe Beame replaced John Lindsay's thousand-watt presence and left immediately after the opening ceremony and speeches.[98]

For Lincoln Center, however, the motivations for the festival had been transformed. Instead of its driving need to improve community relations, it now embraced the mid-1970s refrain of the arts as urban uplift during a fiscal crisis. "At a time when the city's financial problems have left little cause for celebration, John W. Mazzola, managing director of Lincoln Center . . . pointed out 'how rich the city is—rich in talent, rich in people, rich in diversity, rich in the arts.' "[99] Abstract calls for unity run counter to the theory of transcommunality, which, John Brown Childs notes, grows out of "shared, practical action" in constant pursuit and fully cognizant of dispute and difference.[100] The new iteration of the festival privileged the ephemeral and immaterial dimensions of performance practices, and appreciated street theater for its ability to "perform the city," not communicate local complexities of neighborhood identity.

While media coverage occasionally mentioned its street theater roots, Lincoln Center Out-of-Doors soon bore little resemblance to its prior incarnation. In 1977 the *Times* insisted that "though many of the events presented during the three-week celebration are commercial, there remains a sense of the sprawling vitality of New York streets."[101] Rather than Whitaker's vision of "showing New Yorkers what the other parts of New York is doing,"[102] the festival was now described as "a gift" bestowed to the city from the NYSCA, the NEA, and the Exxon Corporation. Clowns, storytellers, and mimes replaced the dozens of street troupes. Companies from Europe, South America, and Asia dominated the schedule of events, and traveled to Lincoln Center with funding from supportive home governments. Rhetorically, the festival still pledged to "reach into every corner of the city," yet its basic composition changed. The *New York Times* reported on only one of four events for children, a play in Spanish. Previously, the street theater companies—comprised largely of youth—sought to speak to all ages and audiences, and bilingual troupes mixed in with all the others. These events now received niche billing, remarked on as exceptional.[103]

Through the city's crisis and the onset of austerity measures, Lincoln Center amplified these new characteristics of the festival. It altered the festival's objectives, and repositioned it as publicity directly connected to its year-round, indoor operations. Seasonal fare appeared in the out-of-doors schedule, as a kind of free tasting menu for gun-shy patrons and out-of-towners. After Robert Wilson's *Einstein on the Beach* sold out at the Metropolitan Opera House that year, the 1977 out-of-doors schedule showcased selections of the music performed by the Philip Glass Ensemble in Damrosch Park. The Tito Puente and Machito orchestras, a blues opera by liturgical jazz composer Paul Knopf, lunch hour with Billy Taylor and the Jazzmobile All-Stars, and a dinner concert performed by the St. Luke's Chamber Orchestra also made the bill. It had expanded into an ambitious summer festival with many merits—yet lacking street theater. By 1979, with tourism picking up, summer visitors ready to spend their money on Rum Rondos at the Avery Fisher Hall bar searched for the "center" of New York. They found it at Lincoln Center, where they could buy Mostly Mozart T-shirts, mugs, tote bags, and neckties, and see the Bolshoi and Stuttgart Ballet free of charge.

By 1983, Lincoln Center organized the festival according to discrete themes: a morning program advertised its "Spanish Flavor," with events like "Caribbean Expressions" featuring Latin arrangements of jazz classics and Fiesta Mexicana with folk dance companies, emceed by actor Carlos Montalbán.[104] Many spectators praised the matured festival, which now covered the entire sixteen-acre domain of Lincoln Center; the face of the Opera House was transformed into an outdoor film screen, and acrobats and jugglers hid around corners. In a sign that the festival had not necessarily come full circle but existed in a distant relationship to its origins, critic McCandlish Phillips described the Lincoln Center plaza during the summer of 1979 as the location where "Coney Island intersects Tuxedo Park."[105] Signs of Coney Island—the neighborhood—were difficult to find in the programming, however, with Phillips invoking nostalgia for Coney Island's public playground, now moved to the Upper West Side.

The transcommunal performance practices of these street theaters in the early 1970s meaningfully produced new definitions of the public space with altered social relations, not merely "accessible," but cogent of the spatial politics of the city. Rather than obscuring the social relations of space, the framing conditions of urgency traveled with the troupes, from their home neighborhoods to the Lincoln Center festival. As a stage to interact with and appear before others, the shift away from the street theater festival and its modes of representation signified a loss for many neighborhoods and artists. By the end of the decade, the arrangement between street theater and Lincoln Center looked more like the performance of altruism on the part of a mildly invested arts complex than a symbiotic relationship. Yet the efficacy of this street theater never stemmed from its ability to revise Lincoln Center's programming, or pressure nefarious real estate interests out of Coney Island, or deliver employment training and needed services. The transcommunal performance of the Everyman Street Theatre and its festival connected neighborhoods and artists, with Lincoln Center as a surprising platform to replace urban dispossession with interconnection.

Ringkamp took pains to clarify the difference between the Everyman Street Theatre and the Everyman festival: "the festival at Lincoln Center is not street theatre. It's taking street theatre out of the streets and giving it a showplace. Where it's most effective and where it's most beautiful is not at Lincoln Center at all."[106] Mical Whitaker maintained the same: "We're not talking about creating street theatre at Lincoln Center. To bring it to Lincoln Center was to give some sign of a commitment from the arts community, of which Lincoln Center represents sort of the crowning achievement."[107] The locus of its change was in interpersonal relationships, between performer and performer, performer and spectator, performer and sanctioned city space. The Out-of-Doors Festival continues to this day, but in the absence of a strong, decentralized infrastructure of neighborhood-based theater companies operating across the city, few aspects of the Everyman-Community Street Theater Festival could be replicated.

Busking

Coney Island lost Everyman, Bread and Puppet, and Marketa Kimbrell's Street Caravan. This reflected a wider dismantling of street performance troupes by the end of the decade. Samuel Hay considers the opening and closing ("like morning glories") of so many African American theaters in the 1970s, their average life span shorter than a pet canary's.[108] The obstacles Hay identifies are applicable across the spectrum of street theater companies: the frequent reliance on a single, highly motivated individual, the inability to mobilize continued support from fractured communities, policy disagreements, and troubles attracting and managing association boards. Prominent in the narrative of the demise of many street theater groups, however, is also the arrival of new municipal priorities for arts organizations, which disregarded the essential role of summer arts funding. The tacit agreement on the part of city officials that street theater could palatably calm the by-products of racial polarization lost much of its political support by the late 1970s, and this dovetailed with the austerity measures of the fiscal crisis. In 1976 the Parks Department announced budget cuts: grasses would not appear lush for the summer, the boardwalk would not be spruced up, and there would be fewer lifeguards and more litter. Vast sections of neighborhood and the amusement district of Coney Island were within the precinct of the Parks Department, which rendered it particularly vulnerable to this curtailment.

The city promised that an outdoor schedule of events in Coney would nonetheless proceed. "The Parks Department, as devastated as all the other city agencies by cutbacks in money and personnel—more devastated, in fact, than some—has managed to pull on its fraying bootstraps and step ahead with a vigorous summer schedule."[109] This rhetorical flourish, which personified the government as an individual in hard times, reflected one strain of urban neoliberal philosophy: the advancement of individual entrepreneurial freedom and skills within an institutional framework characterized by strong private property rights. The same school of thought that blamed spend-happy liberal governance for the city's bankruptcy maligned the artistic forms tethered too closely to liberal policies. If its social welfare provisions were unsustainable, so too were initiatives encouraging streets and parks as public spaces for the articulation of social justice goals that represented the demands of these segments of society. As a form, street theater was also highly susceptible to cuts and regulations: its outdoor performance venues, whether they were parks or playgrounds, suffered from the decline in the supervision or policing of those areas, which suffered from vandalism and disrepair. These realities, in turn, made fund-raising more challenging. The necessity of proper permits from overburdened city agencies also affected the performance that flourished before the fiscal crisis fallout. Street theater companies suffered from cutbacks to arts agencies as well as parks, and there was an ideological component of this retrenchment. While transcommunal arts initiatives were valued in the early part of the 1970s as mechanisms for urban regeneration, a resistance grew among many officials toward artists weaned on a 1960s-style aesthetic and political radicalism.

Political currents and cultural experiments of the 1960s had opened up the parks, but these gains were diminished during the financial crisis and resurgent conservatism. Historians Ray Rosenzweig and Elizabeth Blackmar note that following the evolution of city park spaces into public venues for mobilizing and expressing oppositional politics (during and after the fiscal crisis), these new democratic uses were largely foreclosed. After a decade of unprecedented expansion into parks through new forms of community control of public facilities, "the fiscal crisis of the 1970s provoked a questioning of such experiments and sharply undercut the city's commitment to public services—the maintenance of public parks among them."[110] After a 60 percent cut in Parks appropriations between 1974 and 1980, the department cut the summer workforce from 6,000 to fewer than 2,700.[111]

In the summer of 1976 corporations pulled up the bootstraps of the Parks Department, and increasingly focused their donations on large-scale urban revitalization projects. Pressure on corporations to improve levels of philanthropic donations had ramped up throughout the 1960s and early 1970s, and the exhortations of organizations like the Business Committee for the Arts had an effect.[112] Corporate arts foundations like Exxon philanthropic donated broadly—from Sunday radio broadcasts of the New York Philharmonic to tours of Merce Cunningham's dance group to a mural project on the Lower East Side—yet still routinely rejected applications for rough language or irreverent use of the American flag.[113] Street theater, with its fledgling infrastructure and raw subject matter, proved more suited to direct funding from city agencies than private foundations with little knowledge of individual neighborhood dynamics.

With 23 percent of Parks personnel lost along with $40 million in its capital budget funds, Parks Commissioner Martin Lang augmented its operations with scattershot private industry sponsorship. In Coney Island, Rheingold funded street Olympics, Pepsi backed a mobile tennis unit and a bike race, Mobil Oil sponsored a series of youth games, and French's Mustard offered a bike safety check. As the government increasingly turned to corporate interventions to fill the budgetary gaps of weakened agencies like the Parks Department, the media spin on the ailing amusement area of Coney Island worsened. The paper of record rarely deviated from the "bootstraps" discourse to describe the pitiful state of municipal provisions in the city, and this ideological frame enforced a larger message: just as the government would muster the determination of an individual down on his luck, so too should the citizens of the metropolis. But behind this turn of phrase was a literal draining of funds and continued systematic impoverishment of many outer-borough neighborhoods.

Another clear articulation of the sea change in the municipal attitude toward street theater across the decade is found in a city-produced book, *On the Streets: A Guide to New York City's Buskers*, released around 1979 by the Department of Cultural Affairs (DCA). The book opens on a populist note with an epigraph from a Pablo Neruda poem and an introduction from the DCA commissioner extolling the "liveliness and spirit" of the streets of New York City.[114] Yet the guide reports that the concept of street theater had already changed, "in that most of the groups are now hired to perform in set sites by groups such as Lincoln Center or the Department of Cultural Affairs."[115] It also suggests that the entire phenomenon had been swallowed by official mechanisms of the state and the monolithic civic center. The book's final section, "Theatrical Groups," includes blurbs for only seven street theater groups, alongside a concise explanation for the limited listing:

> The reason is that most theatrical groups are no longer performing informally and extemporaneously on local corners. They have come of age. Groups are organized with administrators and directors and they actively pursue public grants. These grants enable various funding organizations to program the theatre groups so that the South Bronx and South Ferry are served equally. . . . Historically, street theatre has been largely political in nature. The actor can assault the king, attack the taxes, or wreck Westway with comedy and symbols, without having to resort to directly pointing fingers or making speeches.[116]

This questionable narrative references new mechanisms that provide a more equitable distribution of public art funds when there was, in fact, a slow accrual of uneven development of performance practices across neighborhoods. The DCA's *Busking* publication acknowledged the tacit association of inner city performance with street agitation, but the text divorces performance from any place-based imperative or social concern. It expresses ambivalence about the overt political edge of much street theater, and fails to disguise a discomfort with the ability of street theater to animate the public dimension of the streets. It also omits one of the primary conceits of the form: to develop arts directly in underserved communities, and to represent resident-performers in their own territory. Street performance tapped into anxieties regarding the distribution of power in the city, particularly as experienced by the populations that bore the brunt of austerity measures.

By the end of the decade, the government was eager to redevelop Coney Island as a site more appropriate for casino speculation than populist performance efforts. Its residents suffered 20 percent unemployment and further degradation of Surf Avenue, fully aware of the contrast between city efforts elsewhere—that same summer, subway car interiors were repainted as the city polished its tarnished image. The city's political establishment could only be viewed through a prism of broken promises, men who "had let burned-out buildings stand and had allowed Surf Avenue to become a flea market on one side and a sleazy honky tonk on the other."[117] The long-standing problems persisted: from poorly maintained housing stock to police harassment to the lack of basic neighborhood amenities to limited funding for community organizations to few cultural options for youth, compounding systems of structured unevenness in the working-class neighborhood, and in the cultural life of Coney Island beyond its roller coasters. Meanwhile, as New York sweltered in record 101-degree temperatures, pleasure-seekers were heading to Coney Island in a phenomenon the press dubbed "half a tank" leisure: with gas prices spiraling and supply uncertain, Coney Island businesses experienced the best sales days in twenty years.[118]

From its inception in the late 1960s through the next decade, the Everyman Company had resisted the accelerated abandonment of the area through a strategy of linkages. However tenuous, its relationship to the municipal sphere preserved and modeled a form of service provision denied to residents. The Everyman Street Theatre offered a structure that related neighborhood youth to multiple points of the city fabric. As performance that addressed the affective inequalities embedded in the ravages of urban degradation and the compounding factors of fiscal crisis responses, Everyman Street Theatre questioned the logic of failed urban policies and divestment. As municipal enthusiasm for a decentralized model of theater waned, a phase of centralization emerged.

Part Three

✦

The Performance of Neighborhood

Chapter 5

✦

How the Public Became a Public

Joseph Papp's Civic Building

> The theatre, like education, needs the security and comfort, if you will, of inclusion in a Governmental budget. It may be attacked. It may be cut. But it is there to be defended and fought for. Any discussion of freedom of the theatre without considering its permanency is largely academic.
>
> —Joseph Papp, 1960

> All that we ask is that the City share the financial burden equally.
>
> —Joseph Papp, 1967

> We're doing a service to the city—it's like a garbage collection.
>
> —Joseph Papp, 1973

Joseph Papp took over the direction of Lincoln Center's Repertory Theater in 1973 when his reputation was at its height and his financial resources had fallen to a new low.[1] In handing him the keys to the Vivian Beaumont Theater at Lincoln Center, the rarefied world of arts institutions endowed Papp's downtown Public Theater with uptown cachet, and gave the ambitious producer a fund-raising platform for all of his enterprises. Lincoln Center's stalled repertory and the high-profile departure of its previous artistic directors allowed Papp to identify a new mission and aesthetic for the theater. With this coming on the heels of New York City's acquisition of his Public Theater and "selling" it right back to him for one dollar, Papp now ran *three* public arts institutions on city land: the Public Theater on Lafayette Street, the Delacorte in Central Park, and the Vivian Beaumont at Lincoln Center. Papp decided to reposition the Upper West Side's floundering Beaumont as a major and inclusive platform for living playwrights.

Papp's front-page dominance as New York's thespian media darling peaked in the 1970s; he was the ideal cultural spokesperson to lift the city's psyche out of its doldrums. Helen Epstein, his formidable biographer, describes Papp as the "de facto citizens' representative of many New Yorkers in despair over problems ranging from ever-larger potholes to interracial violence."[2] While Papp's admirers already considered him a "municipal hero,"[3] the challenge of establishing a viable theater at Lincoln Center (located at West 65th Street and Broadway) demanded new money and new audiences, and, Papp believed, a turn toward its diverse neighboring communities.

In its troubled first decades, the Beaumont had thrown its own "democratic" aspirations to the winds: as Julius Novick chronicled, "[Robert] Whitehead and [Elia] Kazan did nothing to allay a widespread suspicion that Lincoln Center was to be the exclusive preserve of the upper-middle class and the rich."[4] The fountain in the center of Lincoln Square symbolized the arts and culture of the elite as well as the bulldozing of residential communities in the service of urban renewal. John D. Rockefeller III's vision of "arts for the people" now looked like well-to-do passengers in evening wear stepping out of rows of taxis to attend a Mozart Festival, or the latest opening at the Metropolitan Opera.

For his first production at the Beaumont, Papp compounded his risky decision to produce David Rabe's *In the Boom Boom Room*, a dark play about a victimized go-go dancer, with a surprising pick for its director: Julie Bovasso. As a fixture on New York's avant-garde theater scene since the 1950s, she appeared to be even more incongruous with Lincoln Center's ethos than Rabe, who had won the Tony Award for best play in 1972. Yet Bovasso was cartographically attractive, conferring experimental theater credibility on a Euro-aesthetic shaped via East Village productions of Ionesco, Genet, de Ghelderode, and the recently returned Living Theatre from their edgy American exodus. Papp's production of *In the Boom Boom Room* collapsed dramatically. Most accounts of Papp's dismissal of Bovasso—just before previews—blame the disastrous course of events on Santo Loquasto's set, Julie Newmar's acting, Rabe's overwriting, and Bovasso's direction. At the time, the press attributed the play's difficulties to the implosion of Papp's relationship with Bovasso. Yet a range of social interactions between Lincoln Center and its subscribers, and Papp and his audiences, had foretold of larger troubles.

Papp's crusade to revive the Beaumont reveals the dynamics of theaters as institutions beholden to social, political, and financial constraints. Papp's institutions often required the mobilization of theatrical publics in service of their own survival, and his theaters became a stage for civic discourse about the relationship between residents and city-supported performance. Papp envisioned a theater at Lincoln Center that might tear down the walls of racial and cultural segregation so present across the city. But in order to build such a space, he needed to convince audiences and city power brokers that his theaters already enjoyed—and could attract—the support of a diverse coalition of audiences. Without this, his arguments for the content of his "public" theater—which hinged on access—remained hollow. Rosalyn Deutsche, in her analysis of public art, notes the political contradictions inherent in formulations of democratic aesthetic practices, which can facilitate real critique of dominant ideologies. But, if we

> fail to think of democracy as a social practice challenging the omnipotence of power through the extension of specific rights, discourses of democracy can also be successfully mobilized to compel acquiescence in new forms of subordination. Stuart Hall has described a mobilization of this kind and given it a name—"authoritarian populism."[5]

While Joseph Papp did not subscribe to Hall's "authoritarian populism," the concept provides insight into Papp's contradictory role as a steward of democratic theatrical practices during the early 1970s. In this decade, unlike Papp's earlier interventions in the city's arts landscape, Papp confronted shifting discourses of democracy, and a very different status of public opinion toward the theater as an active space of citizenship.

Hall's term sought to explain a "swing to the right" in Margaret Thatcher's Britain, in which formal representative institutions remained, constructed around active popular consent, with a weakening of democratic forms and initiatives, "but not their suspension."[6] One of the precipitating conditions of this form of the capitalist state was, Hall argued, recession and crisis management. To a degree, Papp recognized similar changes afoot in New York. He operated and expanded his theaters at a period in which the city, desperate to convince its own residents of its livability, challenged Papp's positioning as a populist force. Questions about the public nature of Papp's three theaters became both more entrenched and embattled during the fiscal crisis. In response, the theaters both relied upon and attempted to break down the public/private dichotomies of the theatrical sphere. He targeted those audiences less likely to attend performing arts events in the city's cultural spaces, and yet his appeals for city funding threatened to reshape his theaters toward the interests of the elite and the needs of politicians.

From his earliest efforts producing Shakespeare on the Lower East Side and untested playwrights at his Public Theater on Lafayette Street, he wanted his work to reach audiences "behind the cultural barriers" as "democracy in action."[7] Once installed at the Beaumont, Papp pushed relevant and often controversial subjects to the fore through the work of his young playwrights, but struggled to locate his public as audiences chose their own definitions of the "public space" of Lincoln Center. Despite his attempts to the contrary, his tenure at the arts complex only reified notions of the city's theater institutions as catering to an elite stratum of "Culture Mongers,"[8] and revealed the theater's own board of directors as working at cross-purposes to Papp's democratic ideals.

Yet in desperate times, Papp also defended these theaters as democratic institutions by virtue of their public funding, regardless of social practices.

This formed a pattern across his career at large city-funded organizations, during which he succeeded in securing theater as something to be championed and fought for, but also to be criticized and attacked. In the late 1950s, and again in the mid-1960s, Papp initially sought only cooperation from the city. Its regulations and shifting loyalties signaled a nuisance, and even a loss of freedom. Later, when Papp's operation expanded, residents—anxious about city funds and their equitable distribution—claimed ownership over Papp's production choices. The role of arts institutions in civic society became as embattled as the corollary debate over funding for the arts. Papp produced new plays at the Public Theater that became as much the aesthetic provenance of popular and political opinion as his Broadway musicals.

Surprisingly, there has been little theorizing of director/producer Papp as a cultural power broker who influenced decades of decisions by New York's city and state governments, national and individual philanthropic sources. His intense personality and storied ego combined with his vast accomplishments and have engendered largely hagiographic treatments of his career. A heroic narrative shaped Papp's media reception as early as 1953, when a youthful Papp waged a well-publicized battle with Parks Commissioner Robert Moses. Moses became Papp's bureaucracy-obsessed Goliath when he demanded that Papp charge admission to his free summer Shakespeare festival in Central Park. Papp enjoyed a hard-won victory, and his resistance to Moses made the front pages for nearly a year. Even Papp, however, chafed at the extent to which his feud with Moses, in addition to his musical theater hits, dominated his biography.[9] This treatment of Papp's legacy perhaps speaks to a continued interest in obsolete notions of a public as an essentially coherent space; Papp's achievements in prime real estate acquisition, however, illuminate the social conflicts that produced his performance spaces.

This heroic narrative nestles Papp within a framework of populist theatrical triumphalism and assumed social efficacy. A "poor ghetto kid" from Brooklyn, Joseph Papirofsky gets his start organizing skits in the Navy, on the U.S.S. *Solomons*.[10] From the band shell of the East River Amphitheatre he moves to a traveling flatbed truck, to Central Park, to the Public Theater on Lafayette and East Eighth, and ultimately Broadway. In this telling, his stint at Lincoln Center represents a satisfying culture clash, further evidence that Papp was too *of the people* to placate the stuffy suits on Lincoln Center's board and old-fashioned grey-hairs in the audience. But two of these ambitious ventures—the Public Theater and the Beaumont—offer unique examples of the conjoining of the public and commercial theater realm. Conservatives utilized the fiscal crisis framework to argue that the generous social services endemic to New York's democratic urban culture could no longer be afforded; by that time, Papp had spent decades mounting the case for theater as a social good and city service. This raises larger questions about the culture-state nexus, particularly whether theater defined in Papp's terms necessarily sidestepped the identification of competing publics, and, more importantly, whether his reliance on the language of democracy to further the aims of his theater actually weakened its status.

Papp's Progressive Capitalism

> Joseph Papp has taken over City Hall and is spending New York's entire budget on free Shakespeare. Assistant Mayor Lindsay is running the rest of the town from the Delacorte Theater in the park.
>
> —*New York Times*, 1968[11]

The concept of "public" forms a specter over Joseph Papp's decades of producing theater in New York City, somewhat akin to its usage within performance theory. Though they are not coterminus, conceptualizations of the audience as public have developed from the Habermasian model of the bourgeois public sphere to Michael Warner's notion of alternative "counterpublics," to Janelle Reinelt's defense of cultural practices that create new publics.[12] Raymond Williams advocated a range of classifications of institutions, rather than the narrow formulas of "the artist" and "his public."[13] Christopher B. Balme's *The Theatrical Public Sphere* is one of the few (and most recent) examples of scholarship that directs historiographical attention to the *institution* and its relationship to fragmentation of the public sphere.[14] Balme interrogates the seeming contradiction between institutions as representative of the status quo and theater as subversion, and Papp's iconoclastic producing projects exemplified these tensions.

Papp's short tenure running the Beaumont Theater at Lincoln Center during the early 1970s also supports Balme's contention that debates over theater often express concerns regarding institutional change, rather than responses to the content of specific plays. The hostility Papp inspired attested to the increasingly virulent feelings around the nature of the arts as public or private in New York City. Papp made his appeals for new theatrical structures at a historical moment when the municipal state's ability to deliver public services was under attack, and, as a consequence, released antagonism toward the changing role of theater institutions at this time.

Papp had long dreamt of a municipal theater and civic center that might attract audiences representative of the city's diversity. Papp established his Shakespeare Workshop in 1954 in a small church on the Lower East Side with a few hundred dollars. He began presenting versions of Shakespeare's plays around the city parks in 1956, and in Central Park in 1957. The city-sponsored Delacorte Theater opened in 1962 in Central Park, which provided the New York Shakespeare Festival (NYSF), Papp's umbrella group for his summer theater in Central Park, with a secure foothold. In 1964 Papp added a Mobile Theater Unit to tour the city's five boroughs. Next, Papp began renovating the landmarked Astor Place Library downtown at 425 Lafayette Street to be the home base of operations for the NYSF and his Public Theater.[15] Papp opened the first season at the Public (1967–68) with the wildly successful love-rock musical *Hair*.

Papp had long described his as a "quasi-official" relationship with the city, and, after early funding from the state Education Department, he had approached New York City's Board of Estimate for money as early as 1958.[16] Between 1959 and 1970, the NYSF raised a total of $9,124,700, and the city (through a variety of city agencies and funding mechanisms) contributed only $2,865,500 of that amount; throughout, Papp remained uncompromising in his policy of a free summer theater. The purchase of the Astor Library only exacerbated the Public Theater's constant precariousness, and the NYSF was "desperate" for money throughout this period.[17]

Papp had spent the prior decade insisting that the city should contribute to his free theater, and while he received occasional municipal funds for operating expenses, mayoral administrations preferred to provide operating money to time-weathered institutions in city-owned facilities. Parks Commissioner August Heckscher encouraged Papp to adopt the strategy that had worked at Carnegie Hall in 1960: persuade the city to buy the Astor Library and lease it back to him. In 1965 city law created the Landmarks Preservation Commission, and Papp tapped into the trend toward "adaptive reuse" of threatened structures in order to appeal to the city for help. Heckscher had intimate knowledge of the arcane rules of funding programs: politicians often boasted of the money they spent, and yet, at the same time, had to place enormous obstacles in the way of its disbursement. The capital budget "was a political rather than an economic document, a weird way of communicating with various city constituencies."[18] But what would the acquisition of the Public Theater communicate to which city constituency?

Papp recognized the great difference between "the relative plenty of capital funds, which were raised by bonds, and the scarcity of current spending or tax funds."[19] He devised a plan in which the city would buy the Public Theater building from the NYSF, and Papp in turn would enjoy some consistency of city funding, regardless of administrative whims or the economy's health. Papp's journey to become the city's tenant stretched from March 1967 to April 1971. Papp knew that in return for financial support, publicly owned facilities are mandated "to provide cultural services accessible to all New Yorkers."[20] His NYSF was among the most highly publicized free theater activities in the city—and Robert Moses had helped make it thus. Yet by 1971, Papp's associate producer Bernard Gersten described his and Papp's operating philosophy as one of "progressive capitalism."[21] This philosophy stared down a mood of austerity in the City Council chambers, and from the ensuing friction, Papp's brand of "public" emerged.

Essential components of the unique relationship between Papp's institutions and the city of New York are the ideological contents of progressive capitalism and the brand of public it secured. While structuring at the city level seems perhaps peripheral to performance practices, it is in fact central to Papp's "public," and, more broadly, to the relationship between theaters and the city at this time. The private-public partnership of city-owned cultural institutions in New York began in 1869 and has long been an exclusive club. There exist today only thirty-three of these institutions located on city-owned property, and receiving significant capital and operating support from the city. Major cultural institutions had traditionally been built upon officially designated city parkland that the city provided to a group of patrons, clearing the way for philanthropists to develop an institution of the highest order. These were then considered the primary mechanisms for the delivery of "high culture," located on city land. Papp joined this group of institutions when the city agreed to own the land upon which his institutions sat, no different from the Metropolitan Museum of Art, or the Bronx Zoo. Because of this, Papp eroded the boundaries between commercial theater and public theater spaces, and used the very resources of the city to redefine "public theater" for a municipality in crisis.

Papp needed to persuade the mayor, comptroller, borough presidents, and City Council of the merits of the building purchase. He could only do so with evidence that the Public Theater had the support of the public it claimed to serve. During Papp's quest to secure the Public Theater its own line in the city budget, he criticized the special interest items and pork barrel spending necessary for Mayor John Lindsay to pass a budget, and Papp learned to utilize the media to promote (and occasionally misrepresent) his arrangements with city agencies. Lindsay's assistants argued that the financial burdens of the city prevented them from helping Papp on the scale he desired, and they suggested private, state, and federal financing instead. They also continued to press Papp to charge admission to Shakespeare in the Park, which Papp had long rejected; in addition to Papp's philosophical opposition, he publicly acknowledged that many of his funders gave money precisely *because* it was free, and would abandon the theater if it abandoned its mission. The announcement that Thomas P. F. Hoving would begin to charge admission to the Metropolitan Museum of Art enraged Papp: "What you and they propose is to chip away at this basic freedom in the name of economic policy. . . . A city like New York, which lives and thrives in an environment served in the main by cultural resources—a 2½ BILLION dollar operation if it is necessary to put into money terms—must be served and supported."[22] The text from Papp's letter demonstrates his insight into the government's crisis mentality, as he observed austerity ideology in its earliest incarnations.

Beyond ethical obligation, Papp rightly intuited that the city's image crisis coexisted with its manifold civic and economic crises, within which the fate of his theater might be decided. In a letter to Mayor Lindsay praising the NYSF, two New Yorkers gushed over "moments like the ones at the plays, sitting there in the beautiful outdoor theater," that entice them to "stay in the city despite all the crime and dirt."[23] Lindsay replied to their letter of support with a seemingly unnecessary assurance that the NYSF was not a burden on taxpayers: "Indeed, Mr. Papp and the City are engaged in a partnership to enrich the cultural lives of our citizens at little or no cost to the taxpayer. We plan to continue that endeavor and expand on it whenever possible."[24] This crude philosophy of arts funding—as little financial input as possible, enjoying as many of the benefits as possible—infuriated Papp, who remained bullish in his expectations of city politicians. Papp threatened to dissolve the Public Theater if financial assistance did not arrive in the form of the Astor Library building sale, and he forecast a less livable city: "A tear or two might be shed at our departure; a few voices raised—but in a very short time the overwhelming problems of living in this city will bury all sorrow under an avalanche of polluted air, traffic jams, income tax, race riots and rotten buildings."[25]

"FREE" had become the cry of Papp's revolution. To further induce Lindsay to propose the building acquisition, Gersten and Papp staged an all-night, eleven-hour performance of the play *War of the Roses* (Shakespeare's *The Chronicles of King Henry VI* and *Richard III*) at the Delacorte. The event concluded with a jazz greeting to the sunrise in "celebration of the idea that Free Shakespeare must survive despite war, pollution, and budget cuts."[26] The event publicized what Papp called "a direct threat" to his survival—the construction company renovating the Astor Library would take over the building unless they paid their bills. Mayor Lindsay finally agreed to propose an amendment to purchase the Astor Library building for $5.1 million: $2.6 million for the building, and $2.5 million to pay for the alterations to date and the completed restoration.

Papp and his staff commenced a campaign of political lobbying in preparation for the November 13, 1970, Board of Estimate hearing on the acquisition of the Public Theater. They knew the five borough presidents who sat on the powerful (and now defunct) board would chafe at the idea of providing millions of dollars to purchase a theater building in Manhattan. In response to a letter in support of the sale from literary agent Audrey Wood, Sanford D. Garelik, the president of the City Council, wrote, "although the City still faces a severe financial crisis, I hope the means can be found to continue this valuable program."[27] It is worth noting that Garelik wrote these words in 1970; Papp and Gersten therefore received this "crisis" response to funding requests for years before the "official" fiscal crisis broke in the summer of 1974. By then, Papp was understandably unimpressed by the reasoning the city provided for denying his appeals. Garelik's letter also highlights the ways in which the city's perpetual crisis mirrored the Public Theater's own chronically unstable financial footing. Parks Commissioner Heckscher summed up the city's appraisal of Papp as "constitutionally unable to exist anywhere except the outer limit of a tenuous financial branch—and some thought he made it a practice to saw away at that branch assiduously."[28] The practice of deficits in arts organizations would soon become as politicized as it was on the municipal stage.

The theater elite bombarded the board with letters in support of the city's acquisition of the theater. The letters arrived at City Hall from artists around the world (Peter Brook and Jerzy Grotowski), homegrown celebrities (Barbra Streisand), producers (Harold Prince and Harvey Lichtenstein), and politicians (Congressman Ed Koch and Senator Jacob Javits). Papp designated a group of speakers to appear at the hearing: producers Stuart Ostrow and David Merrick, actors Julie Harris and George C. Scott, and architect Giorgio Cavaglieri. These testimonials established the Public Theater as an internationally respected institution, known from Cairo to Saigon, Paris to Rome. This influence, they argued, stemmed from the people's ownership of the NYSF, made possible by its lack of admission charge. In his remarks, actor George C. Scott conceded "the staggering burdens, the monumental civic and social human problems which face the government of the city of New York today," but proclaimed that without the Public Theater, New York would be a "lesser city, a saddened and deprived citizenry, and a government of disquietude and dissatisfaction with itself and its acts."[29] In the case to justify the expenditure, the cosmopolitan credentials of the NYSF had limited reach; Papp needed to persuade the politicians of the Public Theater's relevance to communities in all of the boroughs.

A gulf emerged between the theory of the people as cooperative owners of the Public Theater and the voices heard by the Board of Estimate. The extensive public debate around the sale occurred largely in opinion pages and via these telegrams from artists of international stature. None of Papp's defenders at City Hall represented the people "behind cultural barriers" to which Papp often alluded. While persuasive to some, the strong showing of the city's artistic elite forced Papp to clearly define his audience, and to satisfy the government's generic demands for "cultural accessibility" in its arts organizations. The challenge was therefore to make that public visible, for the making of the Public Theater would have little to do with international admiration. The Public Theater staked out a rhetorical position in which it was a bulwark against barbarism, as well as an institution that could shore up the city's sense of itself by constituting a form of service provision.

The press and theatrical community had lauded Papp for his policy of interracial casting of Shakespeare; now he needed to prove that his years of presenting these works in the parks and playgrounds of the five boroughs had amassed a diverse following that might organize in the name of the Public Theater. In addition to free Shakespeare mounted at the Delacorte Theater in Central Park, Papp's touring wing of the NYSF, the Mobile Theater Unit, attracted upward of 70,000 people per summer with free performances of classical fare throughout the five boroughs. Papp referenced his traveling summer theater often when rallying the city for funding: "It is unfortunate that the two programs that will be directly effected [*sic*] by budget cuts are the Spanish Language production of *Volpone* on the Mobile Theater and the New York City school tour of *Hamlet*."[30] But while Papp committed early to this model, he was certainly not the only touring outfit in town. Numerous companies jostled for street corners during this period, including the Negro Ensemble Company's street theater workshop, Teatro de Tripas (Gut Theatre), the New York Free Theatre, and the Soul and Latin Theater (SALT). In the pages of *Cue* magazine, Marilyn Stasio frequently described the varying degrees of "committed, enthusiastic amateurism" of street and community theaters, alongside those with "more tangible ties to artistic professionalism," such as Vinnette Carroll's Urban Arts Corps, the Greenwich Mews Spanish Theater, the Afro-American Studio, and Miriam Colón's Puerto Rican Traveling Theatre.[31] Papp was therefore not the only artistic director providing affordable performance events across the city. And he was not alone in demanding the theater respond to the concerns of the streets on stage. He was perhaps the best at translating those activities into the need for a permanent, enclosed theater space.

The absence at the hearings of figureheads from these parallel organizations remains a glaring footnote. Not one of the member theaters of the soon-to-be-formed Black Theater Alliance of New York (BTA)[32] spoke in support of the sale of Papp's theater, nor did representatives from nearby neighborhood performance spaces. This was likely related to competition for new plays; to maintain currency in the landscape of new work, Papp now competed with theaters like La Mama and Theater Genesis, both on the Lower East Side, for the strongest new writers.[33] Papp claimed his theater as *the* Public Theater, but this was, in retrospect, potentially politically unnecessary, as well as disingenuous. It argued for a centralized vision of one public theater, whose reach across a city the size of New York remained debatable. Papp's argument for the building purchase did not attempt to marshal the energies of the stratified landscape of companies, but rather to set aside his operations as deservedly public.

As evidence, Papp enumerated community supporters in Manhattan, Brooklyn, Bronx, Queens, and Richmond, which included the Harlem Cultural Council and the Bronx Council on the Arts.[34] Papp and Gersten arrived at the hearing with twelve talking points focused on its free and low-cost activities. Most drew attention to the representation of people of color in the NYSF's award-winning seasons, and emphasized film and theater events with black writers, actors, and technicians.[35] Papp and Gersten provided the board with materials underscoring the building's "democratic" activities, including the Anthology Film Archives and Cinema; the Photography Workshop for disadvantaged youth under the direction of *Time* photographer Benedict J. Fernandez; and the Cinque Gallery, committed to first exhibition of works by black and minority group professional artists, directed by Romare Bearden and Ernest Crichlow.

Papp's campaign failed to sway the Board of Estimate. The Board rejected Lindsay's proposal to purchase the Public Theater's landmark building, the Astor Library, for $5.1 million, with the intent of leasing it back to Papp for one dollar. Votes on the Board of Estimate were apportioned such that Mayor Lindsay, Controller Abraham Beame, and Garelik each had four votes, and each of the five borough presidents had two. Papp received only the support of Lindsay and Manhattan Borough President Percy Sutton. Papp complained that many of the politicians making the decision—including Mayor John Lindsay—had never seen a performance at the Public Theater.[36] The Board of Estimate was a powerful arbiter of land use issues and budgetary concerns, and it fielded requests for zoning changes, sidewalk cafes, and purchases of buildings for city child care facilities. What did they know of culture?

Further, the issue that would lead to the downfall of the Board of Estimate in a 1989 Supreme Court case—that the most populous boroughs received no greater share of representation than the least populous—certainly fed Papp and Gersten's frustration. Why should Staten Island receive equal say in this decision as Manhattan? The borough presidents responded with skepticism to the mythology of Papp's theater as expanding the cultural opportunities of residents in the outer boroughs. For local politicians, the sale would not be a point of pride; "this was one expenditure they would just as soon soft-pedal in Queens."[37] The protestations of these outer-borough representatives revealed fundamental questions about the role of city funding for a theater whose programming reach they believed remained limited to one borough: Manhattan.

The conflict between Papp's Public Theater and the Board of Estimate therefore held implications beyond the money at stake. Whereas Papp's earlier pleas for funding related to a more recognizably "public" good—theater in the parks—he now suggested that he could create such a theater in a static location, and needed the city's help to pay for the building. This theater met its public not in the space of a park or a playground, but in a singular location; its public had to be constructed discursively, at the hearings, by Papp and his advocates. Garelik and Beame viewed the mayor's proposal on behalf of the Public Theater as "exorbitant,"[38] and felt deceived upon realizing that the money was not for Papp's theater in Central Park, but rather for the Astor Library, a large legitimate theater. The latter still required future stable revenue sources for its sizable array of programming once the building sale and renovation were paid for; would those also come from public sources?

The dynamics of city politics during a turbulent social and financial time also impeded the approval of the building acquisition. The *Times* described a "mood of austerity and asperity" during the vote against the $5.1 million plan; the Board of Estimate voted the same day to withhold support from four Lindsay administration neighborhood programs.[39] This particular vote came with a loaded history: the Board of Estimate had previously acceded to pressure from the Lindsay administration and approved the destruction of fifty-nine homes in Corona, Queens, to make room for a new high school. After major protests, Lindsay unveiled an alternative, leaving board members bruised by the resulting media depiction of Lindsay as the savior of their failed plan. When the board voted to withhold support from four neighborhood projects the same day the Public Theater acquisition decision, they were seeking available means of reprisal against Lindsay: those were his signature projects, part of his attempts to deliver services more directly to neighborhoods suffering from years of neglect. The rejection of Lindsay's proposed amendment to purchase the Astor Library further communicated these political disagreements between members.

The board reiterated its support for free Shakespeare in Central Park (to which the city would still contribute $350,000), an easier arts pill to swallow. Good for publicity and cheaper than a building, summer Shakespeare in the Park carried the distinction of being considered educational theater. The production of new plays at the Public Theater was another matter. The politicians on the board also argued that Papp's deficits since purchasing the Astor Library had nothing to do with the city. The hundreds of thousands of dollars the Public Theater owed to its contractors and on the building's mortgage became a plot point: the *New York Post* denounced Papp as a money-wasting nuisance who wanted the city to take a debt-ridden Off Broadway theater off his hands.[40] All roundly ignored the programming Papp emphasized at the hearing as socially generative. The focus became Papp's debt.

After the original proposal was defeated, Papp and Gersten pared down the Capital Budget Amendment to $2.6 million, the actual cost of the building and renovations, excluding necessary work to be completed. In the media, Papp doubled down on his position that in its rejection of the plan, the city withheld a necessary service. "As long as the garbage is still being collected, our deal with the city must go through."[41] Mayor Lindsay offered lukewarm support for the new plan, but when Papp brought his appeal to the City Council Committee, members questioned why local needs more modest than Papp's request were being denied. Papp argued that positioning needs like park improvements alongside the survival of a cultural institution was a false comparison, but politicians measured every request against their own stalled projects. They were—and not surprisingly, given the imperatives of holding public office—more concerned with their districts and boroughs than with a vision for a centralized public theater. In November 1971 Papp was again told that the deal was off; the city was in a financial crisis and the money was not there for the giving.

Papp's continued attempts to reignite the plan suggest that he recognized the errors in his earlier advocacy. In a letter to the Public Theater's emergency committee in advance of the next vote, Papp recounted that when the amendment was initially defeated, Manhattan Borough President Percy Sutton asked him a pointed question: "Where are your supporters?"[42] The answer, Papp realized, could not take the form of Sir John Gielgud or Helen Hayes.

While he again requested wires from celebrities and esteemed New Yorkers, and wrote urgently to council members across the boroughs, he would not again underestimate the locally savvy political performance required to curry the favor of borough pols.

Papp now framed his fight as a grassroots struggle, not just as theater for the invisible civic sphere. He equated the preservation of the Public Theater building with the protests to preserve the threatened homes in Queens—the contentious issue that dominated the agenda of their first, failed hearing: "People changed the fate of the Corona houses; people can save the Public Theater."[43] Rather than emphasizing the loss of a building, Papp spoke of the loss of "the belief that even in a time of political conflict and economic upheaval there is some quality of life which is worth preserving that we can call cultural—but not in any elitist sense. . . . I see the theater as one of the common amenities of life, like a library or a water supply."[44] This swiftly became the mantra of the campaign—theater not just as free, but provided, as water, or trash collection. Papp's campaign to induce the city to purchase his building seized on a critical narrative: public theater needed to combat urban impoverishment and fiscal conflict.

Convinced of the need to render the Public Theater's constituencies legible, Papp filled the chambers at the next hearing with "his public": he bussed young people to City Hall from all five boroughs while also soliciting letters of support from real estate developers, senators, and Broadway producers. Every one of Papp's advocates attested that his initiatives created positive change across the five boroughs during a time of urban discord. Flyers broadcast his appeal across lampposts and doorways of downtown Manhattan: "Save the PUBLIC THEATER—AGAIN!" In addition to major producers such as the Shubert organization's Irving Goldman and actor Robert Montgomery, Papp brainstormed long lists of acquaintances at every level of city life: Doris C. Freedman of Citizens for Artist Housing, Jacqueline Ceballos of the National Organization of Women and the New Feminist Theater, theater director Osvaldo Riofrancos, Community Planning Board members Ruth Wittenberg and Jerrold Ross, and J. Michael Miller, a dean at New York University's School of the Arts.

For Papp's March 11, 1971, return visit to the Board of Estimate, testimonials of Broadway producers shared the stage with Papp's extensive list of speakers. Director Elia Kazan argued that Papp's theater needed support because of Broadway's diminishment. "If we, the citizens of this city, allow [Papp's] endeavor, the Public Theater, to go down, we will be allowing the image of our city as the artistic center of this country to further shrink."[45] Some of the politicians remained unimpressed, and even took umbrage at theatrics: Deputy Brooklyn Borough President John F. Hayes commented, "I have seen some turkeys produced by some people who have spoken here today, birds that could not even adorn a Thanksgiving table."[46] With this backing of established producers and theater professionals, the Public

Theater resembled a for-profit company supported by the city's white-shoe crowd. Queens Borough President Sidney Leviss asked Papp if any members of his theater's board of directors lived outside of Manhattan, to which Papp responded indignantly. Despite his desire to define his theater within the language of cultural accessibility, Papp realized his audience at the hearing did not understand how the building sale might contribute to the same goals as his neighborhood-hopping Mobile Unit.

The politicians pushed Papp to his limits, and Papp's recollection of their final insult revealed the tensions embedded in his plan: "They were setting up all sorts of conditions and saying they wanted representatives from Queens and from the Bronx to determine this and determine that. That's one thing I cannot tolerate, when someone tries to tell me how to run the organization."[47] Furious, Papp left the hearing room. Gersten took the floor to repair the damage. The board deferred action, but on March 25, they voted unanimously to buy the Public Theater for $2.6 million and lease it back to the Public Theater for one dollar. This final Board of Estimate hearing is remembered for Papp's hotheaded walkout, with Gersten playing "good cop" to his bad. But Leviss's suggestion that so infuriated Papp—representation from his "culturally starved" borough on the Public Theater's board—did not overstate the case. With two million residents and nominal cultural institutions, Queens was nearly famished. Leviss's concerns were clear—what would he have to offer his constituents from the sale, save an invitation to take the subway from Queens to see a potential turkey at the Public Theater?

Papp had successfully negotiated the debate over the mission and objectives of his various theaters to fit the needs of politicians desperate to offer culture to all while raising the city's profile. Flyers for a pro-Public Theater rally at City Hall Park excerpted an open letter from former *Times* critic Brooks Atkinson. He attested to the caliber of the productions and the educational dimension of the Public Theater's operations:

> The young people in the box office, the young ushers, the young men who receive the public at the door are civil, have excellent manners and are personally attractive. The morale of the staff is conspicuously high. There is a reason for that. They know that the Public Theater is on the level and that it does not serve the personal ambitions of any person or the interests of any group but the public. It is a public service organization with the highest motivation.[48]

To the cries for a "public theater," Atkinson added "public service." His oddly phrased pitch signaled the approval of a cosmopolitan elite and the confirmation that the Public Theater offered an experience of spectatorship not dissimilar from Broadway or Lincoln Center. The continued institutionalization of the Public Theater would be accompanied by particular kinds of theatergoing, cultural performance, and interactions. Within that, Atkinson carefully constructed the theater as a public service.

Eventually, Papp's reputation as the man who delivered Shakespeare to the Lower East Side, the city, and even the nation, added to the prestige of the Public Theater as an entity ready to join the storied arts institutions of the city. As Kazin and Scott argued, the Public Theater offered a chance to convince residents—and a skeptical nation—that exciting cultural horizons were still to be found in New York. The decision to commit millions of dollars to Papp's enterprise set the tone for many conversations about the reach and value of "public" theater to come. It also sparked a continuing debate among theater organizations and artists. While many of his contemporaries revered Papp for his bold successes at the helm of the NYSF, others responded bitterly to Papp's "multimillion-dollar dominance over New York theater" that the city amply subsidized.[49] The year that the building sale received approval, the city gave $350,000 to *all* neighborhood arts programs combined, and even those funds were in jeopardy. Mere months after Papp received his one-dollar building, a "city fund crisis" forced the Department of Cultural Affairs to cut its staff from 28 to 6.[50] The Astor Library and Papp's summer productions received many hundreds of thousands of dollars, while the neighboring Lower East Side Community Workshop received just $538 in the 1973–74 fiscal year.[51]

By this period, many independent producers understood commercial producing as the means by which they could support nonprofit operations; yet Papp had the good fortune to leverage a formerly city-owned landmarked building in his efforts to do so. The Public Theater, now on city land, became even *more* public when the city completed its purchase, but not without sacrifice. This strategy of using capital funds for the purchase of the building put many of Papp's more solidly community-oriented programs in jeopardy. Many of the programs Papp described to the board—privately funded projects like the Photography Workshop, the Cinque Gallery, and the Mobile Theater Unit—did not enjoy longevity in the roster of activities at the Public Theater. (The Mobile Unit's operations ceased in 1977.)

Further complications of Papp and Gersten's "progressive capitalism" in practice would soon become clear. On July 27, 1971, a few months after the Board of Estimate decision, Papp's production of a musical comedy adaptation of *Two Gentlemen of Verona* by John Guare and Mel Schapiro, with music by Galt MacDermot (*Hair*), opened at the Delacorte for a three-week run, during which it toured all five boroughs in the Mobile Unit, attracting audiences of over 100,000. Their free love-themed *Two Gents* celebrated interracial romance and friendship. Guare's Verona functions as a stand-in for San Juan, Puerto Rico, and Milan resembles a modern-day, multicultural New York City; actor Raúl Juliá received rave reviews alongside Jerry Stiller's Yiddish accent.[52] The creative team developed the show chiefly through improvisation in rehearsals, up until the Central Park opening. With lyrics like "Boom chika chika chika / Fuck fucka wucka wucka / Cock cocka wocka wocka / Puss pussa wussa wussa," the play echoed the earlier MacDermot musical *Hair*, but ultimately traded urban conflict for fluff; its jubilant finale featured a bicycle, soap bubbles, a basketball, Frisbees, yo-yos, rubber balls, and roller skates.[53] *Two Gents* arrived on Broadway on November 13, 1971, where it won two Tony awards and the Drama Critics award.

With *Two Gents*, the direction of the NYSF changed: the show pioneered a new producing model that used private funds to transfer a show developed in the nonprofit and city-funded arena of the Delacorte to Broadway, under full ownership of the NYSF.[54] This (after the fact) complicated Papp's appeals to municipal officials—should the city provide free rent and capital funding to a theater that would have a Broadway hit on its hands in a matter of months?[55] Could Papp's theater retain its stated mission as it evolved as an institution with one foot pointing toward the Great White Way? Papp's pace of production never slowed; by 1973 the NYSF had already produced 117 plays—66 revivals and 51 new plays.[56] Incredibly, the Public Theater now had more hits on and off Broadway than any other theater company—David Rabe's *Sticks and Bones* and *Two Gents* on Broadway, with Jason Miller's *That Championship Season* poised to make the move as well—and it enjoyed rent-free space at Astor Library and the Delacorte. Papp still had to fight for the money to run the enormous building, and operations money remained hard to find from foundations or government coffers. He necessarily needed to continue to turn to ever-more grandiose boards, more Manhattan-centric programming and decisions—which eventually led him to accept the Lincoln Center position.

Audiences Found and Lost

> In the late nineteen-fifties, the thinly financed Shakespeare Festival and the richly supported plans for Lincoln Center were two points of a V whose convergence could hardly be imagined. Mr. Papp's enterprise was to Lincoln Center what Charlie Chaplin's little tramp was to the feast of the oil barons.
>
> —McCandlish Phillips, 1973[57]

New York critics from McCandlish Phillips to Ada Louise Huxtable shared this view of Papp's distant relationship to Lincoln Center. In her 1971 column about the Public Theater sale, Huxtable aligned the city's purchase of the building with the city planning values necessary to revive downtown Manhattan. Huxtable captures the overriding philosophy that motivated support for the Public Theater, and also made Papp's transition uptown to Lincoln Center so unlikely:

> The Public Theater is much more than a place. It is an urban catalyst. Here is a downtown neighborhood being slowly brought back to life after a long slide downhill, receiving a critical infusion of creative and environmental quality. Between Cooper Union and New York University there are now signs of physical and social revitalization where it is desperately needed, in a city unable to stem decay and despair. The Public Theater is a key piece. This is how culture and creativity should be used as a life-giving force to rebuild the city. How odd that we should put out $200-million for static, symbolic show in Lincoln Center, with debatable cultural and environmental results, and lack $5 million for something that is simply and obviously right.[58]

The city's purchase of the Public Theater included none of the destructive slum clearance that had marred the early development of Lincoln Center. Huxtable exalts the local as a corrective to these missteps of heavy-handed urban renewal; her argument prefigures contemporary discussions of the "place making" powers of the arts within the new "creative city." In 1971 this strategic linkage, rehearsed in the Public Theater building sale, offered Lincoln Center as its foil. Across the city, Lincoln Center had become a kind of metonymic shorthand for a retrograde and Establishment institution, particularly as deployed by proponents of decentralizing arts resources to deprived areas of the city.[59] Papp was now bound for that "static, symbolic show."

When Papp banned Julie Bovasso from the theater, she reminded him, "This is a public building, this belongs to the city of New York," before her agent sent a telegram requesting that her name be stripped from any mention of *In the Boom Boom Room*.[60] In Bovasso's argument, Lincoln Center's "public building" denoted limitations to Papp's role, challenging his dominance as both a public steward and theatrical rebel. Bovasso's comment also revealed the shifting stakes: the emergence of the Beaumont and the struggle to fund theater at Lincoln Center led to the formation of a lively and engaged theatrical public sphere, one that Papp did not anticipate.

Papp established ambitious goals for the Beaumont, yet the social fracturing of New York City at the time made his hoped-for outcomes illusory. In addition to Rosalyn Deutsche's warnings against the facile deployment of "public" in the rhetoric of conservative democracy,[61] Janelle Reinelt observes that "the invocation of an idealized equality has not and does not now manifest in the composition of the historical Western public sphere."[62] Declaring the space of an emancipated public sphere often refers to an objective or goal, not a reality—an idealized place of communication where equitable discourse might occur. Bernard Gersten complained that Papp "romanticized the Mobile audience," whereas Gersten remained sensitive to the difficulty of getting "*any* people into the theater, *any* time," let alone the residents of poorer neighborhoods.[63] Yet encoded in the very origin of Lincoln Center is the clashing of modernist visions of the city stage with new ideas about the contribution—and viability—of culture to the urban neighborhood, particularly as the kind of "urban catalyst" of which Huxtable wrote. If not geographically, then in terms of subscriber base, Lincoln Center remained far from Papp's Mobile Unit audiences.

Papp bet on Lincoln Center as a magnet for New Yorkers and suburbanites only willing to venture to well-lighted and well-populated areas of the city. He also stated on many occasions his desire to bring both middle-class black and white New Yorkers to the theater, and to target the evolving Puerto Rican middle class.[64] Across the decade, the city's population continued to fall and, despite media reports to the contrary, census data reflected a city increasingly unattractive to high-income families. The area with the largest increases in high-income households, just a few blocks north of Lincoln Center, could be found between 70th Street and 90th Street in Manhattan.[65] Papp's new artistic home remained a fortress within this protected enclave, yet Papp publicly affirmed continuity between the mission of his plays in the Delacorte, the Mobile Unit, and now Lincoln Center:

> If there is a single driving force which characterizes the New York Shakespeare Festival, it is its continual confrontation with the wall that separates vast numbers of people from the arts. This wall—spawned by poverty, ignorance, historical conditions—is our principal opponent, and as we joust and engage with this "enemy" we distill and shape the nature and style of our theater.[66]

When he assumed leadership of the Beaumont, he framed the choice within ambitious goals: to provide an antidote to the factors threatening theater attendance, to meld together the audiences for the NYSF and that of Lincoln Center, and to find work that responded "to the reality of what is happening in the city."[67] Yet the tastes of a privileged few—the subscribers—supported the theater through ticket sales, not a minor feat given the cost of funding an expansive year-round theater.

This largely white audience base held certain expectations for its programming; Papp yearned to connect with new audiences. This included the increasing numbers of Latino and black residents, but also 25–34-year-olds of various racial identities, living in single-person households who had come of age in the 1960s, many with a high degree of educational attainment.[68] Some had already had contact with street theater, ethnic theater, or some form of Off-Off Broadway performance in the prior decade. By combining these populations, he aimed to "convey to the predominantly middle-class patrons a feeling of togetherness, rather than separateness and isolation with their accompanying fears."[69] Papp wanted to add at least 5,000 black subscribers to Lincoln Center's 40,000 predominantly white ones.[70] This desired shift in the geography of theater attendance and neighborhood identity underestimated the extent to which public support for Lincoln Center had calcified around a rearguard response to institutional changes in theater. To birth "unified" theatergoing experiences out of its geographic centrality relied on a series of fictions about the city's spaces.

These ambitions were designed to alter some of the bedrock aspects of Lincoln Center Papp had long disdained. It was not a mistrust of its money; many of Papp's earlier projects had been made possible by the generosity of wealthy individuals, from George Delacorte to Florence Sutro Anspacher to LuEsther Mertz and even the Astor Foundation. In 1971, Papp had decried the "expansionist, predatory, and imperialistic aims" of the administrative and managerial wings of the Lincoln Center theaters.[71] Two years later, it was Papp's turn to advance his "Theater for the People" at the complex. The cultural capital of the complex signified many other injustices to which Papp remained alive—why should putting on a new play at Lincoln Center be more significant than doing the same at a regional, Broadway, Off, or Off-Off Broadway theater? Papp's rebellion at Lincoln Center took the form of the challenging playwrights in his coterie—Miguel Piñero, Thomas Babe, Michael Weller, Dennis J. Reardon, John Ford Noonan, and David Rabe—coupled with his decision to relegate Shakespeare to the smaller stage of the Forum/Mitzi E. Newhouse Theater.

Due to these producing choices, Papp's 1973–74 season announcement incited a backlash from Beaumont subscribers writing to cancel their memberships even before the season commenced. Some were repelled by Papp's public remarks regarding the solicitation of new audiences, which, when coupled with appeals to long-time subscribers, appeared arrogant: "Mr. Papp, according to the *Times*, dismissed the established patrons as people who did not interest him; instead, he said, he looked to the young and the black. Why, then, in his letter to the old subscribers does he now talk of 'earnestly soliciting' us?"[72] Others interpreted his actions as undermining the "classics," an accusation that no doubt surprised Papp, given his producing history of nearly exclusive Shakespeare productions. The most offensive subscriber defections questioned Papp's allegiance to the classics *and* his stated passion for new plays:

> I do *not* wish the theatre to play a role in urban society and to add minority theatre goers if that means eliminating classic theatre and producing another *Shaft in Africa*. Blacks and Hispanics in the U.S.A. are American and not a separate people. The melting pot of our country has taken numerous minorities, brought them in, and taught them the classics. I believe Euripides, Shakespeare, and Ibsen can present the problems of any people far better than *The Pig Pen* or *The Chickencoop Chinaman*.[73]

Ironically, the plays singled out by this irate letter-writer revolved around questions of stereotyping, identity, and visibility such as Frank Chin's *The*

Chickencoop Chinaman, which examined the performance of radicals and cultural workers in the Red Guard Party. Papp's decision to stage these plays tapped into embodied discomforts alive in the city. Subscribers proved they would sooner avoid the theater than be forced to sit through plays that seemed to signify certain political ideologies, and produced their representative subjects—locating them on a city stage. Subscriber cancelations went from dozens, to hundreds, and eventually, with Miguel Piñero's *Short Eyes*, in May 1974, the subscriber base dropped to 16,000.[74]

This conflagration revealed defensiveness over the classical canon, as well as a sentiment that Papp had somehow tricked spectators into a theatrical exchange with contemporary characterizations of black or Asian characters, particularly at a time in which neighborhood segregation (by class and, even more so, race) remained a reality of urban life. These subscribers valued the stages at Lincoln Center territorially, and viewed Papp's season as a ceding of their authority to determine urban representation, the fear of the visibility of minority communities made real. Ignoring Papp's many public statements about courting middle-class audiences, one subscriber canceled his subscription with a letter that accused Papp of forgetting the "middle class who have for many years supported the theatre."[75] To announce a season with a reference to a new work "by a prominent black playwright" contained the problematic insinuation that the largely white audience of Lincoln Center subscribers would support a show based upon their approval of Papp's curatorial taste and social mission. "To pick a work because it's a 'black play' is idiotic. *In the Boom Boom Room* may very well sound appetizing to small children and morons."[76] Papp underestimated the anger in the civic sphere; his hope for "togetherness" and unity at the onset of his tenure appeared naive.

The consensus of the theatrical public sphere did not match Papp's artistic and political vision for the city and its stages. Christopher Balme highlights the contradictions of theatrical public sphere formation: heavily debated performance can reestablish "contact between the theatrical and the political public sphere," but those performances may not have even yet been performed.[77] Papp's season announcement achieved this, as subscribers fought for stages that upheld a domestic theater mirroring their own private sphere. This reception was not unrelated to the urban anxiety that circulated throughout Broadway producing circles: a strong undercurrent of ethnic conflict and race-based discrimination animated many of the responses to a changing Times Square during the 1970s. It energized the media coverage and conservatized responses to the fiscal strain as pundits and even some city officials blamed jobless New Yorkers—poor whites, many recent immigrants, unemployed blacks and Latinos—as a drain on city funding. The "lost audiences" of Broadway threatened to withhold their patronage of Lincoln Center, too, should the concerns of minority playwrights and performers be made fully visible on stage.

Subscriber complaints were echoed in softer language by mainstream critics who similarly disdained Papp's decision to move classic plays into the smaller Forum Theater, and spitefully predicted that he did not have a large enough store of (quality) new plays to fill stages at both the Public Theater and the Beaumont. Critic Stanley Kauffman's incendiary fifteen-page appraisal of Papp's work in 1974 criticized Papp's "ethnic policy," which led to productions like Charles Gordone's *No Place to Be Somebody* (1970), a play of "small worth" that nevertheless won the Pulitzer and confirmed for Kauffman "that prize's bankruptcy and reverse Uncle-Tomming."[78] Kauffman railed against the politics, aesthetics, and themes of every first-season Beaumont play: *In the Boom Boom Room* was filled with adolescent insights, cliché characters, and clumsy directing; Irish writer Hugh Leonard's *The Au Pair Man* was a "feeble allegory about the decline of the British Empire," and Ron Milner's *What the Wine-Sellers Buy* was merely "a black play by a black playwright" about "ghetto life in Detroit" that contained "deliberate whoring."[79] *What the Wine-Sellers Buy* attracted a 40 percent African American audience, but did not succeed in converting one-time ticket buyers into subscribers.

Simultaneously, Papp received criticism for showering too much attention on a small cohort of writers to the exclusion of many other promising playwrights, yet his initial commitment to new work at the Beaumont signaled a potentially sustainable future for new plays. The Bovasso-Rabe *In the Boom Boom Room* pairing was its trial run. That Papp imagined this play might galvanize new subscribers is as fascinating as it is puzzling; fierce in his dedication to new writers, he also misjudged their ability to rehabilitate the public's perception of Lincoln Center. In Rabe's play, the themes of victimization and violence—communicated through a parade of sadistic male characters who terrorize the guileless Chrissy—made overt the injuries of sexual and gendered disempowerment. As the sexually abused Chrissy longs to make it as a legitimate dancer in New York, the play hovers between her dreams and her decrepit reality, through an abstract exploration of a woman victimized by the myths of success, the politics of display, and the self-serving decisions of the men from whom she desperately *needs*. Audience members dissented; the expressionistic structure of the play did not temper the stark brutality of its message, or reception.

Given Papp's famously overbearing style and Bovasso's storied temper, it is perhaps no surprise that their relationship imploded before previews. Bovasso referred to her downtown artist circle as "the wild men of Second Avenue," who by 1973 thought of Papp's work "as very traditional, old fashioned kind of theater."[80] She had a penchant for absurd, mystifying stage spectacles; critic Dan Isaac described her strength as a dramatist as her "ability to scramble traditional patterns, creating thereby new orders of sense and feeling."[81] Papp desired both for his inaugural play at Lincoln Center. Bovasso directed the play "as a piece of architecture" with an emphasis on height and "a classic stature."[82] The huge thrust stage at the Beaumont enthralled her, as she had just finished directing her play, *Gloria and Esperanza*, at Philadelphia's Annenberg Center with a cast of sixty-two people and the use of multiple stage levels. For Bovasso's production of Rabe's play, Theoni Aldredge designed loud go-go costumes, and Santo Loquasto built an enormously tall set replete with catwalks and cages hanging throughout the stage for the dancers. Bovasso created tapes of music for the show comprised of 1950s and 1960s rock.

Though Papp initially hired Bovasso for these concepts, when he dismissed her and took over as director, Bovasso discovered Papp's *In the Boom Boom Room* had little in common with hers: "Everything was leveled and flattened out, and he began working on it as if it were a social realist play, which it is not. I disagreed with him totally, and artistically."[83] Reviewers panned the production, which is remembered in Public Theater lore chiefly for garnering the *New York Times* review ("chic filth") that incited Papp to personally threaten the critic, Clive Barnes. The episode, however, points to a situational urgency that would define Papp's programming at the Beaumont: Papp later commented that "even if [the play] had been done splendidly. . . . David Rabe would not be acceptable to that audience, no matter what."[84] *That audience*: the calcified, presumptively mostly white and mostly aged supporters of culture as an aspirational place of beauty, who rejected the politics of Papp's enterprise and his belief that new plays might cultivate new forms of urban togetherness. Even more importantly, these skeptical subscribers held the upper hand in the eyes of the city's most powerful, as the concerns about a fleeing tax base dominated every conversation about spending. This conflict therefore became not just about the class struggle cohering around audience preferences, but the very ability of the state to sanction arts for the city public.

Papp had long argued that theaters needed the "luxury of an occasional failure," or else they would fall prey to the "hit" philosophy that demanded profits from every experiment, an argument Papp used in his bid to buy the Astor Library.[85] Whereas the paper of record had once exalted this perspective and hailed Papp's Public Theater as a model national theater, by 1975, critic Charles Marowitz published a full-court critique of Papp's producing choices at Lincoln Center as better-suited to for-profit stages than a national theater built to "tower over and . . . shame the Broadway stage."[86] Papp's creation of "a theater patterned to the needs of poor whites, blacks, and Puerto Ricans" represented a "laudable intention . . . not reconcilable with the needs of a professional, privately subscribed artistic enterprise."[87] For an institutionalized theater to devote itself to "the disenfranchised" amounted to inverse snobbery. Many critics and audience members shared this interpretation of the Beaumont as a not-for-profit, *private* theater—noncommercial yet professional. At the height of the fiscal crisis, the rhetoric of art reaching beyond the privileged at Lincoln Center had faded into the archives of the

Rockefeller Foundation, as had sustained public deliberation about the mission of the performing arts on city land.

Papp's persuasive construction of Theater for the People during the Astor Library hearings held little resonance for potential theatergoers at Lincoln Center; they wanted their stages preserved and protected, not changed and renewed. To them, Papp's commitment to stage works by playwrights of color amounted to the overtaking of the central space of municipal cultural production with a leftist political agenda, inspired by the same 1960s radicalism that had rendered their city so unintelligible. Supporters of the city's most famous public stage could not accept Papp's attempt to sever its connection to the romantic myth of high art—produced in an unvarnished merit-based system, insulated from the demands and fluctuations of radical movements and progressive demands. As "theatre's high extroversion meets the habituated introversion of race privilege,"[88] the real negotiation of race and the boundaries of public theater hit up against the transfer of Papp's "Public Theater" philosophy to a ticket-paying venue. Audience members and critics, stinging from the revelation that a city stage had been usurped, celebrated their latitude as ticket-buyers and reviewers to vent the full force of their venom about the state of the city.

Miguel Piñero's *Short Eyes*, directed by Marvin Felix Camillo and produced at the Beaumont in 1974, demonstrates this displacement of anxieties. A typical profile of the Puerto Rican-born Piñero began with a discussion of audience members walking out of *Short Eyes*—"they're always middle-aged or elderly white people who don't quite see this play as 'culture,'" explained an usher.[89] The play originated in a theater workshop in Sing Sing prison, where Piñero served time for armed robbery after a youth spent on the Lower East Side. Playgoers felt assaulted by the brutal depiction of life in jail. Racial and class-based prejudices motivated attacks in the media and betrayed specific grievances: bitter stereotyping of the playwright, the old-fashioned snobbery of reviewers, and even a defensive posture against the perception of new audiences in the house. The negative reviews of *Short Eyes*, Fiona Mills contends, reflect "a larger race and class bias intrinsic to New York theater during the 1970s," particularly in their "unspoken yet palpable mandate for a specifically middle- to upper- class mode of theatergoing behavior that is decidedly Anglo/Western in its foundation."[90] Interestingly, Mills refers to the Beaumont as "Broadway," and frames her argument in relation to the reviewers' discomfort with the "new phenomenon" of Latino plays on Broadway at the time of Piñero's debut. The reviews Mills analyzes—which frequently critiqued audience members, more so than the actual play—are even more potent when placed in their full context at Lincoln Center, produced by Papp, in a theater that Arthur Miller once hoped would be an "alternative to the commercial Broadway theatre."[91]

However, to understand Papp's transformation of the Beaumont as a failure is to assume that its process and eventual outcome should have—or could have—been free of conflict. Papp's years at Lincoln Center offered the strongest reflection of a theater's role in a crisis that had changed "the nature of the terrain itself on which struggles of different kinds are taking place."[92] Stuart Hall made this observation about Britain during a similar period in the 1970s; as he points out, these ideological and political class struggles "have a purchase on practice."[93] Positioned at one of the geographic centers of culture in New York, Papp confronted a new logic of discourse, and the methods by which it was being accomplished. A subscriber from the Bronx announced her decision not to renew her subscription, explaining:

> I am not one bit interested in the "trials and traumas" of a Philadelphia Go-Go girl. . . . The third play, listed merely as a new work 'by a prominent black playwright' has caused me nausea. If I were black, I'd be furious, for this sort of advertising smacks of patronizing condescension! Are we to presume that because a play is written by a member of a minority group, that it will be worth producing and seeing? For shame! Let us judge a play on its merits as a work worthy of production, rather than because a black or a Puerto Rican or a jew [*sic*] wrote it.[94]

The writer assumes that *she* is being addressed by these plays; just as George C. Scott maintained that free Shakespeare in the Park made audiences feel ownership over the enterprise, so too did the Lincoln Center subscribers assert their own belief in the ticketed transaction as one of ownership. They interpreted Papp's season not as ethically geared toward multiple audiences, but rather as capitulation to an Other that already overran their stages, screens, and city coffers.

An alternate reading suggests that Papp had strayed from his stated mission, focused too much on expansion to conduct a sober appraisal of Lincoln Center's stages. He stubbornly pushed his pet playwrights to produce while the houses remained half-full. The plays galvanized a response, to be sure, but also unwittingly tagged the playwrights as Papp's undercooked talents, or messengers of his liberal agenda. Papp's eagerness to right the ship of the Beaumont transferred into a residue of mistrust that marred his first season, and prepped both audiences and critics to disparage later productions. The protracted brush-up over each controversial Beaumont play served to both underscore and obscure the economics at the heart of the theater transaction in the tradition of public arts. The individual's right of refusal as a subscriber revealed one layer of fundament, but regardless of subscriptions, Papp's overarching problem remained the economic dilemma at the foundation of Lincoln Center's operations, evident since its inception.

Composer William Schuman, the former president of Juilliard and the president of the entire complex between 1961 and 1969, argued for a policy of budget deficits in order to maintain programming integrity: deficits in the performing arts exist to provide latitude for experimentation. His "Schuman's Law and Postulates" held that "nonprofit institutions in the performing arts compromise their reason for being in direct proportion to the programs and policies which are adopted for fiscal reasons extrinsic to artistic purpose."[95] To John D. Rockefeller III, a deficit philosophy signaled unsound financial planning and the eventual downfall of Lincoln Center. The Executive Committee chastised Schuman for his provocative statements, but for years many of Lincoln Center's programs had operated with a growing deficit. Schuman had expressed a principle already in practice, but was considered too publicly unpopular to voice.

Lincoln Center did not just want "safe" plays—it also wanted fiscal safety, another matter entirely. Arthur Miller observed with dismay the skittishness over arts funding, stemming from a Lincoln Center Board clueless as to the actual cost of supporting the culture that Rockefeller once imagined would offer "a new kind of city therapy."[96] After they poured millions into the building in which a repertory was to be housed, the board took a miserly approach to the actual company, revealing themselves as arts aficionados who craved monuments, not theaters with actual operational budgets. Miller inveighed against this prevailing funding philosophy that nickel-and-dimed the cultural life of the metropolis into extinction: "We're becoming a utilitarian society in the crudest sense, namely, that which is not bought cannot be art. Whole sections of the New York Public Library . . . are closed. Museums have short hours. Even the hospitals have to curtail their services and are threatened with closing because they have no money."[97] According to Miller, this doomed Lincoln Center's Repertory Theater before Papp arrived; now, with Papp, disagreements over "deficit" ideologies in arts funding reemerged as the decisive issue facing New York's cultural production.

Papp managed all of his theater projects with major deficits. He claimed that he and Gersten were in fact "fiscally conservative," and joked publicly that if Jules Irving, one of the previous artistic directors of the Beaumont, "had run up a healthy two million dollar deficit instead of his chickencrap $500,000 he wouldn't be in such trouble at Lincoln Center, because you can't live like a beggar in a castle."[98] This was one of Papp's great performances; while he knew that any theater he ran without consistent governmental funds would remain unsustainable, he continued to expand them.

His resolve, however, weakened as his list of grievances grew: the Lincoln Center Board refused to commit funds for Papp's $6.5 million renovation plan for the Beaumont. He disliked his NYSF productions pumping money into his uptown productions; Papp fed $2 million of *A Chorus Line* profits into Lincoln Center every year. The fact that Papp's financial predicament continued even when he had four palpable hits confounded even his supporters. Ntozake Shange's *for colored girls who have considered suicide/ when the rainbow is enuf* was a Broadway success; the David Rabe play *Streamers*, directed by Mike Nichols at the Mitzi Newhouse Theater, was a sellout, as was Richard Foreman's *Threepenny Opera*. Papp's most sizable triumph, Michael Bennett's *A Chorus Line*, ran simultaneously in companies at the Shubert Theater on Broadway, in Los Angeles, and in London.[99] Papp explained the underlying financials of operating an expensive institution year-round: "The more we do, the more it costs, because the price of a ticket never covers the cost."[100]

In August 1976 Papp reduced by half the 1976–77 season of plays at the Beaumont. He abruptly turned to staging the classics at Lincoln Center, blaming critics and audiences for not appreciating his experiments with new plays. He found a string of successes through a spate of these newly conceived classics; Andrei Serban's *Cherry Orchard* opened in February 1977 and was nominated for five Tony Awards, and Liz Swados's production of *Agamemnon* opened in May 1977. Still, in June 1977, Papp announced his departure from Lincoln Center, decrying its artistically oppressive environment and fiscal difficulties.[101] He attributed partial blame for his exit on a bedeviled combination of audience, location, critical reception, and finances. He could not run expensive theaters through ticket sales or subscriptions alone, and argued that even if his plays averaged 90 percent capacity audiences, there would still remain untenable annual shortfalls. Papp left Lincoln Center with a $1.6 million deficit, and, on the occasion of his exit, released a financial statement that showed that government support of his Lincoln Center operations accounted for only 14 percent of income over the four years he operated the theaters, and only 5 percent during his final year.[102]

In New York in 1977, Papp's indignation held far less sway than it had seven years earlier. The conversation in New York altered dramatically over those years; Papp, still a municipal hero, now looked impervious to the fiscal drama of the city. Papp had changed, as anyone would across decades of producing, yet now Lincoln Center forced him to abandon his belief in the motivating mission behind a city theater. Papp had ambitiously embraced numerous institution-building projects that threatened to implicate him in a model of top-heavy monuments to antiseptic democratic art. His delicate balancing act at the helm of public theaters during the fiscal crisis left him newly critical of the rhetoric of populist participation, and the romantic possibility that a centralized theater might reconfigure audience attendance in the city.

In a revealing speech given in January 1976, Papp had strong words for arts centers on the scale of Lincoln Center:

> We find that these civic institutions, erected with tax money, on tax free ground, still retain an air of elitism. . . . Building concentrated arts centers in a single geographic location, we lend aid and comfort to the colonialist enclave theory—"defending the last bastion of western civilization against a hostile native population." To tolerate class division is antithetical to the primary social purpose of your art center. [103]

Papp argued instead in favor of "decentralization of art buildings" better suited to continuity with the mission of his earliest producing. Yet in the arena of competition for resources, Papp frequently orchestrated relentless public relations campaigns that did nothing to disperse additional arts funding across the five boroughs, and in fact centralized the flow of monies to his two primary projects, the Public Theater and the Beaumont; both enjoyed money, security, and legitimation as beacons of centralization, but their raison d'être derived from Papp's decentralized mission—theater for the people. Along with the fiscal issues Papp gave the press as the reasons for his departure from the Beaumont, the narrative also must include his irresolvable tension between location and audiences. For Papp, Lincoln Center's unspoken boundaries of reception had solidified a framework of impossibility that blocked Papp's vision of public theater.

As biographers have chronicled, 1977 closes Papp's expansionist period. In the following years, Papp recommitted himself to the Public Theater on Lafayette Street, and focused on new artists and new plays, writers like Adrienne Kennedy, Wallace Shawn, Jessica Hagedorn, Tina Howe, and Liz Swados. But it also signaled an era of changed relationships and initiatives in the city, as well as in Papp's life. He had lost credibility in certain circles; though Papp hired artists—Argentine director Osvaldo Riofrancos and singer and administrator Novella Nelson—to maintain a "pipeline" to communities underrepresented in mainstream talent, it was unclear where that pipeline led. Helen Epstein describes a generational shift; by the late 1970s, a more streetwise generation "saw the producer in a different light, calling him 'Massa Joe,' referring to the Festival as 'Papp's Plantation.' "[104] Acrimony had been growing for some time; in his annual theater review in *Black World/ Negro Digest*, critic Peter Bailey wrote bleakly that 1972 was the high point "for Black Theater at the Public Theater, which is only right since we pay taxes, and the city practically gave Papp the place, but it seems to have been too Black for old Joe to deal with."[105] Competing theaters resented Papp's budget and visibility, and press outlets chastised him for leaving his responsibilities to various constituencies unfulfilled. These pressures resembled those of a Board of Estimate politician more closely than an artistic director. A number of his long-standing collaborations—David Rabe, Andrei Serban, Sam Shepard, Bernard Gersten—fell apart due to feuds and hurt feelings.

Once dubbed "Mayor Papp" for his perceived carte blanche to city funds, in 1974 Papp made front-page news when the Parks Department opposed his proposed $3-million, 2,500-seat theater to replace Central Park's aging Delacorte Theater.[106] The scope and depth of the city's money problems remained under debate, but that summer, the headlines were dominated with news of independent audits of the city's comptroller's office.[107] Mayor Beame, a former city comptroller himself, took to the airwaves to convince the citizens of New York City that the reports amounted to distortion and manipulation. Still, anxiety increased in financial circles, interest rates for bonds began to rise, and the collision course toward the brink of financial collapse had been set. After an initially sunny announcement of Papp's new open-air theater, the Parks administrator, Edwin L. Weisl Jr., attributed his change of opinion to the negative public reaction to the plans and the deterioration of the larger park landscape: "Particularly in light of the city's fiscal situation this seems to be the best policy to follow."[108]

Genius, leader, bully, egotist: profiles often describe these titles as recognizably Papp—part of a personality whose quirks were essential to persevere in the industry and consolidate so much theatrical real estate. Yet it was also Papp's particular political ruthlessness that enabled him to convince the city during a time of retrenchment that the Public Theater was a unique good for the people, one that deserved—required—establishment as part of the city's permanent cultural infrastructure. His loyalty to new playwrights and willingness to take risks on untested talent meant that countercultural voices of all political persuasions found a greater platform on his stages. Yet the favored anecdotes encapsulate the go-it-alone ethos for which Papp became known, entirely separate from his role in transforming the arts institutions of the city.

Three mayors—Lindsay, Beame, and Ed Koch—spoke at Papp's 1978 surprise birthday party, but Papp's alliances with politicians always proved frustratingly mercurial. "You are *sui generis*. No one else could do what you are doing," is scrawled in then-Congressman Ed Koch's own handwriting at the bottom of a 1970 letter to Papp.[109] Though Papp's summer Shakespeare Festival received city funding continually through the fiscal crisis, once Koch moved into Gracie Mansion in January 1978, he cut $3.5 million from the city's Cultural Affairs budget, and, with it, all of the NYSF's city funding.[110] For the first time in four administrations, Papp's Shakespeare in the Park would not have public monies behind it; when the Cultural Affairs commissioner created an emergency Summer Arts Fund from corporate donations, Papp refused the $323,000 offered to him. It was the municipality's responsibility to fund the Delacorte.

Of all the candidates in New York's 1977 mayoral election, Koch had "used the harshest rhetoric, blaming the crisis on unions, leftists, and 'poverty pimps,'"[111] yet his prior support of Papp's initiatives left the producer blindsided by his cuts. With the aim of restoring municipal credit, voters responded to Koch's neo-managerial proposals carved from the necessity of austerity, particularly after looting and unrest in the city during the Blackout summer of 1977. Public financing proved harder than ever in the climate of the 1980s. This polluted Papp's interrelation with the city, as politicians abandoned the same theater that they so often intoned in the press as one of New York City's most vibrant and redeeming institutions.

Some aspects of these changed interactions mirrored a changed relationship between the public and the theater across the 1970s. The Lincoln Center area needed to be safeguarded; downtown, near the Astor Library, needed to be revived. Papp wisely concentrated on the latter, a building that prefigured many later efforts to rebuild the edges of neighborhoods through the arts. As Ada Louise Huxtable had argued in 1971, the Public Theater's best defense could be mounted in an architecture column, as an "urban catalyst," not the theater section. This becomes centrally important to the Public Theater and its continued existence today, where similar contradictions and tensions persist. The Public Theater is unquestionably among the most fearless and uncompromising venues for new plays, while also being a treasured city institution with a strong orientation toward Broadway stages.

In 2012, after a $40-million capital campaign (of which the City of New York contributed $28.5 million), the Public Theater undertook a massive renovation, including cosmetic improvements, increased accessibility, reconfigured electrical systems, and a new lobby bar and restaurant, "The Library." Theater critic Alexis Soloski noted that "the latter has higher price points than a purely public-minded venture might entail,"[112] suggesting that the Public Theater's brand of public continues to be recast: from public theater to a public service to a public-minded venture.

The Public Theater reinvigorated its long-dormant Mobile Unit in 2011 to present "free Shakespeare to prisons, homeless shelters, centers for the elderly, and other community venues throughout the five boroughs."[113] The original rallying cry of "free" has shifted, largely due to the dynamics of theater in a vast city that must relegate "accessibility" to the Mobile Unit, while ticket prices for Public Theater productions are comparable to other major Off Broadway theaters. Further, the media reception to the Mobile Unit indicated a state of affairs nearly unchanged from decades before, as in this article in the Theatre Development Fund's online magazine:

> But if you're a prisoner, or you're homeless, how many chances will you get to see Shakespeare? Or how about if you're a senior citizen who can't physically travel to a matinee? Or if you live on the outskirts of New York, where Manhattan can seem like a foreign country? And if communities like these don't have access, then what happens to the theatre? . . . If they think of it at all, will it seem unwelcoming? Will the theatre itself seem like a locked door they can't enter?[114]

Most striking is the fact that the Public Theater is *still* the institution expected to right the wrongs of uneven cultural development across the city, and surmount the obstacles created by a centralized theater system that creates outskirts and centers, both geographic and economic. The primary issues at play in Papp's lobbying for millions of dollars for his theaters—inter-borough inequities, disputed access to arts facilities, and the arcane decision-making processes of municipal government—remain.

Papp's achievements and failures during the 1970s galvanized debates related to commercial versus independent theater and the responsibility of the latter to address local concerns. He vacillated between decentralized principles and centralized funding streams, diminishing state support and increasing publicity desperation, urgent coalitions and hostile politics. Papp understood theater as a social force, and viewed himself as radicalizing the environments in which he worked—commercial television, Central Park, Lincoln Center, or Broadway. Yet he pursued a socially dynamic vision of theater that revealed the medium itself as conservative, and at times, even outmoded. In the spaces of the city the most resistant to change, Papp argued for—and occasionally achieved—transformed cartographies of both production and reception.

Chapter 6

✦

The Brooklyn Syndrome

BAM and Outer-Borough Arts

> Among the crowds in the lobby at BAM, where spectators scurry about smoking and planning when to walk out, you wonder what the purpose of performance has become. Has the ritual of communication in a communal space—however faulty its basis now seems—been reduced to seeing and being seen in the lobby or the aisles?
>
> —Jill Dolan, 1986

In 1986 theater scholar Jill Dolan inveighed against the avant-garde egoists that dominated New York's "it" stages, such as the Next Wave Festival at the Brooklyn Academy of Music (BAM), where Robert Wilson's *The Golden Windows* received its American premiere in 1985. Theater critics penned largely hagiographic reviews of the works Dolan critiqued as empty spectacles: Tadeusz Kantor's *Let the Artist Die* at La Mama E.T.C., Sam Shepard's *Lie of the Mind* at the Promenade Theatre, Wilson's *The Golden Windows* at BAM, and Richard Foreman's *The Birth of the Poet* (also at Next Wave). Dolan discerned a "self-congratulatory air" permeating the lobbies where patrons toasted their "being in the right place seeing exactly the right work,"[1] and she was not alone in her complaints about BAM's fall avant-garde celebration. As Gerald Rabkin wrote in 1985, while Next Wave claimed very real achievements, its title mislabeled them; Next Wave constituted "a particular form of inter-arts collaboration whose scale demands financial support almost impossible outside of an institutionalized framework."[2] This formula did not necessarily affirm unsettling or provocative work, but rather ensured the continuity of experimental arts and collaboration between the all-stars of the avant-garde.

The Brooklyn Academy of Music began to use the acronym BAM in 1973, when it had little to lose after its years of post–World War II decline, and steadily built a new institution out of its staid programming of adventure travelogues and lecture series. The Next Wave series debuted in 1981, and became a full-fledged fall festival in 1983. The popular origin story of BAM's twentieth-century renaissance starts here, when it ascended to cultural prominence on the strength of Next Wave experimental productions, with rotating players that included Laurie Anderson, Tricia Brown, Lucinda Childs, Meredith Monk, Remy Charlip, Philip Glass, Robert Wilson, Pina Bausch, Merce Cunningham, John Cage, Steve Reich, Bill T. Jones/Arnie Zane, and John Zorn. Next Wave signified the institutionalization of radical modes of art, and, occasionally, the surprising tepidness of contemporary experimental performance. The festival did not reliably look toward the *next*—a revival of the 1976 Glass/Wilson collaboration, *Einstein on the Beach*, headlined the 1984 Next Wave festival.

For performance in Brooklyn and BAM's position within the larger cultural landscape of New York City and beyond, Next Wave signaled a future of a different kind. It secured BAM's placement as a venue for "downtown performance" in Brooklyn, and the image of a cross-disciplinary, avant-garde institution, not in competition with Manhattan but on the level of it. This replaced BAM's prior cultural identification with racial tensions and urban blight of the 1970s. Next Wave recast Brooklyn itself as relevant after a period of cultural obsolescence: if the segregation of communities and the pathetic funding landscape could be conquered by the great possibilities of BAM, theater in Brooklyn could fulfill a new vision of urban outer-borough performance.

Yet BAM almost did not survive the 1970s. To do so, the institution needed to overhaul the borough's arts reputation from what it was—outer—to what it was not yet: a center. While BAM's physical plant sat at the transit hub of Atlantic and Flatbush Avenues, prior to Next Wave it was considered, as playwright Charles Mee remembers, "a big, old, dark, neglected pile of stones off Flatbush Avenue where no one I knew ever thought to go."[3] To change this, BAM laid a new foundation, in tandem with smaller companies and organizations that worked within and near BAM's premises; Gautam Dasgupta notes that Next Wave coincided with the departure of companies that "helped define a purpose and a philosophy" for BAM.[4] If Next Wave marked a clear shift—described variously as abandonment, selling out, moving forward, and stepping back—one accompanying question is, from what?

BAM's executive director, Harvey Lichtenstein, adjusted his focus on dance in the late 1960s to tap into new theater companies, playwrights, and performance experiments. Audience members filed into refurbished performance spaces to see new plays by Ed Bullins and Amiri Baraka, the street theater of the Everyman Company, translations of Polish avant-garde dramatists, and Peter Brook's multinational company of artists, the International Centre for Theatre Research. As an arts center on city land, BAM—not unlike Joseph Papp's Public Theater building—was uniquely positioned to fill a perceived cultural void. Lichtenstein inaugurated a curatorial phase that incorporated the work of both avant-garde artists and grassroots cultural formations inspired by philosophies of community control. This led to an atypical interplay of local and centralized cultural organizations, which fostered new relationships as well as new causes for dissension between BAM, its neighbors, and the broader landscape of theater in Brooklyn. Throughout, the "Brooklyn Syndrome" that had stood in the way of BAM's progress in the past began to recede, and, along with it, the strength of the neighborhood's working-class associations. Across New York neighborhoods in the early 1970s, the growth of theater and performance in Brooklyn's downtown area emerges dynamically from the historical record, and redefines the spaces and stages of outer-borough performance.

Be a BACA Backa'

Next Wave contributed considerably to the inspired overhaul of the country's oldest performing arts center, the Brooklyn Academy of Music. The Academy opened in its original building on Montague Street in 1861, erected by the city of Brooklyn to present musical, literary, and scientific diversions. A debate over the propriety of its theatrical presentations commenced almost immediately; the Academy's directors favored grand operas accompanied by their Philharmonic Orchestra, with occasional lectures and Horticultural Society flower shows.[5] Yet "the people and the press desired the drama."[6] The directors of the Academy relented, and audiences responded enthusiastically after its first theatrical production, *Hamlet*, appeared in 1861, with productions of Sheridan and Goldsmith following. Through the next decades, Mark Twain, Booker T. Washington, and Edwin Booth visited its stages, until a mysterious fire in 1903 forced the Academy to relocate to a new building on Lafayette Avenue, when Enrico Caruso and the Metropolitan Opera performed at its 1908 gala opening.

Caruso exemplified Academy offerings into the first decades of the twentieth century, when Arturo Toscanini, Martha Graham, Amelia Earhart, and Franklin D. Roosevelt also appeared. The Great Depression of the 1930s led to audience and funding declines, a trend that persisted for decades to come; for the next twenty years, the Academy struggled against a downward spiral. It hosted ballet companies, modern dancers, and dramatic recitals, often without success. The programs between 1957 and 1967, under Director William McKelvy Martin, added solo musical programs, a jazz series with Count Basie, the Brooklyn Philharmonic, and the Brooklyn Opera Company, with theater represented to a more limited extent.[7] When Harvey Lichtenstein arrived in 1967, the programming again shifted. He turned to theater, and often to daring international companies, making decisions in tune with avant-garde influences. Jerzy Grotowski's Polish Laboratory Theatre produced three shows with BAM in 1969 (*The Constant Prince, Acropolis*, and *Apocalypse*), and Lichtenstein charted a course for his institution that "featured less Puccini and Beethoven and more jazz and calypso."[8] Lichtenstein's work to diversify might have fallen short without the concomitant efforts of neighboring arts organizations with a mutually affirming goal: the dismantling of the "Brooklyn Syndrome," or the prejudice that the borough was a cultural backwater. As an aggrieved theater director complained to the *New York Times*, "What goes on in Manhattan is known all over the world. The boroughs are very slighted."[9] The emergence of borough cultural councils represents one major piece of this movement; these organizations sought to organize and connect theater companies in neighborhoods. They countered the image of the outer boroughs as cultural wastelands, and also saw little distinction between cultural development and other local improvement initiatives.

In 1969 Charlene Victor, a former Broadway actress and wife of a Brooklyn politician, formed the Brooklyn Arts and Culture Association (BACA) as an arts advocacy organization in her Flatbush basement. The Parks Department's plans to celebrate the Prospect Park Centennial with little more than a maypole dance infuriated Victor, who gathered a team to organize visual art exhibits and student performances for the centennial. BACA expanded steadily to become the umbrella council for more than 500 civic, educational, cultural, and business institutions that promoted cultural programs in the borough—professional, nonprofessional, and somewhere in between. BACA proved to be a highly adaptive pan-neighborhood organization, and conjoined with the larger movement of borough arts councils and coalitions, like the Harlem Cultural Council, the Brooklyn Association of Theater Arts, and the Boardwalk Arts and Theatre Association (BATA). The performing arts arm of BACA, the Alliance of Brooklyn Theatres, was formed in 1972, and grew to a membership of over 100 groups. These new borough-specific organizations began to demand a share of public funds that had previously supported only established institutions of the "high" arts.

For this reason, BACA forged a complex relationship with its neighbor, BAM. Large or small, all organizations had two main preoccupations: the need for space, and the need to cultivate local audiences. These organizations stood on unequal footing, due to a disparity in their potential for funding and support; the city still directed the bulk of public monies toward older institutions on city property, which BAM was. Despite the best intentions of some of its administrators, the machinery of Cultural Affairs was not nimble enough to serve the decentralized model of organizations that had emerged during the explosion of 1960s theatrical movements.

Should they have been more prepared? By 1970, the *New York Times* covered lively new theater and dance companies cropping up in all boroughs, with simultaneous reporting on the needs of the new arts constellation. A *New York Times* article covering cultural activity in the outer boroughs reported that "poorer sections" of the city were "stirring."[10] Yet even after Mayor Beame—a Brooklyn native—successfully detached Cultural Affairs from the Parks Department, a move intended to liberate the constraints on supporting the arts, there still remained structural hurdles before the balance could be tipped away from the traditional arts institutions on city land.[11] Still, Cultural Affairs began to realize that the cultural life in New York City stretched far beyond institutions built on city property (and therefore with access to the city capital funds), and they expanded their mission through the decade. The recognition of Cultural Affairs as its own economic driver was crucial to BAM's ability to access both city and federal program money.[12]

Concurrently, social equity movements pushed the visibility of arts access to the forefront of cultural debates and sought municipal and state support. A report by Alvin H. Reiss attested to the reality that predominantly affluent, educated, white-collar or professional people attended cultural performances in Manhattan. Reiss described an "indigenous arts impulse" that could lead to a mutually beneficial relationship for "the so-called established arts" if they "would pay it more heed."[13] Since Brooklyn was a bastion of blue-collar workers and a former stronghold of industrial labor production, mainstream publications condescended to cultural events in Brooklyn as analogous to working-class arts. As a consequence, by the mid-1970s, frustration mounted on the part of Brooklyn's institutions. With 2.6 million people, Brooklyn had 33 percent of the city's population but received only 19.8 percent of the funds for institutions. Additional city and state funds for cultural programs went to Manhattan in the greatest number—41.8 percent, and the Bronx, 29.5 percent.[14] Motivated by principles of community representation, outer-borough cultural agencies demanded grant and funding opportunities as well as expanded resources for resident artists in the form of available space.

Shannon Jackson's notion of "infrastructure avowal" acknowledges "interdependent systems of support that sustain human beings, even though we often feel constrained by them," and provokes reflection on the "opportunity and inconvenience of our enmeshment in systems of labor, ecology, able-bodiedness, social welfare, public infrastructure, kinship and more."[15] Jackson's formulation articulates the inevitability of infrastructure support for even antiestablishment or "independent" artists. It also highlights the underlying reason for why artists and theaters linked to a public infrastructure in crisis discover both opportunities and inconveniences through the alliances within these systems. Many outer-borough arts advocates argued against the austerity conditions that were constraining the growth of their operations, and continued to make demands of their officials. When confronted with inflexible defenders of budget cuts and the fiction of a centralized arts landscape, they simultaneously built parallel infrastructures of support, and labored to connect audiences and performers within it.

In fact, some theater artists argued that it was in fact this "enmeshment" in Jackson's interdependent systems of support that would see neighborhood theaters through the fiscal crisis. Woodie King envisioned "multi-conceptional" theaters:

> The ideal theater center there would be a theater run by Robert Macbeth, Leonard Parker, myself, Dorothy Maynor, Barbara Ann Teer, Ernie McClintock, and whoever else. That's the only way it's going to work, because one person does not have the answer. A lot of people think they really know, but this is the age of merging. Everybody's merging. If ITT and ATT can merge, Black people can merge. They have to merge, otherwise, nothing's going to happen.[16]

Macbeth worked in Harlem at the New Lafayette; Maynor founded the Harlem School of the Arts; Teer founded the National Black Theatre; McClintock directed Harlem's Afro-American Studio for Acting and Speech; Parker was a Harlem-based acting teacher. King imagines a theater of transcommunal performance, in which locally determined arts resources facilitate logistically complex and artistically nuanced strategies of cultural production, a "coordinated heterogeneity." Neighborhood-based arts transcended the polarity of centralization versus community control that the city traditionally understood (and funded). New methods of borough-based organizing upturned the usual "discourse of dependency."[17] King and BACA pushed against the myth (and hubris) of autonomous organizations capable of single-handedly reviving an ailing neighborhood, an urban planning philosophy that echoed the "avant-garde egoists" that Dolan critiqued: artistic directors-impresarios who rendered the labor of others invisible.

BACA grew quickly as a booster organization producing a new ethos for Brooklyn: its members refused to accept characterizations of the borough as a rotting appendage on the body of a bruised city. They instead intoned a vibrant (but distant) legacy of theaters in Flatbush, Brighton Beach, and Downtown Brooklyn, with glittering stars and great plays. "Brooklyn is a theater town!!" Each exclamation point was filled with the hope that the injustices of daily life—the trash piles, the teacher layoffs—could be remedied. "For decades, the City of Brooklyn has remained entrenched as a major fortress of live theater, with its output second only to the mainstream legitimate houses of Manhattan."[18] Since many of these individual fortresses no longer operated as theater venues, in their place BACA discovered new, often itinerant, theater companies recently formed in (or migrating to) the borough.

The working class, a category much maligned in media accounts during the fiscal crisis, emerged alternately as a desired or neglected audience for theaters in the 1970s. BACA's promotional materials communicated a bounty of diverse cultural interests, from student dance troupes to community theaters to professional arrivals like the Chelsea Theater Center at BAM. They also employed the rhetoric of outer-borough folksiness. An urban toughness and immigrant pride coexisted with BACA's insistence on a level of professionalism to which many companies aspired; these were not exclusively "community theaters." Yet a palpably working-class undercurrent remained constitutive of BACA's identity; their bumper stickers ("Be a BACA Backa'") playfully alluded to the dialect of Brooklynese. Joshua B. Freeman describes this 1970s phenomenon in which the working class as "a distinct class" became associated with marauding hardhats and Archie Bunker, symbols of Vietnam-era backlash.[19] The BACA materials smoothed over tensions of race, class, gender, and even geospatial differences: its small, printed listings of performances and companies and enthusiastic "theater spotlight" lacked privileging of cultural hierarchy, with political affiliation and location neutralized.

The great hope of organizations like BACA was that the public institutions of society—the churches, theaters, museums, parks—could convince the people of their own health. In an effort to alleviate the hardships facing arts groups during the crisis, BACA departed from its original function as a programming organization and began to offer free workshops about fiscal survival. Within a few years of its founding, BACA joined the austerity debates, and protested the cuts that threatened neighborhood libraries, school arts programs, and upstart theaters. Beginning in late 1973, the usual enthusiasm of the BACA newsletter theater spotlight gave way to pessimism about the future of theatrical production in the borough. By December 1975, BACA warned against "LIFE WITHOUT THE ARTS" unless readers pressured their city officials: "Inform them of the fact that, during a fiscal crisis, the arts are an anchor in the maintaining of civic equilibrium."[20] However, as many protesters argued, in the years prior to the fiscal crisis, this "equilibrium" was not a given for all residents. With basic and nonbasic services persisting under the threat of cuts, civic dissonance resulted from the fears that outer-borough arts would be entirely abandoned.

The Brooklyn Prejudice

In BAM's evolution through the 1970s, its location between multiple retail and residential neighborhoods functioned decisively. So too did its position amid numerous sites of local activism on- and offstage, which responded to the context of the city's "planned shrinkage" policy and its forced reductions in public services. In the predominantly middle-class black neighborhoods near BAM, residents took action against cutbacks to services as basic as trash collection. The laying off of more than 10 percent of the sanitation workforce due to the fiscal crisis (a reduction that led to a 50 percent cut in collection) directly affected these streets.[21] In nearby Crown Heights, residents living at the intersection of Brooklyn Avenue and Dean Street endured nine days without garbage pickup before infuriated protesters piled plastic bags of trash and metal cans in the middle of the street, obstructing traffic and forcing sanitation workers (and the press) to take notice.

Between the years 1972 and 1976, Crown Heights and other largely minority neighborhoods faced impending fire destruction and abandonment, aggravated by dramatic reductions in fire service. Throughout the decade, these neighborhoods were "dismembered and displaced into adjacent middle-class communities, while these themselves crumbled and were dispersed."[22] Urban decay produced both housing and health crises, as massive population shifts accompanied burnout—a "contagious urban decay" that numerous city officials foresaw yet largely ignored, recognizing them as "beyond the fiscal capabilities" of the city.[23] Municipal cutbacks inspired urban activism, as already underserved New Yorkers fought local battles for the maintenance of city services. Yet a significant segment of residents "felt shortchanged even before the reductions came into effect."[24]

The Crown Heights garbage blockade attracted a flicker of press to a neglected area, but as heaps of refuse crowded street corners, the city proclaimed that more had to be done with less. Fed up with curtailed services, boarded-up apartment buildings, and muggings after dark, leaders like Shirley Chisholm fought for improvements and the destruction of racial and gender barriers in nearby districts. Community advocates argued for increased autonomy: to rely on city services was an inner-city fool's errand at a time when "cutback" was rapidly becoming "the most odious word in the lexicon of our daily lives," as editor Charles Reichenthal wrote in a 1977 BACA newsletter. "We must analyze, to a man, the priorities of our society—and, of vast importance, to project the effect of today's cutback on tomorrow's community."[25] This tension between desires for autonomy in the face of neglect and increased community-building to advocate more effectively, extended to the realm of cultural production.

BAM sought to halt the coterminous decline of its audiences. The venue initiated a performance-based dialogue with local concerns, often by featuring the work of playwrights directly plugged in to the drama of urban neglect, such as Roger Furman's *The Long Black Block*, produced in two short runs in BAM's Lepercq Space: in 1973, and then again at the onset of 1975. *The Long Black Block* dramatizes the realities of spatial segregation as well as the public and private, material and psychological, repercussions of political corruption and official negligence. Furman wanted to move beyond overly didactic theater to theater that dealt "directly with the life of the black community, such as housing, drugs, welfare," and to do so he crafted present panoramas that "told of the community's problems, of its hopes and dreams."[26] *The Long Black Block* captured the frustrations of residents in a row of dilapidated brownstone houses in Harlem, an indictment of its decay in full view of the polis.

Furman's play opens with a blues prologue that laments the youth of the neighborhood who have been sent off to fight the Vietnam War, and those left behind with dope pushers marauding the streets. Chorus cries of "What is the Ghetto made of?" are answered with, "Let me go away from here."[27] The building's super, Mrs. Zelda R. Howards, is a tired guardian who watches over the house and the block. She lives in a lonely basement flat with the water pipes clanging beside her. She bitterly condemns the neighborhood malaise as she sweeps her stoop: "We ain't got no real leaders so to speak. We don't have any kind of real Black power like they've been talking about. And you know damn well that we don't have any money."[28] We meet a young couple whose plans for escape diverge. Lottie dreams of the theater and of one day performing alongside her stage idols, Ruby Dee, James Earl Jones, Diana Sands, and Diahann Carroll. Her boyfriend, Van, plots a path of political action: community control that could take over the derelict buildings. Lottie mocks Van's "Mickey Mouse revolutionary jive," and when she reveals that she might have an opportunity to go on the road with a touring production of a play, Van retaliates:

> You know damn well niggers ain't raising no hell on Broadway or any other way. Girl, you know you've got to have a big name to make it in this country. Why don't you join the little theatre group over at the women's Y? At least you'll be doing something that you like. Forget all about that big time stuff.[29]

The Long Black Block implicates the audience in a particularly bleak performance of neighborhood; the stoop encompasses the life of the bar, laundromat, beauty parlors, the junkie looking to jive, the pusher looking to ensnare youth. A hopefulness edges into the frame to occasionally soften the conditions in the broken-down apartment building, usually in the form of the matriarchal Super. The characters disagree in philosophy, but all provide unsparing analyses of the urban power dynamics, political will, and artistic visions in the places where the cutting of city services signified a deepening of long-standing spatial injustices.

When the play was first presented in Brooklyn as part of BAM's 1973 Black Theater Alliance (BTA) festival, Mel Gussow's review in the *New York Times* critiqued overly long scenes and "too broad" characters with repetitive themes; still, he singled out Furman's play as clearly deserving of "an extended engagement," though he did not review the show's brief return to BAM in 1975.[30] Furman mounted the show at BAM after its runaway 1972 success at the New Heritage Theatre in Harlem.[31] A review in the *Amsterdam News* praised the "wild experience" of the play, and discussed specifically the resonance of its venue:

> So we understand this powerful thing they're doing at the New Heritage Theatre on 125th Street near Madison Avenue. We understand that Black people had to take an old loft with wall-to-wall mess and turn it into a clean, comfortable theatre so that they could produce plays that we can relate to. Now we can sit there and share this experience with the audience and the players. We surely KNOW the characters in *The Long Black Block*.[32]

A second review in the same newspaper described the capacity of the play to diminish the separation between art and its audience; the spectators collaborated in upending the conventions of Western theater. "How do you review an audience that becomes its own performance?" The critic acknowledges the intersections of place and performance in his wish for the play: "I hope this play will remain in the community, not running off, as some theatre exercises have recently, to become show business casualties."[33] Yet the material challenges faced by Furman at his New Heritage Repertory Theatre, Harlem's oldest active theater company, likely made an extended run at BAM an attractive option.

Furman started the New Heritage in 1964 as a street theater with Haryou-Act, the federally financed antipoverty program. Acquiring stable rehearsal and production space posed a distinct problem after the years of its Great Society funding. The BTA had been formed to address exactly these issues: it sought to increase box office revenue and audience base with stronger publicity, fund-raising, and advertising. [34] At a forum on black theater in 1971, Furman described his plight, shared between so many BTA companies:

> We have to pay $300 a month, and we miss the rent one time and that man, you know what to call him, is going to be there to put our ass out—chairs, seats, scenery, flats—right on the street. So, to sit and talk and say how beautiful it is . . . all the people in my company are working like hell. They are all workers, they have no money. We put in our own dues to pay the rent, to get the lights on, to get our scenery, to get the scripts mimeographed off, and we even pay our authors royalties—we have the nerve to give somebody a royalty.[35]

City governments and funding organizations sought bargain basement ways to remedy the problems of urban decline, while the oldest theater in Harlem remained unfunded. Furman's argument echoed a larger debate, trenchant at the time. Some federal, state, and city officials viewed the funneling of arts money to troubled neighborhoods as downright irresponsible—"at best the idea sounds wide-eyed, at worst like putting inmates in charge of the asylum."[36] Yet those same officials and pundits considered the upkeep of city-owned arts facilities like BAM an urban investment. This argument suggested that a livable city would arise not from the guidelines of legislative action, but from a refurbishment of neighborhood landmarks, given a new setting and status.

A short subway ride separated BAM from the trash revolt block in Crown Heights. Yet throughout the 1960s the cultural center remained largely invisible as an arts resource for the surrounding residents, and BAM resolved to reverse that state of affairs.[37] Throughout the late 1960s and 1970s, the institution underwent a phase of self-reflection regarding its relevance to the "community," in an effort to improve flagging audience numbers. This self-reflection, however, proved a difficult task for leaders in downtown Brooklyn who still clung to the top-down approach to urban and cultural development that had once been ascendant. In the early 1960s, the area that was to be the symbolic and geographic heart of the borough's industrial renaissance struggled mightily; some even suggested that the Academy be demolished.[38] BAM (then still known as the Academy of Music) shared in the reputation of its streets as unsafe. Local boosters begged businesses to remain in the area. The many single-screen cinemas that had thrived in the neighborhood closed down in favor of large multiplexes, leaving behind darkened streets and few patrons for restaurants. In 1965, then director William McKelvy Martin blamed the low attendance on the exodus of middle-class residents out of the area. In his 1962 annual report, he expressed doubt that the borough even wanted such an institution.[39] Martin's predecessor, Julius Bloom, blamed audience erosion between 1948 and 1957 on "the Brooklyn Prejudice," which led audiences to see the same artists perform in Manhattan, but not in Brooklyn.

Martin hewed closely to this narrative, but with a slight variation. By 1965, the flight of the white middle class became the target of city officials hoping to foster a resurgence of elite cultural goods in the area. The head commissioner of city planning, Elinor C. Guggenheimer, argued that unless they enhanced life in Brooklyn, "the borough would become a tremendous lower income bedroom, a desert of urban renewal projects and a vast concentration of unsolvable racial segregation."[40] She praised small bursts of neighborhood enthusiasm in Park Slope, Brooklyn Heights, Cobble Hill, Coney Island, Bedford-Stuyvesant. But the "hub" was of concern—the area around the Long Island Rail Road depot, right near the Academy, where stretches of Flatbush Avenue were popular corridors for prostitutes and drug peddlers, and crime was on the rise. Administrators at the Brooklyn Institute of Arts and Sciences (the Academy was underneath the Institute's umbrella until 1971) adopted this sociological explanation for the institute's difficulties. In 1968 John R. H. Blum, the vice president of the board, tried to imagine the Institute as a constructive force that might "resolve many of the biting animosities that divide the City."[41] In addition to budget cuts, the Academy faced "the resentment stirred by militant demands for minority control," and "underlying feelings of opportunity long denied."[42] In truth, attendance at the Academy's "enrichment" programs had been ailing well before Blum acknowledged the need to reconsider programming in light of its social and cultural context. "Travel and adventure" still received top billing, and a group of all-male, all-white faculty members at Brooklyn College led a lecture series. The Academy's arts programming included the Brooklyn Opera Company, the Brooklyn Philharmonic, Paul Taylor Dance Company, and some evidence of collaborations that presaged its later focus, including the McCarter Theatre Repertory Company of Princeton.

Administrators at the Academy and Institute, however, resisted a focus on new residents—and those who remained throughout the suburban exodus—in favor of activating a population they feared losing to the suburbs entirely. Julia Foulkes describes the extent of the population redistribution that had occurred when the neighborhoods of Fort Greene and Bedford-Stuyvesant changed from Irish, Italian, and Scandinavian families to predominantly African American, Puerto Rican, and Caribbean families.[43] The African American population grew from 7.6 percent of the total population in the borough in 1950 to 32 percent in 1980—but "the increase in African American and Puerto Rican residents on the streets directly around BAM was even more divergent, becoming close to sixty percent of the population there by 1970."[44] Veiled behind arguments for the resuscitation of the Academy was, then, the nationwide belief that investing in a performing arts center could reverse population decline. Guggenheimer believed that the "Brooklyn Syndrome" or "Brooklyn Prejudice" could be mitigated with funding and attention to unique cultural attractions. Others felt that BAM's target audience—Manhattan theater patrons—would never be attracted to an outer borough for serious theater.

Even before Lichtenstein arrived, the city had been relatively generous with money for the Academy throughout the 1960s. In 1962, Mayor Wagner and the Board of Estimate approved a $750,000 rehabilitation project at the Academy; in 1964 they upgraded the building's heating systems, equipment, staircases, and dressing rooms.[45] This constituted a municipal leap of faith, and in 1967, when the board hired Lichtenstein as director, Mayor Lindsay approved more money from city coffers, in addition to Ford Foundation funds.[46] The Academy hoped Lichtenstein's administrative experience could revive its subscriber numbers; tellingly, Lichtenstein arrived at BAM from Lincoln Center, where, during an internship for cultural administrators sponsored by the Ford Foundation, he initiated and ran the 1964–65 subscription campaigns for the New York City Ballet and the New York City Opera.[47] Even better, Lichtenstein was a Brooklyn Boy. The child of Polish and Russian immigrants who settled in Bushwick, and the brother of the painter Roy Lichtenstein, he discovered dance while a student at Brooklyn College and abandoned his plans to study engineering. He later studied modern dance and ballet with Merce Cunningham, Martha Graham, and at the experimental Black Mountain arts school.[48] Still, in the years to come, audiences and media perceived a growing chasm between Lichtenstein, who came from working-class immigrant stock, and the new working-class immigrant arrivals in the neighborhood.

Historian Suleiman Osman describes this moment of demographic and cultural change, when the borough's once thriving industrial economy faded and large numbers of working-class white residents anxious about the changing racial composition of the area and declining work opportunities fled for the suburbs.[49] At the same time, African American and Puerto Rican migrants arrived, only to find themselves trapped in "decaying tenements surrounded by abandoned townhouses," with few job prospects. Osman stresses the postindustrial elements over deindustrialization:

> Rather than the site of a bipolar conflict between black and white, Brownstone Brooklyn was a multiethnic, multiclass, and polyglot landscape with multiple and shifting conflicts and coalitions. . . . Rather than a flat space, Brownstone Brooklyn's deindustrialized landscape was a layered landscape that retained the imprints of previous eras of economic structuring. The palimpsest of empty factories, waterfront piers, and Victorian townhouses was a repository of symbolic value for white-collar enthusiasts, black power activists, white ethnic homeowners, and a variety of neighborhood groups.[50]

The development of postwar urban history that led to the influx of white-collar professionals into low-income central city areas brought a flood of "Brownstoners" distinguished by cultural and social capital. Arts organizations in Brooklyn found themselves at the crosshairs of this conflict; the multiethnic, multiclass, and polyglot communities did not fit easily into binaries of cultural consumption. David Savran argues that the economic, social, and cultural hierarchies implicated in matters of taste are always determined by many different factors; highbrow taste is not the exclusive province of the upper classes, or even those with the most education. "It is, in fact, more often than not associated with intellectual rather than economic elites," but hierarchies of taste become intelligible only when linked to class relations.[51] Osman argues that these Brownstoners (a term Osman uses interchangeably with geographer David Ley's "new middle-class") did have a specific sense of identity and consumption/lifestyle patterns, and it is here that issues of taste, class, and proximity collide.

BAM needed to adjust to these changing patterns of social class and ethnicity in the city. New cultural structures, forms, and hierarchies threatened to render the programming of large institutions obsolete. For Savran, the breakdown of clear taste hierarchies in the 1950s and early 1960s represents "the very end of the era during which hierarchy of taste was a useful and accurate guide to the disposition of economic, educational, and cultural capital in the United States."[52] Political and social radicalism, cultural nationalisms, a youth culture explosion, Pop Art, Minimalism—all of these trends (and more) challenged the opposition between elite and mass culture. The Academy administrators were tastemakers coping with the twin problems of their own increasing cultural isolation and an urban environment that they perceived as unsettled by heterogeneity. The stewards of theater spaces worked to redefine their audiences, which were bifurcated by disparate cultural expectations.

Nearby to BAM, the renovation of homes in dilapidated neighborhoods gained momentum. Longtime and new residents constituted this movement, with rebuilding efforts aided by private entities like ConEdison. Seth Faison, chairman of BAM's board, identified "a new potential audience . . . out there among the brownstoners and the black middle-class in the surrounding neighborhoods."[53] Soon, BAM marketed directly to the sensibilities of potential home buyers, as in an ad in the 1976 program for the Everyman Company of Brooklyn's *Everyman and roach*, performed in the Lepercq Space: "The rebirth of the city has begun in Brooklyn. It was incubated in the brownstone houses of Brooklyn. Nurtured by energetic people creating new homes, new neighborhoods and a new Brooklyn."[54] The ad lauded the five "Cinderella" restoration projects that Brooklyn Union Gas had undertaken in the borough, and its most recent project, Cinderella V, underway on St. Felix Street, adjacent to BAM. "The rebirth of the city," the copy explained, was "sparked by people who with paint brush and hammer are creating a bright future for themselves and the community."[55] BAM's potential and the city's potential had become one. There existed an inspiring symmetry between this vision of Brooklyn and the spirit of the Everyman company, which typified the "wealth and vitality" of the do-it-yourself street theater movement.[56] Brother Jonathan Ringkamp, a high school teacher and Franciscan brother, ran the Everyman Theatre Company, which began working with youth on street corners in Coney Island. Many small Brooklyn theater companies cycled through BAM's offbeat, intimate Lepercq; others found refuge in the neglected physical plants of community spaces that increasingly hosted theaters.

Could BAM aid the goals of the neighborhood arts movements—and appeal to new populations—while also re-creating itself as an international cultural destination? Would BAM transform into a performing arts center for Osman's "multiple and shifting conflicts and coalitions," or adhere to a definition of culture and leisure to attract the white, "young marrieds with children"?[57] Could particular models of theater producing begin to achieve both? A refashioned and refurbished cultural jewel was the kind of civic monument that the borough needed to convince the city—and the nation—that it was more than the sum of its bad press. While the burgeoning brownstone movement (augmented by tax policies and support from corporations like Con Edison) grew, a question remained: for whom were they renovating the Academy?

The Specter of Social Work

BAM's production history from the 1970s shows compelling variety and a nearly frenetic embrace of a wide range of companies across styles, political interests, and definitions of "professional" theater. At the time, the Ford Foundation offered grants for the establishment of resident companies and artists. Early in his tenure, Lichtenstein expressly wanted a black theater to be in residence; he renovated the lecture hall used to present travelogues to senior citizens to make way for a new repertory company.[58] His first choice for its artistic director, Robert Macbeth, instead founded his New Lafayette Theatre in Harlem, and Lichtenstein continued to search. Intrigued by the Chelsea Theater Center's mounting of thirty-six plays in three years, Lichtenstein decided to commit to Robert Kalfin's company. When Lichtenstein invited the Chelsea to be the resident company at the Academy for its 1968–69 season, George Bari, one of the theater's cofounders, feared that the move to BAM's facility would destroy their momentum: "There was no there there."[59] By 1971, the *Times* declared the Chelsea Theater Center at the Brooklyn Academy of Music "the most exciting new theatre in America."[60]

The company's record of producing work in nontraditional venues far from the theater district, and its successful building of diverse audiences, matched with Lichtenstein's goals. Their previous productions—including Archie Shepp's jazz allegory, *Junebug Graduates Tonight!*—garnered both critical attention and political controversy, and proved that the bold company could devise collaborations not likely to be encountered elsewhere. In one of their earliest performance spaces, an Episcopal church in Chelsea, on 28th Street and Ninth Avenue, sandwiched between predominantly Jewish and Puerto Rican housing projects, Kalfin staged *Las Ventanas* by Roberto Rodriguez, and transformed the inside of the church into a Puerto Rican tenement. Admission was free, the performances were full, and local audiences raved. Because of this adventurous production history, BACA heralded the arrival of the Chelsea Theater Center at BAM as a natural extension of a "cultural revolution" that debunked "that long unquestioned misconception that Manhattan holds all the franchises on exciting theatre."[61]

The Chelsea won further goodwill early in its tenure at BAM through its free performances in the comfortable, refurbished Third Theatre. Once installed, the company mounted controversial imports, newly translated international works, and political theater: *Christophe* by John Gay (1968), Edward Bond's *Saved* (1971), *The Water Hen* by Polish dramatist Stanislaw Ignacy Witkiewicz (1971), Leonard Bernstein's *Candide* (1974), and Megan Terry's *Hothouse* (1974). The plays attracted diverse audiences; the theoretically attuned Amiri Baraka entrusted his *Slave Ship* to the theater after the play had languished unproduced for four years. Baraka appreciated BAM's location "on the edge of Bedford-Stuyvesant," and black audiences made up 60 to 70 percent of each house.[62] Howard Clurman described the audience for the Chelsea's 1969 *Black Quartet*, a series of short plays produced by Woodie King and written by LeRoi Jones (Amiri Baraka), Ed Bullins, Ben Caldwell and Ronald Milner as "composed [of] nearly as many teenaged blacks as of older white and black folk," laughing and applauding "in rapturous glee."[63] A 1972 collaboration between BAM and the Chelsea led to *Lady Day: A Musical Tragedy*, written by Harlem playwright Aishah Rahman and directed by Paul Carter Harrison, which revived Kalfin's collaboration with musician Archie Shepp. Tellingly, *Lady Day* was the opener of the season in the 1,200-seat music hall, not the quirky Lepercq black box; this demonstrated an institutional commitment to works that positioned black concerns and creative teams centrally.[64] In 1973, El Teatro Campesino chose the Chelsea as the inaugural indoor stop for *La carpa de los Rasquachis* before launching an outdoor tour of the city's parks.[65]

In his theatrical migration to Brooklyn, Robert Kalfin transformed the Chelsea from a primarily new play workshop into a major professional theater that eventually ran full productions for three weeks and charged admission. "When we moved to Brooklyn, it was not our ambition to get Manhattan to come to Brooklyn," explained Kalfin. "We looked to Brooklyn and its people. But we found that if we did something that was exciting people would come from everywhere."[66] In 1971, 70 percent of the Chelsea's audience (average age: twenty-six) came from Brooklyn—equally divided among residents of Park Slope, Brooklyn Heights, Flatbush, and Bedford-Stuyvesant, with the rest from Connecticut, Westchester, New Jersey, and other boroughs.[67]

Throughout the full span of the Chelsea's tenancy at BAM (1968–78), the company bridged the Brooklyn institution to the Manhattan performance scene in ways previously unimaginable and frequently contentious. At BAM, the Chelsea acquired a courtesy Off Broadway classification in theater listings; it transcended the "Brooklyn Syndrome" while it also gathered strength from its position as outsider. "The word 'Manhattan' means what we want it to mean, *Alice in Wonderland*-wise, when we include Brooklyn's Chelsea Theater Center and Academy of Music programs" in Off Broadway listings, wrote critic Otis Guernsey, commenting on the disappearing borders between "professional" and "semi-professional," Off Broadway and location.[68] With shows like a five-hour long, Obie-winning production of Genet's *The Screens* (with more than forty players) Manhattan theatergoers could be tempted to the seats of BAM, and later return on a bus chartered for the purposes of shuttling them back. Lichtenstein instituted the bus service between Brooklyn and Manhattan in 1968, and it incited complaints from Brooklyn residents (notably, Alvin Ailey), who desired bus service between BAM and *other* neighborhoods in the borough.[69]

The realities of the neighborhoods outside of the doors weighed heavily on a company (and an institution) already preoccupied with both audience analysis and critical reception. Kalfin's eclectic approach to theater was anachronistic at a time when many theater companies in Brooklyn claimed definite political positioning and community alliances. While Kalfin made daring and often brilliant artistic moves, his mentality remained, as Napoleon argues, *in* Brooklyn but never was "of Brooklyn."[70] This distinction might seem imprecise, but within the broader salience of the cultural activity near BAM at the time, it has resonance:

> Kalfin did not ignore the larger society beyond the stage door—Chelsea plays often spoke to or about it—but he treated it with a respectful distance, as a president of one country might treat the population of a bordering country with which he wanted to maintain good relations.[71]

The Chelsea had presented itself as a theater company that could ably fill the gap between uneven Off-Off Broadway and the commercialized Off Broadway. They even managed to create this "middle world" in the imaginations of audiences, as well as in the official regulations governing small theater operations: the Chelsea began as an OOB house but arranged a special contract with Actors' Equity that put it "mid-way between Off-Broadway and Off-Off," and allowed it to produce longer runs with transfers to Manhattan.[72] Yet while articles claimed the theater was "free of any aspirations to Broadway or anywhere else," in 1972 the Chelsea signed a ten-year lease for a building on West 43rd Street as a "Manhattan annex" for its activities.[73]

This decision to produce plays in Brooklyn *and* on the West Side of Manhattan proved a logistical and artistic undertaking so ambitious that it nearly broke the company. In 1974 their large-scale environmental production of Leonard Bernstein's *Candide*, directed by Harold Prince, removed all 1,800 seats of the Broadway Theatre, positioned the audience on fixed stools, and turned the pit into "the jungle of El Dorado."[74] In 1975 the Chelsea had three productions at BAM, two at its Westside Theatre, and Broadway runs of *Yentl* and *By Bernstein*, a work celebrating Bernstein's lost theater music. By 1976, the financial problems intimated in media reports as early as 1971 had finally reached a breaking point: the maverick company had been showered with acclaim, but never reached even a moderate level of financial stability.[75] The Chelsea wanted to maintain an interactive sense of audience and theater space, but the "specter of social work" haunted its stormy decade at BAM as Kalfin struggled to balance creative vision with the politics of place. Pressure surged for the Chelsea to mount work for "social reasons," and coexisted with unrelenting financial pressures.[76] As part of their original agreement, Lichtenstein committed to work with Kalfin to maintain the Chelsea's free admission policy, which had clearly been a great help in attracting past diverse audiences, but this policy could not be sustained.[77] The press loudly hailed the Chelsea's bold choices—producing plays considered nearly impossible to stage—while the company itself operated within a desperate financial situation.

The administrators of the Chelsea maintained that working in three locations—Brooklyn, the West Side, and Broadway—did not "undermine its Brooklyn background," and sought to cast this proliferation of shows as a direct result of its success. Their choice of plays, however, now appeared aimed more squarely at Broadway producers than at residents culled from multiethnic neighborhoods. Productions of Lodewijk de Boer's epic four-part *The Family*, Tankred Dorst's drama about a Nazi collaborator, *Ice Age*, the classic German play, Heinrich von Kleist's *The Prince of Homburg*, and Edward Brewster Shelton's 1911 melodrama *The Boss*—were often chosen with subscriber packages in mind.[78]

Alongside the "three phrases" often emphasized in BAM's rejuvenation (dance, theater, Next Wave), there were concurrent phases related to its community engagement approach: first "passive" (discounted tickets for schoolchildren), then a deeper partnering with minority companies and presenting of work from "alternative" communities, and, ultimately, a diminished attention toward neighborhood arts showcases in favor of avant-garde programming. Throughout, BAM negotiated the friction between the representation of difference on stage and the needs of the institution. The intellectual and critical establishment—some of whom held comparatively conservative ideas of a night out at the Academy—remained essential to its rebuilding. The Chelsea Theater's productions constituted one major step in the transformation of BAM's spaces from its previous offerings of lectures and travelogues. While the company continued to mount shows in its upstairs space, Lichtenstein continued to experiment with the forms, genres, and artists most suited to the new BAM. Its multiple stages allowed BAM to host exciting instances of cross-pollination between so-called community groups and Lichtenstein's avant-garde fare. Perhaps tellingly, these are still much overlooked, even in BAM's own institutional history.[79]

The Tyranny of Manhattan

The buses ferrying Manhattanites to BAM, the decision of the Chelsea Theater to split operations between the West Side and Brooklyn, the mobilization of cultural organizations making demands on the city support networks: all were variations of resistance to the attrition of cultural development across the outer-borough neighborhoods. On a national scale, Alvin Reiss remained resolute that small, local efforts would have long-standing impact on the country's flailing cities: "Grants should be given openly to culture, not disguised as grants for training, education, or anything else. A performing arts group in the ghetto is providing an essential service to the community, not unlike welfare, education or health care. It should not be seeking a handout, but reimbursement for its services."[80] Brooklyn's working-class and "ghetto" labels threatened to unsettle stable barriers between Off-Off, Off Broadway, and location; could it thrive both as something for the "dems" and "douse" to enjoy in the outer boroughs, and for powerful Manhattan boards to save and exalt? Was there physical space and political viability for distinct outer borough performance practices in a protracted funding landscape? These provided the context for the development of BAM, and for the centralization of theater resources—BAM, Broadway, and the Public Theater—that occurred during the 1970s. Geography intersected with issues of taste and class to create a potent conflict during the fiscal crisis, one that inflamed the passions of theater artists who glimpsed a future for performance practices not centrally located or controlled, but still very much a functioning piece of the official machinations of New York City's culture.

The June 1974 First American Congress of Theatre (FACT) showcased these confrontations as outer-borough voices protested perceived tyrannies on the map of culture. The reductive "center" versus "edges" geographic imaginary positioned Manhattan—and large, centralized theater spaces—as the dominant force silencing an increasingly inclusive and pluralistic theater hierarchy. FACT is chiefly remembered as an overture by commercial theaters seeking to align themselves with regional theaters, although the antics of notorious anti-establishment figures feature prominently in accounts.[81] Yet the four-day event at Princeton's Woodrow Wilson School of Public and International Affairs also aired perspectives on decentralization and its relationship to aesthetics. Was the legendary producer David Merrick the most important figure in the American theater, or was it parolee-playwright and "ghetto activist" Miguel Piñero?[82] The allocation of tangible and intangible resources as well as the territorial effects of belonging and exclusion dominated many of the panels and discussions.

Some of the key players on Broadway created the FACT organization to counteract what producer Gerald Schoenfeld called theater's "urban environment problem."[83] Deep aesthetic and political divisions frequently overshadowed the ambitious goal of the event, which was for the theater community to speak with "one voice on all matters concerning public subsidy and other forms of aid," especially given the "the disastrous conjunction of inflation and economic recession, the need to relate to and stimulate more effectively the young and minority audiences," rising production and operating costs, and the unpredictable nature of financial support.[84] FACT proceeded with the assumption that "one voice" was possible and desirable.

The strategy of urban regeneration through culture did not have clear application in a landscape as striated as New York. The suspicion among independent theater-makers grew: were commercial producers using the "urban deterioration" as an excuse to curry favor with funding outlets? During the conference, Joan Sandler, the head of the BTA, described the economic plight of "the disenfranchised theaters"; Woodie King of the New Federal Theatre praised future-oriented producers, and criticized those who "[kept] doing what they were doing," to the detriment of the city.[85] André Gregory argued with Richard Barr's contention that all artists fix their dreams in Broadway: "we must not deal with fantasies. . . . It is no longer true that Broadway is the goal."[86] For a new generation of artists, trained on the stages of Off-Off Broadway, the status quo of Broadway—as a nexus for professional goals and a space of dreaming—no longer held a deadlock on their geographic imaginations. As a consequence, they challenged FACT's Manhattan-centric focus and chafed at the limits of exclusionary conversations. They homed in on the specific prejudices that circulated around race, class, space, theatergoing, and theater-funding. Hazel Joan Bryant, the founder of the Afro-American Total Theatre and the secretary of the BTA, critiqued the dissonance between the conference plenaries and her own work, which was focused on rebuilding communities:

> While it's true that some theaters are in poor neighborhoods and you're afraid to go there, that doesn't mean that it is not important what goes on there . . . if you would take off those words that make some of us pure and some of us illegitimate or a little bit dirty or I wouldn't go there. . . . Even the word "alternative" is a word like "white" and "non white," "real" and "not real," words like that are being used and making it impossible for some people who are looking for new ideas to come to the places where there are also very interesting things being done.[87]

She was not speaking of BAM; she was speaking of the neighborhood theaters, the street theaters, the professional theaters crammed into community centers for lack of space. She argued for changed definitions of audience and theater districts: where work was made, seen, scouted, and legitimized.

The recommendations that survived the conference intact related most directly to producers and theater owners in Times Square. FACT's summer meeting after the June conference developed a list of priorities cherry-picked from—and not always representative of—the Princeton conference. Initiatives included a coordinated lobby for all theater that would make it available to congressmen and other legislators, especially Mayor Ed Koch; a fund to support a massive survey by economist William Baumol to look at the economics of Broadway; a "continuing personnel group" to provide information on federal, state, and local taxes for theaters; a tax incentive for theater investors; a proposal to remove theater from antitrust laws; a push to repeal real property tax laws affecting theaters; a second TKTS discount ticket booth on Wall Street; the pursuit of a system of selling block tickets to business interests; and an affiliation with the *New York Times* to produce directories of plays. Each item centered on the needs of Broadway and the strengthening of the economic model and cultural system in place. Among the issues widely discussed at FACT but neglected in the post-conference review: support for playwrights, labor issues, the meaning of the "nonprofit" designation, the specific challenges that faced black theaters, the role of small theaters around the country, the paucity of theater in youth education, and the importance of theater in rebuilding communities around the five boroughs. Although small theaters multiplied at a rapid clip, the search for solutions common to both Sandler's and Shubert's theaters proved elusive.

Broadway producers and outer-borough theaters were not the only organizations discovering that the demographic makeup of their constituencies had changed. The religious institutions of downtown Brooklyn faced similar challenges to arts groups. Their underused facilities, however, held the potential to reach the mix of cultures converging in these neighborhoods. In addition to the Everyman Street Theater Company, over a dozen theater companies collaborated with churches to present plays around the borough. By 1975, collaborations between theater companies and ecumenical institutions reached a zenith for theater troupes in search of stages: the Festival Repertory Company, producing at the Flatbush Y; On Stage Repertory Company, located at the Church of the Advent; Encore Studio, at the Windsor Terrace Church; and Master Works Laboratory Theater, at Spencer Memorial Church. In the next years, this list grew; the Clinton Hill Repertory Company produced a version of Peter Copani's well-reviewed street theater musical, *Street Jesus*, at Emmanuel Christian Center on St. James Place, and the Flatbush Repertory Company and the Dorchester Masquers operated out of the Flatbush-Tompkins Church. Neither amateur nor Off-Off Broadway, this vestigial and transcommunal performance movement held clear benefits for all involved, and shielded many companies from the instability that accompanied the fiscal crisis symptoms FACT identified: the conjunction of inflation and economic recession, the need to reach young and minority audiences, and rising production and operating costs. It did little, however, to solve the larger unpredictability of financial support during a fiscal crisis, or to create permanent facilities for local arts organizations.

One of these theaters in downtown Brooklyn, the Big Apple Theater (BAT), formed in the wake of a negative artistic experience at the Public Theater. Jan Barry, a poet and a founder of Vietnam Vets Against the War, moved to Brooklyn in the late 1960s with his future wife, theater director Paula Kay Pierce. Pierce had adapted Barry's poetry collection about the war into dramatic form, which was scheduled for production at the Public Theater before producer Joseph Papp abruptly canceled the show during previews. (According to Barry, Papp wanted to replace Pierce as director, and the couple refused to comply.) This and other forays into the theater by director and actor Pierce motivated the couple to create BAT with a mission to counteract race and gender stereotyping and the exploitation of theater talent they found in Off Broadway houses.

In April 1975 BAT began a residency at the Lafayette Avenue Presbyterian Church, at the corner of South Oxford Street in Fort Greene, down the street from BAM's Lafayette Avenue building. In a news profile of BAT, "Brooklyn Theater Is Trying to Be Different," Pierce described their desire "to be involved with the theater of ideas and social comment."[88] One of the earliest productions at the church was Lorraine Hansberry's second and infrequently produced play, *The Sign in Sidney Brustein's Window* (1964). Its themes connect racial discord with ideological hypocrisies during the fallout from 1960s idealism. The play's protagonist, Sidney Brustein, is nearing forty and clings to his left-wing political ideals even as a succession of his ambitious ventures fail. He impulsively buys a radical weekly newspaper and campaigns earnestly for a reform candidate running against a machine politician in Greenwich Village. His marriage crumbles along with his faith in his candidate, who is revealed to be a puppet for the political machine. The play, then a decade old, proved Hansberry prescient in her depiction of a crisis in one New York City neighborhood: fractious and distrustful communities sorting through the remains of short-circuited activism. Robert Nemiroff understood the play in relation to Hansberry's earlier *A Raisin in the Sun*, in which the Younger family had decided to risk all for the new home in the white middle-class neighborhood. With *Sidney Brustein*, Hansberry "was saying that that house was on fire, the community a disaster area of the soul, and that a great deal of rebuilding would have to be done from the ground up if the neighborhood was to be fit for the Youngers to live in at all."[89]

Hansberry's depiction of 1960s radicals awakening to the dysfunction of their streets and local political system and the fragmentation of their ideals resonated with the Brownstoner movement, while also capturing something of the zeal underlying progressive neighborhood reform. Not merely a restoration fad, Suleiman Osman describes this as a cultural revolt that shunned suburbia, actively sought "diversity, authenticity, community, historicity," and led to renovated housing as well as block associations, food cooperatives, tree planting, and all forms of betterment.[90] As Barry recalls, a minister's wife in their neighborhood who led writing classes for area children impressed both him and Pierce. The energy from BAM's renewed theater programming also influenced the couple, and their first organized neighborhood poetry event "was meant to try to see how we could add to that sense of making neighborhoods livable communities through the arts."[91] Even as the murder rates remained alarmingly high, Pierce and Barry quickly identified a cluster of people looking to "connect with the neighborhood in every way, including block associations, poetry readings, and plays."[92] BAT received small grants from BACA, but Pierce supported these activities and the $300–400 production costs with her job at an advertising agency.

The diversity of institutional structures and arrangements for theater provision at this moment demonstrates the evolving relationships between modes of performance practices in the neighborhood, often with shared objectives. BAM received large sums from public and private sources, and it presented itself as a cultural center meeting community needs. In 1974 Lichtenstein pushed the Brooklyn borough president for a 100 percent funding increase for the coming year—from $700,000 to $1.5 million.[93] "With our newly established alliance with the School of Performing Arts at Brooklyn College," Lichtenstein explained, "we are of more and more service to the community. With increased capital over the next five to ten years, the building could be utilized doubly, air-conditioned, and more programs made available at a lower price."[94] BAM's building acted as a crucial stabilizer, and its intangible neighborhood resources became the same. A lack of available money for groups who remained precariously pitched toward insolvency and looked to secure their own performance spaces created an inequitable contrast with BAM's historically privileged status as a city institution enjoying rent-free accommodations and deficit spending. Lichtenstein's demands irked some of these companies who received a fraction of that funding for their own community alliances. But his circumstances also required boldness, particularly if his institution was to make it through the challenges of the city's fiscal environment. Renovations in the nearly 72-year-old Academy building were costly. BAM may have had access to capital funds for building improvements because of its location on city-owned property, but every aspect of its programming and operations required considerable investment. Marlyn Baum describes BAM's deficit spending in great detail, and in its own publications BAM acknowledges this practice as a kind of quirk of its daring leader, whose habit of overreaching was "often abetted by larger economic crises in the city and the country."[95] This acceptance of deficit spending among arts institutions quickly took on ethical dimensions: which arts groups survived the fiscal crisis period through deficit spending, and which could not?

Exceptionalism

Throughout the 1970s BAM reinvented its physical space, cushioned by its philosophy of budgetary exceptionalism. In the years between 1971 and 1973, BAM endured its most challenging financial period. In the years after the fiscal crisis, however, BAM rebounded, thanks to a newly proactive board of directors, Lichtenstein's leadership, and steps taken by the city government to bolster its support. In its 1974–75 annual report, BAM explained that a positive business approach helped to decrease its accumulated deficit. Three years later, Lichtenstein admitted that he and his colleagues at times felt "deeply depressed and pessimistic about BAM, its ability to attract an audience, and its financial viability."[96] Nonetheless, an ambitious and long-planned renovation of the entire building was underway. In 1976 BAM redesigned the smaller of two ground-floor theaters to create the 1,000-seat Carey Playhouse (now BAM Rose Cinemas). This evolution is significant; the BAM Café and the BAM Rose Cinemas ultimately displaced two theaters dedicated to live performance, leaving only the two larger performance spaces. While grand (and beneficial in terms of optimizing ticket sales), they have neither the flexibility nor the intimacy of the Lepercq or the Carey. Even after the building suffered major flooding in 1977, when its financial resources were at its lowest, a high-profile relief committee stepped in with support.[97]

During the height of the fiscal crisis, BAM contributed to the myriad cultural dimensions of Downtown Brooklyn; it later received recognition as a vehicle for the expansion of the artistic life of the entire borough, and, arguably, the city. Indeed, Lichtenstein's tenure decisively contributed to the redefinition of Brooklyn—and its neighborhoods—as generative performance spaces. Its transformation is justifiably viewed as a success story of urban arts revival, deficit spending, historic preservation, marketing, and arts administration, but BAM's rebirth depended upon the energies of many local theater groups working in tandem with cultural coalitions that consciously dispersed theater across the networks of urban spaces. As arts initiatives multiplied and expanded across the borough, they created a wide geographic net of artists who entered into reciprocal arrangements with new and old organizations. At BAM, artists of the downtown avant-garde were offered a chance to frame their work in a proscenium setting, no longer confined to the small lofts where they shared their first experiments. Lichtenstein was not just a prescient administrator; his foresight mixed with intuition and a daring to gamble on artists who initially did not draw crowds, and were occasionally critical failures, as well. Moreover, BAM invested wisely and heavily in its visual identity and outreach innovations; by 1979, BAM's marketing department numbered fifteen with a $1,250,000 budget.[98]

But as Julia Foulkes argues, BAM's involvement in urban development (including the achievement of historic district designations for both Fort Greene and the area immediately surrounding BAM) remained strong even as its relations with neighbors through education and youth programming grew less visible.[99] Many have remarked on the inverse relationship between the Next Wave box office gross and its willingness to challenge subscriber audiences; others have perceived a failure to engage or acknowledge an audience in any way.[100] A less common critique is the absence of companies relevant to audiences on a more local scale: community-based theatrical groups that tethered BAM to the surrounding neighborhoods. These companies felt the municipal crisis acutely, and struggled for the material means to engage in extended experimentation. Those theatergoers who "met" BAM through its Next Wave Festival missed a decade of experimentation that showcased a changing Brooklyn through the lives of its residents. But as Next Wave became the centerpiece of BAM's season, the question of "the local" lost its currency—or, rather, was rebranded with the changing ethics and demands of audience development. The popularity of the Next Wave Festival only "reinforced the gap" between BAM's programming "and its culturally, economically, and ethnically diverse neighbors."[101] A growing schism in its operations in turn created a bifurcation between its community ties and embodied theatrical practice.

When journalists accentuate the "lonely crusade" of BAM's "presiding genius" Lichtenstein,[102] many other, perhaps even lonelier crusaders, drop from the frame. The neighborhood theater arts movement faded from the landscape of Downtown Brooklyn after the fiscal crisis, when new austerity policies championed the transformation of urban space for uses leading to "culture as enterprise."[103] By the 1980s, divisions grew once again between the zones of elite tastes versus neighborhood arts practices. This transformation cannot be delineated as a simplistic "Manhattanization" of Brooklyn's formerly working-class associations. BAM's exceptional success suggests that dedicated investment in an institution during times of fiscal austerity will in fact pay increasing returns. It also raises questions regarding municipal policy: if smaller organizations are neglected during lean periods, what will remain of the delicate ecosystem of urban performance within which BAM grew?

BAM tapped into the credibility of Manhattan's avant-garde for its transformation and rallied political support eager to invest in a known model of cultural development around a preeminent arts center. Coextensive circumstances were equally instrumental in this process: the diminished opportunities to be found Off Broadway, the dissolution of theatrical hierarchies, the demands for decentralized cultural resources around the boroughs, and the formation of vestigial theaters and new cultural councils in the area. All were energized by the prospect of BAM's success, and in turn, animated BAM. It did not constitute a stable center of rebirth, but rather locked into overlapping zones of performance activity that reshaped contested urban spaces.

Conclusion

✦

The Myth of Self-Sufficiency

> Obviously the crisis does not in itself give rise to a new type of society, but it does contribute to the destruction of the old one and it can also prevent a new type of society from developing.
>
> —Alain Touraine

The city government utilized socially destructive short-term tactics to increase investor confidence and "muddle through" fiscal stress in the 1970s: groups most recently the beneficiaries of long-deferred rights—and some measure of power—met renewed deprivation. This both redrew and deepened fractures between neighborhoods, and extended uneven cultural development across communities variously valued or undervalued. Historians, economists, and political scientists identify the period spanning 1974 and 1982 as a turning point in the city's political and economic history for many reasons, but, most relevant to our contemporary performance context, these years set in motion the inequalities now endemic to the city's economy. "Neoliberal New York was birthed by fiscal crisis," writes William Sites.[1] The development of this economic paradigm is not only pertinent to New York City's urban history. Many phenomena tracked in this study relate to the rolling back of 1960s achievements and philosophies, and this occurred on a national level, as well. New York City enacted a rehearsal for a larger, national restructuring.[2] Municipal agendas echoed from the city's fiscal crisis as a model for the policies of presidents Ford, Carter, and Reagan.

The new dynamics of urban economies were increasingly dependent upon international financial speculation. As described by David Harvey, the "neoliberal city" refers to a restructuring of the urban economy around "financial activities, ancillary services such as legal services and the media, and diversified consumerism (gentrification and neighborhood 'restoration' playing a prominent and profitable role)."[3] The clearly uneven development of culture as demonstrated across the full arc of this book set the stage for some of these attendant processes, particularly as related to a homogenization of cultural production. This only intensified the need for the different models of culture across the city that had been constrained through the crisis itself.

The fiscal prosperity of the 1980s reversed New York City's population decline, but as much research on income inequity now shows, it benefited a lucky minority: during the "boom" years, the top percent of income earners doubled their share of the city's total income, while the vast majority of the city saw median hourly wages shrivel.[4] The rhetoric of self-sufficiency as applied to theater companies and other arts organizations complemented the crisis discourse. Officials sought distance from perceived past errors of profligate liberal governance, and ignored the innovations promoted by Martin E. Segal and the warnings of economist William Baumol, as well as the protestations of theater artists Joseph Papp and Vinnette Carroll. All four disputed the myth of self-sufficiency through the 1970s: budgets were inherently political documents and "cost disease" was real. The price of this continued myth lands squarely on the shoulders of under-resourced artistic communities.

New York's spaces of performance—on and offstage—bear the mark of transformations that occurred through the 1970s. In some of the case studies found in this book, the course of institutionalization that theaters pursued during the 1970s created a surprising safety net for the continuation of certain performance practices, such as Ellen Stewart's work at La Mama. Yet there are very few instances of what might be called "local Broadway"—Vinnette Carroll's development of Broadway shows (and performers) from across the city's five boroughs. As David Savran notes, in a world of mainstream theater now dominated by multinational corporations, plays often cannot be linked to a single metropolis, let alone a single borough. His explication of the transnational musical and attendant "deterritorialized Broadway" holds vast implications for local arts initiatives in urban areas.[5] It points to a growing chasm between Broadway and grassroots theatrical fare originating in New York City, but it also demonstrates the ways in which sharp delineations between "community theater" and "professional theater" are regressive as well as constraining to a theatrical public sphere.

After the fiscal crisis, in many spheres of civic life, art for the public good became another luxury that the city's poorer neighborhoods could not prioritize, let alone demand. The desire for tourists who could plump up the city's coffers dominated the attention of arts leaders and economic policy strategists alike. Austerity packages most directly weakened neighborhood arts organizations catering specifically to low-income or minority populations. Sponsorships from corporations went from supplement to necessity. By 1983, the deadlock of austerity ideologies had set the parameters of conversations around culture. That year, Mayor Ed Koch proposed limiting the city's financial contributions to cultural institutions to 50 percent of their budgets. He callously warned arts groups: "There's nothing like a gap in your budget to concentrate your attention. . . . Better get cracking."[6] The new commissioner of cultural affairs, Bess Myerson—who later resigned amid an ethics scandal—acknowledged that the limit would affect small institutions, but reasoned that the cap incentivized funding sources to give more.

Outer-borough neighborhood organizations committed to increasing attendance among minority populations knew that the policy hurt them most directly; arts administrator Lloyd Hezekiah of the Brooklyn Children's Museum argued that the new policy might "eliminate a whole segment of the population" if his museum charged increased entry fees.[7] The vice chairman of the Mayor's Advisory Commission for Cultural Affairs maintained that the change promoted self-sufficiency so that institutions "can withstand whatever the winds of politics are."[8] This arrangement still exists: spatial inequities dictate that in some neighborhoods, when cuts are made, these winds are gale force; in others, their reach is tempered. The ethical and philosophical challenges articulated by theater artists in the mid-1970s in New York continue to reverberate today: Richard Schechner's questioning of the logic of Broadway, "Why should we be working to decentralize the theatre and then centralize it again?" or Douglas Turner Ward's skepticism of major theaters ignoring demographic change and new audiences, "Who are they playing to?"[9]

The cultural capital of arts institutions—both prestige and resources—played a major role in the rebound of the economy. Under the coalition of Mayor Koch, elite cultural institutions helped New York keep its "competitive edge" as a global city.[10] This book has questioned the assumption that elite cultural organizations could have achieved any measure of success without transcommunal networks of smaller organizations and the prior administrative frameworks of support for theater. In fact, the conflict between centralized "elite" cultural destinations and decentralized theater programming becomes decisive to the production of social space in the 1970s and beyond. The generative opposition between these two forms is part of the simultaneously economic and symbolic power relations investigated in *Drop Dead*. Yet in the discourse about New York City's emergence from the fiscal crisis, the cultural assets most frequently understood as important are those institutions that could be classified under Pierre Bourdieu's "large scale" productions.[11]

Throughout the 1970s, two of the characteristics of the "global city"—elite cultural organizations and diversity—intersected in ways that renewed and redeveloped the very conception of the city itself. Across the plurality of publics in the global city, both "large scale" and "small scale" productions—and everything in between—confer forms of capital upon neighborhoods. Jim Sleeper described the concomitant expulsion of cultural and other nonprofit institutions throughout the 1980s as a final uprooting of perceived "low culture," with many officials and developers understanding cultural institutions merely as "loss leaders that soften the big boom's rapacity into something like verve."[12] In the years to come, the competition for resources and the rise of place marketing using the city as a "stage" both generated and revealed deep fissures between artists, theaters, and the communities in which they lived and performed.

Progressing on a parallel track, theories related to the "creative city" and the cultural economy exploded in the mid-1980s: the use of cultural planning and programming as an urban development strategy was widely heralded throughout the 1990s and 2000s.[13] Formal arts districts continue to be introduced through zoning or districting for the purposes of economic development; even the East Fourth Street area that Julie Bovasso once boasted was "inaugurating theatres left and right"[14] converted into an official East Fourth Street Arts district comprised of twenty-eight member arts groups, known as the Fourth Arts Block (FAB). When city officials design strategies and allocate resources according to an ahistorical "creative city" agenda, they frequently neglect the complex legacy of theater as a force for advocacy, activism, and community autonomy. Rather than "cookbook approaches" to cities, urban policies must, as Andy Pratt has argued, challenge normative approaches that are too often both universal and ignorant to difference.[15] Much of the artistic work that bridged the 1960s to the 1970s offers a framework of alternatives and counter-histories to today's urban revitalization programs.

Drop Dead suggests also that the 1970s laid the groundwork for some of our strongest—and at times destructive—assumptions about the instrumentality of theater. The substitution of an economic rationale for social welfare as the guiding force behind government spending made an imprint on theater and performance. A 2008 panel sponsored by the Martin E. Segal Theatre Center, *Surreal Estate: Artists, Urban Development and the Future of New York*, occurred coincidentally just days after the collapse of Lehman Brothers, the takeover of Fannie Mae and Freddie Mac, and the federal bailout of American International Group.[16] The discussion was at once abstracted from these events, and yet inextricably linked to the mega-crisis felt in every global economic center. The panel of artists, administrators, and representatives from city government feared a "mass migration" of their peers leaving New York due to the real estate market, and the contradictions of the "creative economy" emerged as a touchstone; before the 2008 financial crisis, the city experienced its largest building boom since the 1960s.[17] All panelists described increased reliance on corporate support, but whereas the representatives from a real estate development company and the city focused exclusively on the ability of the arts to feed the municipality's economic engines, the artists chafed under constant pressure to prove the financial impact of their aesthetic experimentations. To understand the role of the artist within urban development, they measured economic contributions with little consideration of any other variable. (Just six years later, in 2014, one of the panelists, Robert Elmes, made headlines when he announced he would move his Galapagos art space to Detroit after twenty years in Brooklyn, due to rental prices.)[18] As this book demonstrates, artists can play a role in identifying and mitigating the effects of *uneven* cultural development, yet their contributions rarely exempt them from worsening precariousness.

Housing and financial livelihood are topics of concern for a great many New Yorkers, and the ability of the global city to retain its more vulnerable residents is increasingly treated with skepticism. Given that artists are frequently seen—and often function as—agents of the processes known as gentrification, lamentations about the plight of "the creatives" risks a kind of tunnel-vision analysis that boils neighborhood identity down to arguments between displaced and displacers. The institutionalized racism and decision-making that have led to dramatic cultural and economic transformations of neighborhoods in turn motivated narratives of loss that made it to the stages of New York, as in Danny Hoch's *Taking Over* (the Public Theater, 2008), Seth Zvi Rosenfeld's *Handball* (the New Group, 2009), Bruce Norris's *Clybourne Park* (Playwrights Horizons, 2010), and Jackie Alexander's *Brothers from the Bottom* (Billie Holiday Theatre, 2010).

Yet as Christopher Balme has argued, it is often far from the proscenium stage—through connections with new media and a move outside theater buildings—that the political and social efficacy of theater is reactivated in urban centers.[19] Balme concedes that leaving the private space of the modernist black box can create new black boxes in derelict factories and spark gentrification, but he identifies the more radical (re)occupation of theater buildings as enabling theater to "engage more directly with the political public sphere."[20] In New York, the labors of 1970s theater artists made possible the existence of these projects, which have little to do with classical canon delivery and everything to do with disrupting the public sphere to create new interactions between residents. For example, while the "cooling the streets" philosophy that motivated much support of neighborhood arts was in many senses misguided, its architects were a multiracial coalition who, instead of bringing "culture" to the people of the inner city, or bussing youth to elite performance events, began to trust community artist-leaders themselves. This was not a naive approach to the animosities between communities and local authorities, or a belief in theater games as a cure-all for police misconduct. Some of the more successful arts initiatives in this book allowed theater workers, community leaders, *and* civil authorities to explore alternative ways of being present on the streets. They expanded the boundaries of representation for neighborhoods and residents. And the participants and spectators involved found a new apparatus for communicating issues of local concern to the government.

Following in the footsteps of these projects, contemporary artists collaborate directly with both centralized and neighborhood institutions in order to counteract the monetization of arts participation. One of the more potent examples of how performance can mediate the processes shaping cities and also illuminate patterns of space and sociability is the work of Theaster Gates, a sculptor with a background in urban planning. Gates's brand of art for social practice has included the renovation of houses, the curation of community arts centers, and an overall inter-arts approach with clear citations of 1970s community autonomy and pride movements. Artist Rick Lowe's prior work on the Watts House Project and the contemporary Project Row Houses in Houston present other examples of this type of "performance of neighborhood," in which artists and residents (and artist-residents) create development goals together. While acknowledging the challenges inherent in Gates's site-specific performance projects and architectural experiments, Hesse McGraw has described his novel strategies for engaging local communities through scalable and replicable cultural planning as "regenerative interventions" in the service of neighborhood transformations.[21]

These and other experiments appeal to governments and funding sources eager to embrace "placemaking" through the arts. However, the historical case studies in this book remind us that the phenomenon of "placemaking" is historically situated, attendant with particular ideologies about urban public space and visibility. A 1968 Rockefeller report on the arts noted sloganeering behind the charged vocabulary popularized in the decade: "relevance," "participation," "involvement," and "creativity."[22] All could, even then, be evacuated of meaning, or represent important bulwarks in the struggles for more equitable visions of the arts. Joe Papp's successes in theatrical "placemaking" during the city's fiscal crisis, for example, owed much to the unpredictable perception of deficits in the city's arts organizations: necessary evil or in need of reform?

Critic Clive Barnes defended Papp's Public Theater as "a civic theater—perhaps even a national theater—on European lines but adapted to American manners. This costs money; it involves public subsidy. Do we as a city or a state wish to have this?"[23] We today repeat the same questions when our local municipalities are driven to the edge of financial disaster. Vallejo, California; Central Falls, Rhode Island; Detroit, Michigan—three very different localities in the United States that all experienced financial crises in the 2000s. In the debate over the Detroit Art Museum collections, fiscal stress immediately triggered questions about art institutions as a luxury too expensive to afford. Even as the global financial "mega-crisis" of 2008 prompts research on the topic of austerity in the twenty-first century, many of our global, national, and local conversations respond more to the rhetoric than to the political regimes of austerity, and gloss over the specific, situated, cultural ramifications.

In many cities in North America, these dialogues exist concurrently with the overwhelming trend to fund, support, and define the arts based upon their economic value to the operations of the city center. Yet any economic analysis of performance practices—as with our financial systems—must be tempered and balanced with the social and cultural. Particularly to address accompanying spatial transformations in cities, we need to continue to find new ways to identify and communicate the role of the arts as more than a buzzword of revitalization. The enhancement of city branding is the low-hanging fruit; the case studies analyzed in this book suggest the variety of ways in which theater and performance function as generative public infrastructure.

Austerity transforms the theater in varying ways, and the specific relationship between the two can take many figurations. Some of the theaters discussed in this book offered an escape or a refuge from the ideologies of austerity; others became *part* of austerity, through cuts or as extensions of policy. Alain Touraine has observed similarities between responses to crises at different historical moments; sometimes, social actors who are socially excluded or marginalized as a result of a crisis are "incapable of reacting politically."[24] While this was to some extent true in New York in the 1970s, this book presents examples in which theaters did not respond to social crisis with rebellion, but rather with a deepening complexity of connections with (and as) institutions. In doing so, these companies demonstrated both resilience and support for state intervention.

The conclusions that can be gleaned from this book should therefore not be restricted to the explicit circumstances of bankrupt municipalities, but can be applied more broadly to the spaces of our postindustrial cities today. The April 2015 death of Freddie Gray in Baltimore brought worldwide attention to the injustices related to the criminalization of African American men in the United States, but also to Gray's neighborhood, Sandtown-Winchester/Harlem Park. The rapid dissemination of statistics attested to the area's dismal homicide, juvenile arrest, unemployment, and mortality rates. News coverage featured residents eager to express pride in their community, but also to protest the conditions of persistent neglect and the daily realities of living in under-resourced neighborhoods. Diverse mechanisms for arts provision across urban forms of the size and scale of Baltimore or New York preclude any singular conclusion. Yet in many cities today, conditions persist that diminish spaces of representation for neighborhoods, and contribute to the draining of both social welfare and strong cultural infrastructures.

While residential racial segregation in the United States has been declining, it remains high—and residential segregation by income has risen sharply since 1970.[25] Concurrently, social science researchers have detailed the close relationship between local environment (and amenities) and the physical and emotional health of residents. Significant correlations have been found between intergenerational mobility and income inequality, economic and racial residential segregation, and other neighborhood economic and cultural conditions. Recent analyses of the federal government's Moving to Opportunity antipoverty experiment offer evidence of the (somewhat intuitive) role of neighborhood and geography in social inequality.[26] As Vinnette Carroll argued decades ago, without thoughtful interrelationships (and investment) between these areas of social and civic life, all urban residents remain impoverished.

Demands for increased funding alone—for individual theaters alone—do not succeed in achieving the kind of long-lasting, sustainable coalitions that other efforts might. To build and rebuild institutions across neighborhoods requires more than the fair distribution of resources. It necessitates the development of connections between institutions, across the spaces of the city, in order to transform the conditions identified and combated by artists throughout the 1970s. It involves a reshaping of assumptions about the relative value of performance and theaters in neighborhoods. Increasingly, our understanding of the "performance of neighborhood" will necessarily push past large and small, commercial and community, to find new language for the various ways that communities interact with city governments through performance.

NOTES

Introduction

EPIGRAPHS: "History," Urban Arts Corps Records, New York Public Library, Schomburg Center for Research in Black Culture, 1; Micki Grant and Vinnette Justine Carroll, *Don't Bother Me, I Can't Cope* (Electronic Edition, Alexander Street, 1970, 2014, 34.) The latter was also published in *Don't Bother Me, I Can't Cope: A Musical Entertainment* (New York: Samuel French, 1972).

1. "Early Enforcement Efforts," Equal Employment Opportunity Commission, http://www.eeoc.gov/eeoc/history/35th/1965-71/early_enforcement.html.

2. As quoted in Joshua B. Freeman, *Working-Class New York: Life and Labor since World War II* (New York: New Press, 2000), 259–60. Criticizing New York–style liberalism posed an opportunity for Ford, who feared a challenge within the Republican Party, from Ronald Reagan.

3. For a comprehensive account of the activities of MAC during the 1970s, see Robert W. Bailey, *The Crisis Regime* (Albany: State University of New York Press, 1984); Martin Shefter, *Political Crisis/Fiscal Crisis* (New York: Columbia University Press, 1992); William K. Tabb, *The Long Default* (New York: Monthly Review, 1982).

4. Steven R. Weisman, "How New York Became a Fiscal Junkie," *New York Times*, August 17, 1975, 9.

5. Robert Fitch, *The Assassination of New York* (London: Verso, 1993), vii–viii.

6. The term fiscal "crisis" could be enveloped in inverted commas throughout this book; some scholars disagree with its use, and prefer other options (fiscal "stress" or fiscal "strain"). Peter Marcuse, "The Targeted Crisis, On the Ideology of Urban Fiscal Crisis and Its Uses," *International Journal of Urban and Regional Research* 5 (September 1981): 330–55. See also Roger Friedland, Frances Fox Piven, and Robert R. Alford, "Political Conflict, Urban Structure, and the Fiscal Crisis," *International Journal of Urban and Regional Research* 1 (March-December 1977): 447–71.

7. Quoted in Ellen Noonan, "Interview with Mike Wallace," *Radical History Review* 79 (Winter 2001): 49–74.

8. For more on the effects of the crisis on public spaces in Athens, see the volume from the conference, "The City at a Time of Crisis." Jaya Klara Brekke, Dimitris Dalakoglou, Christos Filippidis, and Antonis Vradis, eds., *Crisis-scapes: Athens and Beyond*, 2014, http://www.crisis-scape.net.

9. See Rebecca Bramall, *The Cultural Politics of Austerity: Past and Present in Austere Times* (Houndsmills, Eng.: Palgrave Macmillan, 2013), 37–58.

10. Craig Browne and Simon Susen, "Austerity and Its Antitheses: Practical Negations of Capitalist Legitimacy," *The South Atlantic Quarterly* 113 (Spring 2014): 221.

11. Jaime Peck, "Geography and Public Policy: Constructions of Neoliberalism," *Progress in Human Geography* 28 (2004): 392–405.

12. Freeman, *Working-Class New York*, 335.

13. Will Kaufman, *American Culture in the 1970s* (Edinburgh: Edinburgh University Press, 2009), 169. Wolfe, Christopher Lasch, and Lester Thurow argued that the "rights revolution" led people to act selfishly and retreat away from the liberal tenets of social purpose. See Edward D. Berkowitz, *Something Happened: A Political and Cultural Overview of the Seventies* (New York: Columbia University Press, 2006), 158; and Stephanie A. Slocum-Schaffer, *America in the Seventies* (Syracuse, N.Y.: Syracuse University Press, 2003), 129.

14. Matthew Gandy, "Rethinking Urban Metabolism: Water, Space, and the Modern City," *City* 8 (December 2004): 373.

15. There has been an influx of work within theater scholarship that takes into account the social quality of space as essential to understanding artistic production. Recent edited collections include D. J. Hopkins and Kim Solga, eds., *Performance and the Global City* (Basingstoke, Eng.: Palgrave Macmillan, 2013); Nicolas Whybrow, ed., *Performance and the Contemporary City: An Interdisciplinary Reader* (Basingstoke, Eng.: Palgrave Macmillan, 2010); Michael McKinnie, ed., *Space and the Geographies of Theatre* (New York: Theatre Communications Group, 2007); Marina Peterson and Gary W. McDonogh, eds., *Global Downtowns* (Philadelphia: University of Pennsylvania Press, 2012).

16. Judith Hamera, *Dancing Communities: Performance, Difference, and Connection in the Global City* (New York: Palgrave Macmillan, 2007), 3.

17. Lara D. Nielsen, "Introduction: Heterotopic Transformations, The (Il) Liberal Neoliberal," in *Neoliberalism and Global Theatres: Performance Permutations*, ed. Lara Nielsen and Patricia Ybarra (London: Palgrave Macmillan, 2012), 1–2.

18. Jason Hackworth, *The Neoliberal City: Governance, Ideology, and Development in American Urbanism* (Ithaca, N.Y.: Cornell University Press, 2007). Hackworth advocates an approach in which institutional-urban domains are used to examine the processes of neoliberalization.

19. "Excerpts from Statements of New York and Federal Officials to Senate Committee," *New York Times*, June 8, 1978, B11.

20. Ruth Gilmore, *Golden Gulag: Prisons, Surplus, Crisis, and Opposition in Globalizing California* (Berkeley: University of California Press, 2007), 131.

21. Ibid., 54.

22. Bernard R. Gifford, "New York City and Cosmopolitan Liberalism," *Political Science Quarterly* 93 (Winter 1978–79): 562.

23. As an example of this shift, Arlene Dávila examines the development of Taller Boricua and El Museo del Barrio, two institutions founded in the late 1960s. Arlene M. Dávila, "Culture in the Battlefront: From Nationalist to Pan-Latino Projects," in *Mambo Montage: The Latinization of New York,* ed. Agustín Laó-Montes and Arlene M. Dávila (New York: Columbia University Press, 2001), 167.

24. Mariana Mogilevich, "Arts as Public Policy: Cultural Spaces for Democracy and Growth," in *Summer in the City: John Lindsay, New York, and the American Dream,* ed. Joseph P. Viteritti (Baltimore: Johns Hopkins University Press, 2014), 198.

25. Ibid.

26. For more on the Lindsay mayoralty, see Vincent J. Cannato, *The Ungovernable City: John Lindsay and His Struggle to Save New York* (New York: Basic Books, 2001); and Sam Roberts, ed., *America's Mayor: John V. Lindsay and the Reinvention of New York* (New York: Museum of the City of New York and Columbia University Press, 2010).

27. Joseph Wesley Zeigler, "Centrality without Philosophy: The Crisis in the Arts," *New York Affairs* 4 (Winter 1978): 17.

28. Max Page, *The City's End: Two Centuries of Fantasies, Fears, and Premonitions of New York's Destruction* (New Haven, Conn.: Yale University Press, 2008), 28.

29. See Shefter, *Political Crisis/Fiscal Crisis*, 139. William Tabb describes the trickle-down to nonprofit organizations and community groups. Tabb, *The Long Default*, 43.

30. Gifford, "Cosmopolitan Liberalism," 560.

31. Shannon Jackson, *Social Works: Performing Art, Supporting Publics* (New York: Routledge, 2011), 14–15.

32. See Leonard Wallock and Dore Ashton, *New York, Culture Capital of the World, 1940–1965* (New York: Rizzoli, 1988); Samuel Zipp, *Manhattan Projects: The Rise and Fall of Urban Renewal in Cold War New York* (New York: Oxford University Press, 2010).

33. Robert A. Mayer, "New York: The State of Art," *New York Affairs* 4 (Winter 1978): 7.

34. Fred Ferretti, *The Year the Big Apple Went Bust* (New York: Putnam Books, 1976), 415.

35. Much of this recent popularity can be traced to Richard Florida's trademarked term "creative class," explicated in his books, *The Rise of the Creative Class* (2002) and *The Flight of the Creative Class* (2007). See Ann Markusen, "Urban Development and the Politics of a Creative Class: Evidence from the Study of Artists," *Environment and Planning A* 38, no. 10 (2006): 1921–40.

36. Arlene Dávila, *Culture Works: Space, Value, and Mobility across the Neoliberal Americas* (New York: New York University Press, 2012), 189.

37. Laura Levin and Kim Solga, "Building Utopia: Performance and the Fantasy of Urban Renewal in Contemporary Toronto," *TDR: The Drama Review* 53 (Fall 2009): 38.

38. Quoted in McCandlish Phillips, "Candidates Assess City's Arts Future," *New York Times*, November 1, 1973, 50.

39. Ibid.

40. David Harvey, *A Brief History of Neoliberalism* (Oxford: Oxford University Press, 2005), 118. For more on Harvey's concept of uneven development, see 87–119. Harvey takes 1970s New York as a central case study in his book. During this period, monetary policy changes in China, the United States, and the United Kingdom created a new economic configuration that followed the principles of privatization, deregulation, and the withdrawal of the state.

41. Joseph Papp, "To Break Down 'The Wall,'" *New York Times*, July 22, 1973, 89.

42. Jean-François Pradeau, *Plato and the City*, trans. Janet Lloyd (Exeter, Eng.: University of Exeter Press, 2002), 2–3.

43. Manuel Castells, "Class and Power in American Cities," *Contemporary Sociology* 13 (May 1984): 270.

44. Edward Soja, *Thirdspace: Journeys to Los Angeles and Other Real-and-Imagined Places* (Oxford: Basil Blackwell, 1996), 12.

45. For more on the dominant theories related to how theater produces urban meaning, see Jen Harvie, *Theatre and The City* (London: Palgrave Macmillan, 2009), 1–11; and Jen Harvie, *Staging the UK* (Manchester: Manchester University Press, 2005).

46. Shannon Jackson, "Working Publics," *Performance Research* 16 (2011): 10.

47. Ibid.

48. Neil Brenner and Nik Theodore, "Cities and the Geographies of 'Actually Existing Neoliberalism,'" *Antipode* 34 (July 2002): 375.

49. Mike Sell, *Avant-Garde Performance and the Limits of Criticism* (Ann Arbor: University of Michigan Press, 2008), 16–18. Sell also enumerates the many needs that countercultural performance addressed in that decade, as both practice and discourse.

50. Between 1962 and 1969, over 60 percent of all government, foundation, and private funding dedicated to the performing arts was earmarked for the construction of facilities. See Rachel Shane, "Negotiating the Creative Sector: Understanding the Role and Impact of an Artistic Union in a Cultural Industry: A Study of Actors' Equity Association and the Theatrical Industry" (dissertation, Ohio State University, 2006).

51. James M. Harding and Cindy Rosenthal, "Between Characteristics, Continuities, and Change—Theorizing the Legacy of Radical Theaters," in *Restaging the Sixties: Radical Theaters and Their Legacies* (Ann Arbor: University of Michigan Press, 2006), 5.

52. Ibid.

53. Kaufman, *American Culture in the 1970s*, 72.

54. Theodore Shank, *Beyond the Boundaries: American Alternative Theatre* (Ann Arbor: University of Michigan Press, 2002); Christopher Bigsby, *A Critical Introduction to Twentieth-Century American Drama,* vol. 3: *Beyond Broadway* (Cambridge: Cambridge University Press, 1990); and Arnold Aronson, *American Avant-Garde Theatre: A History* (New York: Routledge, 2000).

55. Stephen J. Bottoms, *Playing Underground: A Critical History of the 1960s Off-Off-Broadway Movement* (Ann Arbor: University of Michigan Press, 2006), 348, 364. Caffe Cino closed in 1968; the Open Theatre closed in 1973; Theatre Genesis in St. Mark's Church lasted until 1978; Judson Poets' Theater continued with a pared-down slate of programming and formally closed its theater programming in 1981.

56. Aronson, *American Avant-Garde*, 159.

57. Herbert Blau, "Spacing Out in the American Theater," *The Kenyon Review* 15 (Spring 1993): 28; Shank, *Beyond the Boundaries,* 155–99.

58. For more on the costs of Off Broadway producing before the end of the 1960s, see Judith Marechal, "Off-Broadway: A Limited Engagement," *TDR: Tulane Drama Review* 10 (Fall 1965): 78–88; and Samuel L. Leiter, *Ten Seasons: New York Theatre in the Seventies* (Westport, Conn.: Greenwood, 1986), 26–30.

59. Allan Tannenbaum, *New York in the 70s* (New York: Overlook, 2011), 6.

60. Andreas Killen, *1973 Nervous Breakdown: Watergate, Warhol, and the Birth of Post-Sixties America* (New York: Bloomsbury Publishing, 2006), 146.

61. Tannenbaum, *New York in the 70s*, 6.

62. Elizabeth Currid-Halkett, *The Warhol Economy: How Fashion, Art, and Music Drive New York City* (Princeton, N.J.: Princeton University Press, 2007), 28–29. Others have investigated the romanticization of artists as "urban pioneers," another aspect that contributes to the popular representation of artists thriving during recessions. David B. Cole, "Artists and Urban Redevelopment," *Geographical Review* 77 (Oct. 1987): 391–407.

63. Kimberley Johnson, "Community Development Corporations, Participation, and Accountability: The Harlem Urban Development Corporation and the Bedford-Stuyvesant Restoration Corporation," *The Annals of the American Academy of Political and Social Science* 594 (July 2004): 110.

64. Sell, *Avant-Garde Performance*, 244.

65. Kimberly Phillips-Fein, "New York's Fiscal Crisis," YouTube Video, posted by John Jay College of Criminal Justice, 2013, https://www.youtube.com/watch?v=XynqDxJAdZ0. See also Kimberly Phillips-Fein, "The Legacy of the 1970s Fiscal Crisis," *The Nation*, April 16, 2013, http://www.thenation.com/article/173873/legacy-1970s-fiscal-crisis#.

66. Jan Cohen-Cruz, *Local Acts: Community-Based Performance in the United States* (New Brunswick, N.J.: Rutgers University Press, 2005), 6.

67. Hazel Bryant, quoted in Stuart W. Little, *After the FACT: A Report on the First American Congress of Theatre* (New York: Arno, 1975), 55–56.

68. Don Mitchell, "There's No Such Thing as Culture: Towards a Reconceptualization of the Idea of Culture in Geography," *Transactions of the Institute of British Geographers* 20 (1995): 102.

69. Robert W. Bailey, *The Crisis Regime: The MAC, the EFCB, and the Political Impact of the New York City Financial Crisis* (Albany: State University of New York Press, 1984), 11.

70. Roger Starr, "Build Another East Village in the Dakota Badlands," *New York Times*, September 24, 1972, SM94.

71. Marvin Carlson, *Places of Performance: The Semiotics of Theatre Architecture* (Ithaca, N.Y.: Cornell University Press, 1993), 92.

Chapter 1

EPIGRAPH: Ellen Stewart, quoted in Lionel H. Mitchell, "Ellen Stewart: La Mama's Defiant Trailblazer," *Amsterdam News,* October 24, 1981, 64.

1. Dan Sullivan, "At Café La Mama, A Floor Show in Hell," *New York Times*, February 1968, 29.

2. Julie Bovasso, *The Moon Dreamers* (New York: Samuel French, 1969), 9.

3. See Bottoms, *Playing Underground*, 272–75.

4. John Greenfeld, "Their Hearts Belongs to La Mama," *New York Times*, July 9, 1967. For a description of the development of La Mama's distinctive identity through the 1960s, see Bottoms, *Playing Underground*, 90–104.

5. Cindy Rosenthal, "Ellen Stewart: La Mama of Us All," *TDR: The Drama Review* 50 (Summer 2006): 14.

6. Bottoms, *Playing Underground*, 275.

7. Brian Massumi, "Urban Appointment: A Possible Rendez-Vous with the City," from *Making Art of Databases*, ed. Joke Brouwer and Arjen Mulder (Rotterdam: V2 Organisatie/Dutch Architecture Institute, 2003), 31.

8. Ibid., 30.

9. Erin Manning and Brian Massumi, "A Perspective of the Universe," *Inflexions* 6, "Arakawa and Gins" (January 2013): 449.

10. Massumi, "Urban Appointment," 30.

11. Dolores Hayden, "Making Women's History Visible in the Urban Landscape," *City & Society* 10 (June 1998): 9.

12. Roberta Brandes Gratz, *The Living City: How America's Cities Are Being Revitalized by Thinking Small in a Big Way* (New York: John Wiley and Sons, 1994), 177. These areas were also hit hard by President Nixon's 1973 decision to impose austerity on domestic programs. See Andreas Killen, *1973 Nervous Breakdown*, 204–10.

13. Joanne Tompkins, "Space and the Geographies of Theatre: Introduction," *Modern Drama* 46 (Winter 2003): 538.

14. Rosenthal, "La Mama of Us All," 18.

15. Ibid., 25, 40.

16. David Savran, "The Death of the Avantgarde," *TDR: The Drama Review* 49 (Fall 2005): 10–42. Savran's assessment of the consecrated avant-garde notes that the same names are repeatedly intoned, forming a lineage: beginning with Black Mountain College, the Living Theatre, John Cage, and Allen Kaprow; culminating in the Open Theatre, the Performance Group, Mabou Mines, Robert Wilson, and Richard Foreman; and ending with The Wooster Group.

17. Randy Gener, quoted in Wendell C. Stone, *Caffe Cino: The Birthplace of Off-Off-Broadway* (Carbondale: Southern Illinois University Press, 2005), 181–82.

18. Bottoms, *Playing Underground*, 327.

19. Ibid., 272–75.

20. Stewart, quoted in Jack Poggi, *Theater in America: The Impact of Economic Forces, 1870–1967* (Ithaca, N.Y.: Cornell University Press, 1968), 202. Other figures in the movement, like Murray Mednick of the Theatre Genesis and Bread and Puppet Theater, expressed ambivalence about accepting funding from any institution.

21. Starr, "Build Another East Village in the Dakota Badlands," SM94.

22. Stewart's storied reticence about her personal history has created discontinuity in her biography. I am utilizing Cindy Rosenthal's superb appraisal of Stewart as the definitive biographical source. Rosenthal, "La Mama of Us All," 12–51.

23. Roger Starr, "Making New York Smaller," *New York Times*, November 14, 1976, 225.

24. There is persuasive research arguing that these policies represent a larger orientation toward neighborhoods defined as "blighted." For planned shrinkage as predominant urban development thinking nationwide, see Gratz, *The Living City*, 175–92.

25. Freeman, *Working-Class New York*, 277.

26. Bottoms, *Playing Underground*, 40–41, 322.

27. For more on Amiri Baraka's evolving frustration with the West Village bohemian scene, see Jerry Gafio Watts, *Amiri Baraka: The Politics and Art of a Black Intellectual* (New York: New York University Press, 2007), 44–171.

28. Ellen Stewart and Glenn Loney, "La Mama Celebrates Twenty Years," *Performing Arts Journal* 6 (1982): 10.

29. David A. Crespy, *Off-Off Broadway Explosion: How Provocative Playwrights of the 1960s Ignited a New American Theater* (New York: Backstage Books, 2003), 77.

30. Stewart described the impact of racism as "always affecting her." George W. Anderson, "Visiting La Mama's Founder: An Interview with Ellen Stewart," *America*, February 8, 1997, 31.

31. Rosenthal, "La Mama of Us All," 19. See also Stewart and Loney, "La Mama Celebrates Twenty Years," 9.

32. Louis Calta, "Fund Will Buy Tickets to Aid Two New Shows," *New York Times*, December 4, 1969, 68.

33. Jerry Tallmer, "Jottings by an Off-Broadway Critic," *Encore* (March/April 1963): 10.

34. Ethan Persoff and Scott Marshall, "John Wilcock: Sneaking Julie Bovasso into McSorley's 'Men's Only' Saloon," *Boing Boing*, May 20, 2014, http://boingboing.net/2014/05/20/john-wilcock-sneaking-julie-b.html.

35. Greenwich Village lies due west of the Lower East Side (with Fourth Avenue the border between the two). Fourteenth Street is the northern border of the LES, and Houston Street borders on its southern edge; these are also the borders of Alphabet City, a subsection of the East Village. The latter nomenclature includes two of the neighborhood's three most westerly zones. For details on these changes, see Janet L. Abu-Lughod, ed., *From Urban Village to East Village: The Battle for New York's Lower East Side* (Oxford: Blackwell, 1994).

36. See Tom Angotti, *New York for Sale: Community Planning Confronts Global Real Estate* (Cambridge: MIT Press, 2008); and Marci Reaven, "Citizen Participation in City Planning: New York City, 1945–1975" (dissertation, New York University, 2009).

37. Any sketching of the postwar contours of Lower East Side demographic changes would be incomplete without mention of its significance as a historical center of Jewish identity, as the survivors of older immigrant communities were joined by new groups of Ukrainians and Poles. Abu-Lughod, *Urban Village*, 8.

38. The name also refers to Loíza, a town on the island of Puerto Rico. For an analysis of Nuyorican performance activism in New York City, see Patricia E. Herrera, "Nuyoriquenas in the House: Performing Identity through Hip Hop, Poetry, and Theatre" (Ph.D. dissertation, City University of New York, 2008).

39. Rosalyn Deutsche and Cara Gendel Ryan, "The Fine Art of Gentrification," *October* 31 (Winter, 1984): 97.

40. Mario Maffi, *Gateway to the Promised Land* (New York: New York University Press, 1995), 215.

41. Jerry Tallmer, "Watering the Off-Broadway Garden," *Village Voice*, May 6, 2005, http://www.villagevoice.com/2005–05–03/theater/watering-the-off-broadway-garden.

42. Tallmer, "Jottings by an Off-Broadway Critic," 9.

43. Bovasso, *The Moon Dreamers*, 44.

44. "15 Receive 'Obies' for '68-'69 Season," *The Village Voice*, May 29, 1969, http://blogs.villagevoice.com/runninscared/2010/07/its_the_1969_ob.php.

45. Jerry Tallmer, quoted in Bottoms, *Playing Underground*, 337.

46. Julie Bovasso, *Gloria and Esperanza* (New York: Samuel French, 1969), back cover.

47. Bottoms, *Playing Underground*, 336.

48. Kevin O'Connor, quoted in "Portraits in Words," *Performing Arts Journal* 6 (1982): 27.

49. Robert Heide, "These Playwrights Did Get into a Room," *New York Times*, October 15, 1972, D6.

50. Fornes quoted in Scott T. Cummings, *Maria Irene Fornes* (New York: Routledge, 2012), 52.

51. Julie Bovasso, "Letter to Dr. William Bradley," July 3, 1969, Julie Bovasso folder, La Mama E.T.C. archives.

52. Richard Schechner, "Ford, Rockefeller, and Theatre," *TDR: Tulane Drama Review* 10 (Fall 1965): 30.

53. Ibid., 24.

54. Lizbeth Goodman, *Contemporary Feminist Theatres: To Each Her Own* (London: Routledge, 1993), 24. Goodman dates the council's founding to 1972; Fornes and Kennedy both date the founding to 1971 in their website biographies.

55. Mel Gussow, "New Group to Offer Plays by Women," *New York Times*, February 22, 1972.

56. Tom Eyen, "The Discreet Alarm of the Off Off Broadway Playwright," *New York Times*, September 23, 1973, 3, 15. Eyen refers to the "Playwrights Strategy," known elsewhere as NYTS.

57. "Off-Off and Running," *New York*, May 14, 1973, 80. The festival ran from May 16 to June 17, 1973, at the Manhattan Theater Club, then located at Stage 73, 321 East 73rd Street.

58. Eyen, "The Discreet Alarm," 15.

59. Julie Bovasso, "A New Breed of New York Actor," *New York*, February 11, 1974, 41.

60. Ibid., 44.

61. Ibid.

62. Clive Barnes, "Billy Noname, Uneven Musical, Begins Run: Bright Cast Pictures Growing Up Black, Production Is First for Off Broadway House," *New York Times*, March 3, 1970, 37.

63. Clive Barnes, "Anthony Perkins Directs *Steambath*: Friedman Casts Diety as a Bath Attendant," *New York Times*, July 1, 1970, 49.

64. "Off Stage," *Village Voice*, July 3, 1973, 58.

65. Ellen Stewart, quoted in Julius Novick, "La Mama Rekindles the Fire of Ancient Greek Drama," *New York Times*, November 17, 1974, 5.

66. Stewart quoted in Mel Gussow, "La Mama's Latest Production Is Annex, Just Two Doors Down," *New York Times*, September 12, 1974, 47; Rosenthal, "La Mama of Us All," 25–29.

67. "Staff Report on Transactions in Securities of the City of New York: Introduction and Summary, October 1, 1974—April 8, 1975," vol. 1, Securities and Exchange Commission, August 26, 1977, https://www.sec.gov/info/municipal/staffreport0877.pdf.

68. Libraries in these areas sustained 20 percent cuts in the fiscal year that started July 1, 1975: shorter hours and fewer books, classes, movies, and services. Tom Buckley, "About New York: Dimming a Beacon," *New York Times*, June 13, 1975, 19.

69. Ron Nessen, quoted in John Krinsky, *Free Labor: Workfare and the Contested Language of Neoliberalism* (Chicago: University of Chicago Press, 2007), 273, note 73.

70. Starr, "Making New York Smaller," 225.

71. Ibid. See also Roger Starr, "Refusal to Face Facts a Peril to City," *New York Times*, October 3, 1976, 225.

72. While there were suspicions of "East Villagers"—professionals and single women who had moved there from elsewhere—artists played a role in the community planning. Reaven, "Citizen Participation," 91.

73. Val Orselli, interview with author, December 19, 2011.

74. Ibid.

75. William Sites, *Remaking New York: Primitive Globalization and the Politics of Urban Community* (Minneapolis: University of Minnesota Press, 2003), 81.

76. Stuart W. Little, "What Makes Off Off Broadway Off Off?" *New York Times*, December 22, 1974, C1, 5.

77. Michiko Kakutani, "Ellen Stewart Works Hard to Keep La Mama Going," *New York Times*, April 5, 1980, 14.

78. Ellen Stewart, quoted in Thomas Lask, "A World of Theatre at La Mama," *New York Times*, March 4, 1977, 50.

79. Mel Gussow, "Zoe Caldwell Enjoying *Colette* and East 3rd Street," *New York Times*, June 2, 1970, 34.

80. Ibid.

81. Julie Bovasso, *Standard Safety* (New York: Samuel French, 1976), 37.

82. Ellen Stewart, quoted in Kakutani, "Ellen Stewart Works Hard," 14.

83. Ari L. Goldman, "Lower East Side Is Standing Trial in Custody Case," *New York Times*, January 18, 1979, B1.

84. Neil Smith, Betsy Duncan, and Laura Reid, "From Disinvestment to Reinvestment: Tax Arrears and Turning Points in the East Village," *Housing Studies* 4 (1989): 239.

85. Charles H. Levine, Irene S. Rubin, and George G. Wolohojian, *The Politics of Retrenchment: How Local Governments Manage Fiscal Stress* (Beverly Hills, Calif.: Sage Publications, 1981), 17.

86. Don Adams and Arlene Goldbard, *Creative Community: The Arts of Cultural Development* (New York: Rockefeller Foundation, 2001), 54.

87. Erika Munk, "Scowls," *Village Voice*, October 8, 1979, 114.

88. Richard Goldstein, "Sites," *Village Voice*, April 9, 1979, 43.

89. See David G. John, "The First Black Gretchen: Fritz Bennewitz's *Faust I* in New York," *Monatshefte* 94 (Winter 2002): 447–63.

90. Ibid., 450.

91. Ibid., 454.

92. Novick, "La Mama Rekindles the Fire of Ancient Greek Drama," 5.

93. There were attempts to create a mutual cultural association that would function under a collective ownership model, but some organizations did not

support teaming relatively well-off groups with weaker organizations. The favored model was to purchase buildings from the city for one dollar in as-is condition that would leave the groups free to engage in individual fund-raising for renovation and operations. When the Department of Housing Preservation and Development sold arts groups buildings *plus* adjacent vacant lots that had previously been intended for affordable housing, tenants were outraged. Val Orselli, interview with author, December 9, 2011.

94. Yvonne Rainer, *The Films of Yvonne Rainer* (Bloomington: Indiana University Press, 1989), 180.

95. See *Report to the Mayor's Committee on Cultural Policy* (New York: New York City Mayor's Committee on Cultural Policy, 1974); *Growth in New York City Arts and Culture: Who Pays?* (New York: Cultural Assistance Center, 1976); and *Public and Private Support for the Arts in New York City* (Cultural Assistance Center, 1980).

96. Christopher Mele, *Selling The Lower East Side: Culture, Real Estate and Resistance in New York City* (Minneapolis: University of Minnesota Press, 2000), 165. See also 25–27.

97. Jack Kroll, "Life with La Mama," *Newsweek* 73 (April 28, 1969): 109, quoted in Barbara Lee Horn, *Ellen Stewart and La Mama: A Bio-Bibliography* (Westport, Conn.: Greenwood, 1993).

98. See, for example, Connie Grzelka, "Broadway Mama," *The Washington Post*, March 27, 1977, 133; Dan Sullivan, "Ellen Stewart Nurtures Theater," *Los Angeles Times,* October 4, 1971, F1.

99. Richard Schechner, "Ringing the Bell for Ellen Stewart: 1919–2011," *TDR: The Drama Review* 55 (2011): 9.

100. Shannon Jackson, *Professing Performance: Theatre in the Academy from Philology to Performativity* (Cambridge: Cambridge University Press, 2004), 174.

101. Massumi, "Urban Appointment," 32, emphasis in original.

102. Gratz, *The Living City*, 176.

103. The city's population declined by about 800,000 people across the 1970s. Frank F. DeGiovanni and Lorraine C. Minnite, "Patterns of Neighborhood Change," in *Dual City: Restructuring New York,* ed. John H. Mollenkopf and Manuel Castells (New York: Russell Sage Foundation, 1992), 267.

104. For an example of this exodus narrative, see Ronald Sukenick, *Down and In: Life in the Underground* (New York: Beech Tree Books, 1997).

Chapter 2

EPIGRAPH: Transcript, banquet and plenary session, First American Theatre Congress, June 2–5, 1974. First American Theatre Congress Records, box 1, folder 4, Billy Rose Theatre Division, New York Public Library.

1. Stuart W. Little, *After the FACT: A Report on the First American Congress of Theatre* (New York: Arno, 1975), 19–21.

2. Margaret Croyden, "Box-Office Boom: Broadway," *New York Times*, May 10, 1981, 1.

3. During the 1968–69 season, the Theatre Development Fund began to aid selected productions on and off Broadway by purchasing subsidized tickets with a combination of federal and private money.

4. Margaret Croyden, *Lunatics, Lovers, & Poets: The Contemporary Experimental Theatre* (New York: McGraw-Hill, 1974).

5. Little, *After the FACT*, 20.

6. Joseph Papp, "To Break Down 'The Wall,' " *New York Times*, July 22, 1973, 89.

7. See Benjamin Chesluk, *Money Jungle: Imagining the New Times Square* (New Brunswick, N.J.: Rutgers University Press, 2007). Samuel Delany identifies the 1960s as the beginning of Time Square's "moral and legal revamping." Samuel R. Delany, *Times Square Red, Times Square Blue* (New York: New York University Press, 2001).

8. Tom Eyen, "The Discreet Alarm of the Off Off Broadway Playwright," *New York Times*, September 23, 1973, 15. Eyen would eventually fulfill his ambition in 1981 when *Dreamgirls* opened at the Imperial Theatre and ran for 1,521 performances.

9. Ibid.

10. Many in the theater industry took part in activism aimed at improving the experience of Broadway theatergoing. In 1975, 200 performers took to the streets with brooms in a street-cleaning demonstration and publicity stunt. Eight thousand people attended massive anti-pornography rallies in 1977, including one that featured the casts of twenty-five Broadway shows in full costumes. Samuel L. Leiter, *Ten Seasons: New York Theatre in the Seventies* (Westport, Conn.: Greenwood, 1986), 2.

11. Elizabeth L. Wollman, *Hard Times: The Adult Musical in 1970s New York City* (Oxford: Oxford University Press, 2012), 198. Wollman's chapter "New York's Financial Crisis and the Adult Musical on Broadway" provides an excellent overview of the impact of the socioeconomic health on Broadway, and concentrates on the 1977 Broadway musical *I Love My Wife*. See 193–222.

12. Irving W. Cheskin, "The 'Taxpaying' Theater: How Has It Fared During Inflation?" in *Inflation and the Performing Arts*, ed. Hilda Baumol and William J. Baumol (New York: New York University Press, 1984), 45.

13. David Kaufman, *Ridiculous!: The Theatrical Life and Times of Charles Ludlam* (New York: Applause Books, 2002), 100–102.

14. Quoted in ibid., 79.

15. Richard F. Babcock and Wendy U. Larsen, *Special Districts: The Ultimate in Neighborhood Zoning* (Cambridge, Mass.: Lincoln Institute of Land Policy, 1990), 27. No new theaters had been built between 1930 and 1960. During Lindsay's eight years in office, many buildings were demolished, and five more high-rises went up in Times Square before the 1972 recession halted demolition and construction. Marc Eliot, *Down 42nd Street: Sex, Money, Culture and Politics at the Crossroads of the World* (New York: Warner Books, 2001), 129; Nicholas Van Hoogstraten, *Lost Broadway Theatres* (Princeton, N.J.: Princeton Architectural Press, 1997).

16. Themis Chronopoulos, *Spatial Regulation in New York City: From Urban Renewal to Zero Tolerance* (New York: Routledge, 2011), 59.

17. Otis L. Guernsey, *Curtain Times: The New York Theater, 1965–1987* (New York: Applause Theatre Books, 1987), 220.

18. "Meeting Minutes," June 23, 1974, box 1, folder 1, Minutes and Correspondence, First American Theatre Congress Records, Billy Rose Theatre Division, New York Public Library.

19. Alexander J. Reichl, *Reconstructing Times Square: Politics and Culture in Urban Development* (Lawrence: University Press of Kansas, 1999), 2–3.

20. Transcript, Banquet and Plenary Session, June 2–5, 1974, box 1, folder 4, First American Theatre Congress Records, Billy Rose Theatre Division, New York Public Library.

21. Guernsey, *Curtain Times*, 213.

22. Cheskin, "The 'Taxpaying' Theater," 46.

23. Ibid., 46–48.

24. Beame, quoted in Eliot, *Down 42nd Street,* 139.

25. Ibid. With seventeen theaters on Broadway owned and operated by his Shubert Organization, Schoenfeld had much at stake. The Nederlander organization, the second largest theater owner in Broadway and the Shubert's main competitor, owned eight Broadway theaters and another seventeen owned or leased out of New York.

26. William Baumol and William Bowen, *Performing Arts: The Economic Dilemma* (New York: Twentieth Century Fund, 1966), 164.

27. William J. Baumol and Hilda Baumol, "What Ails the Fabulous Invalid? It's Not What You Think!" *New York Times*, June 2, 1974, 1, 22.

28. Ibid.

29. Anna Quindlen, "Mayor Gets Some Bad Notices after Second Raid on Times Square Show," *New York Times*, March 26, 1977, 30; Steven R. Weisman, "The AntiCrime Drive: Beame's Stepped-Up Emphasis on Law and Order During an Election Year Raises Some Questions," *New York Times*, April 15, 1977, 26.

30. Walter Kerr, "Can Broadway Move?" *New York Times Magazine*, June 3, 1973, 22–37.

31. Ibid.

32. Ibid.

33. The company was intricately involved in the successive phases of development planning for the area, with decision-making power that nearly paralleled that of the city or state government. William J. Stern, "The Truth About Times Square," *Perspectives on Eminent Domain Abuse* 5 (April 2009): 8–10, http://www.ij.org/stern-perspective; William R. Taylor, ed., *Inventing Times Square: Commerce and Culture at the Crossroads of the World* (Baltimore: Johns Hopkins University Press, 1996).

34. Kerr, "Can Broadway Move?" page unknown.

35. Matthew Gandy, *Concrete and Clay: Reworking Nature in New York City* (Cambridge, Mass.: MIT Press, 2002), 60.

36. Ibid., 52.

37. Reichl, *Reconstructing Times Square*, 61.

38. "Panel 9: Stimulating Creative Resources," June 2–5, 1974, box 1, folder 13, First American Theatre Congress Records, Billy Rose Theatre Division, New York Public Library.

39. Daniel Horowitz, *The Anxieties of Affluence: Critiques of American Consumer Culture, 1939–1979* (Amherst: University of Massachusetts Press, 2004), 203–25.

40. Guernsey, *Curtain Times*, 266. Guernsey believed that the extent and the frequency of crime in the city were exaggerated, and feared the increased police

visibility programs organized by the city and theater committees would negatively affect the district.

41. William Kornblum et al., "West 42nd Street: The Bright Light Zone," Graduate School and University Center of the City University of New York, 1978, 76. The Ford Foundation commissioned this frequently cited study, conducted by a team of social scientists at the City University of New York (CUNY) Graduate Center who undertook a study of the street life of 42nd Street between Sixth and Eighth Avenues. Lynne Sagalyn critiqued the study's methods, as it was designed to assist a specific audience of government and business leaders formulate proposals for investors, and Chesluk critiques the language of fear that pervades the study. Sagalyn, *Times Square Roulette: Remaking the City Icon* (Cambridge, Mass.: MIT Press, 2001), 495; Chesluk, *Money Jungle,* 40–41.

42. Kornblum et al., "The Bright Light Zone," 7.

43. Chronopoulos, *Spatial Regulation in New York City*, 59.

44. Reichl, *Reconstructing Times Square*, 62–65.

45. Papp, "Break Down the 'Wall,' " 8. As I discuss at length in chapter 5, Papp received numerous letters of complaint for these public statements, and the Beaumont Theater at Lincoln Center lost subscribers as a consequence.

46. Judith Cummings, "Blacks Gain on Broadway, Lag in Two Other Arts," *New York Times*, June 6, 1975, 10.

47. Ibid.

48. Ibid. See also Elenore Lester, "We Exist to Create a Real Black Theater," *New York Times*, March 2, 1975, 95; and Ernest Kaiser, "Black Images in the Mass Media: A Bibliography," *Freedomways* 14, "The Black Image in the Mass Media" (1974, 3rd Quarter).

49. Guernsey, *Curtain Times*, 290.

50. Reichl, *Reconstructing Times Square*, 2.

51. Louis Calta, "City Aides Act to Implement Theater Report," *New York Times*, January 27, 1972, 43.

52. Ibid.

53. Hugh Southern of TDF credited Anna Crouse (in collaboration with the Office of Midtown Planning and the League of New York Theatres and Producers) with the original concept for TKTS. James Stevenson, "Cut-Rate Tickets," *New York Times*, March 7, 2009, http://www.nytimes.com/imagepages/2008/03/07/opinion/08oped.ready.html. Marc Eliot credits the inspiration almost wholly to Mayor Lindsay, who thought up a discount ticket booth in collaboration with Gerald Schoenfeld. See Eliot, *Down 42nd Street*, 130.

54. The study used financial and sales data and 1,600 questionnaires filled out in three different months, between 1973 and 1974.

55. There is some evidence that the shoestring start of the TKTS booth has been embellished in contemporary accounts; to establish the booth, individuals and foundations gave over $60,000, including $35,000 from the Ford Foundation. They also received space rent-free and advertising space donated. William J. Baumol and Hilda Baumol, *Last Minute Discounts on Unsold Tickets: A Study of TKTS* (New York: Theatre Development Fund, 1974), 5.

56. "About Us," Negro Ensemble Company, http://www.necinc.org/about/about-us.

57. Edith Oliver, "The Theatre: Welcome Additions," *The New Yorker*, April 7, 1973, 58. For more on the decision to transfer the play from the theater at 145 St. Marks, see Mel Gussow, "Negro Ensemble Finds Hit Play Poses Problem," *New York Times*, February 7, 1973, 30.

58. Baumol and Baumol, *Last Minute Discounts*, 2; Guernsey, *Curtain Times*, 263.

59. "Panel 5: The Audience for the Theatre Today," June 2–5, 1974, box 1, folder 9, First American Theatre Congress Records, Billy Rose Theatre Division, New York Public Library.

60. Ibid.

61. While almost half of their opening budget was spent informing the public about TKTS, "despite all of the publicity received, approximately 40 percent of TKTS patrons learned about the booth from friends, while about 9 percent simply noticed it while passing by." Baumol and Baumol, *Last Minute Discounts*, 6.

62. Cummings, "Blacks Gain on Broadway."

63. Lester, "Real Black Theatre," 95. Audelco was established in 1973 by Vivian Robinson, and is still active.

64. Quoted in Gus Edwards, "On Black Audiences," *The Douglas Ward Quarterly*, March 21, 2012.

65. Guernsey, *Curtain Times*, 406–7; Leiter, *Ten Seasons*, 6–8, 19.

66. Quoted in Edwards, "On Black Audiences." Next Wave refers to BAM's festival of experimental, multidisciplinary arts, launched in 1983.

67. Ward, quoted in Gussow, "Negro Ensemble Finds Hit Play Poses Problem," 30.

68. Baumol and Baumol, *Last Minute Discounts*, ix.

69. Ibid., 35

70. Ibid.

71. Ibid., 36.

72. This Lower Manhattan TKTS opened on William Street and moved to 2 World Trade Center in 1983. It was destroyed on 9/11 and reopened at the South Street Seaport in 2002.

73. Baumol and Baumol, *Last Minute Discounts*, ix.

74. Ibid., 17.

75. Ibid., 13. Adjusted for inflation, the medium income would be roughly $79,000 today.

76. Baumol and Baumol, *Last Minute Discounts*, 6.

77. Ibid., 35.

78. Ibid., 1. TDF, the organization that operates TKTS, has expanded throughout the decades to include a wide range of theatrical advocacy programs.

79. Susan Bennett, "Theatre/Tourism," *Theatre Journal* 57 (October 2005): 411.

80. Reichl, *Reconstructing Times Square*, 16–17; and Sagalyn, *Times Square Roulette*, 5–6.

81. Freeman, *Working-Class New York*, 256–58.

82. See Bart Eeckhout, "The 'Disneyfication' of Times Square: Back to the Future?" in *Critical Perspectives on Urban Redevelopment*, ed. Kevin Fox Gotham (Emerald Group Publishing, 2001); Mark Sussman, "New York's Facelift," *TDR: The Drama Review* 42 (Spring 1998): 34–42; Maura Wickstrom,

Performing Consumers: Global Capital and Its Theatrical Seductions (New York: Routledge, 2006); and Elizabeth L. Wollman, "The Economic Development of the 'New' Times Square and Its Impact on the Broadway Musical," *American Music* 20 (Winter 2002): 445–65.

83. Roger Starr, "The Decline and Decline of New York," *New York Times*, November 21, 1971, SM31.

84. Freeman, *Working-Class New York*, 336.

85. Kati Kormendi, "Darkhorses Win International Competition for TKTS Booth," *Gotham Gazette*, March 1, 2000, http://www.gothamgazcttc.com/article/arts/20000301/1/88.

86. The original design for the TKTS booth won a design award in 1973 from the New York Society of Architects, and a Bard Award in 1975 from the City Club for merit in civic architecture. While preservation advocates believed a case could have been made for granting the booth landmark status, according to the rules, it would not have been eligible to apply until 2003.

87. Ibid. Mayor Rudolph Giuliani established NYC 2000, the official New York City Millennium Committee, to showcase the city's offerings for New Year's Eve 2000.

88. Mark Sussman, "New York's Facelift," *TDR: The Drama Review* 42 (Spring 1998): 37.

89. David W. Dunlap, "A Tough Act to Follow," *New York Times*, July 8, 1999, http://www.nytimes.com/1999/07/08/garden/a-tough-act-to-follow.html.

90. Sagalyn, *Times Square Roulette*, 266.

91. David W. Dunlap, "Atop the New TKTS Booth, Ruby-Red Stairs with a View of the Great White Way," *New York Times*, October 18, 2008, http://www.nytimes.com/2008/10/17/nyregion/17tkts.html.

92. Ibid.

Chapter 3

EPIGRAPH: Louis Calta, "Musical Slated for City's Parks: Pepsi-Cola Will Sponsor 12 Showings of 'I Can't Cope,'" *New York Times*, May 16, 1974, 49.

1. Carroll used the Los Angeles Inner City Cultural Center, one of three educational laboratory theaters funded in part by the NEA, as a model for UAC.

2. Vinnette Carroll, quoted in "Micki Grant: She Can Cope," *Ebony* 28 (February 1973): 100.

3. "Don't Bother Me, I Can't Cope," *Internet Broadway Database*, http://www.ibdb.com/production.php?id=3533. The play won multiple distinctions at the 1972 Obie awards, an Outer Critic's Circle Award, and a Drama Desk Award. For more on Carroll—the first African American woman to direct on Broadway with Langston Hughes's 1961 *Black Nativity*—see Calvin A. McClinton, "Vinnette Carroll: African American Director and Playwright," in *Black Lives: Essays in African American Biography*, ed. James L. Conyers (New York: M.E. Sharpe, 1999), 32–44; and Kimberly K. Harding, "Vinnette Carroll, 1922–2002," in *African American Dramatists: An A-to-Z Guide*, ed. Emmanuel Sampath Nelson (Westport, Conn.: Greenwood, 2004), 88–96.

4. August Heckscher, *Alive in the City: Memoir of an Ex-Commissioner* (New York: Charles Scribner's Sons, 1974), 169.

5. Vinnette Justine Carroll and Micki Grant, *Don't Bother Me, I Can't Cope* (Electronic Edition, Alexander Street, 1970, 2014), 34. Also published as *Don't Bother Me, I Can't Cope: A Musical Entertainment* (New York: Samuel French, 1972).

6. See Sylvie Drake, "'Cope' Director—From Unlikely to Inevitable," *Los Angeles Times*, August 6, 1972, 27.

7. Grant and Carroll, *Don't Bother Me, I Can't Cope*, 10.

8. George Nelson, "Ms. Carroll Brings Black Richness to the Stage," *New York Amsterdam News*, March 5, 1977, D9.

9. Carroll, quoted in Jo Ann Levine, "Actress-Director with 'a Sense of Herself,'" *Christian Science Monitor*, March 15, 1974, 14.

10. James Earl Jones, quoted in "Profile: Life of Vinnette Carroll, Who Died This Week," Washington, D.C., National Public Radio, 2002, http://search.proquest.com/docview/190126731?accountid=14026.

11. Kathleen Lynch and Judy Walsh, "Love, Care, and Solidarity: What Is and Is Not Commodifiable," in *Affective Equality: Love, Care, and Injustice,* ed. Kathleen Lynch, John Baker, and Maureen Lyons (Basingstoke, Eng.: Palgrave Macmillan, 2009), 37.

12. Lynch and Walsh, "Love, Care, and Solidarity," 38.

13. Nora Cole, "Vinnette Carroll: The First Black Woman Broadway Director," *Black Masks* (Summer/Fall 2012): 9, 14.

14. Mariana Mogilevich, "Arts as Public Policy: Cultural Spaces for Democracy and Growth," in *Summer in the City: John Lindsay, New York, and the American Dream,* ed. Joseph P. Viteritti (Baltimore: Johns Hopkins University Press, 2014), 196.

15. Other companies working in a similar model were Miriam Colon's Puerto Rican Traveling Theatre Company, Rosetta LeNoire's AMAS Repertory Theatre Company, Ernie McClintock's Afro-American Street Theater, Mical Whitaker's East River Players, and, later, Pregones Theater.

16. Vinnette Carroll, "To Journey to Each Other," *New York Times*, February 2, 1969, D9.

17. Alvin H. Reiss, "Business: The New Arts Patron," *Cue*, August 21, 1971, 7; see also Poggi, *Theater in America*, 205.

18. The Rockefeller Foundation, *President's Five-Year Review and Annual Report*, 1968, 92.

19. Courtney Callender, "Bringing It All Back Home: Community Access to the Arts," *New York Affairs* 4 (Winter 1978): 90.

20. Arlene Dávila cites the War on Poverty's state-led programs of distribution as directly involved in the "cultural revolution" of Puerto Rican identity through art and cultural initiatives in the late 1960s and early 1970s. Dávila, "Culture in the Battlefront," 162.

21. For a defense and full description of these programs, see Noel Cazenave, *Impossible Democracy: The Unlikely Success of the War on Poverty Community Action Programs* (Albany: State University of New York Press, 2007); and Cedric Johnson, *Revolutionaries to Race Leaders: Black Power and the Making of African American Politics* (Minneapolis: University of Minnesota Press, 2007), 40.

22. Writer Larry Neal described the Black Arts Theatre's radical politics as standing in opposition to "the feeble attitudes about culture of the 'War on

Poverty' bureaucrats." Larry Neal, "The Black Arts Movement," *TDR: The Drama Review* 12, "Black Theatre" (Summer 1968): 32.

23. King, quoted in Kalamu Ya Salaam, "Black Theatre—The Way It Is: An Interview with Woodie King, Jr.," *African American Review* 31 (Winter 1997): 648. King's starting budget for MFY was $575,000.

24. Ibid. In 1964 Roger Furman was appointed field director for the Harlem Youth Opportunity Unlimited (HARYOU), another New York City-based antipoverty agency. He used the funds to form a summer program that grew to become the New Heritage Repertory Theatre Company (NHRTC), Harlem's oldest black nonprofit theater group. In 1965 Lyndon Johnson (through HARYOU) also funded Amiri Baraka's (then LeRoi Jones') Black Arts Repertory Theater School (BARTS), founded in 1964 with Charles Patterson, William Patterson, Clarence Reed, Johnny Moore, and others. Anthony D. Hill and Douglas Q. Barnett, *A to Z of African American Theatre* (Lanham, Md.: Scarecrow, 2009), 198. See also Harry Elam, Jr., *Taking It to the Streets: The Social Protest Theater of Luis Valdez and Amiri Baraka* (Ann Arbor: University of Michigan Press, 1997), 2.

25. Woodie King Jr., *The Impact of Race: Theatre and Culture* (New York: Applause Theatre and Cinema Books, 2003), 35.

26. Woodie King Jr., quoted in Lindsay Patterson, "Black Theater: The Search Goes On," *Freedomways* 14 (1974): 244.

27. Woodie King Jr., *The Impact of Race*, 36.

28. Lonne Elder, III, *Charades on East Fourth Street* (Electronic Edition by Alexander Street, 2014), 10. Also published in Woodie King, Jr. and Ron Milner, eds., *Black Drama Anthology* (New York: New American Library, 1986).

29. Ibid., 12.

30. Woodie King, Jr., *The Impact of Race*, 36.

31. Patterson, "Black Theater: The Search Goes On," 246.

32. Sell, *Avant-Garde Performance*, 22.

33. Clarence Taylor, "Race, Rights, Empowerment," in *Summer in the City: John Lindsay, New York, and the American Dream*, ed. Joseph P. Viteritti (Baltimore: John Hopkins University Press, 2014), 74. Taylor contends that black and Latino New Yorkers supported Lindsay's efforts, and cites a compelling statistic: in his first run for mayor in 1965, Lindsay won 40% of the black vote and 25% of the Puerto Rican vote. In his second run in 1969, he received 80% of the vote in black districts, and 60% in Puerto Rican districts.

34. Callender, "Bringing it All Back Home," 90. Callender also argues that as far as the arts were concerned, the segment of New York's population that was most able to take advantage of Lindsay's brand of open governance was African Americans.

35. Joseph Wesley Zeigler, "Centrality without Philosophy: The Crisis in the Arts," *New York Affairs* 4 (Winter 1978): 12–23.

36. James M. Markham, "Street Theater Troupes Find the Play's Their Thing," *New York Times*, August 6, 1971, 62.

37. McCandlish Phillips, "1,250 Performances Are Given Here During Season," *New York Times*, August 27, 1970, 41. About 980 of the summer's 1,250 free shows were mounted by the Parks, Recreation and Cultural Affairs Administration, working with the Urban Coalition, foundations, block associations, civic

groups, and private donors. For more on the cultural identity and street theater in the 1960s, see Bradford D. Martin, *The Theater Is in the Street: Politics and Performance in Sixties America* (Amherst: University of Massachusetts Press, 2004).

38. Heckscher, quoted in Markham, "Street Theater Troupes Find the Play's Their Thing," 62.

39. Callender, quoted in ibid. For more on Callender's tenure in the position, see Heckscher, *Alive in the City*, 78.

40. Markham, "Street Theater Troupes Find the Play's Their Thing," 62. Troupes often bundled money from the city, national coalitions, and private foundations. The Puerto Rican Traveling Theatre had its street debut in 1967, when it was sponsored by Mayor Lindsay's Summer Task Force and presented *The Ox Cart* in fourteen locations throughout the city. See "Salute of the Week," *Cue*, August 7, 1971, 1.

41. This structure superseded (though by 1973 it had not replaced) the earlier Neighborhood Task Force system, formed in the summers of 1967 and 1968 to anticipate trouble in communities seen as hotbeds of unrest.

42. Quoted in David Greenstone, *Race and Authority in Urban Politics: Community Relations and the War on Poverty* (Chicago: University of Chicago Press, 1974), 42.

43. By 1970 the chairman of NYSCA, Seymour Knox, described the term "ghetto arts" as a "now-disquieting title." Seymour Knox, "NYS Council on the Arts 1969–1970: Chairman's Review" (New York: New York State Council on the Arts, 1970), http://www.experimentaltvcenter.org/nys-council-arts-1969–70-chairmans-review. For more on the Ghetto Arts Program, see Dávila, "Culture in the Battlefront," 167–70.

44. "History," Urban Arts Corps Records, New York Public Library, Schomburg Center for Research in Black Culture, 1.

45. Vinnette Carroll, quoted in Calvin A. McClinton, *The Work of Vinnette Carroll: An African American Theatre Artist* (Lewiston, N.Y.: Edwin Mellen, 2000), 94.

46. Junius Eddy, "Government, the Arts, and Ghetto Youth," *Public Administration Review* 30 (July/August 1970): 402. This was essential given the makeup of the State Arts Council, which had been criticized as a homogenous body representing primarily middle- and upper-middle-class white values.

47. In cooperation with the President's Council on Youth Opportunity, in 1968 the National Endowment for the Arts made matching grants of $25,000 available to support a series of summer workshops in the arts for inner-city youth. The money allowed indigenous artist-leaders to facilitate training and production workshop programs. Eddy, "Government, the Arts, and Ghetto Youth," 399–400.

48. Ibid., 402.

49. Ibid., 401.

50. Vinnette Carroll, quoted in "Vinnette Carroll: Masters of the Stage," American Theatre Wing, Stage Directors and Choreographers Foundation, November 1999, https://player.fm/series/atw-sdcf-masters-of-the-stage/vinnette-carroll.

51. Vinnette Carroll, quoted in Louis Calta, "Vinnette Carroll Gets a State Post: Actress-Director Is Head of Ghetto Arts Program," *New York Times*, March 23, 1968, 23.

52. McClinton, *The Work of Vinnette Carroll*, 96.

53. *Arts and the People: A Survey of Arts and Culture in New York State* (New York: American Council for the Arts in Education, 1973), 91. Similar studies included a NYSCA-funded survey by Tom Lloyd's group, the Community Artists Cultural Survey Committee, backed by Thomas Hoving at the Metropolitan Museum, as well as a survey conducted through the American Association of Museums and funded by the U.S. Department of Housing and Urban Development. See "Museums and the Ghetto," *Newsweek*, vol. 76, August 17, 1970, 93.

54. *Arts and the People*, 28, 92. Common to policy studies at the time, the report made no attempt to distinguish between different races or ethnicities, and has only two categories: white and nonwhite.

55. Ibid., 7, 28.

56. Ibid., iv.

57. "Culture Popping Up in All Boroughs," *New York Times*, March 26, 1970, 56.

58. See Elam, *Taking It to the Streets*, 4.

59. Carroll, "To Journey to Each Other," D9.

60. Sell, *Avant-Garde Performance*, 249.

61. Bertolt Brecht, *Brecht on Theatre: The Development of an Aesthetic*, trans. John Willett (New York: Hill and Wang, 1964), 185.

62. Alvin H. Reiss, "Arts in the Neighborhood: New York's Cultural Center without Walls," *Cue*, June 5, 1971, 9.

63. Mel Gussow, "'Croesus and Witch' Goes to 20th Street," *New York Times*, August 27, 1971, 18.

64. Vinnette Justine Carroll and Micki Grant, *Croesus and the Witch* (Electronic Edition by Alexander Street, 2014), 5, 27.

65. *Step Lively, Boy!* opened on February 7, 1973, at the Urban Arts Theater and later at the New Locust Theatre in Philadelphia, on a double bill with *Croesus and the Witch*. Dan Dietz, *Off Broadway Musicals, 1910–2007* (Jefferson, N.C.: McFarland, 2010), 427.

66. Vinnette Carroll, quoted in McCandlish Phillips, "Urban Arts Corps Offers Two Plays on Negro Life," *New York Times*, August 29, 1969, 25.

67. Robert Macbeth, "Parochialism," *New York Times*, April 11, 1971, D18.

68. Sylvie Drake, "'Cope' Director: From Unlikely to Inevitable," *Los Angeles Times*, August 6, 1972, AB1.

69. See Robert C. Wylder, "'Don't Bother Me' Has Everything: Things Go Superlatively with *Cope*," *Press Telegram*, August 16, 1972, A30.

70. Carroll and Grant, *Please Don't Bother Me, I Can't Cope*, 52.

71. Ibid., 20.

72. Ibid., 15.

73. Phillips, "Urban Arts Corps Offers Two Plays on Negro Life," 25.

74. Clifford Mason, "Vinnette Carroll Is Still in There Swinging," *New York Times*, December 19, 1976, X4.

75. "Beame Agrees to Be Victim of Inner Circle's Lampoon," *New York Times*, February 14, 1975, 42. The cast of *The Wiz* accompanied Beame's rebuttal in 1977. "Inner Circle's Review Lampoons Mayor's Troubles," *New York Times*, March 6, 1977, 37.

76. "Carey and Beame Are Satirized Here by the Inner Circle," *New York Times*, March 2, 1975, 40.

77. Ronald Smothers, "Black Repertory Troupe Is 'Coping' with Success," *New York Times*, March 23, 1975, 49.

78. Mason, "Vinnette Carroll Is Still in There Swinging," X4–X5.

79. Phillips, "Candidates Assess City's Arts Future," 50.

80. Across the landscape of arts in New York City, this amounted to a foundational redefinition of "a cultural institution." Prior to 1976, the agency in charge of Cultural Affairs—and the city's cultural resources—had been lumped with the Department of Parks and Recreation. In 1976 Mayor Beame made Cultural Affairs a separate agency and Claude Shostal became the city's first commissioner of cultural affairs. The cultural institutions housed in city-owned buildings or on city-owned property that received support from the Bureau of the Budget were added to the new agency's budget, known as the Cultural Institutions Group (CIGs). Grace Glueck, "City Council Acts on New Arts Agency," *New York Times*, October 2, 1975, 44.

81. Steven Weisman, "Beame, Naming Advisory Panel on Culture, Plans New Agency," *New York Times*, May 23, 1975, 38.

82. *Report to the Mayor's Committee on Cultural Policy* (New York: New York City Mayor's Committee on Cultural Policy, 1974).

83. Richard F. Shepard, "Beame Is Upbeat Over the Cultural Life of the City," *New York Times*, April 8, 1975, 30.

84. See Miriam Greenberg, *Branding New York: How a City in Crisis was Sold to the World* (New York: Routledge, 2008), 49.

85. Ibid., 161–62.

86. Ibid., 165.

87. Ibid.

88. J. Allen Whitt, "Mozart in the Metropolis: The Arts Coalition and the Urban Growth Machine," *Urban Affairs Review* 23 (September 1987): 16.

89. Ada Louise Huxtable, "Art, Money and Impotence in New York," *New York Times*, December 15, 1974, 151.

90. Janet Langsam, interview with author, January 11, 2012. Langsam was involved in efforts to create artist housing on the Lower East Side. During the course of our conversation, Langsam wondered aloud if incorporating Cultural Affairs under the OED umbrella contributed to hostility toward their initiatives from LES residents. "As I'm sitting here talking about it and thinking about it . . . maybe the [artist housing] experience in the East Village had more to do than I thought or realized with this whole notion of the arts as an economic driver. The arts are out there, trying to survive: 'Why are we attached to the Parks Department? That doesn't really make sense in terms of the whole of what the arts are, so let's move over to the economic development bucket.' . . . Being in the economic development bucket, maybe that turned off those housing folks in the LES."

91. Carter Ratcliff, "The Culture Vulture Flies Higher," *New York*, April 10, 1978, 53.

92. Glueck, "City Council Acts," 44.

93. Ibid.

94. Ratcliff, "Culture Vulture," 53. Ratcliff contends that it was Segal's approach that led Beame to pry Cultural Affairs loose from the Parks Department.

95. Grace Glueck, "Money Isn't Enough at City Culture Unit," *New York Times*, June 24, 1974; Grace Glueck, "Cultural Agencies Reducing Hours and Security: Cultural Services Feel Impact of Cuts," *New York Times*, November 3, 1975, 1. Segal publicly protested these actions.

96. Louis Calta, "City Cultural Affairs Chief Foresees Money Battles," *New York Times*, August 18, 1976, 46.

97. Thomas Willis, "'Too Short to Box with God' Brings the Gospel Home," *Chicago Tribune*, April 9, 1976, B1; Clive Barnes, "Stage: 'Your Arms Too Short . . .'" *New York Times,* December 23, 1976, 19; "'Your Arms Too Short to Box with God' Successful Run at Variety," *Los Angeles Sentinel,* December 6, 1979, B6A.

98. C. Gerald Fraser, "Urban Arts Corps Faces Ouster and Search for a New Theater," *New York Times*, February 25, 1979, 46; see also C. Gerald Fraser, "At Ten, Urban Arts Corps Keeps Pace," *New York Times,* June 24, 1979, 30. UAC leaders (Carroll, Anita MacShane, and choreographer Talley Beatty) found new headquarters at 227 West Seventeenth Street, between Seventh and Eighth Avenues, and began soliciting funds for the raw space renovations and operations.

99. Anita MacShane, quoted in, C. Gerald Fraser, "Urban Arts Corps Faces Ouster and Search for a New Theater," *New York Times*, February 25, 1979, 46.

100. Carroll quoted in Mason, "Vinnette Carroll Is Still Swinging," 5.

101. Smothers, "Black Repertory Troupe Is 'Coping' With Success," 49.

102. Michael McKinnie, *City Stages: Theatre and Urban Space in a Global City* (Toronto: University of Toronto Press, 2007), 86–87. "Edifice complex" refers to a focus on civic centers and/or large theatrical sites.

103. Carroll quoted in Nelson, "Black Richness to the Stage," D9.

104. Guy Flatley, "Don't Worry, Micki Can Cope," *New York Times*, May 7, 1972, 7.

105. Taylor, "Race, Rights, Empowerment," 61.

Chapter 4

EPIGRAPH: Peter Brook, "The Complete Truth Is Global," *New York Times,* January 20, 1974, 3.

1. The bulk of Bread and Puppet performers departed Coney Island in 1972 after two seasons. Charles Denson, *Coney Island: Lost and Found* (Berkeley, Calif.: Ten Speed, 2002), 201; see Stefan Brecht, *Bread and Puppet Theatre* (London: Methuen, 1988), 2:197.

2. See Howard Thompson, "Street Theatre Livens Lincoln Center," *New York Times*, August 20, 1971, 17; George Gent, "Festival to Offer a Parade of Skills by 32 Troupes," *New York Times,* August 22, 1973, 42.

3. Geraldine Fitzgerald, quoted in Janet Noble, "Geraldine Fitzgerald: A Woman for All Seasons," *Irish America Magazine* (January/February 1993): 31.

4. Fitzgerald, quoted in Tom Burke, "Geraldine's Long Journey," *New York Times*, June 13, 1971, 7.

5. Mimi Gisolfi D'Aponte, "*Everyman and roach* in Retrospect: A Study of Street Theatre That Worked," *Journal of Dramatic Theory and Criticism* (Spring 1990): 170.

6. Fitzgerald, quoted in Noble, "Geraldine Fitzgerald: A Woman for All Seasons," 31.

7. D'Aponte, "*Everyman and roach* in Retrospect," 170–71; and Denson, *Coney Island: Lost and Found*, 200.

8. Earl G. Schreiber, "*Everyman* in America," *Comparative Drama* 9 (Summer 1975): 99.

9. Dudley Cocke, quoted in Jan Cohen-Cruz, *Engaging Performance: Theatre as Call and Response* (London: Routledge, 2010), 11. Cocke invokes Wendell Berry to argue that too few practitioners of Augusto Boal's "theater of the oppressed" in the United States employ his methodologies within the context of their own local culture.

10. Clifford Geertz, "Local Knowledge and Its Limits: Some *Obiter Dicta*," *Yale Journal of Criticism* 5 (1992): 132.

11. Mel Gussow, "Festival's Cry: Theater to the People," *New York Times*, August 28, 1972, clippings file, "Lincoln Center—Community / Street Theatre Festival," Billy Rose Theatre Collection, New York Public Library at Lincoln Center.

12. Jonathan Ringkamp, quoted in "A Dialogue on the Street Theatre Festival at Lincoln Center with Geraldine Fitzgerald, Brother Jonathan Ringkamp, Mical Whitaker, Hazel Bryant," videotaped for the Theatre on Film and Tape Archives, August 20 and 22, 1973, Billy Rose Theatre Collection, New York Public Library at Lincoln Center, 1973.

13. Mical Whitaker was the theater coordinator of the Black Theater Alliance (BTA) and founded the East River Players in East Harlem in 1964. Hazel Bryant established the Afro-American Total Theatre in 1968 (later renamed the Richard Allen Center for Culture and Art). Bryant was the president of the BTA, and produced the first Black Theatre Festival USA in the summer of 1979.

14. Mical Whitaker, interview with author, July 9, 2014.

15. "For 30 Sidewalk Troupes, Top Lincoln Center Billing," *New York Times*, August 7, 1972, 22.

16. John Brown Childs, ed., *Transcommunality: From the Politics of Conversion to the Ethics of Respect* (Philadelphia: Temple University Press, 2003), 25.

17. Guillermo Delgado-P., "Transcommunality: Beyond Tolerance, for Understanding," in Childs, ed., *Transcommunality*, 104.

18. Rem Koolhaas, "Delirious New York: A Retroactive Manifesto for Manhattan (Excerpt)," in *Coney Island: The Parachute Pavilion Competition*, ed. Zoë Ryan and Jonathan Cohen-Litant (Princeton, N.J.: Princeton Architectural Press, 2007), 20.

19. I borrow this term from Tracy Metz, "Calculating Leisure," in *Coney Island*, ed. Ryan and Cohen-Litant, 27.

20. Michel Foucault theorized carnivals as "temporal heterotopias," and in part owing to Rem Koolhaas's 1978 evocation of Coney Island in *Delirious New York*, numerous scholars have written about the amusement area as a heterotopic space. See, for example, Eliza Darling, "Nature's Carnival: The Ecology of Pleasure at Coney Island," in *In the Nature of Cities: Urban Political Ecology and the Politics of Urban Metabolism*, ed. Nik Heynen, Mari Kaika, and Erik Swyngedouw (New York: Routledge, 2006).

21. "Why Do New Yorkers Go to Coney Island? Radical and Philosopher Take up the Question—and Settle a Bet," *New York Times*, July 4, 1909, SM10.

22. See John F. Kasson, *Amusing the Million: Coney Island at the Turn of the Century* (New York: Hill and Wang, 1978); and Kathy Peiss, *Cheap Amusements: Working Women and Leisure in Turn-of-the-Century New York* (Philadelphia: Temple University Press, 1986), 4.

23. Woody Register, *The Kid of Coney Island: Fred Thompson and the Rise of American Amusements* (New York: Oxford University Press, 2001), 89–90.

24. Quoted in Denson, *Coney Island: Lost and Found*, 73–76. For additional analysis of Moses and Coney, see Miriam Greenberg, *Branding New York: How a City in Crisis Was Sold to the World* (New York: Routledge, 2008), 47.

25. Marshall Berman, quoted in Gareth Millington, "'Man Dem Link Up': London's Anti-Riots and Urban Modernism," *Sociological Research Online* 17 (November 30, 2012): 2.3, http://www.socresonline.org.uk/17/4/12.html. See also Barbara Hooper, "Urban Space, Modernity, and Masculinist Desire: The Utopian Longings of Le Corbusier," in *Embodied Utopias: Gender, Social Change, and the Modern Metropolis,* ed. Amy Bingaman, Lise Sanders, and Rebecca Zorach (London: Routledge, 2002), 55–79.

26. Denson, *Coney Island: Lost and Found*, 142–43. The *New York Times* led the media thrashing of Coney Island with a full-page article in 1975 that labeled the neighborhood a "war zone" and a "ghost town." See Leslie Maitland, "Air of Uncertainty Dogs Coney Island," *New York Times,* November 3, 1975, 39.

27. Victoria W. Wolcott, *Race, Riots, and Roller Coasters: The Struggle Over Segregated Recreation in America* (Philadelphia: University of Pennsylvania Press, 2012), 288–89, footnotes 54–62.

28. Ibid., 196.

29. D'Aponte, "*Everyman and roach* in Retrospect," 165. D'Aponte has also researched the phenomenal growth of street festivals during the 1970s. Mimi Gisolfi D'Aponte, "Good Friday: Street Theater in New York," *Other Stages* 5 (March 24, 1983): 8.

30. For more on Maryat Lee's life and work, see William W. French, *Maryat Lee's Ecotheater: A Theater for the Twenty-First Century* (Morgantown: West Virginia University Press, 1998).

31. Dan Sullivan, "Theater in East Harlem: The Outdoor Audience Gets into the Act," *New York Times*, August 30, 1968, 101.

32. Richard Faust and Charles Kadushin, *Shakespeare in the Neighborhood: Audience Reaction to A Midsummer Night's Dream as Produced by Joseph Papp for the Delacorte Mobile Theatre* (New York: Twentieth Century Fund, 1965), 61. See also Sandra Schmidt, "Theater in the Street: Looks Arch," *Christian Science Monitor,* July 31, 1965, 4.

33. Faust and Kadushin, *Shakespeare in the Neighborhood*, 8. Some actors disliked performing in Papp's Mobile Unit because of this tense dynamic between performers and audience. See Kenneth Turan and Joseph Papp, *Free for All: Joe Papp, The Public, and the Greatest Theater Story Ever Told* (New York: Anchor Books, 2010), 82–83, 102, 109–10, 121, 179; Helen Epstein, *Joe Papp: An American Life* (Boston: Da Capo, 1996), 178–81.

34. Director Woodie King credited Brand as one of the first to make a real attempt at developing street theater and "guerilla theater." Woodie King Jr., "The Dilemma of Black Theater," *Black World/Negro Digest* (April 1970): 12. See

Richard F. Shepard, "Street Audience Enjoys Moliere," *New York Times,* July 8, 1964, 37; "Theater in Street to Expand Program," *New York Times,* February 3, 1965, 30; and Louis Calta, "Street Theater to Play 51 Dates," *New York Times,* June 15, 1965, 44.

35. Louis Calta, "Unruly 'Actors' Try to Upstage Troupe in Bedford-Stuyvesant," *New York Times*, June 28, 1966, 51.

36. Callender, quoted in, James M. Markham, "Street Theater Troupes Find the Play's Their Thing," *New York Times*, August 6, 1971, 62.

37. Fitzgerald, quoted in Gussow, "Festival's Cry: Theater to the People," *New York Times*, August 28, 1972, clippings file, "Lincoln Center—Community / Street Theatre Festival," Billy Rose Theatre Collection, New York Public Library at Lincoln Center.

38. Vargas quoted in Leticia Kent, "The Gut Theatre Is in the Street," *Village Voice*, August 17, 1967, 3.

39. Ibid.

40. Ibid., 17.

41. Geraldine Fitzgerald, quoted in Noble, "Geraldine Fitzgerald: A Woman for All Seasons," 31.

42. See Denson, *Coney Island: Lost and Found*, 147.

43. Maitland, "Air of Uncertainty Dogs Coney Island," 39.

44. Denson, *Coney Island: Lost and Found*, 147.

45. Dierdre Carmody, "Where New Yorkers Go—and Don't Go," *New York Times*, January 18, 1974, 19.

46. Curtis J. Berger, "Hart et al. v. Community School Board, et al.: Report of the Special Master," United States District Court for the Eastern District of New York, 1974, i–ii, Billy Rose Theatre Division, New York Public Library.

47. Fitzgerald, quoted in Tom Burke, "Geraldine's Long Journey," *New York Times*, June 13, 1971, 7.

48. "A Dialogue on the Street Theatre Festival at Lincoln Center."

49. Jonathan Ringkamp, quoted in Marilyn Stasio, "On the Theatre Scene," *Cue*, September 11, 1971, 13.

50. D'Aponte, "*Everyman and roach* in Retrospect," 170–71.

51. Reichenthal, quoted in Denson, *Coney Island: Lost and Found*, 200.

52. Geraldine Fitzgerald and Jonathan Ringkamp, *Everyman and roach*, undated, unpublished play script, courtesy Mimi D'Aponte, 3.

53. "A Dialogue on the Street Theatre Festival at Lincoln Center."

54. Ibid.

55. *Everyman and roach*, VHS, Billy Rose Theatre Division, Theatre on Film and Tape Archive, New York Public Library, 1972. This production was performed by the Mt. Morris-Everyman Theater; coproduced by Hazel Bryant, Geraldine Fitzgerald, Mical Whitaker, and Brother Jonathan; written by Geraldine Fitzgerald and Brother Jonathan; directed by Hazel Bryant; choreographed by George Faison.

56. Fitzgerald and Ringkamp, *Everyman and roach*, 6.

57. Ibid., 13.

58. See Cohen-Cruz, *Engaging Performance*, 1–16.

59. D'Aponte, "*Everyman and roach* in Retrospect," 171.

60. Howard Thompson, "Rhythm and Satire at Street Festival: Dayton and Brooklyn Troupes Perform," *New York Times*, August 23, 1973, 43.

61. Fitzgerald and Ringkamp, *Everyman and roach*, 37.

62. Ibid., 43.

63. Ibid., 48.

64. D'Aponte, "*Everyman and roach* in Retrospect," 175.

65. Heckscher, *Alive in the City*, 171.

66. Woodie King Jr., "The Dilemma of Black Theater," 14–15.

67. "The Negro Family: The Case for National Action," Office of Policy Planning and Research, United States Department of Labor (March 1965), http://www.dol.gov.

68. Dick Brukenfeld, "Theatre: Mr. Esteban," *The Village Voice*, December 4, 1969, 54.

69. Amy Bingaman, Lise Sanders, and Rebecca Zorachin, *Embodied Utopias: Gender, Social Change, and the Modern Metropolis* (London: Routledge, 2002), 7.

70. Sonja Arsham Kuftinec, "Theatrical Imaginaries in the Balkans and Jerusalem," in *Considering Calamity: Methods for Performance Research*, ed. Tracy C. Davis and Linda Ben-Zvi (Tel Aviv: Assaph Books, 2007), 97–98.

71. Clive Barnes, "From Street Theater, an 'Everyman,'" *New York Times*, October 6, 1971, 42.

72. Peter Brook, "The Complete Truth Is Global," *New York Times*, January 20, 1974, 3.

73. Ibid.

74. Mel Gussow, "To Peter Brook, Audience Is a Partner," *New York Times*, September 28, 1973, 20.

75. Louis Chapin, "Peter Brook in Brooklyn: British Director Has All-day Sessions," *Christian Science Monitor*, October 12, 1973, 14.

76. Peter Brook, quoted in "This Week in BAM History: Peter Brook, Barbra Streisand, and Africa," *BAMblog*, September 16, 2011, http://bam150years.blogspot.com/2011/09/workingthis-week-in-bam-history-peter.html.

77. Brook, "The Complete Truth Is Global," 13. See also "New Performances for Brook's *Birds*," *New York Times*, October 3, 1973, 39.

78. Dan Sullivan, "Called on the Carpet by a Theatre Guru," *Los Angeles Times*, September 2, 1973, 35.

79. "*A Midsummer Night's Dream* Program," Everyman Company, January 2–6, 1974, BAM Hamm Archive.

80. The complex cost $185 million at its completion in 1969, approximately $990 million in 2005. For a thorough analysis that ties the surrounding streets to the stages of Lincoln Center, see Julia L. Foulkes, "The Other West Side Story: Urbanization and the Arts Meet at Lincoln Center," *Amerikanstudien/American Studies* 52 (2007): 227–47.

81. Marvin Carlson, "The Theatre as Civic Monument," *Theatre Journal* 40 (March 1988): 27.

82. See Zipp, *Manhattan Projects*, 159–61; and Julia L. Foulkes, "Streets and Stages: Urban Renewal and the Arts after World War II," *Journal of Social History* 44 (Winter 2010): 413–34.

83. Robert Moses, quoted in Alvin H. Reiss, "Who Builds Theatres and Why?" *TDR: The Drama Review* 12 (Spring 1968): 83.

84. See "Events in Street Theater Festival," *New York Times*, August 28, 1973, 29.

85. Childs, *Transcommunality*, 25.

86. Julia Foulkes, "Streets and Stages: Urban Renewal and the Arts after World War II," *Journal of Social History* 44 (Winter 2010): 415.

87. Quoted in Raymond Ericson, "Changing Lincoln Center's Image," *New York Times*, October 10, 1971, D15.

88. Larrabee, quoted in "Lincoln Center Opens Free Outdoor Festival," *New York Times*, August 21, 1974, 29.

89. Ibid.

90. Mel Gussow, "Theatre: In the Streets: Lincoln Center's Open-Air Festival Ends with Reaffirmations of Black Message," *New York Times*, September 4, 1972, 6; Mel Gussow, "Theatre: Rock vs. Junk: Street Festival Offers Anti-Drug Musical," *New York Times*, August 24, 1972, 52.

91. Copani, a recovering addict, traveled the streets of South Brooklyn to bring Puerto Rican and Italian teenagers together to alleviate tensions after periods of gang unrest. McCandlish Phillips, ". . . Which Will Run for Two Weeks at Lincoln Center," *New York Times*, August 22, 1972, 52; Mel Gussow and Don McDonagh, "*Blind Junkie* Presented at Street Theatre Fete," *New York Times,* September 2, 1972, 14; "Street Action," *New York Times,* August 27, 1973, 28.

92. Heckscher, *Alive in the City*, 172.

93. Foulkes, Robert Bennett, and others have argued that the ideology of the spatial practices employed at Lincoln Center had been previewed at Moses's 1939 World's Fair. See Robert Bennett, *Deconstructing Post-WWII New York City: The Literature, Art, Jazz, and Architecture of an Emerging Global Capital* (New York: Routledge, 2003), 29–30, 49.

94. "A Dialogue on the Street Theatre Festival at Lincoln Center."

95. The budget in 1972 was $53,000, and in 1973 it was projected to be $64,962. When United Brands pulled its sponsorship, the budget was cut to $38,337. See Phillips, ". . . Which Will Run for Two Weeks at Lincoln Center," 52; Edward Hudson, "Festival Leader Is Really Its Juggler," *New York Times*, August 24, 1972, 52; George Gent, "Festival to Offer a Parade of Skills by 32 Troupes," *New York Times,* August 22, 1973, 42.

96. Amyas Ames, "Our Cup Is Broken: What Inflation Is Doing to the Arts," *Music Educators Journal* 60 (December 1973): 16.

97. "A Dialogue on the Street Theatre Festival at Lincoln Center."

98. "Lincoln Center Opens Free Outdoor Festival," *New York Times*, August 21, 1974.

99. John Mazzola, quoted in Leslie Maitland, "Lincoln Center Opens Its Fifth Year of Free Events 'Just Right' for Everyone," *New York Times*, August 13, 1975, 35.

100. Childs, *Transcommunality*, 11.

101. Jennifer Dunning, "Arts and Outdoors Meet at Lincoln Center," *New York Times*, August 19, 1977, 46.

102. Mical Whitaker, interview with author, July 9, 2014.

103. Maitland, "Lincoln Center Opens Its Fifth Year of Free Events," 35. Among many examples of previous bilingual performance at the festival, in 1972, the Henry Street Settlement's New Federal Theatre received praise for its Spanish-language *Abdala-José Martí*, a play adapted by Ivan Acosta and Omar Torres. Mel Gussow, "Poet-Revolutionary Inspires a Drama," *New York Times*, August 23, 1972, 34.

104. See Eleanor Blau, "Lincoln Center Goes Out of Doors," *New York Times*, August 12, 1983.

105. McCandlish Phillips, "Summertime, and the Arts Are Easy at Lincoln Center," *New York Times*, July 8, 1979, D1. Tuxedo Park is a small, wealthy, predominantly white residential community in New York.

106. "A Dialogue on the Street Theatre Festival at Lincoln Center."

107. Ibid.

108. Samuel A. Hay, *African American Theatre: A Historical and Critical Analysis* (Cambridge: Cambridge University Press, 1994), 177. Hay discusses influential "second-stage organizations" of the 1960s that closed due to lack of space, particularly after their founders died.

109. Mary Breasted, "Parks to Bustle Again in Summer," *New York Times*, May 16, 1976, 47.

110. Ray Rosenzweig and Elizabeth Blackmar, *The Park and the People: A History of Central Park* (Ithaca, N.Y.: Cornell University Press, 1992), 471.

111. Ibid., 502.

112. Corporate contributions to arts and culture went from $22 million in 1965 to $109 million in 1980. See J. Allen Whitt, "Mozart in the Metropolis: The Arts Coalition and the Urban Growth Machine," *Urban Affairs Review* 23 (September 1987): 15–36.

113. See, for example, John Brooks, "Fueling the Arts, or, Exxon as a Medici," *New York Times*, January 25, 1976, 71.

114. Wickham Boyle, *On the Streets: A Guide to New York City's Buskers* (New York: New York City Department of Cultural Affairs, 1981?), 4.

115. Ibid., 75.

116. Ibid., 73. "Westway" refers to one of the most contentious planning debates in New York City's history, a proposed $1.16-billion dollar, twelve-lane highway and waterfront development project proposed for the West Side of Manhattan.

117. Colin Campbell, "Beleaguered Coney Islanders Rally with Sense of Affection: The Talk of Coney Island," *New York Times*, August 29, 1981, 25.

118. "'Half a Tank' Leisure: The Latest Boom," *U.S. News & World Report*, August 6, 1979, 41.

Chapter 5

EPIGRAPHS: (1) Joseph Papp, "Government Aid: Sponsor of Free Shakespeare Says It Would Help More Than Hinder," *New York Times*, July 24, 1960, xi; (2) Papp, address to the Board of Estimate, May 9, 1967, New York Shakespeare Festival Records, box 13–7, folder 1, Billy Rose Theatre Division, New York Public Library; (3) Papp, quoted in, McCandlish Phillips, "Papp's Dream Enriches a City," *New York Times*, March 7, 1973, 38.

1. Mel Gussow, "A Playwright's Invention Named Papp," *New York Times*, November 9, 1975, 93. At the time, the Public Theater carried a deficit of $2 million. Helen Epstein, *Joe Papp: An American Life* (Boston: Da Capo, 1996), 277.

2. Epstein, *An American Life*, 7.

3. Stanley Kauffman, "The Stages of Joseph Papp," *The American Scholar* 44 (Winter 1974–75): 117.

4. Julius Novick, *Beyond Broadway: The Quest for Permanent Theatres* (New York: Hill and Wang, 1968), 183. John D. Rockefeller III, in his capacity as president of Lincoln Center for the Performing Arts, Inc., decided that the center should include a repertory theater. Whitehead and Kazan began working full-time as the founders of the repertory in the fall of 1962. The Beaumont Theater opened in 1965, when Herbert Blau and Jules Irving took over. Blau resigned in 1967, and Irving remained until 1971.

5. Rosalyn Deutsche, "Art and Public Space: Questions of Democracy," *Social Text* 33 (1992): 36.

6. Stuart Hall, "The Great Moving Right Show," *Marxism Today* (January 1979): 15.

7. Joseph Papp's address to the Board of Estimate, May 9, 1967, box 13–7, folder 1, New York Shakespeare Festival Records, Billy Rose Theatre Division, New York Public Library.

8. Papp disparagingly called the businessmen on the board of directors at Lincoln Center's Forum Theater "culture mongers" with "expansionist, predatory and imperialistic aims." Joseph Papp, "Is There a Fifth Column at the Forum?" *New York Times*, July 25, 1971, D4.

9. See, for example, Epstein, *An American Life*, 15.

10. Howard Greenberger, *The Off-Broadway Experience* (Englewood Cliffs, N.J.: Prentice Hall, 1971), 81.

11. Arnold M. Auerbach, "If You Don't Like It, Go Fight Mayor Papp," *New York Times*, April 14, 1968, D10.

12. Janelle Reinelt, "Rethinking the Public Sphere for a Global Age," *Performance Research: A Journal of the Performing Arts* 16 (2011): 16–27. See also Robert B. Shimko and Sara Freeman, eds., *Public Theatres and Theatre Publics* (Newcastle-upon-Tyne, Eng.: Cambridge Scholars, 2012).

13. Raymond Williams, *The Sociology of Culture* (New York: Schocken Books, 1982), 56.

14. Christopher B. Balme, *The Theatrical Public Sphere* (Cambridge: Cambridge University Press, 2014).

15. See Epstein, *An American Life*, 193; Stuart W. Little, "Joe Papp's Biggest Real-Estate Deal," *New York*, April 21, 1969, 54–55.

16. Epstein, *An American Life,* 188, 172.

17. Turan and Papp, *Free for All*, 239. For more details on the financial situation at the Public Theater during those years, see Stuart W. Little, "Another Opening, Another Show?" *New York*, June 29, 1970, 6–7.

18. Heckscher, *Alive in the City*, 105.

19. August Heckscher, quoted in Turan, *Free for All*, 239. Because bonds funded the capital budget, and the city had ample bond-issuing authority under the state constitution, capital money was not as tight as operations money.

20. "City-Owned Institutions," Department of Cultural Affairs, City of New York, http://www.nyc.gov/html/dcla/html/funding/institutions_links.shtml.

21. Bernard Gersten quoted in Catherine Breslin, "The Hottest Show in Town Is Joe Papp!" *New York*, November 29, 1971, 36.

22. Papp, quoted in Epstein, *An American Life,* 248–49.

23. Correspondence between Mr. and Mrs. Henry Elghanayan and Mayor John V. Lindsay, September 1, 1972, box 1–96, folder 20, New York Shakespeare Festival Records, Billy Rose Theatre Division, New York Public Library.

24. Ibid.

25. Papp, quoted in Epstein, *An American Life,* 246.

26. John Beaufort, "New York Shakespeare Festival Public Theater: The Difference between Creative Vision and Wishful Thinking," *Christian Science Monitor*, December 10, 1971, 9.

27. Letter from Sanford D. Garelik to Audrey Wood, October 21, 1970, box 1–82, folder 7, New York Shakespeare Festival Records, Billy Rose Theatre Division, New York Public Library.

28. Heckscher, *Alive in the City*, 280.

29. George C. Scott's address to the Board of Directors, October 8, 1970, box 1–82, folder 7, New York Shakespeare Festival Records, Billy Rose Theatre Division, New York Public Library.

30. Joseph Papp's address to the Board of Estimate, May 9, 1967, box 13–7, folder 1, New York Shakespeare Festival Records, Billy Rose Theatre Division, New York Public Library.

31. Marilyn Stasio, "On the Theatre Scene," *Cue*, September 11, 1971, 13.

32. Delano H. Stewart, artistic director of the Bed-Stuy Theater, spearheaded the drive to form the BTA, which officially incorporated in 1971. It initially consisted of Ernie McClintock's Afro American Studio Theater, Hazel Bryant's Afro-American Total Theatre, Roger Furman's New Heritage Repertory Theatre, Lubaba Lateef's Brownsville Laboratory Theater, and Buddy Butler's Theater Black.

33. Stanley Kauffman criticized Papp's overreach and his motivations for wading into new play development at all. See Kauffman, "The Stages of Joseph Papp," 114; Rosenthal, "Ellen Stewart: La Mama of Us All," 25.

34. Fifteen community organizations across the five boroughs were listed in total. Community Supporters of City Acquisition of Public Theater, box 1–82, folder 7, New York Shakespeare Festival Records, Billy Rose Theatre Division, New York Public Library.

35. Black Playwrights Produced by the New York Shakespeare Festival Public Theater, box 1–82, folder 7, New York Shakespeare Festival Records, Billy Rose Theatre Division, New York Public Library. Six black playwrights produced by the Public Theater and fourteen black actors were listed separately from the other distinguished actors.

36. Jack Kroll, "The Public Fights for Life," *Newsweek*, March 22, 1971, clippings file, box 1–92, folder 3, New York Shakespeare Festival Records, Billy Rose Theatre Division, New York Public Library.

37. Breslin, "The Hottest Show in Town Is Joe Papp!" 33.

38. Edward C. Burke, "Board of Estimate Rejects Plan to Aid Shakespeare Theater," *New York Times*, December 4, 1970, 40.

39. Ibid. This included $15,000 for annual leases for three of the mayor's fifty urban task force units and for one of his six neighborhood action program groups.

40. "Papp Theater: To Be or Not to Be?" *New York Post*, March 12, 1971, clippings file, box 1–92, folder 3, New York Shakespeare Festival Records, Billy Rose Theatre Division, New York Public Library.

41. Quoted in Breslin, "The Hottest Show in Town Is Joe Papp!" 33.

42. Letter from Joseph Papp, March 1971, box 1–92, folder 3, New York Shakespeare Festival Records, Billy Rose Theatre Division, New York Public Library.

43. Emergency Committee to Save the Public Theater, March 1971, box 1–92, folder 3, New York Shakespeare Festival Records, Billy Rose Theatre Division, New York Public Library.

44. Papp, quoted in Clive Barnes, "A Plea to Save Papp's Public Theater," *New York Times*, December 18, 1970, 42.

45. Elia Kazan, March 11, 1971, box 1–92, folder 3, New York Shakespeare Festival Records, Billy Rose Theatre Division, New York Public Library.

46. John F. Hayes, quoted in Epstein, *An American Life*, 260.

47. Papp, quoted in Turan and Papp, *Free for All*, 241–42.

48. Brooks Atkinson, March 4, 1971, box 1–92, folder 3, New York Shakespeare Festival Records, Billy Rose Theatre Division, New York Public Library.

49. Courtney Callender, "Bringing It All Back Home: Community Access to the Arts," *New York Affairs* 4 (Winter 1978): 89.

50. Alvin H. Reiss, "Arts in the Neighborhood: New York's Cultural Center without Walls," *Cue*, June 5, 1971, 9.

51. *Report to the Mayor's Committee on Cultural Policy* (New York: New York City Mayor's Committee on Cultural Policy, 1974).

52. Jane Kathleen Curry, *John Guare: A Research and Production Sourcebook* (Westport, Conn.: Greenwood, 2002), 97.

53. Ibid., 99.

54. Gersten and Papp wanted to transfer the play to Broadway, but they did not want investors who would take a profit. LuEsther T. Mertz contributed the money, took a tax deduction as a contribution to a not-for-profit theater, and left the Public Theater as 100 percent owners. Turan and Papp, *Free for All*, 250–56; Curry, *John Guare*, 100.

55. Papp donated 5 percent of profits derived from *Two Gents* to the New York City Cultural Council: he sent Mayor Lindsay a check for $5,750 after its first nine months on Broadway. The coverage of the event described Papp as receiving almost $5 million in subsidies from the city since 1961. "Papp Gives Share of 'Verona' Profits to City in Thanks," *New York Times*, August 23, 1972, 30.

56. McCandlish Phillips, "Papp's Dream Enriches a City," *New York Times*, March 7, 1973, 38.

57. Ibid.

58. Ada Louise Huxtable, "Missing the Point (and Boat) at City Hall," *New York Times*, January 3, 1971, clippings file, box 1–92, folder 3, New York Shakespeare Festival Records, Billy Rose Theatre Division, New York Public Library.

59. See "Museums and the Ghetto," *Newsweek*, vol. 76, August 17, 1970, 93. See also Herschel Post, "The City Politic: Moving in on the Parks," *New York*, March 15, 1971, 6–9.

60. Turan and Papp, *Free for All*, 346.

61. Rosalyn Deutsche, "Art and Public Space: Questions of Democracy," *Social Text* 33 (1992): 34–53. Deutsche is writing in 1992 of particular developments in the art world (and urban development) during the 1980s.

62. Janelle Reinelt, "Rethinking the Public Sphere for a Global Age," *Performance Research: A Journal of the Performing Arts* 16 (2011): 17.

63. Gersten, quoted in Epstein, *An American Life*, 179.

64. Papp, "To Break Down 'The Wall,'" 1; and Mel Gussow, "Papp and the Future of Lincoln Center," *New York Times*, March 9, 1973, 23.

65. Daniel E. Chall, "Neighborhood Changes in New York City during the 1970s: Are the Gentry Returning?" *FRBNY Quarterly Review* (Winter 1983–84): 41.

66. Papp, "To Break Down 'The Wall,'" 1.

67. Ibid.

68. Chall, "Neighborhood Changes," 40.

69. Papp, "To Break Down 'The Wall,'" 1, 8.

70. He also desired an overhaul of its board in accordance with the multinationalism of the city itself. Epstein, *An American Life*, 278–9.

71. Joseph Papp, "Is There a Fifth Column at the Forum?" *New York Times*, July 25, 1971, D4.

72. Subscriber letter, June 10, 1973, Administrative Office: Lincoln Center, box 1–105, folder 9, New York Shakespeare Festival Records, Billy Rose Theatre Division, New York Public Library.

73. Subscriber letter, 1973, Administrative Office: Lincoln Center, box 1–105, folder 9, New York Shakespeare Festival Records, Billy Rose Theatre Division, New York Public Library. *Shaft in Africa* is a 1973 blaxploitation film. *The Pig Pen* is a 1970 play by Ed Bullins, and *The Chickencoop Chinaman* is a 1972 play by Frank Chin.

74. See Epstein, *An American Life*, 299, 313.

75. Subscriber letter, June 12, 1973, Administrative Office: Lincoln Center, box 1–105, folder 9, New York Shakespeare Festival Records, Billy Rose Theatre Division, New York Public Library.

76. Subscriber letter, June 27, 1973, Administrative Office: Lincoln Center, box 1–105, folder 9, New York Shakespeare Festival Records, Billy Rose Theatre Division, New York Public Library.

77. Balme, *The Theatrical Public Sphere*, 138.

78. Kauffman, "The Stages of Joseph Papp," 115.

79. Ibid., 118–19.

80. Turan and Papp, *Free for All*, 340.

81. Dan Isaac, "The Death of the Proscenium Stage," *Antioch Review* (Summer 1971): 241.

82. Julie Bovasso, oral history interview with Julie Bovasso, 1987–05–11 (sound recording), New York Public Library for the Performing Arts, interview by Kenneth Turan.

83. Ibid.

84. Turan and Papp, *Free for All*, 346.

85. Papp, "Government Aid: Sponsor of Free Shakespeare Says It Would Help More Than Hinder," xi.

86. Charles Marowitz, "The Trouble with Papp," *New York Times*, September 21, 1975, 5.

87. Ibid.

88. Jackson, *Professing Performance*, 192.

89. Nat Hentoff, "Piñero: I Wanted to Survive," *New York Times*, May 5, 1974, D1.

90. Fiona Mills, "Seeing Ethnicity: The Impact of Race and Class on the Critical Reception of Miguel Piñero's *Short Eyes*," in *Captive Audience: Prison and Captivity in Contemporary Theatre*, ed. Thomas Fahy and Kimball King (London: Routledge, 2003), 50.

91. Arthur Miller, "Arthur Miller vs. Lincoln Center," *New York Times*, April 16, 1972, 5.

92. Hall, "The Great Moving Right Show," 20.

93. Ibid.

94. Subscriber letter, August 1, 1973, Administrative Office: Lincoln Center, box 1–105, folder 9, New York Shakespeare Festival Records, Billy Rose Theatre Division, New York Public Library.

95. Edgar B. Young, *Lincoln Center: The Building of an Institution* (New York: New York University Press, 1980), 283, 286–87.

96. Zipp, *Manhattan Projects*, 161.

97. Arthur Miller, "Arthur Miller vs. Lincoln Center," 5.

98. Quoted in Breslin, "The Hottest Show in Town Is Joe Papp!" 36–37.

99. See Epstein, *An American Life*, 324–25, 344; and "Joseph Papp, NY Impresario, Says He'll Leave Lincoln Center," *Toledo Blade*, June 14, 1977, 2.

100. Carey Winfrey, "Papp Quits Lincoln Center, Citing Artistic-Fiscal Trap," *New York Times*, June 10, 1977, C17. A major cause was spiraling inflation, plus fewer subsidies as major foundation support dried up.

101. Mel Gussow, "Papp Halves New Season at Beaumont," *New York Times*, August 24, 1976, 20. For more on Papp's reasons for abandoning the Beaumont, see Turan's chapter, "The End of Lincoln Center: Postmortem," Turan and Papp, *Free for All*, 426–33.

102. "Joseph Papp, NY Impresario," *Toledo Blade*, 2.

103. Joseph Papp, "A House Is Not a Home," ACA Conference Ottawa, January 8, 1976, box 13–7, folder 1, New York Shakespeare Festival Records, Billy Rose Theatre Division, New York Public Library.

104. Epstein, *An American Life*, 310–11. Epstein continues: "Accusations of racial or sexual bias at the Festival became routine. Twice, the Puerto Rican Actors Guild formally accused him of discrimination."

105. Peter Bailey, "Annual Round-Up: Black Theater in America," *Black World/Negro Digest*, April 1973, 18.

106. Arnold M. Auerbach, "If You Don't Like It, Go Fight Mayor Papp," *New York Times*, April 14, 1968, D10. Paul Goldberger, "New Theater in Park Is Planned to Replace Delacorte," *New York Times*, August 7, 1974, 1; Paul Goldberger, "Parks Chief Is Now Opposing New Theater for Papp Festival," *New York Times*, September 4, 1974, 1.

107. See Maurice Carroll, "Goldin and Beame Clash Over Audit," *New York Times*, July 24, 1974, 1, 20; John Darnton, "Beame Denounces Goldin's Tactics

as Distortions," *New York Times*, July 29, 1974, 1, 6. For an official report on these early stages of the fiscal crisis, see "Staff Report on Transactions in Securities of the City of New York: Introduction and Summary, October 1, 1974–April 8, 1975," vol. 1, Securities and Exchange Commission, August 26, 1977, https://www.sec.gov/info/municipal/staffreport0877.pdf.

108. Goldberger, "Parks Chief Opposing New Theater," 1. Weisl instead offered an appropriation of $250,000 to rehabilitate the existing structure.

109. Correspondence between Edward I. Koch and Joseph Papp, July 2, 1970, box 1–82, folder 7, New York Shakespeare Festival Records, Billy Rose Theatre Division, New York Public Library.

110. Epstein, *An American Life*, 372.

111. Jonathan Soffer, *Ed Koch and the Rebuilding of New York* (New York: Columbia University Press, 2013), 128–29.

112. Alexis Soloski, "Oskar Eustis Seizes the Moment," *American Theatre* (December 2012), http://www.tcg.org/publications/at/issue/featuredstory.cfm?story=1&indexID=2; see also "Renovated Public Theater to Include New Lounge," *Broadway World*, May 22, 2012, http://www.broadwayworld.com/article/Renovated-Public-Theater-to-Include-New-Lounge-20120522#.U7x3HqhLroc.

113. Alan Feuer, "Murder at Rikers, with Lines by Shakespeare," *New York Times*, July 27, 2012, http://www.nytimes.com/2012/07/29/nyregion/murder-at-rikers-with-lines-by-shakespeare.html?pagewanted=all.; The Public Theater, http://www.publictheater.org/Programs—Events/Mobile-Unit.

114. Mark Blankenship, "What Does a Prisoner Think of *Richard III*?" *TDF Stages* (August 2012), http://wp.tdf.org/index.php/2012/08/what-does-a-prisoner-think-of-richard-iii.

Chapter 6

EPIGRAPH: Jill Dolan, "Seeing and Being Seen: The Avant-Garde and Other Egotists," *Hudson Review* 39 (Spring 1986): 113.

1. Ibid.

2. Gerald Rabkin, "The Academy of Fashion: Beach Hits the Wave at BAM," *Performing Arts Journal* 9 (1985): 47–48.

3. Charles Mee Jr., "Introduction," in *BAM: The Complete Works*, ed. Steven Serafin (New York: Quantuck Lane, 2011), 8.

4. Gautam Dasgupta, "BAM's Next Wave II: The Avant-Garde in the Marketplace: What Next?" *Performing Arts Journal* 8 (1984): 52.

5. Cezar Joseph Del Valle, *The Brooklyn Theatre Index: Vol. II* (New York: Theatre Talks, 2010), 22–26.

6. Henry R. Stiles, *A History of the City of Brooklyn* (Brooklyn: Heritage Books, 1867), 914.

7. See Barbara Parisi and Robert Singer, *The History of Brooklyn's Three Major Performing Arts Institutions* (Lanham, Md.: Scarecrow, 2003), 18–23.

8. Foulkes, "Streets and Stages," 423.

9. Anonymous, quoted in "Culture Popping Up in All Boroughs," *New York Times*, March 26, 1970, 56.

10. Ibid.

11. Janet Langsam recalls occasions when small companies would appeal to Cultural Affairs for help: "While there were things we could help them with through our accessibility to people and to the Mayor, the fact that they weren't in a city-owned building, we weren't able to do much for them. So the rules somehow needed to be changed." Janet Langsam, interview with author, January 11, 2012.

12. One of these was the Comprehensive Employment Training Act (CETA), a job program in which money was dispersed to city agencies to hire people within a year of training. The CETA monies were in the millions of dollars; had Cultural Affairs still been buried in the Parks Department, "that money might have gone for another purpose." Janet Langsam, interview with author, January 11, 2012.

13. Reiss, quoted in "Culture Popping Up in All Boroughs," 56.

14. Louis Calta, "Brooklyn Asks More City Aid for Cultural Institutions," *New York Times*, September 22, 1974, BQLI 1.

15. Shannon Jackson, "Working Publics," *Performance Research* 16 (April 2013): 10–11.

16. Woodie King, quoted in Lindsay Patterson, "Black Theater: The Search Goes On," *Freedomways* 14 (1974): 245.

17. Jackson, *Social Works*, 36.

18. "BACA Newsletter, September 1973," Brooklyn Arts and Culture Association Publications, 1969–1997, Brooklyn Historical Society, Brooklyn, New York. Member companies included the Chelsea Theater Center, Festival Repertory Company, Everyman Company, Gallery Players, Bed-Stuy Theatre, Brownsville Laboratory Theater, the Alonzo Players, Brooklyn Heights Players, Narrows Community Theatre, On Stage Players, Bed-Stuy Drama Workshop, Dorchester Masquers, Harbor East Players, Focus Workshop, Kings Drama Workshop, and Stuy-Heights Co.

19. Freeman, *Working-Class New York*, 325.

20. "BACA Newsletter, December 1975," Brooklyn Arts and Culture Association Publications, 1969–1997, Brooklyn Historical Society, Brooklyn, New York.

21. David Vidal, "City Removes Garbage Tossed in Street Protest," *New York Times*, July 25, 1975, 36.

22. Rodrick Wallace and Deborah Wallace, "Origins of Public Health Collapse in New York City: The Dynamics of Planned Shrinkage, Contagious Urban Decay and Social Disintegration," *Bulletin of the New York Academy of Medicine* 66 (September-October 1990): 392.

23. Deputy Fire Chief Charles Kirby, quoted in ibid., 393.

24. Vidal, "City Removes Garbage," 36.

25. "BACA Newsletter, March 1977," Brooklyn Arts and Culture Association Publications, 1969–1997, Brooklyn Historical Society, Brooklyn, New York.

26. Roger Furman, quoted in McCandlish Phillips, "Message of Street Theater Is Strong," *New York Times*, June 22, 1971, 28. For more on Furman's work, see Mance Williams, *Black Theatre in the 1960s and 1970s: A Historical-Critical Analysis of the Movement* (Westport, Conn.: Greenwood, 1985), 39–46.

27. Roger Furman, *The Long Black Block* (Electronic Version, Alexander Street, 1972, 2012), 3.

28. Furman, *The Long Black Block*, 4.

29. Ibid., 9.

30. Mel Gussow, "Theater: Black Portrait: Furman Work Offered at Brooklyn Fete," *New York Times*, November 17, 1973, 28.

31. M. Cardell Thompson, "New York Beat," *Jet*, March 2, 1972, 63; Peter Bailey, "Annual Round-Up: Black Theater in America," *Black World/Negro Digest*, April 1972, 35.

32. Vivian Robinson, "*Long Black Block* Is Truth in Action," *New York Amsterdam News*, January 29, 1972, D1.

33. Clayton Riley, "Furman's 'Block': Something Fine, Something Real," *New York Amsterdam News*, February 5, 1972, D1.

34. Anthony D. Hill with Douglas Q. Barnett, *A to Z of African American Theatre* (Lanham, Md.: Scarecrow, 2009), 46–48.

35. "Talking of Black Art, Theatre, Revolution and Nationhood, Part II: Black Theatre, A Forum," *Black Theatre 5: Waitin' for the Seventies* (1971): 34.

36. Neil R. Pierce, "And What the Arts Can Do for You," *Pittsburgh Post-Gazette*, September 16, 1977, 10.

37. Julia L. Foulkes highlights Lichtenstein's strategy to remedy this first through programming, and the mixed successes of that approach. Foulkes, "Streets and Stages," 423.

38. Parisi and Singer, *The History of Brooklyn's Three Major Performing Arts Institutions,* 21.

39. Brooklyn Institute Annual Report, 1962, BAM Hamm Archive.

40. Lawrence Farrant, "City Planner Pleads: Do Something Unique," *Brooklyn World Telegram*, Tuesday, November 30, 1965 (B1), clippings file, Downtown Brooklyn Development Association, Brooklyn Historical Society.

41. Brooklyn Academy of Music, Annual Report, 1968.

42. Ibid.

43. Foulkes, "Streets and Stages," 422. In 1963 Fort Greene already had one of the highest populations of African Americans and Caribbean immigrants, 33 percent (topped only by the neighboring Bedford-Stuyvesant, at 70 percent), and its Puerto Rican population had grown to 17 percent.

44. Ibid.

45. Marlyn V. Baum, "The Brooklyn Academy of Music: A Case Study of the Rebirth of an Urban Cultural Center" (Ph.D. dissertation, CUNY Graduate Center, 1983), 52.

46. Baum, "The Brooklyn Academy of Music," 60.

47. Baum, "The Brooklyn Academy of Music," 49; see also Foulkes, "Streets and Stages," 420.

48. "He Introduced Avant-Garde to BAM," *The Brooklyn Eagle*, April 9, 2012, http://www.brooklyneagle.com/articles/day-history-april-9-he-introduced-avant-garde-bam.

49. Suleiman Osman, *The Invention of Brownstone Brooklyn: Gentrification and the Search for Authenticity in Postwar New York* (Oxford: Oxford University Press, 2011), 3.

50. Osman, *Brownstone Brooklyn*, 11.

51. David Savran, *High Brow/Low Down: Theater, Jazz, and the Making of the New Middle Class* (Ann Arbor: University of Michigan Press, 2009), 9.

52. David Savran, *A Queer Sort of Materialism: Recontextualizing American Theatre* (Ann Arbor: University of Michigan Press, 2003), 12.

53. Quoted in Baum, "The Brooklyn Academy of Music," 57.

54. "*Everyman and roach* Program," Everyman Company, May 13–16, 1976, BAM Hamm Archive.

55. Ibid.

56. Kenneth P. Nolan, "Brooklyn Streets Become Stages: Van Arrives, World Is a Stage," *New York Times*, August 19, 1973, 99.

57. Farrant, "City Planner Pleads."

58. Davi Napoleon, *Chelsea on the Edge: The Adventures of an American Theater* (Ames: Iowa State University Press, 1991), 32–33.

59. Quoted in Napoleon, *Chelsea on the Edge*, 32.

60. Martin Gottfried, "America's Most Exciting New Theater?" *New York Times*, February 21, 1971, D3.

61. "BACA Newsletter, March 1969," Brooklyn Arts and Culture Association Publications, 1969–1997, Brooklyn Historical Society, Brooklyn, New York.

62. Gottfried, "America's Most Exciting New Theater?" D3. The Chelsea started charging admission with *Slave Ship*. For an insightful analysis of *Slave Ship* within the context of performativity in the Black Arts Movement, see Sell, *Avant-Garde Performance*, 248–52.

63. Howard Clurman, "Theatre," *The Nation*, May 12, 1969, 612.

64. The issue of black representation within the administration of the theater company emerged from the first day of Chelsea's tenancy at BAM; because "Chelsea was reopening its doors in a ghetto," the Chelsea Board expected the theater company to do more than just represent diversity on stage. Napoleon describes Kalfin's search for a replacement for his Chelsea colleague David Long in 1968, in which the issue of race factored prominently. Napoleon, *Chelsea on the Edge*, 29–30.

65. Mel Gussow, "Stage: Teatro Campesino in Brooklyn," *New York Times*, April 28, 1973, 21.

66. Robert Kalfin, quoted in Louis Calta, "Brooklyn's Chelsea Theater Is Successful, but Unspoiled," *New York Times*, December 5, 1971, A14.

67. See Calta, "Brooklyn's Chelsea Theater," A14. It is difficult to find conclusive numbers regarding BAM's changing audience composition. According to Parisi and Singer, "by 1971, 40 percent of the Academy's audience came from Manhattan . . . a sign of the Academy's success." Parisi and Singer, *The History of Brooklyn's Three Major Performing Arts Institutions,* 31. According to Julia Foulkes, BAM's audience grew a remarkable 600 percent between 1967 and 1976, with the majority of the subscription tickets bought by Brooklyn residents. Foulkes, "Streets and Stages," 424–25.

68. Guernsey, *Curtain Times*, 377.

69. Foulkes, "Streets and Stages," 424–25.

70. Napoleon, *Chelsea on the Edge*, 115.

71. Ibid., 21.

72. Marilyn Stasio, "On the Theatre Scene," *Cue*, March 13, 1971, page unknown.

73. "Brooklyn's Chelsea Troupe Moving across River," *New York Times*, November 4, 1972, 29; Calta, "Brooklyn's Chelsea Theater," A14.

74. B.E., "'Candide' at the Broadway Theatre," *TDR: The Drama Review* 18 (September 1974): 134–35.

75. Mel Gussow, "Chelsea Theater Center Facing Financial Crisis," *New York Times*, January 26, 1976, 28.

76. Napoleon, *Chelsea on the Edge*, 14.

77. He also gave Kalfin access to "special funds available to neighborhood-development projects near Bedford-Stuyvesant," an initiative about which there is little information. See Napoleon, 32.

78. See Phyllis Funke, "Chelsea Theater Spreading to City," *New York Times*, October 19, 1975, 109.

79. The "BAM Highlights" on their website begins in the fall of 1981, and its pre-1975 highlights in theater mention only Robert Wilson, Peter Brook, and the BAM Theatre Company.

80. Alvin Reiss, quoted in Eddy, "Government, the Arts, and Ghetto Youth," 405.

81. Richard Schechner, *Performance Theory* (New York: Routledge, 2003), 135; Steven Adler, *On Broadway: Art and Commerce on the Great White Way* (Carbondale: Southern Illinois University Press, 2004), 102–3.

82. Louis Chapin, "First American Congress of Theater," *Christian Science Monitor*, June 20, 1974, F6.

83. "Meeting Minutes," June 23, 1974, box 1, folder 1, Minutes and Correspondence, First American Theatre Congress Records, Billy Rose Theatre Division, New York Public Library. For a list of steering committee members and registered delegates, see Stuart Little, *After the FACT: Conflict and Consensus, A Report on the First American Congress of Theatre* (New York: Arno, 1975), 21–22, 101–9.

84. Erika Munk, "Second Thoughts on a First Try," *Village Voice*, June 20, 1974, 73.

85. "Panel 9: Stimulating Creative Resources," June 2–5, 1974, box 1, folder 13, First American Theatre Congress Records, Billy Rose Theatre Division, New York Public Library.

86. Ibid.

87. Ibid.

88. Quoted in Phyllis Funke, "Brooklyn Theater Is Trying to Be Different," *New York Times*, July 13, 1975, 77.

89. Robert Nemiroff, "The 101 'Final' Performances of *Sidney Brustein*," in Lorraine Hansberry, *"A Raisin in the Sun" and "The Sign in Sidney Brustein's Window"* (New York: Penguin Books, 1987), 167.

90. Osman, *Brownstone Brooklyn*, 5–6.

91. Jan Barry, interview with author, April 9, 2012.

92. Ibid.

93. Calta, "Brooklyn Asks More City Aid," BQLI 1.

94. Lichtenstein, quoted in ibid.

95. See Baum, "The Brooklyn Academy of Music," 76–100; Serafin, *BAM: The Complete Works*, 76.

96. BAM Annual Report, 1977–1978, BAM Hamm Archive.

97. See Serafin, *BAM: The Complete Works*, 88; and BAM Annual Report, 1977–1978, BAM Hamm Archive.

98. Baum, "The Brooklyn Academy of Music," 4.

99. Foulkes, "Streets and Stages," 426–8.

100. Brian Walsh, "Murder by Timidity: BAM's Next Wave and Classic Revivals," *PAJ: A Journal of Performance and Art* 25 (May 2003): 83–87.

101. Foulkes, "Streets and Stages," 427.

102. James Traub, "The (Not Easy) Building of (Not Exactly) Lincoln Center for (Not Manhattan)," *New York Times*, April 25, 2004, http://www.nytimes.com/2004/04/25/magazine/the-not-easy-building-of-not-exactly-lincoln-center-for-not-manhattan.html.

103. Arlene Dávila uses this phrase to describe a similar process that occurred in East Harlem during the 1980s. Arlene Dávila, "Empowered Culture? New York City's Empowerment Zone and the Selling of El Barrio," *Annals of the American Academy of Political and Social Science* 594 (July 2004): 49–64.

Conclusion

EPIGRAPH: Alain Touraine, *After the Crisis* (Cambridge: Polity, 2014), 3.

1. William Sites, *Remaking New York: Primitive Globalization and the Politics of Urban Community* (Minneapolis: University of Minnesota Press, 2003), 35.

2. See Kim Moody, *Welfare State to Real Estate: Regime Change in New York City, 1974 to the Present* (New York: New Press, 2007).

3. David Harvey, *A Brief History of Neoliberalism* (Oxford: Oxford University Press, 2005), 47.

4. Lizzy Ratner, "Boom Town and Bust City: A Tale of Two New Yorks," *The Nation* (February 14, 2011): 11–14.

5. David Savran, "Trafficking in Transnational Brands: The New 'Broadway Style Musical,'" *Theatre Survey* 55 (September 2014): 318–42.

6. Quoted in Fay S. Joyce, "Koch to Impose Cultural Aid Limit," *New York Times*, July 8, 1983, C17. William Sites and others have depicted Mayor Koch's legacy as one in which the less affluent bore the brunt of economic change. William Sites, "Public Action: New York City Policy and the Gentrification of the Lower East Side," in *From Urban Village to East Village: The Battle for New York's Lower East Side,* ed. Janet L. Abu-Lughod (Oxford: Blackwell, 1994), 189–213.

7. Quoted in Joyce, "Koch to Impose Cultural Aid Limit," C17.

8. Ibid.

9. Transcript, Banquet and Plenary Session, June 2–5, 1974, box 1, folder 4, First American Theatre Congress Records, Billy Rose Theatre Division, New York Public Library; Edwards, "On Black Audiences"; see chapter 2 in this book.

10. John Hull Mollenkopf, *A Phoenix in the Ashes: The Rise and Fall of the Koch Coalition in New York City Politics* (Princeton, N.J.: Princeton University Press, 1992), 53. See also Vera Zolberg, "New York Cultural Institutions: Ascendant or Subsidant?" in *Capital of the American Century: The National and International Influence of New York City,* ed. Martin Shefter (New York: Russell Sage Foundation, 1993), 145–67.

11. Pierre Bourdieu, *The Field of Cultural Production*, trans. Richard Nice, ed. and intro. Randal Johnson (New York: Columbia University Press, 1993), 83.

12. Jim Sleeper, "Days of the Developers," in *In Search of New York*, ed. Jim Sleeper (New Brunswick, N.J.: Transaction, 1989), 36.

13. This includes the planning of arts districts. See Karen Chapple, Shannon Jackson, and Anne J. Martin, "Concentrating Creativity: The Planning of Formal and Informal Arts Districts," *City, Culture and Society* 1 (2010): 225–34.

14. Julie Bovasso, "Letter to Dr. William Bradley," July 3, 1969, Julie Bovasso folder, La Mama E.T.C. archives. See chapter 1 in this book.

15. Andy C. Pratt, "The Cultural Contradictions of the Creative City," *City, Culture and Society* 2 (2011): 123–30.

16. *Surreal Estate: Artists, Urban Development and the Future of New York*, September 25, 2008, Prelude '08, Elebash Theatre, Martin E. Segal Theatre Center, Graduate Center of the City University of New York. Jennifer Wright Cook, executive director of The Field, moderated the event, with panelists Yehuda Duenyas (theater artist), Zannah Mass (Cultural Affairs director, Two Trees Management), Robert Elmes (founder of performance space Galapagos), and Teresa Vasquez (NYC Economic Development Corporation).

17. See Juan Gonzalez, "Lower East Side Rezone Plan Another Mike Boondoggle," *Daily News*, July 16, 2008.

18. Colin Moynihan, "Born in Brooklyn, Now Making a Motown Move," *New York Times*, December 7, 2014, http://www.nytimes.com/2014/12/08/arts/galapagos-art-space-will-make-detroit-its-home.html?_r=0.

19. Balme, *The Theatrical Public Sphere*.

20. Ibid., 17.

21. Hesse McGraw, "Theaster Gates: Radical Reform with Everyday Tools," *Afterall: A Journal of Art, Context, and Enquiry* 30 (Summer 2012): 86–99.

22. Rockefeller Report, 1968, 92.

23. Clive Barnes, "A Plea to Save Papp's Public Theater," *New York Times*, December 18, 1970, 42.

24. Touraine, *After the Crisis*, 2.

25. Sean F. Reardon, Lindsay Fox, and Joseph Townsend, "Neighborhood Income Composition by Household Race and Income, 1990–2009," *The Annals, AAPSS* 660 (July 2015): 78–97.

26. "Moving to Opportunity for Fair Housing (MTO)," U.S. Department of Housing and Urban Development, http://portal.hud.gov/hudportal/HUD?src=/programdescription/mto. In a separate study, after thirty years of tracking the widening disparities in income mobility through the lives of children living in different areas, economists identified a very real "neighborhood gap," akin to the achievement gap long-discussed in education. See Raj Chetty, Nathaniel Hendren, Patrick Kline, and Emmanuel Saez's Equality of Opportunity Project, http://www.equality-of-opportunity.org.

BIBLIOGRAPHY

Abu-Lughod, Janet L., ed. *From Urban Village to East Village: The Battle for New York's Lower East Side*. Oxford: Blackwell, 1994.

Adams, Don, and Arlene Goldbard. *Creative Community: The Arts of Cultural Development*. New York: Rockefeller Foundation, 2001.

Adler, Stephen. *On Broadway: Art and Commerce on the Great White Way*. Carbondale: Southern Illinois University Press, 2004.

"American Experimental Theatre: Then and Now." *Performing Arts Journal* 2, no. 2 (Fall 1977): 13–25.

Ames, Amyas. "Our Cup Is Broken: What Inflation Is Doing to the Arts." *Music Educators Journal* 60 (December 1973): 16–21.

Anderson, George W. "Visiting La Mama's Founder: An Interview with Ellen Stewart." *America*, February 8, 1997.

Angotti, Tom. *New York for Sale: Community Planning Confronts Global Real Estate*. Cambridge, Mass.: MIT Press, 2008.

Aronson, Arnold. *American Avant-Garde Theatre: A History*. New York: Routledge, 2000.

Arts and the People: A Survey of Arts and Culture in New York State. New York: American Council for the Arts in Education, 1973.

Auerbach, Arnold M. "If You Don't Like It, Go Fight Mayor Papp." *New York Times*, April 14, 1968.

Babcock, Richard F., and Wendy U. Larsen. *Special Districts: The Ultimate in Neighborhood Zoning*. Cambridge, Mass.: Lincoln Institute of Land Policy, 1990.

Bailey, Beth, and David Farber, eds. *America in the 70s*. Lawrence: University Press of Kansas, 2004.

Bailey, Peter. "Annual Round-Up: Black Theater in America." *Black World/Negro Digest*, April 1973.

Bailey, Robert W. *The Crisis Regime: The MAC, the EFCB, and the Political Impact of the New York City Financial Crisis*. Albany: State University of New York Press, 1984.

Balme, Christopher B. *The Theatrical Public Sphere*. Cambridge: Cambridge University Press, 2014.

Barnes, Clive. "Anthony Perkins Directs Steambath: Friedman Casts Deity as a Bath Attendant." *New York Times*, July 1, 1970.

———. "Billy Noname, Uneven Musical, Begins Run: Bright Cast Pictures Growing Up: Black Production Is First for Off Broadway House." *New York Times*, March 3 1970, 37.

———. "An Engaging 'Prodigal Sister.' " *New York Times*, November 26, 1974.

———. "From Street Theater, an 'Everyman.'" *New York Times*, October 6, 1971.

———. "A Plea to Save Papp's Public Theater." *New York Times*, December 18, 1970.

———. "Some Love Lincoln Center, Some Feel Unwelcome." *New York Times*, December 30,1973.

———. "Stage: Café La Mama II." *New York Times*, April 5, 1969.

———. "Stage: 'Your Arms Too Short . . .'" *New York Times*, December 23, 1976.

Baum, Marlyn V. "The Brooklyn Academy of Music: A Case Study of the Rebirth of an Urban Cultural Center." Ph.D. dissertation, City University of New York, 1983.

Baumol, William J., and Hilda Baumol. *Last Minute Discounts on Unsold Tickets: A Study of TKTS*. New York: Theatre Development Fund, 1974.

———. "What Ails the Fabulous Invalid? It's Not What You Think!" *New York Times*, June 2, 1974.

Baumol, William J., and William G. Bowen. *Performing Arts: The Economic Dilemma*. New York: Twentieth Century Fund, 1966.

Beaufort, John. "New York Shakespeare Festival Public Theater: The Difference between Creative Vision and Wishful Thinking." *Christian Science Monitor*, December 10, 1971, 9.

Belkind, Lara. "Stealth Gentrification: Camouflage and Commerce on the Lower East Side." *Traditional Dwellings and Settlements Review* 21, no. 1 (Fall 2009): 21–36.

Bennett, Robert. *Deconstructing Post-WWII New York City: The Literature, Art, Jazz, and Architecture of an Emerging Global Capital*. New York: Routledge, 2003.

Bennett, Susan. "Theatre/Tourism." *Theatre Journal* 57, no. 3 (October 2005): 407–28.

———. "Universal Experience: The City as Tourist Stage." In *The Cambridge Companion to Performance Studies*, edited by Tracy C. Davis, 76–90. Cambridge: Cambridge University Press, 2008.

Berkowitz, Edward D. *Something Happened: A Political and Cultural Overview of the Seventies*. New York: Columbia University Press, 2006.

Berman, Marshall. *On the Town: One Hundred Years of Spectacle in Times Square*. New York: Random House, 2006.

Bigsby, Christopher. *A Critical Introduction to Twentieth-Century American Drama*, vol. 3: *Beyond Broadway*. Cambridge: Cambridge University Press, 1990.

Bingaman, Amy, Lise Sanders, and Rebecca Zorach. *Embodied Utopias: Gender, Social Change, and the Modern Metropolis*. London: Routledge, 2002.

Blau, Eleanor. "Lincoln Center Goes Out of Doors." *New York Times*, August 12, 1983.

Blau, Herbert. "Spacing Out in the American Theater." *Kenyon Review* 15, no. 2 (Spring 1993): 27–39.

Bottoms, Stephen J. *Playing Underground: A Critical History of the 1960s Off-Off-Broadway Movement*. Ann Arbor: University of Michigan Press, 2006.

Bourdieu, Pierre. *The Field of Cultural Production.* Edited by Randal Johnson. New York: Columbia University Press, 1993.
Bovasso, Julie. *Gloria and Esperanza.* New York: Samuel French, 1969.
———. *The Moon Dreamers.* New York: Samuel French, 1969.
———. "A New Breed of New York Actor." *New York*, February 11, 1974.
———. *Schubert's Last Serenade.* New York: Samuel French, 1972.
———. *Standard Safety.* New York: Samuel French, 1976.
Boyle, Wickham. *On the Streets: A Guide to New York City's Buskers.* New York: New York City Department of Cultural Affairs, [1981?].
Bramall, Rebecca. *The Cultural Politics of Austerity: Past and Present in Austere Times.* Houndsmills, Eng.: Palgrave Macmillan, 2013.
Brash, Julian. "Invoking Fiscal Crisis: Moral Discourse and Politics in New York City." *Social Text* 21, no. 3 (Fall 2003): 59–83.
Breasted, Mary. "Parks to Bustle Again in Summer." *New York Times*, May 16, 1976.
Brecht, Bertolt. *Brecht on Theatre: The Development of an Aesthetic.* Translated by John Willett. New York: Hill and Wang, 1964.
Brecht, Stefan. *Bread and Puppet Theatre.* 2 vols. London: Methuen, 1988.
Brenner, Neil, and Nik Theodore. "Cities and the Geographies of 'Actually Existing Neoliberalism.'" *Antipode* 34, no. 3 (July 2002): 349–79.
Breslin, Catherine. "The Hottest Show in Town Is Joe Papp!" *New York*, November 29, 1971.
Breslin, Rosemary. "Rent Rises Shock City-Property Tenants." *New York Times*, June 26, 1983.
Brook, Peter. "The Complete Truth Is Global." *New York Times*, January 20, 1974.
Brooks, John. "Fueling the Arts, or, Exxon as a Medici." *New York Times*, January 25, 1976.
Browne, Craig, and Simon Susen. "Austerity and Its Antitheses: Practical Negations of Capitalist Legitimacy." *South Atlantic Quarterly* 113, no. 2 (Spring 2014): 217–30.
Buckley, Tom. "About New York: Dimming a Beacon." *New York Times*, June 13, 1975, 19.
Bullins, Ed., ed. *The New Lafayette Theatre Presents.* New York: Anchor, 1974.
———. *Twelve Plays and Selected Writings.* Edited by Mike Sell. Ann Arbor: University of Michigan Press, 2006.
Bunce, Alan. "The New Truck and Warehouse Theater." *Christian Science Monitor*, March 6, 1970, 4.
Burke, Edward C. "Board of Estimate Rejects Plan to Aid Shakespeare Theater." *New York Times*, December 4, 1970.
Burke, Tom. "Geraldine's Long Journey." *New York Times*, June 13, 1971.
Busà, Alessandro. "Rezoning Coney Island: A History of Decline and Revival, of Heroes and Villains, at the People's Playground." In *The World in Brooklyn: Gentrification, Immigration, and Ethnic Politics in a Global City*, edited by Judith N. DeSena and Timothy Shortell, 147–85. Lanham, Md.: Lexington Books, 2012.
Callender, Courtney. "Bringing It All Back Home: Community Access to the Arts." *New York Affairs* 4, no. 4 (Winter 1978): 87–94.

Calta, Louis. "Brooklyn Asks More City Aid for Cultural Institutions." *New York Times*, September 22, 1974.

———. "Brooklyn's Chelsea Theater Is Successful, but Unspoiled." *New York Times*, December 5, 1971.

———. "City Aides Act to Implement Theater Report." *New York Times*, January 27, 1972.

———. "City Cultural Affairs Chief Foresees Money Battles." *New York Times*, August 18, 1976.

———. "Fund Will Buy Tickets to Aid Two New Shows." *New York Times*, December 4, 1969.

———. "Musical Slated for City's Parks: Pepsi-Cola Will Sponsor 12 Showings of 'I Can't Cope.'" *New York Times*, May 16, 1974.

———. "Rip Torn Dropped from Steambath, a New Play." *New York Times*, June 5, 1970.

———. "Street Theater to Play 51 Dates." *New York Times*, June 15, 1965.

———. "Unruly 'Actors' Try to Upstage Troupe in Bedford-Stuyvesant." *New York Times*, June 28, 1966.

———. "Vinnette Carroll Gets a State Post: Actress-Director Is Head of Ghetto Arts Program." *New York Times*, March 23, 1968.

Campbell, Colin. "Beleaguered Coney Islanders Rally with Sense of Affection: The Talk of Coney Island." *New York Times*, August 29, 1981.

Cannato, Vincent J. *The Ungovernable City: John Lindsay and His Struggle to Save New York*. New York: Basic Books, 2001.

"Carey and Beame Are Satirized Here by the Inner Circle." *New York Times*, March 2, 1975.

Carlson, Marvin. *Places of Performance: The Semiotics of Theatre Architecture*. Ithaca, N.Y.: Cornell University Press, 1993.

———. "The Theatre as Civic Monument." *Theatre Journal* 40 (March 1988): 12–32.

Carmody, Dierdre. "Where New Yorkers Go—and Don't Go." *New York Times*, January 18, 1974.

Carroll, Maurice. "Goldin and Beame Clash Over Audit." *New York Times*, July 24, 1974.

Carroll, Vinnette. "To Journey to Each Other." *New York Times*, February 2, 1969.

Carroll, Vinnette Justine, and Micki Grant. *Croesus and the Witch*. Electronic Edition by Alexander Street, 2014.

———. *Don't Bother Me, I Can't Cope*. Electronic Edition, Alexander Street, 1970, 2014. Also published as *Don't Bother Me, I Can't Cope: A Musical Entertainment*. New York: Samuel French, 1972.

Castells, Manuel. "Class and Power in American Cities." *Contemporary Sociology* 13, no. 3 (May 1984): 270–73.

Cazenave, Noel. *Impossible Democracy: The Unlikely Success of the War on Poverty Community Action Programs*. Albany: State University of New York Press, 2007.

Chall, Daniel E. "Neighborhood Changes in New York City during the 1970s: Are the Gentry Returning?" *FRBNY Quarterly Review* (Winter 1983–84): 38–48.

Chapin, Louis. "Peter Brook in Brooklyn: British Director Has All-Day Sessions." *Christian Science Monitor*, October 12, 1973.

Chapple, Karen, Shannon Jackson, and Anne J. Martin. "Concentrating Creativity: The Planning of Formal and Informal Arts Districts." *City, Culture and Society* (2010): 225–34.

Cheskin, Irving W. "The 'Taxpaying' Theater: How Has It Fared During Inflation?" In *Inflation and the Performing Arts*, edited by Hilda Baumol and William J. Baumol, 71–85. New York: New York University Press, 1984.

Chesluk, Benjamin. *Money Jungle: Imagining the New Times Square*. New Brunswick, N.J.: Rutgers University Press, 2007.

Chevigny, Paul. *Gigs: Jazz and the Cabaret Laws in New York City*. New York: Routledge, 2004.

Childs, John Brown. *Transcommunality: From the Politics of Conversion to the Ethics of Respect*. Philadelphia: Temple University Press, 2003.

Chronopoulos, Themis. *Spatial Regulation in New York City: From Urban Renewal to Zero Tolerance*. New York: Routledge, 2011.

Clurman, Howard. "Theatre." *The Nation*, May 12, 1969.

Cohen-Cruz, Jan. *Local Acts: Community-Based Performance in the United States*. New Brunswick, N.J.: Rutgers University Press, 2005.

———, ed. *Radical Street Performance: An International Anthology*. London: Routledge, 1998.

Cole, David B. "Artists and Urban Redevelopment." *Geographical Review* 77, no. 4 (October 1987): 391–407.

Cole, Nora. "Vinnette Carroll: The First Black Woman Broadway Director." *Black Masks* (Summer/Fall 2012): 9–14.

Comtois, M. E. "New York Shakespeare Festival, Lincoln Center, 1973–1974." *Shakespeare Quarterly* 25 (Autumn 1974): 405–9.

Crespy, David A. *Off-Off Broadway Explosion: How Provocative Playwrights of the 1960s Ignited a New American Theater*. New York: Backstage Books, 2003.

Croyden, Margaret. "Box-Office Boom: Broadway." *New York Times*. May 10, 1981.

———. *Lunatics, Lovers, & Poets: The Contemporary Experimental Theatre*. New York: McGraw-Hill, 1974.

"Culture Popping Up in All Boroughs." *New York Times*, March 26, 1970.

Cummings, Judith. "Blacks Gain on Broadway, Lag in Two Other Arts." *New York Times*, June 6, 1975.

Cummings, Scott T. *Maria Irene Fornes*. New York: Routledge, 2012.

Currid-Halkett, Elizabeth. *The Warhol Economy: How Fashion, Art, and Music Drive New York City*. Princeton, N.J.: Princeton University Press, 2007.

Curry, Jane Kathleen. *John Guare: A Research and Production Sourcebook*. Westport, Conn.: Greenwood, 2002.

Darling, Eliza. "Nature's Carnival: The Ecology of Pleasure at Coney Island." In *In the Nature of Cities: Urban Political Ecology and the Politics of Urban Metabolism*, edited by Nik Heynen, Mari Kaika, and Erik Swyngedouw, 73–90. New York: Routledge, 2006.

D'Aponte, Mimi Gisolfi. "*Everyman and roach* in Retrospect: A Study of Street Theatre That Worked." *Journal of Dramatic Theory and Criticism* (Spring 1990): 165–77.

———. "Fairs and Festivals." In *The Encyclopedia of New York City*, edited by Kenneth L. Jackson, 387–88. New Haven, Conn.: Yale University Press, 1995.

———. "Good Friday: Street Theater in New York." *Other Stages* 5 (March 24, 1983).

Dasgupta, Gautam. "BAM's Next Wave II: The Avant-Garde in the Marketplace. What Next?" *Performing Arts Journal* 8, no. 1 (1984): 52–58.

Dávila, Arlene M. "Culture in the Battlefront: From Nationalist to Pan-Latino Projects." In *Mambo Montage: The Latinization of New York*, edited by Agustín Laó-Montes and Arlene M. Dávila, 159–83. New York: Columbia University Press, 2001.

———. *Culture Works: Space, Value, and Mobility across the Neoliberal Americas*. New York: New York University Press, 2012.

———. "Empowered Culture? New York City's Empowerment Zone and the Selling of El Barrio." *Annals of the American Academy of Political and Social Science* 594, "Race, Politics, and Community Development in U.S. Cities" (July 2004): 49–64.

DeGiovanni, Frank F., and Lorraine C. Minnite. "Patterns of Neighborhood Change." In *DualCity: Restructuring New York*, by John H. Mollenkopf and Manuel Castells. NewYork: Russell Sage Foundation, 1992.

Delany, Samuel R. *Times Square Red, Times Square Blue*. New York: New York University Press, 2001.

Denson, Charles. *Coney Island: Lost and Found*. Berkeley, Calif.: Ten Speed, 2002.

Deutsche, Rosalyn. "Art and Public Space: Questions of Democracy." *Social Text* 33 (1992): 34–53.

Deutsche, Rosalyn, and Cara Gendel Ryan. "The Fine Art of Gentrification." *October* 31 (Winter 1984): 91–111.

Dietz, Dan. *Off Broadway Musicals, 1910–2007*. Jefferson, N.C.: McFarland, 2010.

Dolan, Jill. "Seeing and Being Seen: The Avant-Garde and Other Egotists." *Hudson Review* 39 (Spring 1986): 113–17.

Drake, Sylvie. "'Cope' Director—From Unlikely to Inevitable." *Los Angeles Times*, August 6, 1972.

Eddy, Junius. "Government, the Arts, and Ghetto Youth." *Public Administration Review* 30, no. 4(July/August 1970): 399–408.

Edwards, Gus. "On Black Audiences." *Douglas Ward Quarterly*, March 21, 2012.

Eeckhout, Bart. "The 'Disneyfication' of Times Square: Back to the Future?" In *Critical Perspectives on Urban Redevelopment*, edited by Kevin Fox Gotham, 379–428. Bingley, Eng.: Emerald Group, 2001.

Elam, Harry. *Taking It to the Streets: The Social Protest Theater of Luis Valdez and Amiri Baraka*. Ann Arbor: University of Michigan Press, 1997.

Elder III, Lonne. *Charades on East Fourth Street*. Electronic Edition by Alexander Street, 2014.

Eliot, Marc. *Down 42nd Street: Sex, Money, Culture and Politics at the Crossroads of the World*. New York: Warner Books, 2001.

Epstein, Helen. *Joe Papp: An American Life*. Boston: Da Capo, 1996.

Ericson, Raymond. "Changing Lincoln Center's Image." *New York Times*, October 10, 1971.

"Excerpts from Statements of New York and Federal Officials to Senate Committee." *New York Times*, June 8, 1978, B11.

Eyen, Tom. "The Discreet Alarm of the Off Off Broadway Playwright." *New York Times*, September 23, 1973.

———. *Ten Plays*. New York: Samuel French, 1971.

Farrant, Lawrence. "City Planner Pleads: Do Something Unique." *Brooklyn World Telegram*, November 30, 1965.

Faust, Richard, and Charles Kadushin. *Shakespeare in the Neighborhood: Audience Reaction to A Midsummer Night's Dream as Produced by Joseph Papp for the Delacorte Mobile Theatre*. New York: Twentieth Century Fund, 1965.

Ferretti, Fred. *The Year the Big Apple Went Bust*. New York: Putnam Books, 1976.

Fitch, Robert. *The Assassination of New York*. New York: Verso, 1993.

Fitzgerald, Geraldine, and Jonathan Ringkamp. *Everyman and roach*, undated, unpublished play script, courtesy Mimi D'Aponte.

Flatley, Guy. "Don't Worry, Micki Can Cope." *New York Times*, May 7, 1972.

Foulkes, Julia L. "The Other West Side Story: Urbanization and the Arts Meet at Lincoln Center." *Amerikanstudien/American Studies* 52 (2007): 227–47.

———. "Streets and Stages: Urban Renewal and the Arts after World War II." *Journal of Social History* 44, no. 2 (Winter 2010): 413–34.

Fraser, C. Gerald. "At Ten, Urban Arts Corps Keeps Pace." *New York Times*, June 24, 1979.

———. "Street Theater to End Outdoor Festival." *New York Times*, September 4, 1976.

———. "Urban Arts Corps Faces Ouster and Search for a New Theater." *New York Times*, February 25, 1979.

Freeman, Joshua B. *Working-Class New York: Life and Labor since World War II*. New York: New Press, 2000.

French, William W. *Maryat Lee's Ecotheater: A Theater for the Twenty-First Century*. Morgantown: West Virginia University Press, 1998.

Friedland, Roger, Frances Fox Piven, and Robert R. Alford. "Political Conflict, Urban Structure, and the Fiscal Crisis." *International Journal of Urban and Regional Research* 1 (March-December 1977): 447–71.

Funke, Phyllis. "Brooklyn Theatre Is Trying to Be Different." *New York Times*, July 13, 1975.

———. "Chelsea Theater Spreading to City." *New York Times*, October 19, 1975.

Furman, Roger. *The Long Black Block*. Alexander Street, 1972, 2012.

Gandy, Matthew. *Concrete and Clay: Reworking Nature in New York City*. Cambridge, Mass.: MIT Press, 2002.

———. "Rethinking Urban Metabolism: Water, Space, and the Modern City." *City* 8 (December 2004): 363–79.

———. "Review of *Evictions: Art and Spatial Politics* by Rosalyn Deutsche." *Annals of the Association of American Geographers* 89, no. 1 (March 1999): 164–66.

Garner, Stanton B. "Urban Landscapes, Theatrical Encounters: Staging the City." In *Land/Scape/Theatre*, edited by Elinor Fuchs and Una Chaudhuri, 94–118. Ann Arbor: University of Michigan Press, 2002.

Geertz, Clifford. "Local Knowledge and Its Limits: Some *Obiter Dicta*." *Yale Journal of Criticism* 5 (1992): 129–35.

Gifford, Bernard R. "New York City and Cosmopolitan Liberalism." *Political Science Quarterly* 93, no. 4 (Winter 1978–79): 559–84.

Gilmore, Ruth. *Golden Gulag: Prisons, Surplus, Crisis, and Opposition in Globalizing California*. Berkeley: University of California Press, 2007.

Gilroy, Harry. "Stage: Chelsea Center 'Black Quartet.'" *New York Times*, April 27, 1969.

Glover, William. "*The Moon Dreamers* on Off-Broadway." *Los Angeles Times*, December 11, 1969, H19.

Glueck, Grace. "City Council Acts on New Arts Agency." *New York Times*, October 2, 1975.

———. "Cultural Agencies Reducing Hours and Security: Cultural Services Feel Impact of Cuts." *New York Times*, November 3, 1975.

———. "Money Isn't Enough at City Culture Unit." *New York Times*, June 24, 1974.

———. "No Rush for Reservations." *New York Times*, July 6, 1969.

Goldberger, Paul. "New Theater in Park Is Planned to Replace Delacorte." *New York Times*, August 7, 1974.

———. "Parks Chief Is Now Opposing New Theater for Papp Festival." *New York Times*, September 4, 1974.

Goldman, Ari L. "Lower East Side Is Standing Trial in Custody Case." *New York Times*, January 18, 1979.

Goodman, Lizbeth. *Contemporary Feminist Theatres: To Each Her Own*. London: Routledge, 1993.

Gottfried, Martin. "America's Most Exciting New Theater?" *New York Times*, February 21, 1971.

Gratz, Roberta Brandes. *The Battle for Gotham: New York in the Shadow of Robert Moses and Jane Jacobs*. New York: Nation Books, 2010.

———. *The Living City: How America's Cities Are Being Revitalized by Thinking Small in a Big Way*. New York: John Wiley and Sons, 1994.

Greenberg, Miriam. *Branding New York: How a City in Crisis Was Sold to the World*. New York: Routledge, 2008.

Greenberger, Howard. *The Off-Broadway Experience*. Englewood Cliffs, N.J.: Prentice Hall, 1971.

Greenfeld, John. "Their Hearts Belongs to La Mama." *New York Times*. July 9, 1967.

Greenstone, David. *Race and Authority in Urban Politics: Community Relations and the War on Poverty*. Chicago: University of Chicago Press, 1974.

Growth in New York City Arts and Culture: Who Pays? New York: Cultural Assistance Center, 1976.

Guare, John. "Papp and Circumstance." *New York*. December 13, 1971.

Guernsey, Otis L. *Curtain Times: The New York Theater, 1965–1987*. New York: Applause Theatre Books, 1987.

Gussow, Mel. "Broadway Producers and Institutional Theaters Air Divergent Views at Stage Congress." *New York Times*, June 5, 1974.

———. "Chelsea Theater Center Facing Financial Crisis." *New York Times*, January 26, 1976.

———. "'Croesus and Witch' Goes to 20th Street." *New York Times*, August 27, 1971.

———. "Devoted Audience for Street Theatre." *New York Times*, September 1, 1972.

———. "La Mama's Latest Production Is Annex, Just Two Doors Down." *New York Times*, September 12, 1974.

———. "Negro Ensemble Finds Hit Play Poses Problem." *New York Times*, February 7, 1973.

———. "New Group to Offer Plays by Women." *New York Times*, February 22, 1972.

———. "Papp Halves New Season at Beaumont." *New York Times*, August 24, 1976.

———. "A Playwright's Invention Named Papp." *New York Times*, November 9, 1975.

———. "Poet-Revolutionary Inspires a Drama." *New York Times*, August 23, 1972.

———. "Stage: Teatro Campesino in Brooklyn." *New York Times*, April 28, 1973.

———. "Theater: Black Portrait: Furman Work Offered at Brooklyn Fete." *New York Times*, November 17, 1973.

———. "Theatre: In the Streets: Lincoln Center's Open-Air Festival Ends with Reaffirmations of Black Message." *New York Times*, September 4, 1972.

———. "Theatre: Rock vs. Junk: Street Festival Offers Anti-Drug Musical." *New York Times*, August 24, 1972.

———. "To Peter Brook, Audience Is a Partner." *New York Times*, September 28, 1973.

———. "Zoe Caldwell Enjoying Colette and East 3rd Street." *New York Times*, June 2, 1970.

Gussow, Mel, and Don McDonagh. "Blind Junkie Presented at Street Theatre Fete." *New York Times*, September 2, 1972.

Haberman, Clyde. "The Crusade to Honor Father Duffy." *New York Times*, December 7, 1999. http://www.nytimes.com/1999/12/07/nyregion/nyc-the-crusade-to-honor-father-duffy.html.

Hackworth, Jason. *The Neoliberal City: Governance, Ideology, and Development in American Urbanism*. Ithaca, N.Y.: Cornell University Press, 2007.

Halasz, Judith Rachel. "Questioning Work, Making a Scene: Bohemian Life on the Lower East Side of New York City." Ph.D. dissertation, City University of New York, 2007.

"'Half a Tank' Leisure: The Latest Boom." *U.S. News & World Report*, August 6, 1979.

Hall, Stuart. "The Great Moving Right Show." *Marxism Today* (January 1979): 14–20.

Hamera, Judith. *Dancing Communities: Performance, Difference, and Connection in the Global City*. New York: Palgrave Macmillan, 2007.

Hansberry, Lorraine. *"A Raisin in the Sun" and "The Sign in Sidney Brustein's Window."* New York: Penguin Books, 1987.

Harding, James M., and Cindy Rosenthal, eds. *Restaging the Sixties: Radical Theaters and Their Legacies*. Ann Arbor: University of Michigan Press, 2006.

Harding, Kimberly K. "Vinnette Carroll, 1922–2002." In *African American Dramatists: An A-to-Z Guide*, edited by Emmanuel Sampath Nelson, 88–96. Westport, Conn.: Greenwood, 2004.

Harvey, David. *A Brief History of Neoliberalism.* Oxford: Oxford University Press, 2005.

Harvie, Jen. *Staging the UK.* Manchester: Manchester University Press, 2005.

———. *Theatre and the City.* London: Palgrave Macmillan, 2009.

Hay, Samuel A. *African American Theatre: A Historical and Critical Analysis.* Cambridge: Cambridge University Press, 1994.

Hayden, Dolores. "Making Women's History Visible in the Urban Landscape." *City & Society* 10 (June 1998): 9–20.

Heckscher, August. *Alive in the City: Memoir of an Ex-Commissioner.* New York: Charles Scribner's Sons, 1974.

Heide, Robert. "These Playwrights Did Get into a Room." *New York Times*, October 15, 1972.

Hentoff, Nat. "Piñero: I Wanted to Survive." *New York Times*, May 5, 1974.

Herrera, Patricia E. "Nuyoriquenas in the House: Performing Identity through Hip Hop, Poetry, and Theatre." Ph.D. dissertation, City University of New York, 2008.

Hill, Anthony D., and Douglas Q. Barnett. *A to Z of African American Theatre.* Lanham, Md.: Scarecrow, 2009.

Hill, Holly. "How Do Playwrights Make a Living?" *Theatre Journal* 33 (December 1981): 517–26.

Hopkins, D. J., and Kim Solga, eds. *Performance and the Global City.* Basingstoke, Eng.: Palgrave Macmillan, 2013.

Horn, Barbara Lee. *Ellen Stewart and La Mama: A Bio-Bibliography.* Westport, Conn.: Greenwood, 1993.

Horowitz, Daniel. *The Anxieties of Affluence: Critiques of American Consumer Culture, 1939– 1979.* Amherst: University of Massachusetts Press, 2004.

Hudson, Edward. "Festival Leader Is Really Its Juggler." *New York Times*, August 24, 1972.

Huxtable, Ada Louise. "Art, Money and Impotence in New York." *New York Times*, December 15, 1974.

———. "Missing the Point (and Boat) at City Hall." *New York Times*, January 3, 1971.

"Inner Circle's Review Lampoons Mayor's Troubles." *New York Times*, March 6, 1977.

Isaac, Dan. "The Death of the Proscenium Stage." *Antioch Review* (Summer 1971): 241.

Isin, Engin F., ed. *Democracy, Citizenship, and the Global City.* London: Routledge, 2000.

Istel, John. "Boomtown on the East River." *American Theatre*, December 2004. http://www.tcg.org/publications/at/dec04/boom.cfm.

Jackson, Shannon. *Professing Performance: Theatre in the Academy from Philology to Performativity.* Cambridge: Cambridge University Press, 2004.

———. *Social Works: Performing Art, Supporting Publics.* New York: Routledge, 2011.

———. "Working Publics." *Performance Research* 16 (April 2013): 10–11.

John, David G. "The First Black Gretchen: Fritz Bennewitz's *Faust I* in New York." *Monatshefte* 94, no. 4 (Winter 2002): 447–63.

Johnson, Cedric. *Revolutionaries to Race Leaders: Black Power and the Making of African American Politics*. Minneapolis: University of Minnesota Press, 2007.

Johnson, Kimberley. "Community Development Corporations, Participation, and Accountability: The Harlem Urban Development Corporation and the Bedford-Stuyvesant Restoration Corporation." *Annals of the American Academy of Political and Social Science* 594 (July 2004): 109–24.

Joseph, Miranda. *Against the Romance of Community*. Minneapolis: University of Minnesota Press, 2002.

Kaiser, Ernest. "Black Images in the Mass Media: A Bibliography." *Freedomways* 14, "The Black Image in the Mass Media" (1974, 3rd Quarter).

Kakutani, Michiko. "Ellen Stewart Works Hard to Keep La Mama Going." *New York Times*, April 5, 1980.

Kasson, John F. *Amusing the Million: Coney Island at the Turn of the Century*. New York: Hill and Wang, 1978.

Kauffman, Stanley. "The Stages of Joseph Papp." *American Scholar* 44 (Winter 1974–75): 117.

Kaufman, David. *Ridiculous!: The Theatrical Life and Times of Charles Ludlam*. New York: Applause Books, 2002.

Kaufman, Will. *American Culture in the 1970s*. Edinburgh: Edinburgh University Press, 2009.

Kent, Leticia. "The Gut Theatre Is in the Street." *Village Voice*, August 17, 1967.

Kerr, Walter. "Can Broadway Move?" *New York Times Magazine*, June 3, 1973.

———. "The Most Striking New American Play." *New York Times*, April 4, 1971, 3.

Killen, Andreas. *1973 Nervous Breakdown: Watergate, Warhol, and the Birth of Post-Sixties America*. New York: Bloomsbury Publishing, 2006.

King, Woodie. "The Dilemma of Black Theater." *Black World/Negro Digest* (April 1970): 12.

———. *The Impact of Race: Theatre and Culture*. New York: Applause Theatre and Cinema Books, 2003.

Kirby, Michael, ed. "An Evening in the East Village." *TDR: The Drama Review* 29, no. 1, "East Village Performance" (Spring 1985): 92–101.

———. "The New Theatre." *Tulane Drama Review* 10 (Winter 1965): 23–43.

Knapp, Margaret. "A Historical Study of the Legitimate Playhouses on West 42nd Street between Seventh and Eighth Avenues in New York." Ph.D. dissertation, City University of New York, 1982.

Knowles, Ric. *Reading the Material Theatre*. Cambridge: Cambridge University Press, 2004.

Knox, Seymour. *NYS Council on the Arts 1969–1970: Chairman's Review*. New York: New York State Council on the Arts, 1970.

Kormendi, Kati. "Darkhorses Win International Competition for TKTS Booth." *Gotham Gazette*, March 1, 2000. http://www.gothamgazette.com/article/arts/20000301/1/88.

Kornblum, William, et al. "West 42nd Street: The Bright Light Zone." Graduate School and University Center of the City University of New York, 1978.

Krinsky, John. *Free Labor: Workfare and the Contested Language of Neoliberalism*. Chicago: University of Chicago Press, 2007.

Kroll, Jack. "Life with La Mama." *Newsweek*, April 28, 1969.
———. "The Public Fights for Life." *Newsweek*, March 22, 1971.
Kruger, Loren. "Cold Chicago: Uncivil Modernity, Urban Form, and Performance in the Upstart City." *TDR: The Drama Review* 53, no. 3 (Fall 2009): 10–36.
Kuftinec, Sonja Arsham. "Theatrical Imaginaries in the Balkans and Jerusalem." In *Considering Calamity: Methods for Performance Research*, edited by Tracy C. Davis and Linda Ben-Zvi, 97–113. Tel Aviv: Assaph Books, 2007.
Lachman, Seymour P., and Robert Polner. *The Man Who Saved New York: Hugh Carey and the Great Fiscal Crisis of 1975*. Albany: State University of New York Press, 2010.
Lask, Thomas. "A World of Theatre at La Mama." *New York Times*, March 4, 1977.
Lassell, Michael. "Review: Mert and Phil by Anne Burr." *Theater* 6 (1975): 73–80.
Lefebvre, Henri. *The Production of Space*. Translated by Donald Nicholson-Smith. Oxford: Basil Blackwell, 1991.
Leiter, Samuel L. *Ten Seasons: New York Theatre in the Seventies*. Westport, Conn.: Greenwood, 1986.
Lester, Elenore. "We Exist to Create a Real Black Theater." *New York Times*, March 2, 1975.
Levin, Laura, and Marlis Schweitzer. "Editorial: Performing Publics." *Performance Research: A Journal of the Performing Arts* 16 (2011): 1–6.
Levin, Laura, and Kim Solga. "Building Utopia: Performance and the Fantasy of Urban Renewal in Contemporary Toronto." *TDR: The Drama Review* 53, no. 3 (Fall 2009): 37–53.
Levine, Jo Ann. "Actress-Director with 'a Sense of Herself.'" *Christian Science Monitor*, March 15, 1974.
Little, Stuart W. *After the FACT: Conflict and Consensus, A Report on the First American Congress of Theatre*. New York: Arno, 1975.
———. "Another Opening, Another Show?" *New York*, June 29, 1970.
———. "Joe Papp's Biggest Real-Estate Deal." *New York*, April 21, 1969.
———. *Off Broadway: The Prophetic Theater*. New York: Coward, McCann and Geoghegan, 1972.
———. "What Makes Off Off Broadway Off Off?" *New York Times*, December 22, 1974.
Lloyd, Richard. *Neo-Bohemia: Art and Commerce in the Post-Industrial City*. New York: Routledge, 2005.
Lobenfeld, Eric J. "The 42nd Street Development Project: How Litigation Obstructs Public Goals." *Pace Environmental Law Review* 7, no. 2 (Spring 1990): 347–55.
Lopate, Carol. *Education and Culture in Brooklyn: A History of Ten Institutions*. New York: Brooklyn Educational and Culture Alliance, 1979.
Ludlam, Charles. *Ridiculous Theatre: Scourge of Human Folly*. New York: Theatre Communications Group, 1992.
Lynch, Kathleen, John Baker, and Maureen Lyons, eds. *Affective Equality: Love, Care, and Injustice*. Basingstoke, Eng.: Palgrave Macmillan, 2009.
Maffi, Mario. *Gateway to the Promised Land*. New York: New York University Press, 1995.
Maitland, Leslie. "Air of Uncertainty Dogs Coney Island." *New York Times*, November 3, 1975.

Manning, Erin, and Brian Massumi. "A Perspective of the Universe." *Inflexions* 6, "Arakawa and Gins" (January 2013): 448–55.

Marcuse, Peter. "The Targeted Crisis: On the Ideology of Urban Fiscal Crisis and Its Uses." *International Journal of Urban and Regional Research* 5 (September 1981): 330–55.

Markham, James M. "Street Theater Troupes Find the Play's Their Thing." *New York Times*, August 6, 1971.

Markusen, Ann. "Urban Development and the Politics of a Creative Class: Evidence from the Study of Artists." *Environment and Planning A* 38, no. 10 (2006): 1921–40.

Markusen, Ann, and Anne Gadwa. "Arts and Culture in Urban or Regional Planning: A Review and Research Agenda." *Journal of Planning Education and Research* 29 (2010): 379–91.

Marowitz, Charles. "The Trouble with Papp." *New York Times*, September 21, 1975.

Martin, Bradford D. *The Theater Is in the Street: Politics and Performance in Sixties America*. Amherst: University of Massachusetts Press, 2004.

Mason, Clifford. "Vinnette Carroll Is Still in There Swinging." *New York Times*, December 19, 1976.

Massumi, Brian. "Urban Appointment: A Possible Rendez-Vous with the City." In *Making Art of Databases*, edited by Joke Brouwer and Arjen Mulder, 28–55. Rotterdam: V2 Organisatie/DutchArchitecture Institute, 2003.

Mayer, Robert A. "New York: The State of Art." *New York Affairs* 4, no. 4 (Winter 1978): 7–12.

McClinton, Calvin A. "Vinnette Carroll: African American Director and Playwright." In *Black Lives: Essays in African American Biography*, edited by James L. Conyers, 19–32. New York: M. E. Sharpe, 1999.

———. *The Work of Vinnette Carroll: An African American Theatre Artist*. Lewiston, N.Y.: Edwin Mellen, 2000.

McGowan, Martha. *Growing Up in Brooklyn: The Brooklyn Academy of Music, Mirror of a Changing Borough*. Brooklyn: Brooklyn Academy of Music, 1983.

McGowen, Stephanie. "The Coney Island Experience: A Case Study in Popular Culture and Social Change." Master's thesis, Universitat Bremen, 1994.

McGraw, Hesse. "Theaster Gates: Radical Reform with Everyday Tools." *Afterall: A Journal of Art, Context, and Enquiry* 30 (Summer 2012): 86–99.

McKinnie, Michael. *City Stages: Theatre and Urban Space in a Global City*. Toronto: University of Toronto Press, 2007.

———, ed. *Space and the Geographies of Theatre*. New York: Theatre Communications Group, 2007.

Mee, Charles. "Introduction." In *BAM: The Complete Works*, edited by Steven Serafin, 16–60. New York: Quantuck Lane, 2011.

Mele, Christopher. *Selling the Lower East Side: Culture, Real Estate and Resistance in New York City*. Minneapolis: University of Minnesota Press, 2000.

Metz, Tracy. "Calculating Leisure." In *Coney Island: The Parachute Pavilion Competition*, edited by Zoë Ryan and Jonathan Cohen-Litant, 22–29. Princeton, N.J.: Princeton Architectural Press, 2007.

Miller, Henry D. *Theorizing Black Theatre: Art versus Protest in Critical Writings, 1898–1965*. McFarland, 2010.

Millington, Gareth. "'Man Dem Link Up': London's Anti-Riots and Urban Modernism." *Sociological Research Online* 17 (November 30, 2012), http://www.socresonline.org.uk/17/4/12.html.

Mills, Fiona. "Seeing Ethnicity: The Impact of Race and Class on the Critical Reception of Miguel Piñero's *Short Eyes*." In *Captive Audience: Prison and Captivity in Contemporary Theatre*, edited by Thomas Fahy and Kimball King. London: Routledge, 2003.

Mitchell, Don. "There's No Such Thing as Culture: Towards a Reconceptualization of the Idea of Culture in Geography." *Transactions of the Institute of British Geographers* 20, no. 1 (1995): 102–16.

Mitchell, Lionel H. "Ellen Stewart: La Mama's Defiant Trailblazer." *Amsterdam News*, October 24, 1981.

Mogilevich, Mariana. "Arts as Public Policy: Cultural Spaces for Democracy and Growth." In *Summer in the City: John Lindsay, New York, and the American Dream*, edited by Joseph P. Viteritti. Baltimore: Johns Hopkins University Press, 2014.

Mollenkopf, John Hull. *A Phoenix in the Ashes: The Rise and Fall of the Koch Coalition in New York City Politics*. Princeton, N.J.: Princeton University Press, 1992.

Moody, Kim. *From Welfare State to Real Estate: Regime Change in New York City, 1974 to the Present*. New York: New Press, 2007.

Moynihan, Colin. "Born in Brooklyn, Now Making a Motown Move." *New York Times*, December 7, 2014. http://www.nytimes.com/2014/12/08/arts/galapagos-art-space-will-make-detroit-its-home.html?_r=0.

Napoleon, Davi. *Chelsea on the Edge: The Adventures of an American Theater*. Ames: Iowa State University Press, 1991.

Neal, Larry. "The Black Arts Movement." *TDR: The Drama Review* 12, "Black Theatre" (Summer 1968): 28–39.

Negra, Diane, and Yvonne Tasker, eds. *Gendering the Recession: Media and Culture in an Age of Austerity*. Durham, N.C.: Duke University Press, 2014.

Newsom, Barbara Y., and Adele Silver, eds. *The Art Museum as Educator: A Collection of Studies as Guides to Practice and Policy*. Berkeley: University of California Press, 1978.

Nielsen, Lara D. "Introduction: Heterotopic Transformations, The (Il)Liberal Neoliberal." In *Neoliberalism and Global Theatres: Performance Permutations*, edited by Lara Nielsen and Patricia Ybarra, 1–25. London: Palgrave Macmillan, 2012.

Noble, Janet. "Geraldine Fitzgerald: A Woman for All Seasons." *Irish America Magazine* (January/February 1993): 31.

Nolan, Kenneth P. "Brooklyn Streets Become Stages: Van Arrives, World Is a Stage." *New York Times*, August 19, 1973.

Noonan, Ellen. "Interview with Mike Wallace." *Radical History Review* 79 (Winter 2001): 49–74.

Novick, Julius. *Beyond Broadway: The Quest for Permanent Theatres*. New York: Hill and Wang, 1968.

———. "La Mama Rekindles the Fire of Ancient Greek Drama." *New York Times*, November 17, 1974.

Ocejo, Richard E. "The Early Gentrifier: Weaving a Nostalgia Narrative on the Lower East Side." *City & Community* 10, no. 3 (September 2011): 285–310.

Osman, Suleiman. *The Invention of Brownstone Brooklyn: Gentrification and the Search for Authenticity in Postwar New York*. Oxford: Oxford University Press, 2011.

Page, Max. *The City's End: Two Centuries of Fantasies, Fears, and Premonitions of New York's Destruction*. New Haven, Conn.: Yale University Press, 2008.

Papp, Joseph. "Government Aid: Sponsor of Free Shakespeare Says It Would Help More Than Hinder." *New York Times*, July 24, 1960.

———. "Is There a Fifth Column at the Forum?" *New York Times*, July 25, 1971.

———. "To Break Down 'The Wall.'" *New York Times*, July 22, 1973.

Parisi, Barbara, and Robert Singer. *The History of Brooklyn's Three Major Performing Arts Institutions*. Lanham, Md.: Scarecrow, 2003.

Patterson, Lindsay. "Black Theater: The Search Goes On." *Freedomways* 14 (1974): 242–46.

Peck, Jaime. "Geography and Public Policy: Constructions of Neoliberalism." *Progress in Human Geography* 28 (2004): 392–405.

Peiss, Kathy. *Cheap Amusements: Working Women and Leisure in Turn-of-the-Century New York*. Philadelphia: Temple University Press, 1986.

Persoff, Ethan, and Scott Marshall. "John Wilcock: Sneaking Julie Bovasso into McSorley's 'Men's Only' Saloon." *Boing Boing*, May 20, 2014. http://boingboing.net/2014/05/20/john-wilcock-sneaking-julie-b.html.

Peterson, Marina, and Gary W. McDonogh, eds. *Global Downtowns*. Philadelphia: University of Pennsylvania Press, 2012.

Phillips, McCandlish. "Candidates Assess City's Arts Future." *New York Times*, November 1, 1973, 50.

———. "Message of Street Theater Is Strong." *New York Times*, June 22, 1971.

———. "1,250 Performances Are Given Here During Season." *New York Times*, August 27, 1970.

———. "Papp's Dream Enriches a City." *New York Times*, March 7, 1973.

———. "Summertime, and the Arts Are Easy at Lincoln Center." *New York Times*, July 8, 1979.

———. "Urban Arts Corps Offers Two Plays on Negro Life." *New York Times*, August 29, 1969.

———. ". . . Which Will Run for Two Weeks at Lincoln Center." *New York Times*, August 22, 1972.

Phillips-Fein, Kimberly. "The Legacy of the 1970s Fiscal Crisis." *The Nation*, April 16, 2013. http://www.thenation.com/article/173873/legacy-1970s-fiscal-crisis#.

Pierce, Neil R. "And What the Arts Can Do for You." *Pittsburgh Post-Gazette*, September 16, 1977.

Poggi, Jack. *Theater in America: The Impact of Economic Forces, 1870–1967*. Ithaca, N.Y.: Cornell University Press, 1968.

Poland, Albert, and Bruce Mailman, eds. *The Off Off Broadway Book: The Plays, People, Theatre*. New York: Bobbs-Merrill, 1972.

Post, Herschel. "The City Politic: Moving in on the Parks." *New York* (March 15, 1971): 6–9.

Pratt, Andy C. "The Cultural Contradictions of the Creative City." *City, Culture and Society* 2 (2011): 123–30.

President's Five-Year Review and Annual Report, 1968. New York: Rockefeller Foundation, 2003.

Public and Private Support for the Arts in New York City. New York: Cultural Assistance Center, 1980.

Quindlen, Anna. "Mayor Gets Some Bad Notices after Second Raid on Times Square Show." *New York Times*, March 26, 1977.

Rabe, David. *In the Boom Boom Room*. New York: Samuel French, 1986.

Rabkin, Gerald. "The Academy of Fashion: Beach Hits the Wave at BAM." *Performing Arts Journal* 9, no. 1 (1985): 47–53.

Rainer, Yvonne. *The Films of Yvonne Rainer*. Bloomington: Indiana University Press, 1989.

Rancière, Jacques. *Dissensus: On Politics and Aesthetics*. Edited by Steven Corcoran. London: Continuum, 2010.

Ratcliff, Carter. "The Culture Vulture Flies Higher." *New York*, April 10, 1978.

Ratner, Lizzy. "Boom Town and Bust City: A Tale of Two New Yorks." *The Nation*, February 14, 2011.

Reardon, Sean F., Lindsay Fox, and Joseph Townsend. "Neighborhood Income Composition by Household Race and Income, 1990–2009." *The Annals, AAPSS* 660 (July 2015): 78–97.

Reaven, Marci. "Citizen Participation in City Planning: New York City, 1945–1975." Ph.D. dissertation, New York University, 2009.

Register, Woody. *The Kid of Coney Island: Fred Thompson and the Rise of American Amusements*. New York: Oxford University Press, 2001.

Reichl, Alexander J. *Reconstructing Times Square: Politics and Culture in Urban Development*. Lawrence: University Press of Kansas, 1999.

Reinelt, Janelle. "Rethinking the Public Sphere for a Global Age." *Performance Research: A Journal of the Performing Arts* 16 (2011): 16–27.

Reiss, Alvin H. "Arts in the Neighborhood: New York's Cultural Center without Walls." *Cue*, June 5, 1971, 9.

———. "Business: The New Arts Patron." *Cue*, August 21, 1971.

———. "Who Builds Theatres and Why?" *TDR: The Drama Review* 12, no. 3 (Spring 1968): 75–92.

Report to the Mayor's Committee on Cultural Policy. New York: New York City Mayor's Committee on Cultural Policy, 1974.

Riley, Clayton. "Furman's 'Block': Something Fine, Something Real." *New York Amsterdam News*, February 5, 1972.

Rivero, Juan. "Coney Island: Planning Nostalgic Space." Master's thesis, Columbia University, 2004.

Roberts, Sam, ed. *America's Mayor: John V. Lindsay and the Reinvention of New York*. New York: Museum of the City of New York and Columbia University Press, 2010.

Robinson, Alice M., Vera Mowry Roberts, and Milly S. Barranger, eds. *Notable Women in the American Theatre*. Westport, Conn.: Greenwood, 1989.

Robinson, Vivian. "*Long Black Block* Is Truth in Action." *New York Amsterdam News*, January 29, 1972.

Rosenthal, Cindy. "La Mama of Us All." *TDR: The Drama Review* 50, no. 2 (Summer 2006): 12–51.

Rosenzweig, Ray, and Elizabeth Blackmar. *The Park and the People: A History of Central Park*. Ithaca, N.Y.: Cornell University Press, 1992.

Sagalyn, Lynne B. *Times Square Roulette: Remaking the City Icon*. Cambridge, Mass.: MIT Press, 2001.

Salaam, Kalamu Ya. "Black Theatre—The Way It Is: An Interview with Woodie King, Jr." *African American Review* 31 (Winter 1997): 647–58.

Sassen, Saskia. "Analytical Borderlands: Race, Gender and Representation in the New City." In *Re-presenting the City: Ethnicity, Capital and Culture in the 21st Century Metropolis*, edited by Anthony D. King, 183–202. New York: New York University Press, 1996.

Savran, David. "The Death of the Avantgarde." *TDR: The Drama Review* 49, no. 3 (Fall 2005): 10–42.

———. *High Brow/Low Down: Theater, Jazz, and the Making of the New Middle Class*. Ann Arbor: University of Michigan Press, 2009.

———. *A Queer Sort of Materialism: Recontextualizing American Theatre*. Ann Arbor: University of Michigan Press, 2003.

———. "Trafficking in Transnational Brands: The New 'Broadway Style Musical.'" *Theatre Survey* 55 (September 2014): 318–42.

Schechner, Richard. "Ford, Rockefeller, and Theatre." *TDR: Tulane Drama Review* 10 (Fall 1965): 23–49.

———. *Performance Theory*. New York: Routledge, 2003.

———. "Ringing the Bell for Ellen Stewart: 1919–2011." *TDR: The Drama Review* 55, no. 2 (Summer 2011): 9–10.

Schechter, Joel. "On Not Offending the Audience: Brecht at Lincoln Center: A Review of *The Threepenny Opera*." *Theater* 8 (1976): 74–77.

Schmidt, Sandra. "Theater in the Street: Looks Arch." *Christian Science Monitor*, July 31, 1965, 4.

Schreiber, Earl G. "*Everyman* in America." *Comparative Drama* 9, no. 2 (Summer 1975): 99–115.

Scott, Allen J. *Social Economy of the Metropolis: Cognitive-Cultural Capitalism and the Global Resurgence of Cities*. Oxford: Oxford University Press, 2009.

Sell, Mike. *Avant-Garde Performance and the Limits of Criticism: Approaching the Living Theatre, Happenings/Fluxus, and the Black Arts Movement*. Ann Arbor: University of Michigan, 2008.

Serafin, Steven, ed. *BAM: The Complete Works*. New York: Quantuck Lane, 2011.

Shane, Rachel. "Negotiating the Creative Sector: Understanding the Role and Impact of an Artistic Union in a Cultural Industry: A Study of Actors' Equity Association and the Theatrical Industry." Ph.D. dissertation, Ohio State University, 2006.

Shank, Theodore. *Beyond the Boundaries: American Alternative Theatre*. Ann Arbor: University of Michigan Press, 2002.

Shefter, Martin. *Political Crisis/Fiscal Crisis*. New York: Columbia University Press, 1992.

Shepard, Richard F. "Beame Is Upbeat Over the Cultural Life of the City." *New York Times*, April 8, 1975.

Shimko, Robert B., and Sara Freeman, eds. *Public Theatres and Theatre Publics*. Newcastle, Eng.: Cambridge Scholars Publishing, 2012.

Sites, William. *Remaking New York: Primitive Globalization and the Politics of Urban Community*. Minneapolis: University of Minnesota Press, 2003.

Sleeper, Jim, ed. *In Search of New York*. New Brunswick, N.J.: Transaction Publishers, 1989.

Slocum-Schaffer, Stephanie A. *America in the Seventies*. Syracuse, N.Y.: Syracuse University Press, 2003.

Smith, Neil, Betsy Duncan, and Laura Reid. "From Disinvestment to Reinvestment: Tax Arrears and Turning Points in the East Village." *Housing Studies* 4, no. 4 (1989): 238–52.

Smith, Michael. "Caffé Cino." http://michaeltownsendsmith.com/caffe-cino.

———. "The Good Scene: Off Off-Broadway." *Tulane Drama Review* 10, no. 4 (Summer 1966): 159–76.

Smothers, Ronald. "Black Repertory Troupe Is 'Coping' with Success." *New York Times*, March 23, 1975.

Soffer, Jonathan M. *Ed Koch and the Rebuilding of New York City*. New York: Columbia University Press, 2012.

Soja, Edward. *Thirdspace: Journeys to Los Angeles and Other Real-and-Imagined Places*. Oxford: Basil Blackwell, 1996.

Staff Report on Transactions in Securities of the City of New York: Introduction and Summary. October 1, 1974–April 8, 1975. Vol. 1, Securities and Exchange Commission, August 26, 1977. https://www.sec.gov/info/municipal/staffreport0877.pdf.

Starr, Roger. "Build Another East Village in the Dakota Badlands." *New York Times*, September 24, 1972.

———. "The Decline and Decline of New York." *New York Times*, November 21, 1971.

———. "Making New York Smaller." *New York Times*, November 14, 1976.

———. "Refusal to Face Facts a Peril to City." *New York Times*, October 3, 1976.

Stasio, Marilyn. "On the Theatre Scene." *Cue*, March 13, 1971, page unknown.

———. "On the Theatre Scene." *Cue*, September 11, 1971, 13.

Stephens, Julie. *Anti-Disciplinary Protest: Sixties Radicalism and Postmodernism*. Cambridge: Cambridge University Press, 1998.

Stern, William J. "The Truth about Times Square." *Perspectives on Eminent Domain Abuse* 5 (April 2009): 8–10, http://www.ij.org/stern-perspective.

Stevenson, James. "Cut-Rate Tickets." *New York Times*, March 7, 2009. http://www.nytimes.com/imagepages/2008/03/07/opinion/08oped.ready.html.

Stewart, Ellen, and Glenn Loney. "La Mama Celebrates Twenty Years." *Performing Arts Journal* 6 (1982): 6–17.

Stone, Wendell C. *Caffe Cino: The Birthplace of Off-Off-Broadway*. Carbondale: Southern Illinois University Press, 2005.

Sukenick, Ronald. *Down and In: Life in the Underground*. New York: Beech Tree Books, 1997.

Sullivan, Dan. "Called on the Carpet by a Theatre Guru." *Los Angeles Times*, September 2, 1973.

———. "Ellen Stewart Nurtures Theater." *Los Angeles Times*, October 4, 1971.

———. "Theater in East Harlem: The Outdoor Audience Gets into the Act." *New York Times*, August 30, 1968.

———. "Theatre: Junebug Graduates Tonight!" *New York Times*, February 27, 1967.

Survey of Arts and Culture in New York State. New York: American Council for the Arts in Education, 1973.

Susser, Ida. *Norman Street: Poverty and Politics in an Urban Neighborhood*. Oxford: Oxford University Press, 1982.

Sussman, Mark. "New York's Facelift." *TDR: The Drama Review* 42, no. 1 (Spring 1998): 34–42.

Tabb, William K. *The Long Default: New York City and the Urban Fiscal Crisis*. New York: Monthly Review, 1983.

"Talking of Black Art, Theatre, Revolution and Nationhood." *Black Theatre 5: Waitin' for the Seventies* (1971): 18–37.

Tallmer, Jerry. "Jottings by an Off-Broadway Critic." *Encore* (March/April 1963): 8–13.

Tannenbaum, Allan. *New York in the 70s*. New York: Overlook, 2011.

Taylor, Clarence. "Race, Rights, Empowerment." In *Summer in the City: John Lindsay, New York, and the American Dream*, edited by Joseph P. Viteritti. Baltimore: Johns Hopkins University Press, 2014.

Taylor, William R., ed. *Inventing Times Square: Commerce and Culture at the Crossroads of the World*. New York: Russell Sage Foundation, 1991.

Thompson, Howard. "Rhythm and Satire at Street Festival: Dayton and Brooklyn Troupes Perform." *New York Times*, August 23, 1973.

———. "Street Theatre Livens Lincoln Center." *New York Times*, August 20, 1971.

Tompkins, Joanne. "Space and the Geographies of Theatre: Introduction." *Modern Drama* 46 (Winter 2003): 537–41.

Touraine, Alain. *After the Crisis*. Cambridge: Polity, 2014.

Turan, Kenneth, and Joseph Papp. *Free for All: Joe Papp, the Public, and the Greatest Theater Story Ever Told*. New York: Anchor Books, 2010.

Valle, Cezar Del. *The Brooklyn Theatre Index, Volume I*. New York: Theatre Talks, 2010.

Van Hoogstraten, Nicholas. *Lost Broadway Theatres*. Princeton, N.J.: Princeton Architectural Press, 1997.

Vidal, David. "City Removes Garbage Tossed in Street Protest." *New York Times*, July 25, 1975.

Von Hoffman, Alexander. *House by House, Block by Block: The Rebirth of America's Urban Neighborhoods*. New York: Oxford University Press, 2003.

Wald, Richard C. "City to Accept $20,000 for Free Shakespeare: Lyons, While Voting 'Yes,' Uses Occasion to Question the Americanism of Papp." *New York Herald Tribune*, June 26, 1959.

Walker, Joseph. *The River Niger*. New York: Hill and Wang, 1973.

Wallace, Deborah, and Rodrick Wallace. "Origins of Public Health Collapse in New York City: The Dynamics of Planned Shrinkage, Contagious Urban Decay and Social Disintegration." *Bulletin of the New York Academy of Medicine* 66, no. 5 (September-October 1990): 391–434.

Wallock, Leonard, and Dore Ashton. *New York, Culture Capital of the World, 1940–1965*. New York: Rizzoli, 1988.

Walsh, Brian. "Murder by Timidity: BAM's Next Wave and Classic Revivals." *PAJ: A Journal of Performance and Art* 25, no. 2 (May 2003): 83–87.

Walsh, Thomas. "Street Scenes: The Art and Science of Street Theatre." *Back Stage* 28 (July 1989): 1A+.

Waren, Stanley A. "The City and the Theatre." *Performing Arts Journal* 4, no. 1/2 (May 1979): 118–24.

Watts, Jerry Gafio. *Amiri Baraka: The Politics and Art of a Black Intellectual*. New York: New York University Press, 2007.

Weisman, Steven R. "The AntiCrime Drive: Beame's Stepped-Up Emphasis on Law and Order During an Election Year Raises Some Questions." *New York Times*, April 15, 1977.

———. "Beame, Naming Advisory Panel on Culture, Plans New Agency." *New York Times*, May 23, 1975.

———. "How New York Became a Fiscal Junkie." *New York Times*, August 17, 1975.

Whitt, J. Allen. "Mozart in the Metropolis: The Arts Coalition and the Urban Growth Machine." *Urban Affairs Review* 23 (September 1987): 16.

Whybrow, Nicolas, ed. *Performance and the Contemporary City: An Interdisciplinary Reader*. Basingstoke, Eng.: Palgrave Macmillan, 2010.

Wickstrom, Maura. "Commodities, Mimesis, and *The Lion King*: Retail Theatre for the 1990s." *Theatre Journal* 51, no. 3 (October 1999): 285–98.

———. *Performing Consumers: Global Capital and Its Theatrical Seductions*. New York: Routledge, 2006.

Williams, Mance. *Black Theatre in the 1960s and 1970s: A Historical-Critical Analysis of the Movement*. Westport, Conn.: Greenwood, 1985.

Williams, Raymond. *The Sociology of Culture*. New York: Schocken Books, 1982.

Willis, Thomas. "'Too Short to Box with God' Brings the Gospel Home." *Chicago Tribune*, April 9, 1976.

Wilmeth, Don B., and C. W. E. Bigsby, eds. *The Cambridge History of American Theatre, Volume III*. Cambridge: Cambridge University Press, 2000.

Winfrey, Carey. "Papp Quits Lincoln Center, Citing Artistic-Fiscal Trap." *New York Times*, June 10, 1977.

Wolcott, Victoria W. *Race, Riots, and Roller Coasters: The Struggle over Segregated Recreation in America*. Philadelphia: University of Pennsylvania Press, 2012.

Wolf-Powers, Laura. "Up-Zoning New York City's Mixed Use Neighborhoods: Property-Led Economic Development and the Anatomy of a Planning Dilemma." *Journal of Planning, Education and Research* 24, no. 4 (June 2005): 379–93.

Wollman, Elizabeth L. "The Economic Development of the 'New' Times Square and Its Impact on the Broadway Musical." *American Music* 20, no. 4 (Winter 2002): 445–65.

———. *Hard Times: The Adult Musical in 1970s New York City*. Oxford: Oxford University Press, 2012.

Wylder, Robert C. "'Don't Bother Me' Has Everything: Things Go Superlatively with Cope." *Press Telegram*, August 16, 1972.

Wyszomirski, Margaret J. "Arts Policymaking and Interest-Group Politics." *Journal of Aesthetic Education* 14 (October 1980): 28–34.

Young, Edgar B. *Lincoln Center: The Building of an Institution*. New York: New York University Press, 1980.

Zeigler, Joseph Wesley. "Centrality without Philosophy: The Crisis in the Arts." *New York Affairs* 4, no. 4 (Winter 1978): 12–22.

Zipp, Samuel. *Manhattan Projects: The Rise and Fall of Urban Renewal in Cold War New York*. Oxford: Oxford University Press, 2010.

Zolberg, Vera. "New York Cultural Institutions: Ascendant or Subsidant?" In *Capital of the American Century: The National and International Influence of New York City*, edited by Martin Shefter, 145–67. New York: Russell Sage Foundation, 1993.

Zolotow, Sam. "La Mama Opens at New Home April 2." *New York Times*, March 19, 1969.

Zukin, Sharon. *Loft Living: Culture and Capital in Urban Change*. New Brunswick, N.J.: Rutgers University Press, 1989.

INDEX